Family Violence

Explanations and Evidence-Based Clinical Practice

David M. Lawson

AMERICAN COUNSELING
ASSOCIATION
5999 Stevenson Avenue ▪ Alexandria, VA 22304
www.counseling.org

Family Violence

Explanations and Evidence-Based Clinical Practice

10 9 8 7 6 5 4 3 2 1

American Counseling Association

5999 Stevenson Avenue, Alexandria, VA 22304

Director of Publications ▪ Carolyn C. Baker

Production Manager ▪ Bonny E. Gaston

Production Assistant ▪ Catherine A. Brumley

Copy Editor ▪ Kimberly Kinne

Text and cover design by Bonny E. Gaston.

Library of Congress Cataloging-in-Publication Data

Lawson, David M.
Family violence:explanations and evidence-based clinical practice/David M. Lawson.
  pages cm
  Includes bibliographical references and index.
  ISBN 978-1-55620-317-6 (alk. paper)
1. Family violence.   2. Family violence—Treatment.   I. Title.
HV6626.L39 2013
362.82'92—dc23   2012047565

Table of Contents

Preface

Family violence has a long and painful history, likely extending back to the inception of the family. Child abuse and woman abuse were recognized to varying degrees in the mid-1800s, but it was not until the 1960s and 1970s, respectively, that they began to receive recognition as critical social problems touching the lives of many in society. In particular, the women's movement in the mid-1970s resulted in changes in laws to protect women. Furthermore, women's shelters began to open throughout the United States during the mid-1970s, bringing increased attention to the plight of abused women. As a result, scholars and the general public began to take a greater interest in family and intimate violence during this time. After the 1970s, other types of family violence were recognized, including violence against male intimate partners, same-sex intimate partner violence, dating violence, and violence toward elders. As a result, research has proliferated, shining a light on the many aspects of family violence. Some research has led to controversy, such as distinguishing between victims and perpetrators, identifying female-to-male intimate partner violence, and identifying best clinical practices.

Family violence occurs in approximately one in four families in the United States (American Academy of Family Physicians, 2000). Many of these individuals present for counseling assistance and yet fail to receive adequate services because many providers lack appropriate training to identify and treat family violence. The majority of graduate training programs provide little if any training in family violence, and they provide only slightly more exposure to child maltreatment (Champion, Shipman, Bonner, Hensley, & Howe, 2003). Thus, counselors often have little exposure to the field of family violence, its effects, and evidence-based treatments in their training. This book provides valuable information for counselors-in-training (e.g., in courses related to crisis intervention and marital and family counseling), for professional counselors who have little background in the field of family violence, and for professional counselors and educators who are knowledgeable about some but not all areas of family violence.

Family Violence: Explanations and Evidence-Based Clinical Practice provides an overview of the major issues and controversies in the field of family violence along with relevant information on assessment and treatment. The text covers a wide range of topics related to family violence, such as the historical and cultural context, major explanations for family violence, and incidence and descriptions of family violence, but always with an eye toward enhancing counselors' ability to assess and treat each major type of family violence (i.e., both heterosexual and same-sex intimate partner violence, child maltreatment, dating violence, stalking, and elder maltreatment). Material is presented within the context of existing research and scholarly opinion. Case examples are offered to illustrate various issues such as types of family violence, clinical cases, and research. Furthermore, summaries and suggested readings are provided for each chapter. This book is unique in its inclusion of materials pertaining to major issues in the field of family violence plus clinically relevant material on assessment and treatment issues. For example, the cultural/historical information provides a logical segue into explanations for family violence, types of family violence, and finally interventions for family violence.

The first three chapters provide a current and historical context for family violence. Chapter 1 provides material on the prevalence, economic costs, types, and cultural issues of family violence. The latter part of the chapter presents an overview of family violence historically, with a special focus on women and children, followed by a discussion of a more contemporary and controversial issue: intimate partner violence against males. Chapter 2 discusses major explanations for family violence, including those models that influence treatment, such as social cognitive theory, feminist theory, and attachment theory. Chapter 3 addresses specific cultural factors and explanations that influence the manner by which family violence is maintained, interpreted, and addressed clinically.

Chapters 4 through 9 address specific types of and treatments for adult intimate partner violence and include case examples. Chapter 4 focuses on male-on-female intimacy violence, including risk and protective factors, abuser typologies, consequences for victims, and treatment implications. Chapter 5 addresses female-on-male intimate violence, with topics similar to those in Chapter 4. Chapter 6 is devoted to same-sex violence, Chapter 7 to assessing for intimate partner offenders, Chapter 8 to treatment of intimate partner offenders, and Chapter 9 to providing assessment and treatment for victims of intimate partner violence.

The final chapters, 10 through 13, cover the remaining types of family violence. Chapter 10 examines issues related to dating violence, sexual assault, and stalking as well as treatment and prevention. Chapter 11 is devoted to child maltreatment issues, including a wide variety of topics such as types, prevalence, explanations, victim and perpetrator characteristics, Internet exploitation of children, and consequences of child maltreatment. Chapter 12 focuses on assessment and treatment of child maltreatment. Chapter 13 is devoted to elder abuse, the least researched type of family violence.

Working in the field of family violence is demanding and often leaves its imprint on a counselor's physical and emotional life. And yet the work can be satisfying and life changing for both counselor and client. It is my hope that in conjunction with good supervision and practice, readers will find this book helpful in becoming better prepared to work with family violence issues.

Acknowledgments

I want to express my appreciation to Carolyn Baker, director of publications, and her colleagues from the American Counseling Association, including the American Counseling Association Publications Committee, for their support, expertise, and attention to detail in helping produce this book. For their helpful reviews, thank you to Lee W. Shefferman, PhD (University of Northern Colorado), and Marie B. Francois-Lamonte, PhD (Compton Central Health Clinic, California).

I am particularly grateful for the support of my wife, Peggy. In addition, I am blessed to have children Paul and Brittney, Joel and Camille, and grandchildren Ashton, Paeton, and Keirstyn.

About the Author

David M. Lawson, PhD, is a professor in the Department of Human Services and teaches in the master's program in clinical mental health and the doctoral program in school psychology at Stephen F. Austin State University in Nacogdoches, Texas. He has published extensively on intimate partner violence (IPV) abuser characteristics, predictors of IPV, and treatment of IPV. Current research interests include integrative treatments for physically and sexually abused and traumatized mothers and their children, complex posttraumatic stress disorder, and childhood sexual abuse. He serves on the editorial board of several professional journals, including the *Journal of Family Violence, Journal of Counseling & Development,* and *Psychotherapy.* He also maintains a private practice working primarily with survivors of interpersonal trauma. He received his doctorate in counseling from the University of North Texas.

chapter 1

Introduction to Family Violence

Family violence occurs across all socioeconomic and racial/ethnic lines (M. C. Black et al., 2011). It has become institutionalized in most cultures over the millennia of human existence. In the United States, family violence has been implicitly supported or permitted as a means of influencing other family members' behavior (Damant et al., 2008). Furthermore, until recently, family violence largely has been shrouded by a belief in the sanctity of family privacy, including beliefs such as the supremacy of parental rights above children's rights and the belief that families will act in the best interest of their members (Malley-Morrison & Hines, 2004). This belief has been reinforced by the government's hesitancy to get involved in relationships within the family (Harrington & Dubowitz, 1999). In addition, the media has supported the acceptance of many types of violence with little consideration of its serious effects on the culture (Harrington & Dubowitz, 1999). For example, research consistently has found that exposure to violence through television, movies, and video games causes increased aggressive behavior, especially in children and adolescents (Huesmann, Moise-Titus, & Podolski, 2003), often contributing to the acceptance and use of violence. Aggressive and violent behavior continues into dating and long-term relationships (Marquart, Nannini, Edwards, Stanley, & Wayman, 2007; Tjaden & Thoennes, 2000). Furthermore, the objectification of women as sex objects and victims[1] through television, video

---

[1]The reader will note that the terms *victim* and *survivor* are used throughout the text, most often in a corresponding manner. However, each term carries a different connotation and even political meaning and may elicit quite different emotions and reactions from the reader. Even though I acknowledge their different connotative and denotative meanings, I use the terms in an interchangeable manner largely because both terms are used in this manner in the family violence literature.

games, movies, and the Internet supports a societal expectation that encourages devaluation and abuse toward women (Stankiewicz & Rosselli, 2008).

This chapter provides an overview of salient issues that define the context for family violence. These issues include prevalence and costs, definitions of types of family violence, common elements across explanations for family violence, cultural issues, controversies within the field, and a brief history of family violence.

Prevalence and Economic Cost of Family Violence

The recurrence and support of family violence over time has established cultural norms that have become woven into the fabric of our society. These norms are influenced by both long-held beliefs about the family (e.g., sanctity of family privacy) as well as more recent counter movements, such as feminism. As a result of historical and current cultural norms, many unsupported beliefs about family violence have emerged. For example, many in our culture believe that it is acceptable for a wife to be raped under certain circumstances (Russell, 1990) or that there are times when hitting a spouse/partner is permissible (Mills & Malley-Morrison, 1998). Furthermore, some hold that women cannot physically abuse men (L. E. A. Walker, 1999). Although the vast majority of people in the United States would openly condemn and deny the legitimacy of using violence in the family, national studies offer overwhelming evidence of its pervasive presence in our culture.

Family violence occurs in approximately one in four families in the United States (American Academy of Family Physicians, 2000). Of the victims of family violence, one in four women (24.3%) and one in seven men (13.8%) in the United States experience severe intimate partner violence (IPV; e.g., hit with a fist or beaten) in their lifetime (M. C. Black et al., 2011). In addition, one in five women will experience rape or attempted rape in her lifetime, with 1.4 million women being victims of rape or sexual assault each year (M. C. Black et al., 2011). Non-White and mixed-race men and women are much more likely to experience IPV than White men and women (M. C. Black et al., 2011). Adults are not the only victims of family violence, as between 800,000 to 1 million children were determined to be victims of abuse or neglect in 2005 (U. S. Department of Health and Human Services [DHHS], 2007). These figures do not include the 10% to 20% of children who are exposed to adult intimacy violence each year (Carlson & Dalenberg, 2000) or the 16% of adolescents who report some form of dating violence (Marquart et al., 2007). Finally, one third of college students and college-age young people report some kind of dating violence (Hines & Saudino, 2003). The financial cost of family violence nationally has been estimated to be between $6 billion and $10 billion for adult victims (Max, Rice, Finkelstein, Bardwell, & Leadbetter, 2004).

Although there is less research on intimacy violence in the gay, lesbian, bisexual, and transgender (GLBT) communities, some data indicate that it approximates the same levels of intimacy violence as in heterosexual communities (i.e., 25% to 35%; Bourg & Stock, 1994; National Coalition of Anti-Violence Programs [NCAVP], 1998), whereas more current data suggest prevalence estimates range from a low of 11% to as high as 73% (Craft & Serovich, 2005). Finally, although there are few official estimates of elder abuse, several national surveys suggest that between 565,747 and 2 million elders are abused yearly, most by family members (National Center on Elder Abuse, 1998; Teaster et al., 2006). As alarming as these figures may be, some hold that they are likely underestimates, as victims and their families often fail to report family abuse (e.g. Finkelhor, Hotaling, Lewis, & Smith, 1990; U.S. DHHS, National Center on Child Abuse, Neglect, 1996). Furthermore, some scholars estimate that approximately one half of professionals who are mandated to report child abuse fail to report cases that they identify as abuse (Sedlak, 1991).

In addition to the enormous cost of pain and suffering to humans, family violence exacts a substantial cost in health-related services and worker productivity. Health-related costs attributed to family violence exceed $1 trillion each year in the United States, including medical care, mental health services, and lost work productivity (Dubble, 2006). Victims of IPV lose almost 8 million days of work each year. The vast majority of these victims are women.

The cost of child abuse is even higher. Estimates indicate that the United States spends $103.8 billion annually related to child abuse (Wang & Holton, 2007). This figure is a conservative estimate, as calculations were based on the most stringent definitions of abuse and neglect according to the Harm Standard of the Third National Incidence Study of Child Abuse and Neglect (NIS-3; Sedlak, & Broadhurst, 1996) rather than the less stringent Endangerment Standard. Moreover, this figure includes only costs related to victims and does not include services for victims' families or perpetrators. In addition, research indicates a strong link between child abuse and long-term health effects, such as increased risk of teen pregnancy and/ or sexually transmitted disease, central nervous system damage, speech problems, inhibited growth, mental and emotional disturbances, delayed language development, low self-esteem, and aggressive tendencies (Chalk, Gibbons, & Scarupa, 2002; Kelley, Thornberry, & Smith, 1997).

Defining Family Violence

The term *interpersonal violence* is often used to refer to the various forms of family and intimate partner violence such as child maltreatment, partner abuse, and elder abuse. It is also applied more broadly to include types of community, school, and gang violence that occurs between acquaintances or strangers. In a general sense, interpersonal violence refers to any violence inflicted by an individual or a small group of individuals on another individual or small group (Dahlberg & Krug, 2002). On the other hand, family violence is a subtype of interpersonal violence that includes violence among intimate partners (including dating violence), family members, and people known by the family who are often viewed as friends or extended family members (whether or not they are actual family members by birth, marriage, or adoption). Although perpetrators of child maltreatment, stalking, and elder abuse may be an unknown person to the victim, the overwhelming percentage of perpetrators of such abuse are family members or, to much less extent, family friends or, in the case of elder abuse, staff in assisted living facilities.

Reaching consensus on what constitutes family violence has been difficult to achieve. For example, the terms *maltreatment*, *abuse*, *battering*, and *violence* appear in the family violence literature but often are used interchangeably without any attempt to distinguish between them. Some definitions of family violence provide a limited definition, such as "an act or omission by persons who are cohabitating that results in serious injury to other members of the family" (Wallace, 2005, p. 2). Emery and Laumann-Billings (1998) defined family violence by distinguishing between levels of violence. They delineated between two types of *abuse* in the family: *maltreatment* (i.e., mild to moderate levels of violence, such as slapping, pushing, or hitting) and *violence* (i.e., severe violence, such as physical and sexual abuse that endangers health). *Abuse* is used in a more general, inclusive manner for all types of family violence, whereas *maltreatment* and *violence* are subcategories of abuse. Conversely, Hines and Malley-Morrison (2005) used the term *maltreatment* to encompass a broad range of violence-related terms—including corporal punishment, family violence, partner abuse, domestic violence, spousal abuse, and elder abuse—occurring on a continuum from mild to severe.

Based on several sources, family violence is defined here to include the following: physical and sexual assault; threats and intimidation (psychological abuse); withholding necessary support and sustenance for children and elderly (neglect); and endangerment by acts of omission or commission in intimate relationships, including parent–child, adult and/or aging parent, marital and cohabiting, and GLBT relationships (American Academy of Family Physicians, 2000; Malley-Morrison & Hines, 2007). Dating relationships are included in this definition, as they include to varying degrees intimacy-demanding relationships.

Intimate Partner Violence

Until recently, the majority of family violence literature largely focused on what has been referred to as wife battering, domestic violence, and/or marital/partner violence. Currently, the term *intimate partner violence* (IPV) has become the term of choice for violence between people, family or not, who have or have had a close personal relationship (often romantic) that also has a private component (O. Barnett, Miller-Perrin, & Perrin, 2005). The preference for the term *intimate partner violence* is reflected in its use by the U.S. Bureau of Justice and the Centers for Disease Control and Prevention (M. C. Black et al., 2011). IPV refers to violence between spouses, former spouses, or separated spouses; cohabitants and former cohabitants; boyfriends or former boyfriends and girlfriends or former girlfriends; and same-sex partners or former partners.

As with family violence, different types of IPV have been identified. Neidig and Friedman (1984) distinguished between *expressive* and *instrumental violence*. These distinctions focus on both severity and intention of violence. *Expressive violence* is largely a function of escalating emotional arousal between partners with identifiable precipitants. The violence often occurs as a result of intense emotions such as anger. There is often mutual violence, and participants are more prone to express remorse for their actions and intentions to stop violence in the future. This violence tends to be mild to moderate and occurs infrequently. Prognosis for treatment is typically positive. In contrast, *instrumental violence* is most often perpetrated by men rather than women, with the purpose of control, intimidation, and punishment.

Often, there are no clear precipitants for the violence and the escalation process is sudden. This violence tends to be moderate to severe, with perpetrators showing little or no remorse for their actions. Most important, those who use instrumental violence often lack empathy for the victim and possess little motivation to change. Understandably, the prognosis for change is poor. Neidig and Friedman referred to men who engage in this type of violence as *partner batterers* as distinct from *partner abusers*, who do not use violence to control or terrorize their partners.

Similar to Neidig and Freidman, M. P. Johnson and Leone (2005) identified two types of IPV: common couple violence (CCV) and terroristic violence. *Common couple violence* is characterized by mild, reciprocal violence within the general population and is similar to expressive violence. *Terroristic couple violence* is often found with women's shelter populations and is similar to instrumental violence in that its use is intended to control, dominate, and punish. Research has generally supported the presence of these types of violence for both men and women, with terroristic violence representing a very small but dangerous percentage (4%–5%) of all IPV (D. G. Dutton & Nichols, 2005; M. P. Johnson & Leone, 2005; Laroche, 2005). Table 1.1 presents descriptions of these two types of intimacy violence as bimodal; however, these descriptions are best viewed as anchors that form two ends of a continuum of violent behavior and intentions.

More recently J. B. Kelly and Johnson (2008) identified four types of IPV: situational couple violence, mutual violence, violent resistance, and intimate terrorism as variations of terroristic and CCV. Types were based on three dimensions: severity of violence, control, and whether the violence was unidirectional or bidirectional.

Table 1.1
Examples of Bimodal Types of Intimacy Violence

Expressive/Common Couple Violence	*Instrumental/Terroristic Couple Violence*
Primarily a manifestation of emotion (e.g., anger, mistrust, hurt)	IPV that is used primarily as a means to achieve an outcome and social influence
May be reciprocal; victim and aggressor roles not set	Primarily unilateral IPV; victim and aggressor roles set
IPV often occurs within a context of increasing discord	IPV used to punish and/or control partner
Resulting IPV follows a predictable pattern of progression	Abrupt and speedy progression to IPV
Reciprocal conflict, distress, and aggravation typically precede IPV episode	Low provocation for IPV episode
Partner(s) experience sincere regret and sadness; they view IPV as inconsistent with their values and express desire to control IPV	Insincere, manipulative contrition if any; IPV is consistent with ideology
Often unpredictable but with a high probability for intensification and unintended harm	Probability of violent revenge, homicide, or suicide
IPV often results in low to no prolonged psychological consequences.	IPV results in severe psychological and physical consequences

Note. IPV = interpersonal partner violence. Information is from Neidig & Friedman (1984).

Regardless of the definition used, researchers studying family violence consider context factors such as personal history, causes, motivations, frequency, and intensity in determining whether or not an act is labeled as violence or abuse (Hines & Malley-Morrison, 2005). For example, an open-hand slap or a push may not be viewed as abusive or violent if it does not occur with any regularity or intensity. On the other hand, if someone was raised in a nonviolent home and experienced a milder form of violence, such as being grabbed by the arm(s) in such a way as to control or intimidate, this person may view this action as violent and abusive. More often than not, defining what is considered violent and/or abusive grows out of a cultural context (Malley-Morrison & Hines, 2004). Cultural values, often viewed as distal causes of family violence, are critical shared values that identify acceptable and unacceptable behavior. Thus, to understand family violence one must understand the culture and subculture in which it occurs. Finally, there has been much debate over whether parents spanking their children or sibling violence (pushing, hitting, and so forth) should be defined as family violence. Violence as discipline for a child is still a strongly debated issue (Malley-Morrison & Hines, 2004; Straus, 2005). This issue is addressed more fully in Chapter 11.

In this book, the term *family violence* refers to violence between family members, whereas *IPV* refers to a specific kind of family violence between spouses, partners and ex-spouses and ex-partners, and both same-sex and opposite-sex couples. Specific references are used to identify particular kinds of family violence, such as child maltreatment or dating violence. *Psychological abuse* refers to controlling a partner or family member by domination and/or isolation, verbal abuse such as name-calling and insulting, and threatening to harm the partner.

Cultural Issues and Family Violence

Culture refers to beliefs, traditions, practices, values, expression of emotion, and behaviors that are common to members of a group. Culture provides the foundation for the expression of roles, routines, and—unfortunately — family violence. It defines one's perceptions of how to address various forms of abuse as a member of a family and community (Yoshioka & Choi, 2005). Additional dimensions of culture include the intersection between race/ethnicity, gender, socioeconomic class, and sexual orientation. Assuming that abuse is experienced the same by all people regardless of their culture greatly oversimplifies and obfuscates important differences between people that will hamper effective interventions.

Historically, people representing diverse groups have not found treatment providers for victims of family violence to be culturally sensitive (Malley-Morrison & Hines, 2007). Therefore, counselors working with culturally different clients must consider not only the role a client's culture plays in the dynamics of family violence, but also elements of society that may create obstacles for minority groups, such as racism, sexism, poverty, limited education, and other forms of oppression that may exacerbate the effects of family violence (Richie, 2005). Cultural competence is essential to effective treatment of the various types of family violence. Sue and Torino (2005) defined cultural competence as follows:

Cultural competence is the ability to engage in actions or create conditions that maximize the optional development of the client and client systems. Multicultural counseling competence is achieved by the counselor's acquisition of awareness, knowledge, and skills needed to function effectively in a pluralistic democratic society (ability to communicate, interact, negotiate, and intervene on behalf of clients from diverse backgrounds) and on an organizational/societal level, advocating effectively to develop new theories, practices, policies, and organizational structures that are more responsive to all groups. (p. 8)

In addition, cultural competence includes valuing diversity, having an awareness of one's own cultural biases, and possessing "the ability to use the knowledge acquired about an individual's heritage and adaptational challenges to maximize the effectiveness of assessment, diagnosis, and treatment" (Whaley & Davis, 2007, p. 565). Issues related to culture and family violence are more fully addressed in Chapter 3.

Controversy in the Field of Family Violence

Currently, a controversy exists regarding the definition and measurement of IPV (Gelles & Loseke, 1993; Straus, 1999). This controversy permeates the literature on IPV at multiple levels and has led to the identification of at least two positions that are distinct but not necessarily mutually exclusive or irreconcilable (see Straus, 1999). One group largely composed of academics, feminist activists, and service providers prefers a broader definition of violence that emphasizes injury, including all forms of maltreatment (e.g., physical and sexual assault, psychological intimidation, sexual coercion); the oppression of women in general; and the view that IPV is instigated almost solely by males because of societal-sanctioned patriarchy and male dominance (Loseke & Kurz, 2005).

Conversely, another group largely composed of family studies academics focuses more on maltreatment, which is often addressed in family conflict studies (Straus, 2005). This group points to a large number of studies indicating that men and women perpetrate physical assault at almost equal rates (i.e., gender symmetry) and that the most prevalent pattern of assault is mutual violence (Archer, 2000; Fiebert, 2004). However, they acknowledge that males perpetrate more sexual abuse than females and produce more injuries, death, and fear than female perpetrators (Straus, 2009). Straus (2007, 2009) has claimed that some academics and researchers who support the broader definition often deny and conceal data (e.g., publish survey results on male perpetration of IPV even though data on female IPV perpetration are also available) in order to support their position.

Each group has a specific moral and political agenda (see D. G. Dutton & Corvo, 2006; Loseke, Gelles, & Cavanaugh, 2005). Service providers and activists often have a goal of ending all types of oppression to women; thus, their broader definition of violence translates into larger numbers of victimized women and, in turn, greater support and resources for this cause. Family conflict researchers often focus more on the widespread nature of IPV, including both men and women, with the goal of ending IPV regardless of who the perpetrator is. This group tends to view IPV as having multiple causes (D. G. Dutton & Corvo, 2006). Sometimes these two groups express strong opposition and even hostility toward each other (N. Gilbert, 2005; Loseke & Kurz, 2005). For example, feminist activists often view research that indicates gender symmetry of IPV as an impediment to their ultimate goal, with such research providing ammunition to those opposing their agenda (Straus, 2009). Conversely, *some* family conflict researchers view research that presents women as the primary victims as being in opposition to their wider goal of ending all IPV regardless of gender (Hines & Malley-Morrison, 2005; Straus, 1999). This issue is addressed in later chapters.

Straus (1999) has suggested that both groups' agendas are important in our society to the degree they move toward ending IPV. However, he has offered little hope for a "peaceful" resolution between the sides, although some scholars call for more openness to different points of view on the issue (Yllo, 2005). Unfortunately, obtaining political support and resources for research and for victims' programs necessitates maintaining a high profile via increasingly dramatic offender statistics (Malloy, McCloskey, Grigsby, & Gardner, 2003). Doubtless, a considerable temptation exits for each group to focus on research that supports their position and ignores, minimizes, or discredits research that appears contradictory to their cause. This unfortunate bias is unlikely to change in the current "squeaky wheel gets the most grease" environment.

History of Family Violence

A historical perspective is critical in understanding the cultural origins (see Chapter 3, Culture, Family Violence, and Cultural Competence) and current political landscape that influences societies' thinking about family violence with respect to research, treatment, and social justice. Although members of society express a strong distaste for any type of family violence, their views on its treatment and their levels of tolerance for some forms of family violence (e.g., spanking children, female-on-male violence) are influenced by previous cultural inheritances.

Historical evidence indicates that societies were aware of the negative effects of child maltreatment and IPV against women in the 17th, 18th, and 19th centuries (Ashcraft, 2000; Pleck, 1987). However, most scholars identify the 1800s as a critical time in the United States for the emergence of significant political and social activism against violence directed at children and wives (Ashcraft, 2000; S. J. Pfohl, 1977). Nevertheless, it was not until early 1900 for children and the 1960s for women that significant state and national legislation was passed criminalizing abuse of children and women. However, many complained that government interference in the family in any way was antifamily (Pleck, 1987). Prior to this time, women and children largely were viewed as property with no legal existence apart from the husband/father (Dobash & Dobash, 1979).

Most laws in the United States pertaining to the treatment of children and women were based on English law. A man was responsible for controlling the actions of his wife and children (Sigler, 1989). Therefore, the law gave men considerable latitude in their use of force to maintain control in the home. Violence within the home was considered private and noncriminal, and outside interference from any source was viewed as intrusive (D. G. Dutton, 2006).

Western culture can trace the influence of violence against children and women most directly to the times of the Roman Empire. The Roman civil law of *patria protestas*, or patriarchy, denied legal status to women and children—making them the property of husbands/fathers. Husbands had absolute power of life or death over them. Because Roman law viewed women and children as property of husbands, any offense against them was seen as an offense to the husband, not the women or children. The husband could then seek compensation or retribution against those offenders. Nevertheless, children were tortured, beaten, abandoned, and killed (Sagatun & Edwards, 1995). They were often sacrificed as a part of rituals and ceremonies such as the dedication of a public building or bridges.

Violence Against Children

The current view of childhood as a special time that warrants the provision of love, protection, nurturance, and special treatment from adults and society has emerged only in the last 200 years (O. Barnett, Miller-Perrin, & Perrin, 2011). In previous centuries, children were viewed as small versions of adults who could either contribute or detract from the family's survival (Empey, Stafford, & Hay, 1999). The prevalence of short life spans, disease, suffering, and the struggle to survive life's harshness led to the general devaluation of life (O. Barnett et al., 2011). This devaluation was particularly true for children, who were often viewed as an economic burden (Wolfe, 1991). These conditions created a context that resulted in little or no tolerance for a child. Violation of family rules resulted in harsh physical punishment or death, all within acceptable limits of the existing societal legal structure. As children were considered an economic burden, especially female children, infanticide was often viewed as contributing to the welfare of society (Iverson & Segal, 1990). Early Greek culture condoned infanticide for many circumstances, such as physical deformity, questionable health, illegitimacy, and for simply being an additional strain on economic resources (Gosselin, 2003). Sexual abuse of children was also commonplace within and outside the family (Lascaratos & Poulakou-Rebelakou, 2000).

The influence of Judaism, and later, in the fourth century, Christianity, protected the right of life for a child, regardless of the child's physical condition or contribution to society. In particular, the commandment "Thou shalt not kill" became a prohibition against the infanticide that was common in other cultures (Gosselin, 2003). Furthermore, because a woman's primary role was to bear children, infanticide resulted in harsh consequences. Likewise, abortion was considered murder and was accompanied by severe punishment (Pushkareva, 1997).

Although the courts in medieval Britain were supposed to be operating in the best interests of children, as late as the early 1800s records indicate that deaths of infants by drowning, suffocation, starvation, burning, and scalding were common practice (Radbill, 1987). The practice of infanticide is considered by many scholars to have been the most frequent crime throughout Europe and remained such until the early 1800s (Piers, 1978).

In the United States, it was during the 17th century that Protestant reformers implemented the first laws against child abuse in Massachusetts (Pleck, 1987). However, because of the combination of views both extolling the value of children in God's eyes and yet proclaiming the child's inclination toward evil, these laws were enforced inconsistently. That is, the laws were enforced only with evidence that the child was totally blameless in his or her behavior toward the parent. Cursing or striking a parent could be punishable by death for a child age 16 and older (Pleck, 1987).

The "house of refuge movement" was viewed as a significant movement beginning in the early 1800s in New York. It was viewed as a reaction to growing industrialization and urbanization in which children were often left to fend for themselves or abused by working long, hard hours in factories. Neglected and abused children or those who were delinquent or runaways could be committed to a house of refuge (S. J. Pfohl, 1977). However, these houses of refuge were characterized by harsh discipline and "rebellious" responses by the children committed there. Often these children later returned to their communities as criminals (Gosselin, 2003). In 1874, the Societies for the Prevention of Cruelty to Children (SPCC) were established. The SPCC workers conducted investigations and home searches and warned family members about unlawful treatment of children (Gordon, 1989). The SPCC also attempted to pressure the police force into enforcing the existing child protection laws but to little avail.

The cause of protecting children was further promoted during the 20th century by the increasing number of helping professionals (e.g., social workers, nurses, teachers) and the increased power that women achieved in society (Finkelhor, 1996). Both groups pressed state legislatures to pass child protection statutes making child maltreatment a criminal act (Pleck, 1987). By the 1960s, every state had laws mandating the reporting of child abuse. In 1974 the Child Abuse Prevention and Treatment Act (CAPTA) was passed by Congress (O. Barnett et al., 2011), making funding available to states for fighting child abuse (B. Herman, 2007).

Even with the current laws against child maltreatment, there still exist minority views that hold that children should be able to determine with whom they engage in intimate relationships. One such group is the North American Man/Boy Love Association (NAMBLA; 2002), which was founded in 1979. This group opposes all laws restricting consensual relationships between men and boys. "You can also take a children's liberationist viewpoint—that is to say that children insofar as is possible—should be given liberty to run their own lives as they choose, including the ability to determine how and with whom they should have sex" (Hechler, 1988, pp. 1993–1994). Recently, websites have been identified that appear to promote erotic relationships between women and young girls (see "Meet Women's Auxiliary for NAMBLA" for discussion; http://www.wnd.com/news/article.asp?ARTICLE_ID=28336). Many of these sites have been closed down, but experts such as Judith Reisman, a former principal investigator for the U.S. Department of Justice pertaining to child sexual abuse (CSA) and crimes, expresses concern about websites such as "Butterfly Kisses" that promote sexual relationships between women and children, including mothers and daughters (http://www.wnd.com/?pageId=14612). Advocacy groups such as Making Daughters Safe Again "support and advocate for survivors of mother–daughter sexual abuse (mdsa), to educate professionals and the general public, and to inspire action, knowledge, healing and hope" (Making Daughters Safe Again, 2010, http://mdsa-online.org/). The commonality between both adult males and females who advocate for sexual relationships with children is the belief that children are being oppressed by adults who have taken away their right to fully express their sexuality as they choose. The promotion of such beliefs and actions is clearly illegal and not in the best interest of the child (Finkelhor, 1994).

Violence Against Female Intimates

Down through history and up until the last 100 years, women have had few rights and have been dominated by men. Many believe that this inequality has been the basis for the vast majority of IPV against women (L. E. A. Walker, 2009). The early practice of patriarchy (Greek for "father as ruler") set both the legal and social practice course from thousands of years ago to the present. Both the idea of keeping IPV private and the hesitancy of law enforcement involvement have their roots in this age-old concept.

Some believe that patriarchy was intended to oppress and control women, whereas others believe it initially was instituted for survival and structure based on the belief that women were intellectually and physically inferior to men (Gosselin, 2003). Regardless of its origins, the outcome has been the same: a perceived inequality between the sexes.

Greek and Roman Influences

In many ways, the history of the abuse of women parallels that of children. Both were valued less than males, and as the sole property of the husband they were without power or personal authority. Furthermore, in early Greek and Roman societies, because women had no legal standing other than being property of the husband, they could not appeal to the courts for assistance when abused (Gosselin, 2003). During the Middle Ages, theological writings and teachers supported the belief in women's inferiority and added the view that women were especially susceptible to the influence of the devil and in need of beatings to diminish demonic influence. This view continued to influence later common law and treatment of women.

British and French Laws

Later, under British and French laws, life was somewhat better for women. Although men were still allowed to beat their wives, they could not kill or permanently maim them (Landes, Siegel, & Foster, 1993). In addition, women were no longer viewed as property. However, laws regarding marriage declared that husband and wife were one based on Adam and Eve's relationship. A wife's legal status became an extension of the husband, who was to protect and guide her (Ulrich, 1991). Husbands had the legal right and duty to discipline their wives, with few limits. The phrase *rule of thumb* comes from English common law in which a man could not use a stick any thicker than his thumb to beat his wife (D. G. Dutton, 2006). Although harsh, it was an improvement over the previous laws that allowed beating "with any reasonable instrument." Wife beating was accepted in English common law until 1829.

Based on the Napoleonic Code, battered women were rarely allowed a divorce unless the courts determined that the violence had reached the level of attempted murder (D. G. Dutton, 2006). The French code of chivalry allowed the husband to severely injure his wife in order to maintain her sense of shame and the husband's power in the family (Dobash & Dobash, 1978).

American Laws

The treatment of women in early America was little better than in Europe. The influence of British law was strong in America, with the rule of thumb being an integral part of common law. The Puritans, however, opposed wife abuse. They were the first American group to prohibit wife beating through legislation. Ironically, this crime was punishable by whipping, fines, or both (Gosselin, 2003). In addition, neighbors were required to report any violation of the law. However, the rest of America largely tolerated and supported a man's right to beat his wife, largely because husbands were expected to control their wives. Although there were restrictions, wife beating was rarely prosecuted. Records indicate that between 1633 and 1802, only 12 cases of wife beating were prosecuted (Pleck, 1989). States were often innovative in circumventing laws against wife battering. Many states held to the *stitch rule,* that is, husbands were arrested for wife beating only if the wife's injuries warranted stitches. North Carolina prohibited police interference with wife beating until she had been permanently injured, the so-called *curtain rule* (Belknap, 1992). The North Carolina Supreme Court declared in *State v. Oliver*, "If no permanent injury has been inflicted, nor malice, cruelty nor dangerous violence shown by the husband, it is better to draw the curtain, shut out the public gaze, and leave the parties to forget and forgive" (70 NC 60, 1974, as cited in Gosselin, 2003).

Influence of the Women's Movement

Coinciding with the women's movement in the mid to late 1870s, a few states enacted legislation to protect women against wife abuse. Alabama concluded in *Fulgham v. the State* (46 AL 146-47, 1871, as cited in Gosselin, 2003) that married women had a right to protection under the law. Massachusetts enacted a similar law in the same year. In 1882, Maryland enacted the first state law that made wife beating a crime. Oregon enacted a similar law in 1906 (T. Davidson, 1977). However, between 1915 and the 1960s supportive state legislation was largely absent. Courts rarely got involved with wife abuse cases during this time. The major focus for women's rights during the early 1900s was obtaining the right to vote, which occurred in 1920.

Wife abuse and child abuse once again became prominent social issues in the 1960s, although domestic violence still occurred behind closed doors of the home as it was still viewed as a "private affair" (Gosselin, 2003). The women's movement brought a renewed interest in domestic violence but largely through its focus on the subjugation and inequality of women (Pleck, 1987). The first shelter for battered women opened in 1971 in England (Chiswick Women's Aid). The founder, Erin Pizzey, wrote an influential book titled *Scream Quietly or the Neighbors Will Hear* (see Bala, 2008). Subsequently, shelters were opened in the United States: Rainbow Retreat in Phoenix, A Woman's Place in Illinois (1972), Women's Advocates in Minnesota (1973), Transition House in Boston (1974), and Women Together in Cleveland (1976). The number of shelters grew from 800 in 1985 to over 2,000 by 1994 (Carden, 1994).

In 1976, the National Organization for Women vigorously promoted ending wife abuse as one of their top agenda issues in America. A task force was formed to study the issue and to promote government support and funding of shelters and programs (O. Barnett et al., 2011). The National Coalition Against Domestic Violence was founded in 1978, which led to further national exposure of the battering problem. Their efforts to raise the consciousness of the nation led to greater support for social services and, most important, changes in the legal system that had hampered adequate protection of women against partner violence (Studer, 1984).

As the movement against wife battering gained momentum, greater pressure was exerted on police departments through civil actions to implement mandatory arrests of perpetrators. Rapid arrest of perpetrators was strongly supported as a deterrent to future abuse (Gosselin, 2003). Several studies have been conducted testing the efficacy of arrest, separation, or counseling (Buzawa & Buzawa, 1996; Sherman & Schmidt, 1993) but with mixed results. In the first study, Sherman and Schmidt (1993) found that arrest of the male abusers compared with other interventions resulted in the least repeat violence by the abuser with the same victim. Replications of Sherman and Schmidt's study resulted in mixed results indicating the need for varied responses depending on the perpetrator (Sherman & Rogan, 1992).

Violence Against Male Intimates

In the 1970s, Straus, Gelles, and Steinmetz (1980) conducted a community-based study on domestic violence that shook the field. Their results found that women and men were equally violent, and that women used severe violence on a scale equal with men. Subsequently, over 200 studies have supported gender symmetry of IPV (Straus, 2009). Many advocates for battered women expressed not only disbelief, but in some cases rage and threats toward the researchers because of the results (Straus, 1999). This study was the first to note wife-to-husband violence. The study also noted that women sustain greater physical injury than men as well as experience more fear than men. Little information on this topic had appeared in the literature up to this time.

Possible factors contributing to a lack of pre-1970s documentation on husband abuse (besides the view that husband abuse is nonexistent) are as follows:

1. Consistently, research has shown that male-on-female IPV leads to a greater number of injuries than female-on-male violence (Straus, 2009; Tjaden & Thoennes, 2000).
2. The United States is generally tolerant of female aggression toward males (Douglas & Straus, 2006).
3. Men are hesitant to report violence toward them by their partners (Hines & Malley-Morrison, 2005).
4. Men are often too ashamed and embarrassed to acknowledge that their female partners are violent toward them, calling into question their masculinity (Straus, 1999).

Although both men and women are reluctant to label their intimate partners' violence toward them as a crime, men's reluctance is more marked than women's. This research suggests that some young, educated American males and females tend to either minimize or even support female-on-male IPV and view less favorably male-on-female IPV. Perhaps a concern about IPV is less an issue than the likelihood of injury; therefore, females are given a pass regarding their aggression toward males.

Summary

The prevalence of family violence is quite high in American culture. Family violence occurs in approximately one in four families in the United States. Of the victims of family violence, one in four women and one in seven men experience severe IPV in their lifetime. In the GLBT community, IPV levels approximate heterosexual IPV levels (i.e., 25% to 35%). Furthermore, one in five women will experience rape or attempted rape in her lifetime, with 1.4 million women being victims of rape or sexual assault each year—most of which is perpetrated by an intimate partner. In addition, between 800,000 to 1 million children are identified as victims of abuse or neglect each year. These figures do not include the 10% to 20% of children who are exposed to parent IPV each year or the 16% of adolescents who report some form of dating violence. Furthermore, one third of college students and college-age students report some kind of dating violence. Finally, national surveys suggest that between 565,747 and 2 million elders are abused yearly, most by family members.

Some experts believe that these figures likely are underestimates, as victims and their families often fail to report family violence. In addition, approximately one half of professionals who are mandated to report child abuse fail to report cases that they identify as abuse. The national financial cost of family violence has been estimated to be between $6 billion and $10 billion for adult victims and $103.8 billion annually for child abuse.

Family violence has a long history dating back to ancient times in Europe, the Middle East, and beyond. Women and children in particular have been oppressed, abused, and murdered for a large part of human history, often with the blessing of religious institutions and the government of the time. The last 250 years has been a time of reversing the brutal and oppressive attitudes and behavior toward women and children in an attempt to elevate them to a valued status in society equal to men. In particular, during the last 40 years we have witnessed increasing attention paid to abuse of women and children, which has resulted in significant decreases in their incidence. The feminist movement has played the primary role in bringing the abuse of women in intimate relationships to light as a major problem in society. However, most research has focused on male-to-female battering rather than the more frequently occurring CCV (mild to moderate severity).

More research needs to be conducted to (a) identify rates of violence and factors associated with same-sex intimacy violence, (b) improve earlier identification procedures and treatment for childhood physical and sexual abuse, (c) increase the focus on the identification and treatment of CCV, and (d) address the sexual abuse and psychological abuse of women within intimate relationships.

Suggested Readings

Barnett, O., Miller-Perrin, C. L., & Perrin, R. D. (2011). *Family violence across the lifespan: An introduction* (3rd ed.). Thousand Oaks, CA: Sage.

Bent-Goodley, T. B. (2005). Culture and domestic violence: Transforming knowledge development. *Journal of Interpersonal Violence, 20,* 195–203.

Dutton, D. G. (2006). *Rethinking domestic violence.* Vancouver, British Columbia, Canada: UBC Press.

Hattery, A. J. (2009). *Intimate partner violence.* New York, NY: Rowman & Littlefield.

Hines, D. A., & Malley-Morrison, K. (2005). *Family violence in the United States: Defining, understanding, and combating abuse.* Thousand Oaks, CA: Sage.

Johnson, M., & Leone, J. (2005). The differential effects of intimate terrorism and situational couple violence: Findings from the National Violence Against Women Survey. *Journal of Family Issues, 26,* 322–349.

Loseke, D. R., Gelles, R. J., & Cavanaugh, M. M. (Eds.). (2005). *Current controversies on family violence* (2nd ed., pp. 117–130). Thousand Oaks, CA: Sage.

Malley-Morrison, K., & Hines, D. A. (2007). Attending to the role of race/ethnicity in family violence research. *Journal of Interpersonal Violence, 22*, 943–972.

Straus, M. A., Gelles, R. J., & Steinmetz, S. (1980). *Behind closed doors: Violence in the American family.* Garden City, NY: Anchor.

Tjaden, P., & Thoennes, N. (2000). *Full report of prevalence, incidence, and consequences of intimate partner violence: Findings from the National Violence Against Women Survey.* Retrieved February 2005 from http://www.ncjrs.org/pdffiles1/nij/181867.pdf

chapter 2

Explanations and Models of Family Violence

Explanations for family violence range from influences related to the individual (e.g., psychopathology), to psychosocial influences (e.g., social learning), to sociocultural influences (e.g., cultural norms), and to genetic influences (Hines & Malley-Morrison, 2005). A model of family violence including all the above types is the nested ecological model (Belsky, 1993; D. G. Dutton, 1985) based on Bronfenbrenner's (1979) view that human development and behavior are affected by a series of social factors represented by a number of individual and environment contexts: microsystem, mesosystem, exosystem, and macrosystem. Belsky (1993) added an individual development level he called *ontogenetic*. Boundaries between these contexts are permeable in that events and relationships in one context can affect events and relationships in other contexts. An understanding of family violence from the nested ecological model provides counselors with a basis for understanding family violence and a model for planning interventions for one or more levels, contingent on clients' needs and willingness to change.

This chapter provides an overview of the major theories explaining family violence and its treatment. The major theories include social cognitive learning theory, feminist theory, attachment theory, and family systems theory as well as Bronfenbrenner's ecological model.

Nested Ecological Model

Ontogenetic/Individual

Ontogenetic factors influence family violence through biological and contextual elements that shape an individual's responses to microsystem and exosystem stressors. Biological/genetic factors are modified by the influence of nature and nurture (Belsky, 1993).

Behavioral Genetics

Hines and Saudino (2009) conducted a twin study of genetic and nonshared environmental influences and concluded that shared genes, not shared environments, accounted for 20% of the variance in IPV. Genetic factors may influence a person's tendency to be involved in aggressive romantic relationships and to choose aggressive partners. Genetic influences are probabilistic, not deterministic, factors of aggression and are contingent on environmental factors for expression of violence in relationships (Hines & Saudino, 2009).

Biological Factors

Biological factors such as low serotonin levels (Royce & Coccaro, 2001) and high levels of testosterone (Soler, Vinayak, & Quadagno, 2000) are associated with IPV and child abuse. Head injuries are found with a large portion of male abusers (Pinto et al., 2010). These injuries damage the frontal lobes, which are related to aggression.

Nonbiological Factors

Nonbiological ontogenetic factors include insecure attachment of the male partner-abuser (Lawson, 2008), disorganized and insecure attachment of the child-abusing mother (George, 1996; Moncher, 1996), social skills deficits of the partner abuser (Holtzworth-Munroe, 2000), history of having witnessed interparental violence as a child (Onyskiw, 2003; Wolfe, Crooks, Lee, McIntyre-Smith, & Jaffe, 2003), personality characteristics of partner abusers (D. G. Dutton, 2007), and psychopathology of elder abusers (Collins & O'Connor, 2000).

Microsystem

The microsystem refers to the relationships and interactions between family members (e.g., communication skills) and identified risk factors for violence (e.g., insecure attachment). Number of children, family members with disabilities, and marital discord increase the risk of partner and child abuse, with the absence of these factors decreasing the risk of abuse (Malley-Morrison & Hines, 2004). For example, husbands who perceived themselves with less power in the marital relationship were more abusive to their wives (Babcock, Waltz, Jacobson, & Gottman, 1993), whereas mothers who abused their children reported more stress due to life events and a higher rate of depression and anxiety than nonabusive mothers (Whipple & Webster-Stratton, 1991). Finally, social exchange theory explains elder abuse as occurring from an imbalance of power between caregivers and elders resulting in dependency on caregivers and a tendency to exploit and abuse the elderly (Nelson, 2000).

Exosystem

The exosystem refers to social structures external to individuals that affect them, such as occupational settings, religious groups, mass media, friendships, and support groups. These groups create expectations for choices that people make within these social contexts (Belsky, 1980). For example, environmental stress (e.g., job demotion, family separation; Cano & Vivian, 2001) and social isolation such as absence of social support have been associated with husband-to-wife violence in rural settings (Lanier & Maume, 2009) and elder abuse (Vandecar-Burdin & Payne, 2010). Male-on-female violence tends to be higher in economically disadvantaged neighborhoods and lowest in less economically disadvantaged neighborhoods (Bassuk, Dawson, & Huntington, 2006). Likewise, child abuse is related to poverty, family disruption, and high violence (Korbin, Coulton, Lindstrom-Ufuti, & Spilsbury, 2000).

Macrosystem

The macrosystem includes the impact of cultural values on attitudes and beliefs on ontogenetic development, the microsystem, and the exosystem. An example would be in some societies' acceptance of men's use of violence against women (Yllo, 2005) and children (Seymour, 1998) to maintain their power in relationships.

As D. G. Dutton (1995) stated, "What is done about wife assault, depends in part, on how it is explained; that is, on how it is seen to be caused" (p. 60). The following section discusses specific explanations for family violence based on the various levels of the nested ecological model. These models have greatly influenced treatment approaches.

Models of Family Violence That Most Influence Treatment

While the nested ecological model provides broad-based categories for explaining family violence, only a limited number of specific theories within the ecological model have influenced treatment models. The following discussion addresses these theories and accompanying research. For over three decades, the major explanations and treatment models have been based on social learning theory and feminist theory. More recent treatment models have also included family systems therapy, attachment theory, and, most recently, integrated models of treatment. Placing these models within the nested ecological model provides the counselor with additional information for conceptualizing violence cases as well as for choosing specific interventions.

Social Cognitive Theory

Social cognitive theory falls within the ontogenetic/individual and microsystem categories of the ecological model. From this perspective, family violence is learned through classical conditioning, operant conditioning, and observational learning (Bandura, 1979). Individuals learn that relational violence is effective in resolving conflicts and for maintaining control over a partner. This model assumes violent behavior can be unlearned and replaced with more effective interpersonal behaviors that do not include interpersonal violence. Generally, physical/biological factors (physical size, strength) increase the probable use of violence by men against women and set the limits on the use of violence by women toward men. These factors influence the males' learning curve in the use of IPV. In particular, social cognitive theory views IPV as being transmitted across generations as children learn through witnessing interparental violence (Ehrensaft et al., 2003; McCloskey & Lichter, 2003).

Research largely supports the theory of intergenerational transmission of violence. Childhood exposure to interparental violence and/or direct physical or sexual abuse greatly increases the possibility that children will grow up to show aggression in adulthood (McCloskey & Lichter, 2003; Murrell, Cristoff, & Henning, 2007) toward their own children (Gershoff, 2002) and toward their elderly parents (Yan & Tang, 2003). This increased possibility for violence is especially true for boys who observe their fathers abusing their mothers—such boys are more likely to grow up to be men who use violence against their female partners (Corvo & Carpenter, 2000). Frequency and severity of violence as well as psychopathology all increase as the amount of childhood exposure to interparental violence increases (Murrell et al., 2007). Of particular note, men abused as children are more likely to abuse their own children as well as to commit more violence in general (Murrell et al., 2007). In fact, between 60% and 70% of abusive males were physically or sexually abused as children (Delsol & Margolin, 2004). These individuals have an increased probability of being both victims and perpetrators in intimacy violence (Ehrensaft et al., 2003). However, not all males who observe interparental violence become violent. J. G. Kaufman and Zigler (1987) concluded that approximately 30% of children who witness violence become violent themselves, leaving 70% who do not. Observing interparental violence may be a stronger predictor of later IPV then being physically abused (D. G. Dutton, 2000; Hotaling & Sugarman, 1986).

Other theories place a primary emphasis on the cognitive elements in the process of learning to use violence in the family. Similar to social cognitive theory, social control theory posits that children learn from parental models that the use of force, including violence, is an effective means to obtain compliance from less powerful family members (Gelles, 1983; Goode, 1971). In the same vein, social information processing theory holds that perpetrators of IPV possess deficits in decoding relationship information, which results in misattributions and unrealistic expectations for children and partners (Hastings, 2000; Holtzworth-Munroe, 2000). Treatment models for perpetrators based on social cognitive theory and social exchange theory assume that family violence is caused by (a) a lack of behavioral skill that impede the appropriate expression and processing of feelings, leading to maladaptive behavioral expression of anger; and (b) a lack of cognitive skills, resulting in distorted cognitions and statements about oneself and one's intimate partner (Murphy & Eckhardt, 2005). Treatment approaches emphasize cognitive restructuring, emotional regulation, and relationship skills training (Murphy & Eckhardt, 2005). Focal elements of treatment regime include motivation to change, commitment to nonviolence, implementation of time-out procedures, exploration of (or updating of) attitudes toward women and violence, examination and challenging of maladaptive beliefs, responsibility plans, anger and stress management, relaxation training, communication skills, and appropriate assertiveness. Chapters 7 and 8 in this book address assessment and treatment of offenders in greater detail.

Feminist Theory

Though similar conceptually to social cognitive theory, feminist theory attends to the broader sociocultural influences (macrosystem) regarding male-on-female

IPV and abuse of children and elders. Radical feminist sociocultural theory holds that almost all family violence is based on the patriarchal values of our society (Damant et al., 2008). These values are sanctioned by a culture in which male domination of women and children is both covertly and overtly reinforced (Bograd, 1988; G. Kaufman, 1992). Men possess more social, economic, and political power and standing in the culture than women. As a result, men consider themselves to be superior to women and children and entitled to use whatever means necessary to maintain this status. Thus, violence is considered a normative reaction to the male socialization process (Bograd, 1988; L. E. Walker, 1984). From this perspective, the male's sense of entitlement and gender inequality are the main causes of IPV and child abuse (O. Barnett et al., 2011). Feminist models typically view IPV as normal male behavior and not an indication of psychopathology or dysfunctional relationship interactions (Murphy & Eckhardt, 2005). Therefore, male IPV largely is seen as a criminal act and should be addressed through the criminal justice system.

Other feminist perspectives view IPV from a broader perspective. For example, *intersectional feminism* views IPV as one form of oppression, with multiple factors intersecting to cause IPV, such as race, class, gender, sexual orientation, prejudice, class differences, and heterosexual bias. *Postmodern feminist theory* deemphasizes male–female differences but highlights power differentials among all people, with a greater emphasis on individualism rather than collective political action, as is the case with radical feminist theory (Damant et al., 2008).

Some research has found a significantly higher rate of IPV among men who hold patriarchal ideologies and approve of violent attitudes toward a female partner (Kantor & Straus, 1989; Stith & Farley, 1993). Also, Straus (1994) found that higher levels of wife abuse occurred within a context of social inequality between men and women. Moreover, increasing male control and domination in the family is associated with a greater possibility of child abuse (Bowker, Arbitell, & McFerron, 1988). However, some scholars have noted several challenges to an exclusively feminist explanation of family violence: (a) IPV exists in gay and lesbian relationships (Tjaden & Thoennes, 2000), (b) unprovoked abusive behavior by some female perpetrators exists (Gelles, 1995), (c) the frequency of unidirectional "severe" female IPV is equal to or slightly higher than male unidirectional IPV (Archer, 2000), (d) as many females as males are violent in community samples (Straus, 1999), (e) men who abuse their partners are no more likely than non-partner-abusive men to support sexist beliefs about women (Eckhardt & Dye, 2000), (f) there are large numbers of males in a patriarchal society who do not engage in IPV (D. G. Dutton, 2007), and (g) more women than men physically abuse their children (U.S. DHHS, 2007). A large portion of research has not supported patriarchy as the most significant predictor or correlate with IPV (Archer, 2000; D. G. Dutton & Nichols, 2005). Intimacy and psychological factors are more significant than gender in many studies (D. G. Dutton & Nichols, 2005; Ehrensaft, Cohen, & Johnson, 2006).

Consistent with its ideology, feminist-based treatments largely are psychoeducational, emphasizing resocialization and egalitarian relationships between males and females (Pence & Paymar, 1993). Interventions focus on changing attitudes that support male privilege, dominance, power tactics, intimidation, and self-justification for abuse (Murphy & Eckhardt, 2005). Social and political action is viewed as a large part of the change process, with a focus on institutions and male privilege (Worell & Remer, 2002).

Patriarchy is a significant but not sufficient explanation or risk marker for all family violence. As noted from the outset of this chapter, family violence is likely caused by a number of factors rather than there being one exclusive causal explanation. This is an important concept to remember for counselors working with family violence. Failure to acknowledge multiple causes and influences can hamper effective treatment. The issue of integration is addressed more fully in the Theory Convergence section and throughout subsequent chapters.

Psychopathology

The presence of significant psychopathology distinguishes a large portion of partner-violent men from non-partner-violent men. Research suggests that between 50% and 90% of court-ordered partner abusers have distinct personality disorder traits (Dixon & Browne, 2003; D. G. Dutton, 2007). Of particular note, research indicates that personality factors and psychopathology are the strongest predictors of IPV and violence severity (D. G. Dutton & Corvo, 2006; Ehrensaft et al., 2006). Several studies have identified distinct subtypes of male partner-abusers characterized by one or more of the following personality features: antisocial, borderline, narcissistic, dependent, and passive–aggressive (Holtzworth-Munroe, Meehan, Herron, Rehman, & Stuart, 2003). Antisocial and borderline features have been the primary defining characteristics found in the majority of these studies. Men with antisocial features attempt to control and intimidate partners, and they exhibit significant deficits in empathy and remorse and have disregard for the rights of others (Holtzworth-Munroe & Mehan, 2004). Men with borderline features are characterized by unstable self-concepts and identities, impulsiveness, and anxiety-based rage related to rejection or abandonment (D. G. Dutton, 2007).

Personality features also distinguish partner-violent from non-partner-violent men, with partner-violent men displaying more personality disorder features than non-partner-violent men (Hamberger, Lohr, Bonge, & Tolin, 1996; Lawson et al., 2003). Other psychological problems related to IPV include mood disorders, bipolar disorder, and emotional dysregulation. The origins of these problems often are addressed within the context of insecure attachment, trauma, and psychodynamic theory. It is interesting that research suggests a relationship between borderline personality disorder and anxious attachment and between antisocial personality disorder and avoidant attachment (Mauricio, Tein, & Lopez, 2007).

Psychodynamic/Attachment Theory

Psychodynamic explanations for family violence emphasize the quality of early parent and child relationships (ontogenetic/microsystem; D. G. Dutton, 2007). In particular, attachment theory views humans as goal directed with basic relational needs of security, protection, and intimacy with a predictable attachment figure (Bowlby, 1988). The development of internal working models of relationships in childhood organizes predictions about availability and receptiveness of attachment figures. In addition, internal working models direct the formation of enduring core cognitive processes that define the self, self in the world, and self in relationships, especially one's worthiness of others' care (Bowlby, 1973). Children develop maladaptive internal working models of relationships when caregivers are consistently unreliable, absent, or unresponsive. Disruptions in the attachment process precipitate intense anger, anxiety, fear, and grief that impede the child's ability to develop a trusting and secure attachment with the caregiver. Long-term disruptions in a predictable, caring, and safe childhood environment create maladaptive models of relating that lead to dysfunctional affective regulation strategies in close relationships (e.g., avoidance, intimidation, and aggression; Bowlby, 1988). These early working models become an ingrained aspect of one's personality and continue their influence into adult relationships (Bretherton & Munholland, 2008; Rothbard & Shaver, 1994).

Evidence links early attachment pattern, IPV, and childhood aggression. Children who are maltreated and/or are exposed to IPV are more likely than other children to exhibit insecure attachment (i.e., anxious avoidant or ambivalent; Cicchetti & Barnett, 1991). In turn, these children display more aggression in general toward their peers (George & Main, 1979) and more aggression in response to distressed peers (Main & George, 1985). Also, disorganized and avoidant behaviors in children predict latter aggression (Lyons-Ruth, Alpern, & Repacholi, 1993).

Several studies support the linkage between adult IPV and insecure childhood attachment. Magdol, Moffitt, Caspi, and Silva (1998) measured various individual and family variables of males in early childhood, middle childhood, and adolescence. They found that weak attachments to parents predicted men's later physical abuse toward an intimate partner. Moffitt, Caspi, Rutter, and Silva (2001) found that early antisocial traits in females were associated with involvement with abusive men, and that antisocial behavior in women at age 15 predicted violence toward male partners at age 21. Finally, Ehrensaft et al. (2006) followed 543 children over 20 years to examine the relationships among exposure to childhood family violence, personality disorder, and adult IPV. They found that conduct disorder was the strongest predictor of IPV for both males and females, followed by exposure to family violence as a child. Other longitudinal studies found similar results indicating that psychopathology for both sexes is the strongest predictor of adult IPV (see Putallaz & Bierman, 2004). As the level of aggression increases, so does the likelihood of a personality disorder (O'Leary, 1993). This information is useful when attempting to quickly assess for severity of psychopathology.

Not surprisingly, nonviolent men achieve higher ratings on secure attachments styles, whereas partner-violent men achieve higher ratings on insecure attachment styles (D. G. Dutton, Saunders, Starzomski, & Bartholomew, 1994). Building on Bowlby's views, D. G. Dutton (2007) proposed that the childhood combination of being shamed (especially by the father), having an insecure attachment with the mother, and witnessing interparental violence produces abusive personality in many males. This subgroup of partner-abusive men exhibit borderline personality features, report trauma symptoms, and exhibit anxious attachment characterized by intimacy anger (D. G. Dutton, 1996). Because of childhood insecure attachment, these men experience anger and anxiety related to intimacy dysregulation but attribute their distress to their partners. These conditions during childhood increase the probability of aggression toward their partners.

Van der Kolk (1988) suggested that many partner abusers were themselves abused as children and, as a result, experienced delayed onset of posttraumatic stress disorder (PTSD). People with PTSD have significantly higher rates of being revictimized as well as being perpetrators of abuse than individuals who do not have PTSD (van der Kolk, 1996). In a similar manner, West and George (1998) suggested that IPV is related to disorganized or unresolved attachment relationships and is associated with a history of childhood trauma or abuse, intense abandonment anxiety, and controlling behavior toward the partner. The attachment patterns learned in childhood carry over into adult patterns of regulating affect, organizing emotional experience, and dealing with negative feelings and distressing situations (Feeney, 1999). These experiences in turn create a continuing hypervigilance and oversensitivity to threat, resulting in rage reactions and difficulty in modulating aggression, especially in intimacy-demanding relationships. Emerging treatment models are beginning to integrate elements of psychodynamic and attachment counseling approaches with cognitive–behavioral therapy (CBT) interventions (Lawson et al., 2001; Sonkin & Dutton, 2003). These models go beyond CBT and feminist approaches to include factors related to abusers' early and current relationships that increase the risk of IPV (D. G. Dutton, 2007).

Family Systems Theory

Family systems theory provides explanations for family violence that posit multiple contributing factors (e.g., family stress, member interactions) from multiple sources (e.g., child to parent, parent to child, husband to wife; Murray, 2006). Factors unique to families make them vulnerable to violence, such as close proximity, emotional investment, privacy issues, and power imbalances (Brinkerhoff & Lupri, 1988; Lambert & Firestone, 2000). These factors contribute to both the maintenance and disruption of family violence (Marcus & Swett, 2003).

Family systems approaches conceptualize family violence as resulting from the interrelatedness of the individual, the family, and the larger sociocultural setting (Sprenkle, 1994). Family systems therapists view behaviors as having multiple causes as well as reciprocal causality in the interactions between people. Family interactions are regulated by family rules and feedback systems that to varying degrees include the influence of all members present in the immediate family as well as extended family and intergenerational influences (Ehrenshaft et al., 2006). Furthermore, family systems purists minimize labels, blame, and good-or-bad dichotomies. A change in one member's behavior is viewed as affecting a change in another member's behavior, whether one is victim or perpetrator. A family systems explanation for IPV has been roundly criticized by feminists who view the cause of IPV as exclusively male and unidirectional (Hammer, 2003; Yllo, 2005). Feminists also strongly object to the reciprocal causality axiom that they believe implicitly blames the abused person for the abuser's behavior.

Many adherents of a family systems view of violence consider the importance of both reciprocal causality and personal responsibility (Lawson, 2003; Sprenkle, 1994). General systems concepts (e.g., homeostasis, feedback mechanisms, closed systems) can complement the individually oriented explanations and treatments for violence and need not conflict with holding abusers accountable for their violence or maintaining a nonblaming stance with survivors (Lawson, 1989). In addition, it is important to acknowledge the contribution of such systems concepts as the demand–withdrawal pattern that characterizes many couple conflicts (Christensen & Heavey, 1990). Research indicates that most often women are demanding and men are withdrawing. Research suggests that during conflict, withdrawing partners may experience pressure from their demanding partner to remain engaged (Berns, Jacobson, & Gottman, 1999). With some couples this pattern escalates to IPV by the withdrawing partner. Although having a demanding wife or partner is not a valid reason to use violence, it is important for counselors to realize that nonviolent demanding partners can contribute to the setting conditions for IPV. In addition, this pattern can also be reversed, with males demanding and females withdrawing. Therefore, counselors must be cautious about assuming that any one pattern or partner role fits all circumstances; in particular, they need to be cautious about adhering to rigid gender expectations, such as the assumption that all perpetrators are men and all victims are women.

Intimate Relationships

Finally, some research suggests that intimacy-demanding relationships, regardless of sexual orientation, increase the risk of violence for some individuals. For example, research indicates rates of IPV in gay and lesbian relationships are similar to those of heterosexual relationships (Greenwood et al., 2002; Turell, 2000). This phenomenon is often overlooked because it conflicts with explanations that purport unequal power between men and women as the cause of most IPV (Letellier, 1994). In addition, D. G. Dutton (1998) suggested that intimacy generates abusiveness in borderline men, regardless of sexual orientation. "Partner assault here is not an issue of 'male dominance,' it is an issue of intimate anger" (D. G. Dutton, 1998, p. 89). For these men, the fear of actual or perceived abandonment by a partner triggers anxiety, anger, jealousy, and affective instability. These emotions are highly correlated with verbal and physical abuse in intimate relationships (D. G. Dutton, 1994; D. G. Dutton & Starzomski, 1993). Table 2.1 summarizes the major explanations for family violence.

Theory Convergence

Although single-factor theories (e.g., feminist theory, learning theory) are the most prominent explanations for family violence, the exceptions to what the theories predict (e.g., approximately 60% to 70% of children who witness violence do not become violent, the large number of males who are not violent, the high rate of abuse with gay and lesbian couples) have led to criticism of single-theory explanations for family violence (D. G. Dutton, 2007). Each of the individual explanations fails to provide a stand-alone explanation for violence.

However, each of the theories provides a meaningful part of the whole in explaining family violence. Psychodynamic theories, and particularly attachment theory,

Table 2.1

Major Explanations for Family and Interpersonal Violence

Explanation	Focus	Major Concepts
Biological/Individual Explanations		
Behavioral genetics	Intimacy violence is partially accounted for by genetic transmission.	Genetic factors influence involvement in aggressive romantic relationships and the choice of aggressive partners; genetic factors are probabilistic, not deterministic factors of violence (Hines & Saudino, 2004, 2009).
Biological abnormalities: physiological reactivity, brain abnormalities, low serotonin, high testosterone, and head injuries	One or more biologically based abnormality is associated with partner violence and child abuse. Neuropsychological impairment is associated with incest.	Individuals with biological abnormalities are at increased risk for behaving violently, although these variables interact with the environment (Hucker et al., 1988; Pinto et al., 2010; Rosenbaum & Hodge, 1989; Royce & Coccaro, 2001; Soler et al., 2000; Wolfe et al., 1983; Wright et al., 1990).
Nonbiological Explanations		
Insecure attachment and personality characteristics	Insecure attachment and certain personality characteristics are associated with intimacy violence.	Insecure attachment creates a fear of abandonment, and violence is one attempted solution to keep the partner from leaving (Bowlby, 1988; Tweed & Dutton, 1998). The combination of insecure attachment and either antisocial or borderline personality disorders is linked significantly to partner violence (D. G. Dutton, 1998; Holtzworth-Munroe, & Meehan, 2004).
Social information processing	Relationship between social skills deficits and physical aggression	Inadequate or maladaptive social skills, such as difficulty recognizing various emotions and misattribution of hostile intent to partner, increase the risk of violent behavior toward a partner.
Social cognitive theory	Interpartner violence and intergenerational transmission of violence	Partner abuse is learned through observing that relational violence, particularly between parents, is effective in resolving conflicts and for maintaining control over a partner (i.e., vicarious leaning; Bandura, 1979; D. G. Dutton, 1995).

(Continued)

Table 2.1 (*Continued*)

Major Explanations for Family and Interpersonal Violence

Explanation	Focus	Major Concepts
Feminist theories	The feminist view on the causes of intimacy violence	The male's sense of entitlement and gender inequality, based on the patriarchal values of our society, are the main causes of male-on-female violence (Barnett, 2000) and child abuse (Candib, 1999). These values are sanctioned by a culture in which male domination of women is both covertly and overtly reinforced (Bograd, 1988; G. Kaufman, 1992)
Family systems theories	Family violence	Family systems theory proposes multiple contributing factors (e.g., family stress, interactions between members) from multiple directions (e.g., child to parent, parent to child, husband to wife, etc.; Gelles, 1983). Particular causes of family violence include identified power imbalance, family isolation, and status incompatibility as significant risk markers for couple violence (Gelles & Cornell, 1990).
Intimate relationships	The context of intimacy	Some research suggests that intimacy-demanding relationships, regardless of sexual orientation, increase the risk of partner violence for some individuals. For example, research indicates rates of physical violence in gay and lesbian relationships are similar to those of heterosexual relationships (Greenwood et al., 2002; Letellier, 1994; Turell, 2000).

provide an explanation regarding how early maladaptive personality development provides a relational context for later violence, whereas social learning theory, cognitive based theory, and feminist theory provide explanations for why one chooses to use violence and how this choice is reinforced in a cultural and societal context (Hines & Malley-Morrison, 2005; Malley-Morrison & Hines, 2004). Furthermore, family systems theories and exosystem variables (e.g., religious groups and mass media) must be considered as providing setting conditions for family violence. For example, early research by Hotaling and Sugarman (1986) identified the following social and demographic factors associated with a higher risk of perpetrating IPV: low occupational status, low income, and low educational achievement. Current research corroborates earlier research linking IPV to low income, minority status, gender, and poverty (Rennison & Welchans, 2000; Waters, 2000).

Currently, the general agreement among researchers is that interpersonal violence has multiple causes at multiple levels (e.g., individual, family, society; D. G. Dutton, 2007). Integrative explanations such as the nested ecological model and family systems models attempt to account for the relationships between multiple factors (e.g., psychological, interpersonal/family, societal/cultural; Carden, 1994; Giles-Sims, 1998). Integrative explanations for family violence may offer the most promising model for both explanation and treatment at the present time (Lawson, 2003). Research is needed to test the functionality of these models.

Summary

Researchers have offered a number of explanations for family violence. The four theories that have had the greatest influence on the treatment of family violence are social cognitive learning theory (violence learned through observation), feminist theory (violence based on male patriarchy and gender inequality), attachment theory (violence used to regulate intimacy), and family systems theory (violence as a result of family and environmental stress). More recently, researchers have posited a nested ecological model that includes concentric circles of individual and social influence: ontogenetic, microsystem, exosystem, and macrosystem. Relationships at any one level affect all other levels in a reciprocal fashion. The most promising explanations are ones that allow the integration of several explanations addressing different individual and relational spheres. Each theory provides a unique perspective that when added to the other theories, offers a more comprehensive and complete profile of the causes of family violence and thus a stronger basis for effective treatment.

Together, these explanations offer researchers and clinicians working models to help understand and intervene more effectively with family violence cases. However, future research must provide evidence for efficacy of integrated models for explaining and intervening with family violence.

Suggested Readings

Damant, D., Lapierre, S., Kouraga, A., Fortin, A., Hamelin-Brabant, L., Lavergne, C., . . . Lessard, G. (2008). Taking child abuse and mothering into account: Intersectional feminism as an alternative for the study of domestic violence. *Affilia: Journal of Women and Social Work, 23*, 123–133.

Dutton, D. G. (2006). *Rethinking domestic violence*. Vancouver, British Columbia, Canada: UBC Press.

Dutton, D. G. (2007). *The abusive personality* (2nd ed.). New York, NY: Guilford Press.

Hattery, A. J. (2009). *Intimate partner violence*. New York, NY: Rowman & Littlefield.

Lawson, D. M. (2003). Incidence, explanations, and treatment of partner violence. *Journal of Counseling & Development, 81*, 19–32.

Loseke, D. R., Gelles, R. J., & Cavanaugh, M. M. (Eds.). (2005). *Current controversies on family violence* (2nd ed., pp. 117–130). Thousand Oaks, CA: Sage.

Walker, L. E. A. (2000). *The battered woman syndrome* (2nd ed.). New York, NY: Springer.

Walker, L. E. A. (2002). Politics, psychology, and the battered women's movement. *Journal of Trauma Practice, 1,* 81–102.

chapter 3

Culture, Family Violence, and Cultural Competence

The influence of the larger culture or macrosystem provides the context in which beliefs about family violence are supported, repudiated, or ignored. Cultural norms also influence the government's involvement in sanctioning and enforcing particular laws pertaining to family violence. Unfortunately, child maltreatment and IPV are as high or higher in the United States than in the majority of industrialized nations (Hemenway, Shinoda-Tagawa, & Miller, 2002). Although significant legislation has been enacted to prevent various forms of family violence, it continues to be tolerated to some degree by both majority and minority cultures in the United States and worldwide.

This chapter addresses how culture influences family violence, with a specific focus on issues related to gender, class, and race/ethnicity. In addition, the chapter provides a brief overview of the empirical literature on counselor cultural competence and how it can be applied to family violence. Particular challenges in providing culturally competent counseling are (a) sensitivity to the distinction between underrepresented racial/ethnic groups and the dominant culture, (b) the vast differences within each racial/ethnic group, and (c) the unique contribution of neighborhoods and communities that often are more important influences than generic ethnic group characterizations. Defining and addressing cultural differences largely based on group-specific differences (i.e., African American vs. Euro American) often overlooks intraculture and individual differences. These finer-grain differences are based on each person's local social world that represents the relevant subculture within a particular family and/or community (Lakes, Lopez, & Garro, 2006). This chapter also addresses the three challenges to culturally competent counseling as well as the unique demands that family violence places on underserved and underrepresented groups as pertains to gender, class, and race/ethnicity. The group-specific descriptions below should be viewed as broad-brush descriptions that provide generalities but not absolute characterizations of all members identified with a particular culturally defined group.

Minority and Majority Groups

Individualism Versus Collectivism

Culture-relevant factors that affect victims of family violence include structure of the family, degree of acculturation, immigration status, community response, and history of oppression (Kasturirangan, Krishnan, & Riger, 2004). In addition, gender interfaces with social identities such as race/ethnicity, sexual orientation, social class, economic status, and disability status (Lee, 2000). These factors strongly influence one's worldview and, in turn, what one views as acceptable or unacceptable beliefs and behaviors within a culture. These beliefs include deep-seated values about oneself and others, one's priorities in life, and how one defines how to belong to a particular culture.

One critical means through which worldview is expressed is where a culture falls along the continuum from individualism to collectivism (Yoshioka & Choi, 2005), including tolerance for diverse behavior (Triandis & Suh, 2002). Historically, Latinos, African Americans, Asian Americans, American Indians, and many Middle Eastern countries tend toward a collectivistic orientation as opposed to Euro Americans, who often identify with a more individualist orientation—although there are variations within and between the groups on these dimensions. Collectivist cultures tend to value deference and accord within the group and thus have less tolerance for deviation from specific norms. Conversely, individualist cultures place greater value on personal achievement and autonomy and therefore have a higher level of tolerance for individual choice and lifestyle options (Yoshioka & Choi, 2005). When faced with conflict, tightly controlled collectivist cultures tend to invoke the power of group norms through social sanctions such as shame to control and punish anyone who deviates from the norm. By contrast, more individualist cultures tend to allow members to use confrontation and challenge to defend themselves and maintain some sense of personal face, although they also experience sanctions from their culture for extreme deviations (Triandis & Suh, 2002).

Culture defines what is and is not abuse or maltreatment toward an intimate partner, child, or elder and what is or is not an acceptable use of violence (Malley-Morrison & Hines, 2004). In turn, these cultural constraints affect victims' perception of acceptable options available for dealing with violence. For example, women in tight collectivist cultures may not view divorce or separation from an abusive partner as an acceptable alternative to remaining in the relationship because of strong sanctions against divorce that reflect negatively on her identity group (Hassouneh-Phillips, 2001). In such cultures women are required to be under the authority of either their father or husband; divorce and/or independent living is not an acceptable role for these women, which limits their options for dealing with IPV (e.g., there are few roles for unmarried women in Muslim culture; Hassouneh-Phillips, 2001). However, the women's shelter system in the United States is based on a loose individualistic worldview developed around the assumptions that (a) adult women have the right to live independently from their families if they choose, and (b) divorce or separation are highly preferred over living in an abusive relationship (Yoshioka & Choi, 2005). Women from tight collectivist cultures, both minority and majority populations, risk losing status in the family and in some cases risk losing their family and children.

A challenge for counselors is not to indiscriminately impose a particular perspective on a client's circumstances without first exploring options within the client's cultural constraints. This process may involve thinking outside the box and considering options available for clients who continue to remain in abusive relationships. For example, when a female victim of IPV is in an unsafe relationship but is hesitant to leave, counselors may need to take a developmental perspective realizing that it may take several small incremental changes to finally reach an acceptable and safe solution, one of which may be remaining in the relationship even if it continues to be a dangerous one. Honoring the client's ability to choose (even if the counselor does not necessarily agree with the client's choice) likely will strengthen the counselor–client alliance, affording more leverage to encourage changes in the future—one being the option of leaving the relationship if the client chooses, on her or his terms.

Similarly, adults or children may be reluctant to report CSA by a family member because it would bring shame on the adult perpetrator and as a result the family (e.g., *familism* for Hispanic culture; Comas-Diaz, 1995; Ullman & Filipas, 2005). In such circumstances, if an adult or child reported the abuse he or she may be seen as disloyal to the family and possibly lose family support and inclusion. This possibility applies to some subgroups of the Euro American culture as well. Yet, in cases of child abuse, counselors in the United States must report the abuse first and attempt to deal with the consequences of dealing with the family second.

Acculturation Status

Another layer of cultural context is acculturation status (Yoshioka & Choi, 2005). A woman who was reared in a country or community that holds tight collectivist values but who is living as a new immigrant in a larger society that holds individualist values experiences an additional layer of demands. If she is a victim of IPV seeking services in the host country, she may experience an unsustainable double-bind as her culture of origin rejects divorce/separation or arrest of the abuser while the host country promotes these actions. Recent immigrants and those isolated from support systems in the host country risk losing their only support system. Language barriers may add to her isolation. These factors may push her away from services available in the host culture (Kasturirangan et al., 2004). Factors such as level of acculturation, immigration status, size of the cultural community of origin, language fluency in the host country, and history of oppression can create many challenges and risks for women and children who are victims of family violence (Yoshioka & Choi, 2005). Recognizing and accounting for these factors is critical for providing effective counseling services. Building a trusting relationship with such clients is crucial and likely involves more than 1 hour a week in the counselor's office.

Interpreting Family Violence Statistics

Another issue related to culture is the different rates of family violence found in certain ethnic groups and how they are interpreted. Research has consistently found different incidence and reoccurrence rates of IPV according to race, with significantly higher rates for African Americans than Euro Americans (Jasinski, 2001; Rennison & Welchans, 2000) and higher, though less dramatic, rates for Hispanics than Euro Americans (Caetano, Field, Ramisetty-Mikler, & McGrath, 2005). The interpretation of this data has a significant effect on how a particular minority culture is perceived and how the problem is treated. One explanation, the subculture of violence ("cultural deviant perspective"; Hampton, Carrillo, & Kim, 2005), posits that certain societal groups are more prone to accept violence as a means of problem resolution (Gelles, 1985) than are other groups because of a deficiency or pathology in values and lifestyle. Violence is viewed as intrinsic to the culture. Another explanation, social-structural theory ("cultural variant perspective"; Hampton et al., 2005) attributes violence not to the culture itself but to social structural conditions, such as racial discrimination, poverty, unemployment, school dropout rate. How counselors interpret such information likely affects their expectations for clients and in turn may affect counselors' effectiveness with clients from a particular cultural background.

Culture: Group Differences

The following discussion addresses current research related to culture similarities and differences with regard to various types of family violence. Although culture is *not* synonymous with ethnicity, the research presented below largely reflects such a connection. In a similar manner, most research fails to address intraculture differences and differences among smaller units such as neighborhoods and communities (Korbin, 2002). These distinctions are addressed here when there is literature available. Korbin (2002) suggested that when culture is based on "phenotype characteristics, such as skin color, such groupings may not be meaningful designations of culture or ethnicity but instead serve as proxies for socioeconomic status" (p. 638). Therefore, caution must be exercised in applying some of the research below to all members within a particular ethnic group. Furthermore, it is important to keep in mind that level of acculturation, socioeconomic status (SES), and neighborhood variables are significant within-group moderators of most types of family violence. Others factors such as history of oppression, immigration status, and gender are also important within-group moderators of family violence. The literature does not consistently account for these factors when addressing cultural differences; therefore, counselors must be responsible for considering these factors in treating individual cases.

Viewpoints on Child Maltreatment

Corporal Punishment and Physical Abuse
The maltreatment of children is viewed as the precursor to various types of family violence. Some family violence researchers believe that the practice of spank-

ing or corporal punishment is the origin of family violence and is in fact child abuse (Straus, 2005). They cite research indicating that corporal punishment is associated with (a) a slower rate of cognitive development, (b) lower scores on achievement tests, and (c) increased risk of criminal behavior (Straus, 2004). Other studies do not indicate such dire consequences when corporal punishment is used infrequently and in a manner that does not harm or endanger a child (Baumrind, Larzelere, & Cowan, 2002). In general, the United States' adult population strongly endorses the necessity of some form of physical punishment of children under certain circumstances, especially younger children (Straus, Hamby, Finkelhor, Moore, & Runyan, 1998). However, cultures differ on their degree of support. For example, corporal punishment by parents has been outlawed in 26 countries (Greven, 1990). Most of these countries are European.

The distinction between appropriate physical punishment and child abuse often varies between groups. For example, Euro Americans and African Americans do not differ significantly on the use of corporal punishment, although African Americans tend to view as acceptable more severe forms of physical punishment than do Euro Americans (Straus et al., 1998). Asian Americans tend to view corporal punishment as acceptable and in some circumstances use physical punishment that is seen as harsh and even abusive by Euro Americans and Hispanics, such as burning and beating if the child is caught stealing or not doing homework (Hong & Hong, 1991). Hispanics hold the most conservative views on child physical abuse, rating child abuse scenarios as more abusive than Euro Americans or Asian Americans. Less conclusive data exist regarding child abuse with Native Americans, although national surveys indicate reported rates of child abuse as one of the lowest among the various ethnic groups. Some research indicates that Native Americans may have higher rates of child maltreatment than the overall population, although the rates vary greatly between tribes and between Native Americans that live on reservations and those that do not (Malley-Morrison & Hines, 2004). For all five ethnic groups, low-income parents tend to be more approving of corporal punishment than middle-income parents (Heffer & Kelly, 1987).

Child Sexual Abuse

Identified CSA of Native Americans children and self-reported incidents of CSA by adolescents reflect those of the general population (9.5%; U.S. DHHS, Administration for Children and Families, Administration on Children, Youth and Families, Children's Bureau, 2010). However, retrospective reports by adult female Native Americans present a different picture, with some studies indicating rates as high as 56% of females reporting CSA, with the majority of perpetrators being family members (Hobfoll et al., 2002). These high rates of CSA are often attributed to poverty and alcoholism in the tribal communities (Hobfoll et al., 2002). Other research indicates that Latino and Euro Americans have slightly higher rates of CSA (7.4% and 8.8%, respectively) than African Americans, American Indians, and Asian Americans (5.3%, 4.0%, and 5.3, respectively; U.S. DHHS, Administration on Children, Youth and Families, 2005). Some researchers suggest that Asian American and, to a lesser degree, Hispanic children are less likely to report CSA because of cultural norms that value family loyalty and devotion (Comas-Diaz, 1995; Okamura, Heras, & Wong-Kerberg, 1995).

After reviewing studies on the severity of abuse, K. Elliot and Urquiza (2006) concluded that although a few studies have found some variation across ethnic groups, most research indicates little variation across three major ethnic groups: African American, Euro American, and Latino children. A few studies have examined more fine-grain factors. For example, African American children exhibit a greater willingness to report CSA than Euro American children (Pierce & Peirce, 1984). In addition, Latinas waited longer to report CSA than African American girls (Shaw, Lewis, Loeb, Rosado, & Rodriquez, 2001). Little research exists on intra-ethnic groups. Recall that factors such as poverty, immigration status, SES, and racism often are associated with higher rates of family violence. These factors are viewed as risk factors; that is, they provide the setting conditions for abuse but cannot be considered "causal."

Child Neglect

The role that ethnicity and culture play in child neglect has received less attention than the role they play in CSA and physical abuse, even though neglect is the most frequent and widespread type of child maltreatment for all ethnic groups (78.3%; U.S. DHHS, Administration for Children and Families, Administration on Children, Youth and Families, Children's Bureau, 2010). A few studies have shown differences between ethnic groups on severity of neglect. For example, African American and Latino mothers rated several types of child neglect as more serious than Euro American mothers (Rose, 1999), and Latinos judged several examples of child neglect as more serious than Chinese Americans (Hong & Hong, 1991).

Viewpoints on Female Partner Abuse

IPV against women has been more extensively studied and has been the subject of more scholarship than any area of adult family violence. Early writings by feminist scholars emphasized that IPV largely was an issue of dichotomous sex/gender, largely overlooking racial/ethnic diversity among women (Yllo, 2005). The 1990s saw a proliferation of writings addressing this gap in the IPV literature and continues to the present (Hattery, 2009). These writings address the intersection between gender, race, and class and how this convergence creates distinct setting conditions for different women. For example, intervening effectively with an abused, newly immigrated Hispanic female who is attempting to secure legal residence through her husband is likely quite different than working with a Caucasian female who is gainfully employed and a legal U.S. citizen. Furthermore, working effectively with the same Hispanic female is likely quite different than working with a Hispanic female who was born in the United States and is gainfully employed and less dependent on her husband. These factors must be included in tailoring interventions not simply to a particular ethnic group, but to an individual in a particular ethnic group. Having said this, however, it is often helpful to know how IPV affects women in the various racial/ethnic groups to appreciate broad-brush differences. For example, which ethnic groups seem to be the most affected by IPV? What are general attitudes toward women who are victims of IPV within each ethnic/racial group? Are ethnicity and acculturation level associated with help-seeking behavior? These issues are addressed below.

On the basis of a national study by the U.S. Department of Justice (DOJ), Native American females experienced higher IPV rates than any other racial/ethnic group: 23 for every 1,000 women, followed by 11 per 1,000 for African Americans, 8 per 1,000 for Euro Americans and Hispanics, and 2 per 1,000 for Asian Americans (Rennison, 2001). The disproportionately higher rate of IPV for Native American females is particularly curious given the historical significance that women played in many Native American tribes prior to the arrival of Europeans (see the section titled Cultural Protective Factors). African American women experience more physical abuse than Euro American women, which seems to be reflected in some research regarding tolerance of wife abuse. More Euro Americans judged IPV toward female partners as more serious than African Americans, Latinos, and Asian Americans (J. Miller & Bukva, 2001). Some believe such research fails to address issues related to fear and shame, particularly for African Americans, which often leads to misplaced racial loyalty (Hattery, 2009). Conversely, other research indicates that Hispanics and Asian Americans appear to be more tolerant of IPV toward women than African American and Euro American women. Malley-Morrison and Hines (2004) attributed the more tolerant attitude in part to *machismo* (i.e., hyper-masculinity; expectation of dominance and violence) and *familism* (i.e., emphasis on family over individual needs) in the Hispanic culture and to strong patriarchal values, belief in the benefits of suffering, and fatalism in Asian families. Of note, when the various Asian cultures are examined on the issue of IPV, some are less tolerant, such as Filipino Americans and Korean Americans, whereas other Asian communities are much more tolerant of IPV toward women, such as Cambodians and Vietnamese (Agbayani-Siewert & Flanagan, 2001).

Help Seeking

Finally, a major obstacle to recovery from IPV is failure to seek help on the part of some ethnic groups, most notably Hispanic (Lipsky, Caetano, Field, & Larkin, 2006), Asian, and Pacific Islander women (Archambeau et al., 2010). For example, Lipsky et al. (2006) found that Euro American and African American women were more likely to seek assistance than Hispanic women. Furthermore, when examining only Hispanic women, low acculturation level was associated with decreased utilization of social services, especially for abused women. As stated earlier, when researchers lump ethnicities into broad categories and fail to consider finer-grain variables such as acculturation level, it can obfuscate important differences within and between ethnic groups and lead to inaccurate and oftentimes offensive assumptions that greatly impair effective counseling.

Viewpoints on Sexual Assault

Forcing a spouse to have sex against her will was legal until 1977 (Hines & Malley-Morrison, 2005). By 1993, all states had made spousal rape a crime (L. W. Siegel, 1995). Russell (1990) is largely credited for bringing attention to this often-ignored assault. She dispelled two primary myths about intimate partner rape. First, many hold that this type of assault is rare, when in fact it is the most frequent type of sexual assault committed. Second, many believe that the consequences of intimate partner rape are minor. Research indicates that sexual assault by a male intimate is more physically violent and results in more injuries than does sexual assault by males against acquaintances (Stermac, Del Bove, & Addison, 2001).

Intimate partner sexual abuse has been challenging to identify accurately because of definitions and the fact that until 1977 marital rape was not considered illegal. It is also important to disaggregate marital rape from intimate partner rape (of unmarried partner). Most data address marital rape rather than intimate partner rape or sexual abuse. Sexual abuse is highly correlated with physical abuse, with 33% to 59% of physically abused women also being raped by their husbands (J. C. Campbell & Alford, 1989). Accurate prevalence rates between racial/ethnic groups have been sparse. However, a national survey by the DOJ found that females in the United States reported victimization rates over a lifetime as follows: Euro Americans, 24.8%; Native Americans, 37.5%; African Americans, 29.1%; Asian Americans, 15%; and Hispanics, 23.4% (Tjaden & Thoennes, 2000). Less than half of sexual assaults by an intimate partner are reported to police or medical personnel (Duterte et al., 2008). Ethnic minorities are less willing to disclose sexual and physical abuse by an intimate partner than Euro Americans (Zhang, Snowden, & Sue, 1998). In part, the lack of reporting is often attributed to the shame produced by the sexual assault (Bletzer & Koss, 2006) and a reticence to disclose to strangers—particularly those who belong to the majority culture (Aponte & Johnson, 2000) and who may seem culturally insensitive or unavailable (Bauer, Rodriquez, Quiroga, & Flores-Ortiz, 2000). Of all ethnic groups, Latinas are the least likely to report sexual assault by a partner (R. Campbell, Wasco, Aherns, Sefl, & Barnes, 2001). As with physical violence, it is likely that failure to disclosure sexual abuse is related to the Latino culture's emphasis on family well-being over personal well-being (familism), lack of trust of those beyond family and immediate neighborhood, and traditional gender roles in which women are expected to be submissive to husbands, chaste, and pure (*marianismo*; Ahrens, Rios-Mandel, Isas, & Lopez, 2010).

Native American females have the highest reported incidence of intimate partner sexual assault, although figures vary greatly across tribes. These high rates have been attributed to poverty, isolation, alcoholism, and child maltreatment (Malley-Morris & Hines, 2004; Yuan, Koss, Polacca, & Goldman, 2006). These same factors are purported to "cause" the comparatively higher rates of IPV by an intimate partner of Native American females compared with other ethnic groups.

Finally, a long history of acceptance of sexual assault and rape against African American women has often lead to minimizing such crimes in the legal system, resulting in victim disparities in prosecution and an undervaluing of African American women (Seidman & Pokorak, 2011). This attitude is pervasive in the general population and in the African American community, resulting in fewer sanctions against perpetrators of these crimes (Hattery, 2009).

Viewpoints on Abuse of Male Partners

As noted earlier, IPV against men by women has been a controversial issue; however, based on numerous national surveys on IPV, it is clear that this phenomena is widespread in community samples, with both CCV and, to some degree, terror- istic couple violence occurring (Hines & Douglas, 2009). Research also indicates greater tolerance across ethnic groups for IPV by women against men than vice versa (Hines & Malley-Morrison, 2005). Research indicates some differences be- tween ethnic groups on husband physical abuse: Euro Americans, 7.2%; Native Americans, 11.4%; African Americans, 10.8%; Hispanics, 6.5%; and Asian Amer- icans, 3% (Tjaden & Thoennes, 2000). Furthermore, some studies have indicated differences between female perpetrators from different ethnic backgrounds. For example, the National Family Violence Resurvey (Straus & Gelles, 1986) found that Hispanic women were more likely than Euro American women to physically abuse their husbands (16.8% vs. 11.5%) and to engage in more severe physical violence (7.8% vs. 4%). In a similar manner, some studies have indicated that African American husbands experience more physical abuse from their female wives/partners than do Euro American men (Coker, Derrick, Lumpkin, Aldrich, & Oldendick, 2000). Self-defense is neither the only nor the primary reason reported for the abuse of men. Across all ethnic groups, in 16% to 38% of cases, women are the only partners to use IPV; thus, self-defense, which has been posited as a reason for women's violence toward men (L. E. A. Walker, 2000), is not the obvi- ous motivation (Morse, 1995). The primary reasons that women reported using IPV were issues related to jealousy, retaliation for emotional hurt, and an effort to gain control over their partner (Follingstad, Wright, Lloyd, & Sebastian, 1991). What is less clear are the differences between ethnic groups regarding their beliefs about tolerance level and causes of IPV by women against men. Native Americans appear to differ from other ethnic groups regarding the "cause" of IPV. Rather than viewing IPV as a gender issue, they view IPV as a couple or family problem (Malley-Morrison & Hines, 2004).

Acculturation level appears to be a factor in husband abuse by Hispanic wom- en. Women born in Mexico had much lower rates of husband abuse than Mexican American women born in the United States (Sorenson & Telles, 1991). Those born in the United States are less likely to be bound by traditional Hispanic cultur- al norms such as familism, machismo, and marianismo. Often, the more accultur- ated an immigrant is to Western culture, the less tolerant he or she is of traditional cultural values surrounding gender and IPV.

Viewpoints on Elder Abuse

Elder abuse often has been a difficult phenomenon to clearly conceptualize and define, particularly acts of abuse beyond physical abuse. Issues related to neglect and financial exploitation by family members present particular challenges as cultural context may determine whether such acts of omission or commission amount to maltreatment (Malley-Morrison & Hines, 2004). Furthermore, deter- mining at what age one becomes an elder has often been a moving target, with some scholars identifying age 60 and above whereas others denote age 65 and up as constituting elderhood (Wallace, 2005). Again, cultural context often provides both specific and nuanced meanings to the definition of *elder* and, in turn, to the treatment of elderly persons.

In a national survey conducted by the National Center on Elder Abuse (Teaster et al., 2006)—the National Elder Abuse Incidence Study (NEAIS)—77.1% of victims were Euro American, 21.2% were African American, 10.4% were Hispanic, and less than 1% were Native Americans or Asian American/Pacific Islander. Across all ethnic groups, women were the victims in the majority of the abuse cases (65.7%). Of the ethnic groups, Native Americans have received the least attention in the elder abuse literature. Only three of more than 567 recognized tribes in the United States and only one urban Native population have been studied.

Across ethnic groups, poverty, crowded living arrangements, lack of social support, and isolation are common risk factors for elder abuse (Malley-Morrison & Hines, 2004). Euro American and African American overall rates of elder abuse were consistent with their representation in the population. Researchers suggest that the reported incidence of elder abuse among Hispanics, Native Americans, and Asians is likely underreported largely because of shame, tolerance of abuse, fear of family disloyalty, elder fear of losing their support system, and mistrust toward outsiders. Across all ethnic groups, the most common forms of abuse are neglect, financial exploitation, and psychological/verbal abuse (Laumann, Leitsch, & Waite, 2008). Physical abuse was generally the least frequently reported type of abuse among all groups.

Brandl and Cook-Daniels (2002) and the NCEA (http://www.ncea.aoa.gov/ncearoot/main_site/pdf/research/culture.pdf) conducted a review of 12 studies based on interviews with elders and compared attitudes across the following cultural groups: African American, Caucasian/European American, Hispanic, Japanese American, Korean American, Mexican, Native American, Navajo, Puerto Rican, and Vietnamese American. An abuser was a person known by the elder in an ongoing relationship, such as a spouse/partner, family member, or caregiver. The authors drew several conclusions on the basis of their review. Regarding what constitutes elder abuse, Caucasian/European Americans were more likely to tolerate verbal abuse and Korean Americans were more likely to tolerate financial exploitation than any of the other cultural groups. On the basis of a list of abuse items ranging from mild to severe (excluding neglect), Native Americans rated more of these behaviors as abusive than African Americans, who in turn rated the same abusive behaviors as more severe than Caucasian/European Americans. When asked to identify the "worst things that family members can do to elderly," Caucasian/European Americans and Puerto Ricans noted that psychological neglect was worst. Japanese Americans and African Americans rated psychological abuse as worst. In addition, Japanese Americans said emotional support was the most important element family members could provide to elders. Korean Americans were more tolerant of all types of abuse than were African Americans and Caucasian/European Americans. The authors noted that the studies reported a wide range of beliefs between cultures on the responsibility of grown children to provide elder care in general and financial and emotional support in particular.

Finally, most studies reported a strong reluctance by elders to report abuse of any kind. Reasons included shame and embarrassment about the abuse, concern about causing family conflict, and a desire to protect the community's or culture's image. Elderly adults were more willing to talk about the abuse with family members than professionals in adult protective services. One finding of note is that some cultural groups such as Korean Americans were more likely to blame the victim for elder abuse, thus creating a significant conflict for elders and conflict within their communities. This dynamic is much like that of young Hispanic females who are blamed by adults for "causing" their own rape simply by being female. Counselors must consider such beliefs in dealing with reluctance to report elder abuse. If a counselor fails to acknowledge such beliefs and fails to initially work in conjunction with the culture's belief on this issue, the counselor will not only incur resistance from elders and community members but could create a more dangerous setting for the abused elder.

Cultural Competence and the Client's Local World

As previously stated, ethnic lumping often overlooks critical issues related to day-to-day living in a particular community or neighborhood that typically differs from broad overarching characterizations of each major ethnic group. Group-specific information such as the above material distinguishes between ethnic groups and provides a broad context from which a culturally competent counselor may begin to conceptualize a particular client case. However, more detailed information about the client's day-to-day cultural experience is necessary for tailoring interventions that have direct relevance to the client's everyday experience.

Lakes et al. (2006) suggested it is important for counselors to establish a socially informed definition of a client's daily culture and to develop a shared narrative between counselor and client grounded in the client's culture and concern. Such a focus revolves around identifying what is most salient to clients within their local everyday world, not simply the broad parameters of a particular ethnic group. Counselors should then integrate this understanding of a client's everyday life into the clinical process by understanding the client's actions within the context of his or her local social world based on the client's values and sociocultural experience. For example, a recent immigrant from a collectivist culture living in a neighborhood with like-minded immigrants might have difficulty viewing a safe house at a local women's shelter as an acceptable alternative to living with an abusive husband. A less culturally informed counselor might focus only on the woman's safety, insisting that her safety is the most important issue and that she should not live with an abusive husband. This tack fails to consider the client's current cultural world that holds to a traditional view that values family preservation over any one member's well-being or even safety. Conversely, a culturally competent counselor would demonstrate an understanding of this dilemma within the client's immediate cultural context; that is, leaving her husband likely is not a viable option at this time. However, the client may be willing to develop safety strategies that anticipate and reduce the probability of being abused by her husband as an acceptable first strategy. This strategy may be seen by some in the field as capitulating to the husband's abusive behavior, and yet it may be the best intervention considering the client's everyday world.

Conversely, another immigrant woman with an abusive husband may be living in a neighborhood with families from a variety of cultures, many of whom support a woman's right to be free from spousal abuse and who are more acculturated into the U.S. culture. In this setting, the women may view going to a women's shelter as a more viable option earlier in the helping process. The community context helps the counselor identify what is most meaningful to the client in addressing the abuse. The ethnic stereotypes may or may not fit every situation. For example, familism may be the overriding principle defining one woman's choice to stay in an abusive relationship. For other women the health and education of their children may override the importance of familism. What is important is based on a client's values within her everyday cultural environment, which may or may not be directly related to the ethnic group stereotype.

Lakes et al. (2006) contended that this model can accommodate any number of factors that are critical to the client and/or family. Thus, familism may be an important consideration but not as important as an abused woman's children being free from exposure to physical abuse by her husband. Such a view may reflect a more acculturated Hispanic neighborhood. Therefore, this woman may be willing to consider leaving her husband as part of a safety plan but doing it in a manner consistent within her community values. Thus, she may view living with another family member or neighbor as a viable safety plan as opposed to staying in a safe house. The challenge for the counselor is working creatively within the constraints of the client's everyday culture but realizing that the client's initial perceived solutions may evolve over time, thus allowing for additional strategies that were once unacceptable as counseling progresses.

It is important for counselors to distinguish underrepresented groups from the dominant culture and each ethnic group from other groups in order to have the kind of broad-brush information that allows counselors to place family violence within a general context. Some or all of these characterizations may fit a particular case, but their relevancy can be determined only when examined within the context of the client's community and everyday experience. Thus, counselors will not approach all abused African American women in the same predetermined manner based on stereotypes unless such profiles do in fact represent her values and everyday culture. This approach demands greater flexibility and creativity as the counselor tailors interventions to the particular client, not simply to ethnic group characterizations (Lakes et al., 2006).

Historical Macrosystem Influences and Family Violence

The following discussion addresses the influence of culture on the incidence of family violence and specific historical, environmental, and situational contexts that may have influenced violence in a specific culture. In particular, this section goes beyond proximal factors such as patriarchy and psychopathology and examines more distal risk factors that have created a context for family violence. Examples of cultural protective factors against family violence are included in the discussion. Most cultures possess both risk and protective factors regarding family violence. A more detailed discussion of the culture and intimacy violence can be found in *Family Violence in a Cultural Perspective* (Malley-Morrison & Hines, 2004).

Environment and the Culture of Masculinity

Some sociologists and anthropologists suggest that cultures based on masculinity primarily arose because of the harsh realities of survival, beginning with hunting and gathering societies, continuing into horticultural and agrarian societies, and finally persisting into the present industrial period (D. Cohen, 2001; Nolan & Lenski, 2004). Gilmore (1990) maintained that in early societies manhood was based on the three Ps: protection, procreativity, and providing. In geographical areas with harsh environments, such as Europe, the culture of masculinity emerged in which gender differences were accented for survival. Physical toughness, strength, and courage were particularly important characteristics for survival, and these attributes became highly valued. Furthermore, manhood, unlike womanhood, must be constantly achieved, maintained, and defended rather than being an ascribed state of being or a biological distinction. This view of manhood holds consistent across otherwise different cultures (Gilmore, 1990). Challenges to one's manhood must be vigorously defended, often through aggression toward others. Research indicates that threats to manhood trigger physically aggressive thoughts (Vandello, Bosson, Cohen, Burnaford, & Weaver, 2008).

Importance of a Division of Labor

Because men generally were stronger than women, they were hunters. And because women had comparatively less physical strength than men and spent extended time nursing their children (sometimes up to 4 years), women focused on producing and caring for their offspring and engaged in gathering activities around the home. In addition, because of limited resources, men were expected to protect their families and resources from those who would threaten their ability to provide for their families and to procreate. In geographical areas where food and other resources were plentiful and easily accessible and where human enemies were uncommon (e.g., Tahiti), a distinct division of labor was less necessary for survival, and hence more androgyny between the sexes occurred (Gilmore, 1990). After examining male gender roles across a wide range of cultural variations, Gilmore (1990) concluded that "the harsher the environment and the scarcer the resources, the more manhood is stressed as an inspiration and goal" (p. 224).

The division of labor between men and women in survival activities and the fact that men engaged in the more life-threatening tasks of hunting and war (childbearing also carried great risk) reinforced the distinctions between sexes and the related "might-makes-right" mentality. Research across 70 societies found that male-on-female IPV was much more common in cultures that subscribed to strong warrior traditions (Erchak & Rosenfeld, 1994). Conversely, cultures that were isolated and held to less warrior traditions had less IPV. In these cultures, women are seen in a supportive role to men (C. E. Walker, Bonner, & Kaufman, 1988; Wolfe, 1991).

Devaluation of Life

Brutal living conditions, high rates of death, and high rates of disease resulted in a general devaluation of life, which in turn resulted in children being seen as property of the parents, who could treat them in any way they saw appropriate (O. Barnett et al., 2011). These stark early conditions set the pattern for future generations in which the superiority of men was reinforced and supported by the family and culture. In particular, the importance of the family for survival was paramount, which added to the importance of strong and assertive leadership in maintaining the viability of the family. Violence was one way to maintain power and influence.

However, cultural views on patterns, contexts, and limitations on violence against women and children vary greatly across and within cultures (Heise, Pitanguy, & Germain, 1994; Vandello & Cohen, 2003). The setting conditions for acceptance of violence also vary, and yet some contexts for violence against women have taken on particular significance within the culture. Although many of the environmental conditions that once set the stage for the culture of masculinity and violence no longer exist, current cultural norms based on these past structures have become functionally autonomous from the original setting conditions (i.e., cultural lag; D. Miller & Prentice, 1994; Triandis, 1994). One such cultural artifact is the construct of honor.

Origins of Honor Cultures

Cultures of honor developed out of early cultures of masculinity that were based on an "only the strong shall survive" ethos that values strength, courage, and toughness often associated with masculinity. Specific to the U.S. South and West, the early frontier conditions of these regions, such as little or no law enforcement and no stable social organization (Leung & Cohen, 2011), led to a shared view of retributive justice to be carried out by each man. This view held that "a good man must seek to do right in the world, but when wrong was done to him he must punish the wrongdoer himself by an act of retribution that restored order and justice in the world" (Fischer, 1989, p. 765). This belief was sanctioned and strongly reinforced in the culture (Vandello & Cohen, 2003). A man's sense of honor must be acknowledged and validated by others, often through aggressive means. Cultures of *honor* contrast with cultures of *dignity* that hold to one's inherent value at birth. Therefore, in a culture of dignity one's value or worth need not be proven but is internal and guided more by conscience than by external norms as with cultures of honor.

As with hunting and gathering cultures centuries before, strength, toughness, and retributive violence in response to threat were functional in protecting family and resources. These values were supported by families, communities, and religious institutions as a means of imposing some social order on a previously disorganized frontier culture (D. Cohen, 1998). Thus, insults and threats to a man's reputation and family were viewed as a serious threat warranting reprisal by the offended person in order to maintain his place of respect, reputation, and honor in the family and community. The agricultural North, as compared with the herding culture of the South during the same time (i.e., 16th century and following), had greater social organization, had an established law enforcement system, and had an accumulation of food surpluses that led to a more sedentary and less violent lifestyle (Vandello, Cohen, Grandon, & Franiuk, 2009).

In cultures of honor, proximal causes of IPV often result from issues related to jealousy, fidelity, and abandonment (Buss, Larsen, Westen, & Semmelroth, 1992; Daly, Wilson, & Weghorst, 1982). Distal causes of IPV in the United States date back at least to the 15th or 16th century (D. Cohen, 1998). However, cultures of honor are not unique to the United States but are predated by strong cultures of honor in Mediterranean societies (e.g., Greece, Italy, and Spain; Gilmore, 1990), Middle East and Arab cultures (Antoun, 1968; Gilmore, 1990), Latin and South American cultures (L. L. Johnson & Lipsett-Rivera, 1998), and many Asian countries (Kim & Sung, 2000). These cultures are known for generosity, hospitality, and virtue as well as male reputation and family honor. They are characterized by strong, tightly connected families and collectivism that support staying in an abusive relationship regardless of the danger (Becerra, 1988). This situation is evident in Latin American families in that U.S. Latino women often stay in abusive relationships longer than Anglo women and return to their abusive partners more often (Torres, 1987).

Females as the Keepers of Family Honor

Honor norms apply to females but in a complementary fashion. They are expected to be modest and passive and to avoid behaviors that would bring shame to the family. In fact, females are viewed as the keepers of family honor as family honor goes through the female. Thus, female chastity, purity, and modesty are highly valued. Male honor is almost synonymous with female purity. Conversely, the male's sexual prowess and ability to "capture" other women was critical to the male's status and reputation. Women in honor cultures are expected to willingly accept and maintain the constraints placed on them. Women are expected to sacrifice for the good of the family (Vandello & Cohen, 2003).

The code of female loyalty to the family is also prevalent with Asian Americans (Kim & Sung, 2000) but with the added cultural standards of fatalism, perseverance, and self-restraint, further limiting women's initiative to resist oppressive circumstances (Ho, 1990). Unlike with U.S. women, socioeconomic factors are not associated with IPV for Korean women (Kim & Sung, 2000). However, the longer Korean couples live in the United States and the more education they receive, the more egalitarian the couple's relationship becomes and the less husband-to-wife IPV occurs.

In honor cultures, complementary expectations for males and females create pressure for men to be suspicious of other men and to subjugate women for their own "protection" and the maintenance of family honor. Infidelity of females not only denigrates the family reputation, but also compromises social and economic benefits that might be afforded them in the community.

Because honor cultures strongly promote complementary roles between genders, male–female relationships are characterized by undercurrents of tension and mistrust. This tone increases the possibility of violence against women, including honor killings (Beyer, 1999; Glazer & Abu Ras, 1994). Likewise, legal systems in cultures of honor show more lenience toward violence and even murders arising from adultery (Reed, 1981).

Research

Research has generally supported the importance of female honor to the family. In a study comparing college students in Chile and Canada, 72% of Chileans and 36% of Canadians agreed that a "woman must protect the family's good reputation," and 77% of Chileans and 32% of Canadians agreed that "a woman's honor must be defended by the men in the family (Grandon & Cohen, 2002, as cited in Vandello & Cohen, 2003). In a study comparing North American and Brazilian responses, Brazilian students more than Illinois students believed that husbands whose wives have been unfaithful were less manly and less reputable than husbands with loyal wives (Vandello & Cohen, 2003). The Illinois students were more likely to view the wives' infidelity as reflecting poorly on her and not her husband. Furthermore, Brazilian students tended to see men who were violent with unfaithful wives as more manly and honorable whereas the Illinois students saw the same man as less trustworthy and less manly. Brazilians more than the Illinois students believed that men's reputation can be at least partially restored through violence against the unfaithful wife.

A second study found that southern Anglo and Latino males more than northern Anglos believed that wives should remain loyal to their fiancé in an incident of jealousy-related IPV toward the female. Southern Anglos and Latinos had a better impression of a woman who stayed with her fiancé whereas northern Anglos had a better impression a woman who left her fiancé (Vandello & Cohen, 2003).

Some of the above-mentioned research highlights differences between distinct cultures (i.e., North and South), and yet considerable within-culture variation exists (Vandello & Cohen, 2003). Honor culture themes can be found throughout northern regions of the United States just as less honor-based subcultures can be found in the South and West. This variation within a culture can also be the case with more highly patriarchal-based cultures, such as Saudi Arabia. For example, Ghazal and Cohen (2002, as cited in Vandello & Cohen, 2003) found a curvilinear relationship between an emphasis on women/family honor and socioeconomic level. Individuals in high and low socioeconomic levels ascribed more often to the belief that women and family honor are linked (e.g., "The husband's honor depends on his wife's virtue") than middle levels of the society. The authors suggested that an emphasis on family honor might be most important where extended family involvement is valued and less important in the middle levels where opportunities allow for more social mobility, personal achievement, secular education, and individual ambition.

Honor cultures also support more physical violence against children than non-honor-based cultures. Most cultures in the United States support corporal punishment of children, although there are differences from one ethnic group to another regarding what distinguishes appropriate physical punishment from abuse. For example, beating a pre-teenage girl with a cane and burning a mark in her arm for stealing or beating a child for unfinished homework were both viewed as less serious by Chinese Americans than by Latinos and Euro Americans (Hong & Hong, 1991).

Cultural Protective Factors:
Native Americans and West Africans

Just as the culture of honor increases the risk of male-on-female IPV in many countries and areas of the world, other cultural factors provide protective factors against IPV and for family preservation. Historical sources indicate that in pre-slavery and pre-colonial times both Native Americans and West African cultures held women and children in much higher regard than in current times. Although IPV was present in these cultures, a study of 90 societies worldwide indicated that sub-Saharan Africa reported some of the lowest incidences of wife abuse in the world (Levinson, 1989, as cited in Malley-Morrison & Hines, 2004).

Although tribes varied greatly within both groups, the tribes shared common views on community, sharing, interdependence, importance of the family, humility, and success of community rather than success of the individual (Carson, 1995). These norms were necessary for survival and were strongly reinforced in the culture. In Native American cultures, children were viewed as sacred gifts from the creator, and responsibility for child care was shared among the family and tribe (Cross, Earle, & Simmons, 2000). Native American tradition indicated that parents were patient and tolerant in child rearing, and physical punishment was atypical, although some tribes had a designated "whipperman" who would discipline the children (Cross, 1986). In West African cultures, child discipline was often severe, but grandparents played a significant mediating role in advocating for their grandchildren to ensure fair treatment (Foster, 1983). Stern physical punishment was acceptable but not neglect, psychological abuse, or severe physical abuse.

During pre-colonial times women in both of these ethnic groups held leadership roles often equal to men, such as healers and spiritual leaders. For example, in Navajo culture men and women were viewed as having equal rights and status (McEachern, Van Winkle, & Steiner, 1998). Women owned property, and in some Native American tribes, women could initiate a divorce (Powers, 1986). Physical abuse of women, though present, was rare and not accepted by either culture and in many cases was dealt with severely (Chester, Robin, Koss, Lopez, & Goldman, 1994). Particularly in Native American cultures, the earth was viewed as female, and wife abuse was viewed as abusing Grandmother Earth (Chester et al., 1994). For both African Americans and Native Americans, protective factors against family violence include strong kinship networks with extended families, strong women's roles, and strong spiritual/religious convictions (Malley-Morrison & Hines, 2004).

Some believe that current rates of IPV by African Americans and Native Americans represent the influence of Anglo European oppression and slavery over the last several hundred years (Hamby, 2000). For example, Hamby (2000) stated that rates of IPV have risen dramatically in the last 150 years. Although to date no empirical studies have established a direct link between societal racism and IPV, racial discrimination has increased incidences of income disparity, poverty, limited education, mental health problems, drug abuse, and isolation that in turn are predictors of IPV for African Americans (Belle & Doucet, 2003) and Native Americans (Duran, Duran, Woodis, & Woodis, 2008).

Religion and Family Violence

Religion can play an important role in supporting a social structure where violence is condoned as a method for maintaining family stability. T. Davidson (1978) chronicled the Christian Church's centuries-old sanctioning of abuse toward women. He stated that until very recent history, on the basis of the Bible and other religious writings women have been characterized as the cause of the original fall from grace in the Garden of Eden and as being inferior and susceptible to the influence of the devil. As a result, men were responsible for controlling and restraining the evil nature of women by keeping them in submission. This view of women influenced religion, ethics, and law through and beyond the Middle Ages. The overt mandate to keep women in check by rebuke and punishment is no longer overtly taught in mainstream Western religion, and yet the vestiges of this deeply ingrained view of women remains (D. G. Dutton, 1995).

Fundamental Religious Influences

As with all macrocultural factors, much variation exists within and across cultures. With this in mind, research and other scholarly writings indicate that religious systems with more conservative and fundamentalist interpretations of their holy scriptures (e.g., Old and New Testament, Qur'an, Hindu texts) tend to support narrower gender-specific roles for men and women (Hines & Malley-Morrison, 2005), such as a woman's primary responsibility is to work in the home, to raise children, and to be submissive to her husband. The husband's primary responsibility is to provide for his family and exert appropriate authority to maintain gender roles that are based on their interpretation of scripture. Male and female roles tend to be complementary rather than symmetrical. However, even fundamentalist and conservatives have varying views on interpreting scriptures and which scriptures have the most authority pertaining to male and female roles (Bartkowski, 1996). Although many religions may acknowledge gender roles characterized by male leadership and female "follow-ship," some may place a greater emphasis on the husband's responsibility to provide loving and caring leadership whereas others are more hierarchical and patriarchal (Hendricks, 1998; Rahim, 2000). Even though most fundamentalist and conservative churches in Western society do not overtly condone violence against women, feminist writers purport that the patriarchal system established a power hierarchy that implies the use of force, if necessary, to enforce males' authority (Dasgupta & Warrier, 1996; Dutcher-Walls, 1999). However, some view the problem as distorting or misinterpreting religious texts and not religion per se as the culprit (Hines & Malley-Morrison, 2005).

Maltreatment of Children

Researchers have examined the influence of religious views on the maltreatment of children, with a particular focus on corporal punishment. Conservative Protestant denominations tend to more strongly support corporal punishment as well as other more punitive disciplinary practices than do mainline Protestants and Roman Catholics (Gershoff, Miller, & Holden, 1999; Giles-Sims, Straus, & Sugarman, 1995). Conversely, the United Methodist Church supports prohibiting corporal punishment (Knox, 2010). Hines and Malley-Morrison (2005) suggested that religious belief and the strength of that belief may be a more important predictor of aggression than religious affiliation (e.g., Protestant, Catholic, Jewish). Evangelicals believe the Bible is the inerrant Word of God, have more conservative social ideologies, and are more likely to condone the use of physical punishment than those with less conservative theological views (Ellison & Bradshaw, 2009). Within this group some show strong support for corporal punishment (Dobson, 1987), whereas others discourage it (R. Campbell, 1989). Within religious groups who espouse conservative views, African Americans are more supportive of corporal punishment than other ethnic groups (Ellison & Sherkat, 1993).

Beyond corporal punishment, religious views have been used to justify the withholding of needed medical care, severe beatings to rid children of evil, and CSA (Bottoms, Shaver, Goodman, & Qin, 1995; Flowers, 1984). In one study Quaker parents reported using more kicking, biting, and punching to discipline their children than a national sample (Brutz & Ingoldsby, 1984). This finding is interesting for at least two reasons. First, although Quakers traditionally espouse strong nonviolence views, it does not appear to affect their use of severe punishment with children. Second, kicking, punching, and biting tend to be viewed as abusive even by more conservative Protestant groups who condone spanking on a child's bottom as appropriate discipline. In addition, some Latino religious healing practices often put children at risk for physical harm during healing ceremonies, such as shaking a baby (K. K. Hansen, 1997) and passively accepting life-threatening illnesses that could be successfully treated (Kapitanoff, Lutzker, & Bigelow, 2000). Finally, although sexual abuse of children is prohibited by most religious scriptures, it occurs across most denominations (V. E. Gil, 1988).

Religion as a Protective Factor Against Family Violence

Despite a long history of supporting some types of family violence, religion also provides a protective element against violence. The more influential religious values are in family life, the less likely is spousal abuse (D. M. Elliott, 1994). Furthermore, the belief that marriage is ordained and blessed by God is associated with less marital conflict and aggression (Mahoney et al., 1999). In addition, conservative Protestant theological beliefs are positively related to the amount of hugging and praise parents gave to their children (Wilcox, 1998). As well, parents' religiosity is positively correlated with prosocial characteristics of adolescents (Linder Gunnoe, Hetherington, & Reiss, 1999). Finally, abused women with higher levels of religiosity were found to have a greater chance of attaining an abuse-free relationship following abuse (Horton, Wilkins, & Wright, 1988). To make sense of the pros and cons of religion's influence on family violence, Hines and Malley-Morrison (2005) suggested that religion may tend to be a risk factor for violence with more conservative religious groups but a protective factor with more moderate religious groups.

Acknowledging the influence of religion and the culture of masculinity does not excuse family violence. However, these factors provide a meaningful context for identifying risk and protective factors for family violence. A failure to recognize the influence of the culture and religion on family violence may result in erroneously labeling all offenders with some type of individual psychopathology or, at the other extreme, simply attributing all male violence to patriarchy. Excluding from consideration the powerful cultural mandates both to avoid dishonoring one's family and to place great importance on females as the possessors of family honor may lead both researchers and practitioners to draw overly simplistic conclusions about male IPV. A lack of understanding of macrocultural variables and specific community values may account, in part, for the lack of consistent success in the treatment of family violence. By incorporating the influence of macrocultural and historical contexts in treating family violence, counselors can help partner-abusive men find more acceptable means of maintaining a sense of personal and familial honor than violence and intimidation.

Finally, sociologists and anthropologists provide a historical and cultural explanation for the culture of masculinity. This explanation posits that male dominance was necessary for human survival in early societies in harsh environments and led to a culture of honor that held to the credo "only the strong shall survive." Cultures of honor often support the use of violence against women and children to maintain order and family stability. Likewise, religion has also supported a social structure where family violence was often condoned. However, both cultures of honor and organized religion incorporated elements that protected family members from family violence. Although the historical basis for family violence is no longer viable in most modern cultures, the practice continues, maintained by social structure it helped create.

Together, these explanations offer researchers and clinicians working models to help them understand and intervene more effectively in family violence. However, future research must provide an empirical base for the efficacy of integrated models in order to promote their utility.

Summary of Cultural Considerations in Treating Family Violence

- Consider the intersection of gender, race/ethnicity, class, acculturation level, and local/community culture in conceptualizing interventions and treatment.
- Honor victims' right to choose options for safety and treatment, even if the counselor disagrees with the choices.
- In cases of child and elder abuse, counselors must always report to protective services, regardless of cultural values that may contradict reporting.
- Acknowledge differences between broad cultural groups, intracultural groups, and community culture groups.
- Community/neighborhood culture should be given the greatest consideration in conceptualizing violence cases and intervention strategies.
- Most national reports on incidence of any type of family violence likely are conservative estimates, especially for CSA and elder abuse.
- Asian and Hispanics are the *least* likely of any of the cultural groups to report family abuse because of cultural norms that value family loyalty and devotion.

- Ethnic minorities are less willing to disclose and report sexual and physical abuse (especially to those of the majority culture) than Euro American women, whereas African American women are more willing to report abuse than other ethnic minority women.
- Poverty, immigration status, lower SES, and racism are associated with higher rates of family violence.
- IPV toward men occurs at levels similar to IPV toward women across ethnic groups, although men tend to inflict more injury than women.
- The primary reason women use violence against intimate partners across all ethnic groups is not self-defense but, rather, is related to jealously, retaliation for emotional hurt, and control over partner.
- Across all ethnic groups, women comprise the majority of abuse cases.
- The most common forms of elder abuse across ethnic groups are neglect, financial exploitation, and psychological and verbal abuse.
- Of all ethnic groups, Korean Americans were the most tolerant of all types of elder abuse and the most likely ethnic group to blame the victim for elder abuse.
- Focus on understanding a victim's abuse story through the lens of his or her local social world.
- Use interventions and solutions that fit within the worldview of the victim's local social world rather than those that fit general stereotypes of specific ethnic groups.
- Be knowledgeable of both risk factors (e.g., honor cultures, narrow gender roles) and protective factors (e.g., religious values against abuse) related to family violence.

Summary

Cultural variables play a critical role in determining a person's experience of family violence and abuse. Twenty-five years ago culture was not deemed worthy of consideration in scholarly inquiry into family violence. However, an increasing number of studies have supported the role culture plays in family violence. Culture-relevant factors that affect victims of family violence include structure of the family, degree of acculturation, immigration status, community response, and history of oppression. Furthermore, gender interfaces with social identities such as race/ethnicity, sexual orientation, social class, economic status, and disability status. These factors provide a meaningful context for understanding and providing appropriate services to survivors and perpetrators.

The culture of masculinity and honor is the basis for much of the inequities in power between men and other family members. Sociologists and anthropologists provide a historical and cultural explanation for the culture of masculinity. This explanation posits that male dominance was necessary for human survival in early societies in harsh environments and led to a culture of honor that held to the credo "only the strong shall survive." Cultures of honor support the use of violence against women and children to maintain order and family stability. Likewise, religion has also supported a social structure where intimacy violence was condoned.

However, both cultures of honor and organized religion incorporated elements that protected family members from intimacy violence. Although the historical basis for intimacy violence in the family is no longer viable in most modern cultures, the practice continues, maintained by social structure it helped create.

Suggested Readings

Ahrens, C. E., Rios-Mandel, L. C., Isas, L., & del Carment Lopez, M. (2010). Talking about interpersonal violence: Cultural influences on Latinas' identification and disclosure of sexual assault and intimate partner violence. *Psychological Trauma: Theory, Research, Practice, and Policy, 2,* 284–295.

Cohen, J., Deblinger, E., Mannarino, A., & de Arellano, M. (2001). The importance of culture in treating abused and neglected children: An empirical review. *Child Maltreatment, 6,* 148–157.

Elliott, K., & Urquiza, A. (2006). Ethnicity, culture, and child maltreatment. *Journal of Social Issues, 62,* 787–809.

Hattery, A. J. (2006). *African American families.* Thousand Oaks, CA: Sage.

Hines, D. A., & Douglas, E. M. (2009). Women's use of intimate partner violence against men: Prevalence, implications, and consequences. *Journal of Aggression, Maltreatment & Trauma, 18,* 572–586. doi: 10.1080/10926770903103099

Korbin, J. E. (2002). Culture and child maltreatment: Cultural competence and beyond. *Child Abuse and Neglect, 26,* 637–644.

Leung, A. K., & Cohen, D. (2011). Within- and between-culture variation: Individual differences and the cultural logics of honor, face, and dignity cultures. *Journal of Personality and Social Psychology, 100,* 507–526.

Malley-Morrison, K., & Hines, D. A. (2004). *Family violence in a cultural perspective: Defining, understanding, and combating abuse.* Thousand Oaks, CA: Sage.

chapter 4

Male-on-Female Intimacy Violence: Descriptions, Consequences, and Counseling Implications

Although a large number of community-based studies (Straus, 2009) have found that men and women engage in IPV at roughly the same rate, typically it is men who inflict the most serious injuries and cause longer standing psychological problems (Capaldi, Kim, & Shortt, 2007; Straus, 2009). The effects do not stop with the male or female partner but also adversely affect children who witness IPV. These children display a higher number of somatic, psychological, and behavioral problems than children who have not witnessed interparental violence (Margolin, 2005; Paradis et al., 2009). Not only do children experience more psychological and behavioral problems, but 50% of these children are victims of child physical abuse (Straus & Gelles, 1990). In addition, 30% to 40% of those who witness interparental violence go on to perpetrate IPV as adults (J. G. Kaufman & Zigler, 1987; Widom, 1989).

This chapter presents information on sources and kinds of data collected on male-on-female IPV, descriptions of male partner-abusers, consequences of IPV, and possible treatment implications. In addition, the chapter addresses the financial costs to American society in terms of welfare, medical expenses, and the criminal justice system.

Sources of Male-on-Female Violence Data

Researchers have used two primary sources of data to study IPV against women. The first is the U.S. DOJ, which collects data on crime from the National Crime Victimization Surveys (NCVS), the Federal Bureau of Investigation's Uniform Crime Reports, the National Electronic Injury Surveillance System, and Supplementary Homicide Reports. These surveys focus on various types of criminal acts, such as attacks, threats of violence, robberies, rapes, physical violence, and sexual violence. These data often represent cases of the most severe forms of IPV, such as those women seeking services from women's shelters. The second major source of data is academic-based research studies using nationally representative samples of self-report surveys. These studies collect data on the relationship context for IPV and the frequency of violent acts, rather than just on the assaults, themselves. Examples include the National Family Violence Survey (NFVS; Straus & Gelles, 1986), the National Violence Against Women Survey (NVAWS; Tjaden & Thoennes, 2000), and the National Survey of Families and Households (Zlotnick, Johnson, & Kohn, 2006).

The academic-based surveys often use instruments developed specifically to assess types of IPV, such as the Conflict Tactics Scale (CTS 1; Straus, 1979), the revised CTS (CTS2; Straus, Hamby, Boney-McCoy, & Sugarman, 1995), and the Psychological Maltreatment of Women Inventory (PMWI; Tolman, 1989). The CTS counts specific types of conflict and violence within categories of verbal abuse, minor physical abuse, and severe physical abuse. The CTS has been criticized for placing exclusive focus on frequency to the exclusion of context (i.e., perpetrator's motivation, victim's fear; J. W. White, Smith, Koss, & Figueredo, 2000). Some researchers have attempted to address this criticism by adding instruments such as the PMWI. It assesses for seven types of psychological abuse: (a) isolation, (b) monopolization, (c) economic abuse, (d) degradation, (e) rigid sex-role expectations, (f) psychological destabilization (making a woman feel uncertain of her perceptions and feelings), and (g) withholding emotional response.

Each type of survey provides different types of data on IPV. The DOJ surveys represent a narrow segment of the population and report more frequent and severe IPV labeled as a crime. Academic-based surveys are more representative of community populations than criminal surveys (DOJ) and, therefore, tend to report less severe and less frequent IPV. Both types of data are necessary to provide a meaningful picture of IPV in the United States.

Persistence of Partner Violence by Males

Forty percent of men who physically abuse their partner will reabuse their partner within 1 year (Aldarondo, 2002), with approximately 30 assaults occurring before an arrest takes place (Bodnarchuk, Kropp, Ogloff, Hart, & Dutton, 1995). Male-on-female IPV has been shown to be quite stable in early marriage (premarriage to 30 months postmarriage), particularly if the initial violence is severe or frequent (Jacobson, Gottman, Gortner, Berns, & Shorrt, 1996; Quigley & Leonard, 1996) and if it began in the relationship prior to marriage (O'Leary et al., 1989). Conversely, if men had not engaged in IPV during premarriage or at 6–18 months postmarriage, 90% were not violent toward their partners at 18–30 months postmarriage (O'Leary et al., 1989). Results of a national representative survey found that persistent male partner-abusers were more likely to be unemployed, have a lower family income, and engage in more severe IPV (Aldarondo & Kaufman Kantor, 1997). In addition, the men who were most likely to continue IPV over a 3-year period were younger, used more verbal aggression, and were in relationships exemplified by high levels of conflict (Aldorondo & Sugarman, 1996). However, data from the NFVS indicate that from early to later marriage the prevalence of IPV decreases markedly across age spans (ages 20 to 69 years) from 37% to 2%, with the greatest decrease occurring between the 20s and mid-30s (O'Leary et al., 1989). Over shorter periods of time (e.g., 1 to 3 years), IPV is fairly stable, while over decades, IPV decreases markedly.

Descriptions of Male Partner-Abusers

Research focusing on partner-violent men is a relatively recent phenomenon beginning in the late 1970s. Since that time, researchers have examined particular characteristics of intimately violent men to better understand their motivations, personality, and psychopathology in order to more effectively explain, predict, prevent, and treat IPV. The following discussion examines various ways of describing intimately violent men: correlates of male IPV, comparisons between violent and nonviolent men, and violence typologies.

Risk Factors for Partner Violence by Males

Research indicates a number of risk factors associated with male IPV. These factors cannot be considered necessarily causal or equal in their impact, and yet they provide a context for understanding IPV. The strongest and most consistent risk factors are individual and relationship factors, with much less consistent evidence for community and societal factors. Two comprehensive meta-analyses (Schumacher, Feldbau-Kohn, Smith Slep, & Heyman, 2001; Stith & McMonigle, 2009) identified the following individual risk factors for male partner-abusers:

- low levels of education;
- lower social economic level;
- history of CSA;
- history of family violence (witnessing and child victimization);
- high levels of anger, hostility, depression, personality disorders, and insecure attachment; and
- alcohol and drug abuse.

In addition, risk factors associated with lethal or severe IPV include the following:

- victim's fear of IPV,
- perpetrator's history of violent behavior (e.g., increasing frequency and/or severity of IPV, threatening to harm or kill self or others, forcing partner to have sex, choking partner, and abusing partner when she is pregnant),
- perpetrator characteristics (i.e., jealousy or stalking behavior and history of criminal behavior),
- situational factors (i.e., readily available weapons and victim threatens to leave or attempts to leave the relationship), and
- use of power and control.

Relationship risk factors include high levels of couple discord, low marital satisfaction, and emotional/psychological abuse. Furthermore, younger men are at a higher risk to perpetrate IPV than middle-age and older men (Pan, Neidig, & O'Leary, 1994), and men in cohabitating relationships are at a greater risk for IPV than those who are married (Magdol et al., 1998). Finally, childhood factors correlated with later IPV include the following: lower SES, lower educational attainment, poor attachment with parents at adolescence, conduct problems, and exposure to interparental violence (D. G. Dutton & Golant, 1995; Magdol et al., 1998). Childhood predictors of later IPV largely parallel those correlates of adult IPV risks. Thus, many influences on later adult IPV can be identified in childhood and addressed from a preventative model of treatment rather than waiting until remediation is necessary.

Aldarondo, Kaufman-Kantor, and Jasinski (2002) examined the above-mentioned risk factors among Puerto Ricans, Mexicans, Mexican Americans, and Anglo Americans and noted similarities and differences between groups. Intense relational conflict was the most consistent and robust risk factor across all groups. Differences in risk factors included a higher risk for Mexican and Anglo American men exposed to family violence and for Mexican American men with lower SES.

Protective Factors for Partner Violence by Males

Compared with empirical research on risk factors for IPV, research on protective factors against IPV has been more scant. However, two protective factors have appeared consistently: education and social support. Having attended college or completed college is a protective factor against IPV both in one's current life situation and across one's lifetime (Stith, Smith, Penn, Ward, & Tritt, 2004). Social support is a strong antidote to IPV both to prevent it in the first place (Panchanadeswaran, El-Bassel, Gilbert, Wu, & Chang, 2008) and to reduce the probability of reabuse (Goodman, Dutton, Vankos, & Weinfurt, 2005). Sources of support include friends, family, community support, and professional organizations, such as women's shelters and health care professionals.

Abuser Typologies

Early Abuser Typologies

Research has consistently found that male partner-abusers are not a homogeneous group (Huss & Langhinrichsen-Rohling, 2000) but are composed of several types of partner-violent men based on a number of variables (Hamberger et al., 1996; R. J. White & Gondolf, 2000). Typology research has focused on a number of variables for distinguishing partner-violent men. Understanding differences between abuser types informs conceptualization and treatment.

Early studies used statistical analyses, such as factor analysis or cluster analysis, to derive abuser categories. For example, D. G. Saunders (1992) used six variables (i.e., depression, anger, generalized violence, severity of violence, attitudes toward women, and alcohol use) and identified three subtypes: family-only aggressors, generally violent aggressors, and emotionally volatile aggressors. In a similar manner, Hamberger and Hastings (1986) used the Millon Clinical Multiaxial Inventory (Millon, 1983) to determine three personality types that were then compared based on depression and anger measures, which resulted in eight subgroups. Finally, Gondolf (1988) derived three abuser types based on victim reports: sociopathic, antisocial, and typical.

Current Typology Research

Current typology research has become more diversified in methodology than the earlier research. Three additional typologies models have been developed: (a) examining how violence severity, generality of violence, and psychopathology can distinguish abuser types; (b) categorizing abusers based on psychopathology only, followed by comparisons of the groups on violence and related variables; and (c) categorizing abusers based on abuse response styles.

Typologies Formed by Combining the Three Dimensions

On the basis of their literature review of previous research, Holtzworth-Munroe and Stuart (1994) hypothesized three major subtypes of batterers that are based on three dimensions (i.e., severity of violence, generality of violence, and psychopathology/personality disorder): family only (low severity and frequency of IPV, not violent outside the family, and low to no psychopathology), dysphoric/borderline (moderate to severe violence, some extrafamily violence and criminal behavior, and severe pathology based on high parental rejection and exposure to parent violence), and generally violent/antisocial (moderate to severe IPV, generally violent both in and outside the family, and severe psychopathology with low remorse and severe childhood abuse). Based on this typology, the total averages of male partner abusers across studies were as follows: family only, 50%; generally violent/antisocial, 30%; and dysphoric/borderline, 20% (Dixon & Browne, 2003). Subsequent research using volunteer samples has provided some support for the tripartite model (Holtzworth-Munroe, Meehan, et al., 2000; Waltz, Babcock, Jacobson, & Gottman, 2000). Table 4.1 summarizes Holtzsworth-Munroe et al.'s hypothesized model of distal and proximal variables that led to the development of the typologies.

Psychopathology-Based Typologies

Holtzworth-Munroe and Stuart (1994) have been criticized for confounding IPV (i.e., severity and generality of violence) with psychopathology (i.e., antisocial and dysphoric/borderline; Hamberger et al., 1996). Hamberger et al. (1996) suggested first creating typologies based on psychopathology then comparing the categories on violence and other relevant variables. Using this methodology, Hamberger et al. found three primary abuser types: nonpathological, antisocial, and passive–aggressive–dependent. Group comparisons indicated that nonpathological men had the lowest severity and frequency of IPV and limited their violence to intimate relationships. The antisocial and passive–aggressive–dependent men did not differ on violence severity, but the antisocial men were the most generally violent. Passive–aggressive–dependent men had the highest frequency of IPV.

Table 4.1
Hypothesized Distal and Proximal Variables That Lead to Male Abuser Typologies

Variable	Nonviolent/ Nondistressed	Nonviolent/ Distressed	Family Only	Violent Typologies	
				Dysphoric/ Borderline	Generally Violent/ Antisocial
Distal Historical Correlates					
Childhood family experiences	Low	Low	Low–Moderate	Moderate	Moderate–High
Parental violence	Low	Low	Low–Moderate	Moderate–High	High
Child abuse/rejection	Low	Low	Low–Moderate	Low–Moderate	High
Association with deviant peers	Low	Low	Low	Low–Moderate	High
Proximal Correlates					
Attachment	Secure	Secure	Secure or preoccupied	Preoccupied	Dismissing
Dependent	Moderate	Low	Moderate	High	Low
Empathy	High	Moderate	Moderate	Low–Moderate	Low
Impulsivity	Low	Low	Low–Moderate	Modrate	High
Social Skills					
Marital	High	Moderate	Low–Moderate	Low	Low
Nonmarital	High	High	Moderate–High	Moderate	Low
Attitudes					
Hostile attitudes toward women	No	No	No	Moderate–High	High
Attitudes supporting violence	No	No	Low	Moderate	High

Note. Adapted from "Testing the Holtzworth-Munroe and Stuart (1994) Batterer Typology" by A. Holtzworth-Munroe, J. C. Meehan, K. Herron, U. Rehman, and G. L. Stuart, 2000, *Journal of Consulting and Clinical Psychology, 8,* p. 1001. Copyright 2000 by the American Psychological Association. Adapted with permission.

Response-Style-Based Typologies

Typologies of partner abusers that are based on response styles focus on intensity of emotional state and physiological arousal. The first such study examined heart rate of men in a conflict interaction with their partners (Gottman et al., 1995) and indicated two groups of abusers. Type 1 men started with high levels of aggression and decreased these levels, as indicated by decreasing heart rates as marital conflict increased. Type 2 men increased their heat rate as marital conflict escalated. Type 1 men used more severe violence, such as kicking, biting, hitting with a fist, and threatening with a gun or knife. Gottman et al. (1995) suggested that the lowered heart rate may be for the purpose of focusing their attention in order to be more effective in intimidating and controlling their wives.

Another group of researchers (Chase, O'Leary, & Heyman, 2001) used a method that distinguishes reactive from proactive violence. Reactive violence is evidenced by impulsive responses that are high in affect, by high physiological arousal, and by minimal cognitive processing. Conversely, proactive violence is characterized as a planned, deliberate, methodical, goal-oriented response that is accompanied by minimal emotional and physiological arousal. Chase et al. (2001) found that during a 10-minute couple interaction, proactive participants, as compared with reactive participants, were more: (a) dominant and less angry; (b) more antisocial, aggressive, and less dependent; and (c) often classified as psychopaths. In both Gottman et al.'s (1995) study and Chase et al.'s study, the resulting typologies were similar to Holtzworth-Munroe and Stuart's (1994) hypothesized types and Neidig and Friedman's (1984) typology (see Table 1.1). Type 1 and the proactive abusers were similar to the generally violent/antisocial abusers, whereas Type 2 and reactive abusers were similar to the dysphoric/borderline and expressive types. The most dangerous partner abusers, according to Buzawa and Buzawa (2003), are the generally violent men who have a history of arrest. These men tend to be unfazed by arrest and are low on avoidance learning.

In a review of the literature pertaining to some of the above typologies and related issues (including M. P. Johnson's [2006] violence typology), Langhinrichsen-Rohling (2010) concluded that subtypes of IPV do exist but that dimensional (along a continuum) rather than categorical types are likely to be more accurate in accounting for variability among perpetrators.

Criticism

Typology models have been criticized for failing to view IPV as being embedded largely in social dynamics rather than exclusively in individual pathology. Some feminist writers have expressed concerns that by labeling violent men as personality disordered, they will be relieved of personal responsibility for their violence and thus lack genuine motivation to change (Bograd, 1988). The question remains, however, does psychopathology play any part in IPV? A national comorbidity study (Kessler, Molnar, Feurer, & Appelbaum, 2001) found that premarital mental disorders in men, but not in women, predicted IPV. Furthermore, in a 20-year longitudinal study of 543 children, Ehrensaft et al. (2006) found that the presence of a personality disorder was the strongest predictor of IPV, followed by exposure to interparental violence; gender was not one of the primary predictors of IPV. A more balanced view of the relationship between psychopathology and partner abusers is that "psychopathology variables should be viewed as vulnerability factors rather than causal entities" (Rosenbaum & Maiuro, 1990, p. 281). However, few studies have been conducted that examine the individual abuser within a social context or in the interactional context with his or her partner. Such studies have been criticized for failing to distinguish the abuser from the victim and, thus, implying some degree of personal responsibility for the female victim (L. E. Walker, 1995). As with most human activities and processes, seldom does a one-dimensional explanation adequately address the complexity of human dynamics. It is possible to consider the interaction between intimate partners, including psychopathology, for treatment purposes and still hold perpetrators responsible for their behavior without blaming the victim (Sprenkle, 1994).

Consequences of Male-on-Female Partner Violence

The consequences of male-on-female IPV include psychological and physical trauma, permanent injury, family disruption, child trauma, death, and monetary costs exceeding $5 billion per year in the United States alone (Max et al., 2004). Although these outcomes are alarming, a more insidious consequence is the influence on the next generation of relationships. The abuse of women creates an environment that increases the risk of IPV continuing into the next generation. Being abused and/or witnessing IPV as a child is a strong predictor of later IPV for males (Ehrensaft et al., 2006).

Physical Injuries

Research demonstrates the physical effects that IPV has on female partners. The NCVS indicated that 50% of females abused by male partners reported some type of injury, and 20% reported having to seek medical attention (Rennison & Welchans, 2000). In addition, some research indicates that women incur far more injuries and severe injuries than men who are physically abused by women (Straus, 2009), with the most common injuries being blunt-force trauma to the head and face and strangulation (D. J. Sheridan & Nash, 2007). When comparing women and men who were abused in a similar manner (e.g., slapping or shoving), women sustain more serious injuries than men (Cantos, Neidig, & O'Leary, 1994). However, several community studies indicate that female-on-male severe violence was equal to or surpassed male-on-female severe violence, but again injuries were greater for females (Ehrensaft, Moffitt, & Caspi, 2004). One must consider the sample characteristics in interpreting these results. More injuries and severe violence will likely be reported with crime surveys whereas more equal rates between men and women will be found with community samples.

Sexual Assault

Sexual assault (nonconsensual sex act obtained by force) by an intimate partner is experienced by 10% to 14% of women, between 40% and 50% of physically abused women (Martin, Taft, & Resick, 2007), and up to 59% of women in shelter settings. Women who have been sexually assaulted by an intimate partner report high levels of PTSD, depression, gynecological problems, and numerous physical health symptoms. Women who were raped by their intimate partners reported the following injuries: anal or vaginal stretching (36.1%), bladder infections (50.9%), vaginal bleeding (29.6%), leakage of urine (32.4%), missed menstrual periods (25.0%), miscarriages and stillbirths (20.4%), unwanted pregnancies (17.5%), infertility (7.4%), and sexually transmitted diseases (6.6%; J. C. Campbell & Soeken, 1999; Russell, 1990). The psychological consequences of partner rape are damaging and long-term (Culbertson & Dehle, 2001).

Finklehor and Yllo (1987) distinguished between three types of marital rape: (a) *force-only* rape occurs when a partner attempts to gain control over the frequency and type of sexual activity; (b) *battering* rape is the partner's effort to humiliate and degrade; and (c) *obsessive* rape focuses on sexual sadism, fetishes, and forcible anal intercourse. In addition to the resulting trauma-based symptoms (e.g., hypervigilance, reexperiencing, and avoidance), these women must continue to live with their rapists and the terror that accompanies this arrangement.

Homicides

The ultimate partner abuse is when an intimate partner kills his or her partner. DOJ statistics indicate that 9,102 spouses were murdered by their partner in 2002 (Durose et al., 2005). In 58.6% of the cases, the victim/perpetrator relationship was known. Of the known cases, women were the perpetrators in 19% of the homicides whereas men were perpetrators in 81% of the cases. More recent statistics indicate that in 2008, of the 696 spousal homicides in the United States, wives killed 119 husbands (17.10%) whereas husbands killed 577 wives (82.10%; U.S. DOJ, Federal Bureau of Investigation, 2010). Furthermore, approximately 30% to 50% of all female murders and 12% of all male murders were committed by previous or current intimate partners (Fox, 2005). Three quarters of those women who were murdered by intimate partners were also victims of IPV (J. C. Campbell et. al., 2003). Finally, the rates of intimate partner homicide are higher for cohabitating couples (Riedel & Best, 1998) and among minority populations (Rennison & Welchans, 2000).

The most frequent reason given for intimacy homicide committed by men is fear that his wife will leave him and/or that his wife is in a relationship with another man (Cazenave & Zahn, 1992). In one study, researchers found that 75% of women murdered by their male partners and 85% of women severely beaten by male partners had either left their abuser or had tried to leave their abuser during the previous year (Sharps, Campbell, Campbell, Gary, & Webster, 2003). Men who are at greatest risk for committing femicide are poor, jealous, depressed, have personality disorders and histories of drinking and drug use, and have mental health problems in general (J. C. Campbell, Glass, Sharps, Laughon, & Bloom, 2007). These risk factors are critical when considering how to safeguard female victims, including consultation with law enforcement, especially when multiple risk factors exist.

Psychological Effects

The psychological effects of IPV are most often influenced by the type of physical and psychological abuse. Thus, it is helpful to make some distinctions between types of IPV in discussing consequences. Recall from Chapter 1 that intimate terrorism (IT) typically is used to control and intimidate female partners in a systematic, fear-producing, and dominating fashion (M. P. Johnson, 2006). IT is most often found in studies of women in shelters and criminal justice system surveys (O. Barnett et al., 2011). Conversely, common couple violence (CCV) is typically considered minor and is characterized by infrequent, noninjurious mutual pushing and/or slapping and typically occurs in the heat of the moment rather than being planned or purposeful in nature. CCV most often is found in studies of community samples. IT violence occurs much less frequently than CCV and yet accounts for the overwhelming majority of physical and psychological injury. The following discussion emphasizes the effects of IT violence, as most of the research on the psychological consequences of female victims has been conducted with shelter and clinical samples rather than community samples (Hines & Malley-Morrison, 2005).

Frequency, Severity, and Duration of Violence
With few exceptions, studies on male IPV are associated with grave psychological consequences for female partners. IPV that is more frequent, is more severe, and occurs over a long period of time will tend to produce more severe psychological consequences (Straus, 2009). However, even less severe violence results in some degree of negative psychological consequences. The few studies that have addressed the consequences of less severe IPV—such as found with couples in treatment—indicate that abused women are more likely to report more clinical levels of depression anxiety than women in nonabusive relationships (Cascardi, Langhinrichsen, & Vivian, 1992; Follingstad, 2009). However, couples in early marriage who experienced pushing and slapping on only one occasion in the previous year reported little or no reduction in marital satisfaction (O'Leary et al., 1989).

Long-Term Effects
Even after many women leave their abusive partners, fear often continues because of apprehension about future contact (Zorza, 1998), aversive emotional conditioning (Davey, 1992), and fear conditioning that precipitates neurological changes (Pontius, 2002). Although psychological abuse predicts physical abuse (Murphy & O'Leary, 1989), they tend to co-occur (Stets, 1990). However, psychological abuse has a greater overall negative symptom impact than physical abuse (C. S. Lewis et al., 2006). In fact, psychological abuse rather than physical abuse predicts a woman's level of resolve to leave her partner (Arias & Pape, 1999), marital dissolution (Jacobson et al., 1996), low self-esteem (Aguilar & Nightingale, 1994), and the presence and intensity of a woman's fear level (Sackett & Saunders, 2001).

Anxiety and Depression
The most common psychological correlates of IPV are anxiety and depression, including more severe forms of anxiety disorders such as PTSD and the more severe form of PTSD, complex PTSD (CPTSD; Courtois, 2008). Varying degrees

of anxiety accompany most forms of partner abuse. Women who are repeatedly abused both physically and emotionally report high levels of fear, apprehension, and foreboding with the possibility of another assault (Jacobson et al., 1996; Short et al., 2000). Depression occurs in nearly 50% of women abuse cases (Golding, 1999). For both community and shelter samples, the severity of IPV followed by the severity of psychological abuse (i.e., isolating, ridiculing, discounting, ignoring) were the strong predictors of depression (Sackett & Saunders, 2001). Rates were highest and most severe in women's shelter samples.

Risk of Suicide

The risk of suicide is related to depression, with depression and suicide attempts being 4 times more likely in severe cases of IPV compared with nonabused women (Straus & Smith, 1990). These severely abused women report high rates of attempted suicides, 10% to 23%, as well as contemplation of suicide, 50% (Pagelow, 1984; Stark & Flitcraft, 1988). When researchers have combined several samples together (e.g., shelter, community), attempted suicide rates were between 35% and 40% (Stark & Flitcraft, 1995). Rates were highest with shelter samples.

PTSD

PTSD is a more intense form of anxiety disorder and results from a trauma-inducing experience that involves actual or threatened death or serious injury (American Psychiatric Association, 1994), which produces symptoms of intense fear, a re-experiencing of intrusive aversive thoughts about the traumatic experience, an avoidance of trigger situations, emotional numbing, and hyperarousal/exaggerated startle response. Other symptoms that often co-occur with PTSD include depression, disturbed sleep, difficulty concentrating or remembering, anger, guilt and shame, low self-esteem, substance abuse, difficulties in interpersonal relationships, identity problems, and compulsive reexposure to the situations reminiscent of the trauma (Carlson & Dalenberg, 2000; van der Kolk & McFarlane, 1996). Many believe the last three symptoms are better categorized as symptoms of CPTSD (see below).

PTSD has received considerable attention in the IPV research because abused women are at an increased risk for the disorder. Cascardi, O'Leary, and Schlee (1999) reviewed 11 studies and found that the incidence of PTSD with abused women ranged from 31% to 84%. The extent and severity of abuse are related to severity of PTSD symptoms (Follette, Polusny, Bechtle, & Naugle, 1996). For example, up to 89% of women in battered women's shelters met the criteria for PTSD (Kemp, Rawlings, & Green, 1991). Even some forms of psychological abuse and mild IPV can precipitate PTSD symptoms (Woods & Isenberg, 2001). PTSD symptoms often persist long after the woman has left the abuser (Woods, 2000).

CPTSD

A severe form of PTSD is CPTSD. CPTSD, or "disorders of extreme stress not otherwise specified" (DESNOS; Pelcovitz et al., 1997), is a recent diagnostic conceptualization based on the observation that some people who experience repeated, extensive trauma over an extended period of time within significant relationships exhibit symptoms beyond PTSD (Ford & Courtois, 2009; J. L. Herman, 1992). CPTSD consists of many symptoms, including dissociative reactions (i.e., emotional numbing and detachment, diminished awareness of one's environment, depersonalization, and amnesia), somatic and affective symptoms (e.g., depression, anxiety), and three characterological dimensions: disturbance in relationships, changes in identity, and revictimization and/or self-injury (Zlotnick, Zakariski, Shea, & Costello, 1996). Furthermore, these individuals may experience self-hate, shame, self-blame, disregulation of emotions, and high-risk behavior (e.g., self-harm, suicidality, and various addictions; Courtois, 2008).

The similarity between CPTSD symptoms and those associated with borderline personality disorder (BPD) have been noted (Courtois, 2008), with many researchers preferring the less stigmatizing CPTSD/DESNOS diagnosis that they believe better accounts for the trauma reactions (Briere & Scott, 2006; Ford & Courtois, 2009). Courtois (2008) suggested that BPD might be better conceptualized as a "posttraumatic adaptation," particularly when applied to women with extensive interpersonal trauma histories.

The distinctions between PTSD and CPTSD are parallel to the differences between Type I and Type II traumatic events. Type I trauma consists of an unexpected single traumatic event that often meets criteria for PTSD as specified in the *Diagnostic and Statistical Manual of Mental Disorders* (4th ed., text rev.; *DSM-IV-TR*; American Psychiatric Association, 2000): characterized by intrusive thoughts, avoidance, emotional numbing, and hypervigilance. Conversely, Type II trauma is repeated, severe, and ongoing exposure to trauma. Individuals exposed to Type II trauma experience classic PTSD symptoms along with significant denial, dissociation, psychic numbing, emotional dysregulation, personality problems, and mistrust (Ford & Courtois, 2009).

CPTSD and Childhood Abuse

As compared with a PTSD diagnosis, a CPTSD designation provides a more thorough consideration of the complexity of early abuse and subsequent factors such as trauma history development, self-regulatory impairment, personal resources, resilience, and patterns of revictimization (Ford & Courtois, 2009). This syndrome has a strong relationship to a history of early child abuse and is intensified in current abusive relationships. The presence and intensity of these symptoms vary according to the age and stage in which the trauma occurred; the relationship of the victim to the perpetrator; the degree, duration, and complexity of the trauma; and the support received at the time of the trauma and beyond. Research has generally confirmed that CPTSD is specific to trauma (van der Kolk, Pelcovitz, Sunday, & Spinazzola, 2005) and is most often associated with physically abused women and child abuse victims (Ford & Courtois, 2009). Because of the violation of an assumed trust and expected context of safety, this type of trauma is often referred to as *betrayal trauma* (DePrince & Freyd, 2007).

Leaving or Staying in an Abusive Relationship

Women stay in abusive intimate relationships for many reasons. Often reasons for staying or leaving the relationship may be one in the same. For example, the presence of children can both facilitate and impede leaving an intimate abuser as mothers often want their children to be spared exposure to violence and tension on the one hand and yet retain family unity and avoid family instability caused by the involvement of the legal system on the other (Rhodes, Cerulli, Dichter, Kothari, & Barg, 2010). Reasons many stay in an abusive relationship include hope for change in the future, attachment to the partner, excuses for the partner's behavior, children, lack of resources (feeling trapped), concerns about parents' views, religious values, fear of harm, shame, and nowhere else to go (D. K. Anderson & Saunders, 2003). On the basis of Grigsby and Hartman's (1997) barrier model of leaving or staying, many of these factors can be organized into concentric circles, with the outermost being environmental barriers (e.g., material resources), followed by family and social role expectations (e.g., having affection for partner, wanting to maintain family unity), and finally the innermost circle, psychological impact of abuse (e.g., fear, shame). Different weightings may be given to each level and each issue for each woman.

Notwithstanding the above-mentioned factors, most abused women leave or attempt to leave abusive relationships (Gondolf & Fisher, 1988). Factors associated with women leaving include:

- being younger,
- having a protective order,
- having left a previous relationship,
- having psychological/emotional vulnerability,
- needing abuse-related medical care,
- possessing external support,
- being involved in shelter services,
- experiencing severe emotional and physical abuse, and
- having general dissatisfaction related to violence (D. K. Anderson & Saunders, 2003; Koepsell, Kernic, & Holt, 2006; Panchanadeswaran & McCloskey, 2007).

However, simply leaving an abusive relationship does not necessarily ensure a better life. In fact the notion that leaving an abusive partner is always the best choice for all victims is not supported by rigorous research (Bell, Goodman, & Dutton, 2007). Leaving or staying in an abusive relationship is not a simple decision of comparing pros and cons and going with the one with the most support. This decision is a process and often entails a series of leaves and returns, with an average of five to six leaves and returns before finally leaving for good (Stroshine & Robinson, 2003). Abused women are often overwhelmed by ambivalence, noting many of the above-mentioned factors as the source of their approach–avoidance behavior. In addition, each woman will often give different objective and subjective weightings to each issue. Counselors must be aware of both the strong emotional pull to stay and conversely the pull to leave and provide support, as women often vacillate back and forth in making this decision. It is critical to provide emotional support and to process their ambivalence. It would be counterproductive to push for a decision—even if safety is the overriding rationale—without supporting and validating women as they struggle with this decision. Such a decision is neither likely to be made in one session, nor likely to be made with absolute resolve. Furthermore, whatever decision is made may be reversed at some later date. Counselors must be prepared for such a process and realize that the client's vacillation may have less to do with counseling skill and more to do with the gravity of the situation. Counselors must keep in check their desire for clarity and validate the client's ambivalence and the confusion and distress such a process entails.

Treatment Implications for Male Partner-Abusers

On the basis of typology research, men who physically and/or verbally abuse their intimate female partners are not a monolithic group. Research indicates that these men often differ on severity of violence, personality/psychopathology factors, generality of violence, history of family violence, attachment style, control, and attitudes toward women (Dixon & Browne, 2003). Typology research has consistently found between two and four types of partner-violent men. The importance of treatment matching would seem to be a logical conclusion from these results; however, there is a lack of consistent empirical evidence that supports many of the treatment options discussed below. Yet the following suggestions provide counselors with a general starting point in case conceptualization. As with all counseling, regardless of the model, it must be tailored to the individual needs of the client. The men who use the least severe violence, have little or no psychopathology, and tend to have the least hostile attitudes toward women might benefit most from standard treatment for partner-violent men. Their form of violence often includes some degree of CCV that results from escalation of emotionally charged disagreements. Treatment includes some combination of short-term psychoeducation and CBT that focus on anger management and conflict management skills (Murphy & Eckhardt, 2005).

Intimate-partner-violent men who have greater psychopathology, such as the borderline/dysphoric, would likely be less successful with only the psychoeducation and brief CBT models of treatments. These men often use violence to control and punish (i.e., IT), often have poor attachments and low self-esteem, and are extremely jealous (Holtzworth-Munroe, Stuart, & Hutchinson, 1997). Using approaches that focus on personality characteristics would seem to be necessary in addition to psychoeducation and CBT. For the borderline/dysphoric men, such approaches as dialectical behavioral therapy (Linehan, 1993), schema-focused therapy (Young, 1999), and psychodynamic approaches can be integrated with the psychoeducation and CBT (Lawson, Kellam, Quinn, & Malnar, 2012).

Treatment for antisocial men or those with primary psychopathy may be more challenging. Treatment outcomes for these men have not been encouraging (Garrido, Esteban, & Molero, 1996). Those who have more severe psychopathy do not believe they have a problem nor do they see any reason to change their behavior (Gottman et al., 1995; Hare, 1993). Meyer and Deitsch (1996) suggested that individual or group therapy is often a "finishing school" for those with primary psychopathy and only serves to develop a more manipulative psychopathic person. The treatments that have worked tend to be confrontational, behavioral, and highly structured but require some type of coercion, such as institutionalization or close monitoring (Winston et al., 1994). Those with less severe psychopathy may benefit to some degree from CBT. D. G. Saunders (1996) found that antisocial batterers showed better outcome when treatment was combined with feminist CBT as opposed to psychodynamic-process group therapy, which worked better with borderline/dysphoric types.

Gender-specific group treatment would be most appropriate for borderline/ dysphoric and antisocial types. Jennings and Murphy (2000) asserted that group treatment is preferred over other treatment modalities because it provides an opportunity for men to work on male-to-male relationships. They believe that a lack of healthy male-to-male relationships may contribute to men placing an inordinate amount of responsibility on female intimates to meet intimacy needs, which thus contributes to intimacy violence. In addition, most clinicians oppose couples treatment for men who have severe psychopathology as it may endanger the partner and be less effective because of the greater probability of their partner's level of fear and mistrust (Holtzworth-Munroe, Meehan, Rehman, & Marshall, 2002). Couple treatment may be considered once successful gender-specific treatment has been completed, but this must be considered on a client-by-client basis.

The nonpathological men could also benefit from the group treatment modality but may also be appropriate for conjoint couple treatment if they are committed to nonviolence and their female partners are not intimidated or fearful of violent reprisals as a result of couple work. Most experts agree that conjoint treatment is only appropriate with low to moderate violence and if the woman does not expect imminent violence as a result of treatment (Holtzworth-Munroe et al., 2002). Greater detail on treatment for male offenders is provided in Chapters 7 and 8.

The following case examples illustrate two types of partner abusers.

Case Examples[1]

The Emotionally Volatile Wife Abuser

Bill told his wife, Ann, that if she ever went anywhere without first checking with him that she would "force" him to take strong action. Action for Bill means grabbing, hitting, pushing, and intimidating. Ann reported that she could tell when Bill was upset because he would become noticeably tense and alternate between being very quiet and being very loud and intimidating. It could take days or weeks for Bill to reach a level of rage that resulted in violence. Extreme emotions seem to best describe him. He can be extremely nice and caring but also express rage and extreme jealousy. Some might describe Bill as living on an emotional roller coaster. Bill's greatest fear is that Ann will leave him. Bill also reports a relationship history with his parents and previous intimate partners that indicate an insecure attachment style characterized by extreme fear of abandonment and rejection by others. Unfortunately for Ann, Bill uses verbal abuse such as shame and humiliation in an attempt to control her. If this doesn't work, he uses physical violence. However, he typically apologizes for his violence, although at times it seems superficial and disingenuous. As a result, Ann is often confused about her feelings about Bill. On the one hand she says she truly loves him, and yet his cyclical moodiness and use of humiliation and violence cause her to question whether she can stay in the relationship.

[1]Identifying information in all case examples has been limited to protect clients' confidentiality.

Bill's abusive pattern of behavior fits L. E. Walker's (1979) cycle of violence (tension building, violent episode, and remorse) and Holtzworth-Munroe and Stuart's (1994) typology of dysphoric/borderline abuser. He would most likely benefit from some combination of CBT and psychodynamic therapy to address his problems with anger, his distorted beliefs about relationships and women, and his insecure attachment style in romantic relationships. Interventions might include helping Bill gain an awareness of internal and external triggers for his anger and insecure feelings, helping him develop self-regulation skills such as focused breathing, and identifying and changing distorted beliefs about controlling Ann and his sense of insecurity in intimacy-demanding relationships. A strong therapeutic alliance would be important in working with Bill, especially during treatment times that focus on long-held feelings of insecurity in relationships. Treatment should start in a group setting with other male partner-abusers but with the possibility of later conjoint couple treatment if Bill gains greater control over his behavior and emotions and is committed to nonviolence. Furthermore, Ann should be encouraged to make contact with a local women's shelter for support groups and to make contingency plans for safety.

The Psychopathic Wife Abuser

As distinct from Bill, Howard always seemed to keep his emotions under control or used them strategically to manipulate others, including his current wife Nan. In initial conversation he was likable and flattering. However, extended conversations were often full of contradictions and denials of those contradictions if challenged. Howard had a long history dating back to early teenage years of run-ins with the law, including theft, forgery, assault and battery, domestic violence, and breaking and entering. Nan noted that Howard never took responsibility for his actions. He always blamed others and got noticeably defensive and angry when others attempted to hold him accountable for his actions. When confronted about his abusive behavior in a men's abuser group, he typically blamed his wife for "giving him no other choice." Furthermore, he exhibited little empathy for others or regret for harmful actions he had taken, including physically and verbally abusing his wife and two children. Nan stated that although Howard seldom used violence (his intimidating manner most often did the trick), when he did, it was extreme and calculated. Howard threatened that he would kill her if she ever left him.

Based on Howard's history of run-ins with the law and style of using abusive behavior, he most closely approximates Holtzworth-Munroe and Stuart's (1994) generally violent/antisocial abuser as well as Gottman et al. (1995) Type 1 abuser. On the basis of D. G. Saunder's (1996) research, CBT and feminist psychoeducation would be the preferred treatment approach for Howard, although Howard would be considered to have a poorer prognosis as a result of treatment than Bill, on the basis of Gottman et al. (1995). It would be important for counselors both to develop at least a moderately strong therapeutic alliance and to hold Howard accountable for his thinking and behavior. It would be critical to identify and replace Howard's beliefs concerning his "right" to get what he wants from others in whatever way necessary. Consequences for his behavior are especially critical for Howard, such as separation from Nan (assuming he agrees to a separation before an altercation occurs). Initially, group treatment with other similar abusers would be preferred treatment. It would be critical for Nan to receive treatment as well, including contingency plans for safety in cooperation with women's shelters and family and friends. It may also be important to explore the possibility of a protective order for Nan.

Summary

National family violence surveys indicate that men and women are equally violent; however, men's violence is 6 times more likely to produce injury. As a result, more research has been conducted on men who abuse their partners than on women who abuse theirs. This research has determined a moderate degree of consistency with abusers typologies, although many researchers suggest that distinct abuser categories are artificial. Other researchers hold that such categories are critical in effective treatment matching, although to date only one study has found differential treatment effects for different abusers. Considerably more research needs to be conducted to provide legitimate support establishing distinct treatments for different types of abusers.

It is clearer to see the effects of partner abuse by males than to see the effects of treatment matching. Abused women and the children who witness interparental violence are clearly affected in a profoundly negative fashion. For many victims of physical violence, the negative psychological aftermath remains for a lifetime and has ill effects on future relationships, particular for those experiencing the most severe abuse. PTSD and CPTSD, although treatable, leave an indelible mark on abuse victims.

Finally, based on the typology research on male partner-abusers, same-gender group treatment and couple treatment are most effective with men who use less severe violence and have little or no psychopathology. This issue is discussed more extensively in Chapter 7, Assessment of Intimate Violent Offenders.

Suggested Readings

Archer, J. (2002). Sex differences in physically aggressive acts between heterosexual partners: A meta-analytic review. *Aggression and Violent Behavior, 7*, 313–351.

Courtois, C, A., & Ford, J. D. (2009). *Treating complex traumatic stress disorders: An evidence-based guide.* New York: Guilford Press.

Dixon, L., & Browne, K. (2003). The heterogeneity of spouse abuse: A review. *Aggression and Violent Behavior, 8*, 107–130.

Dutton, D. G., & Bodnarchuk, M. (2005). Through a psychological lens: Personality disorder and spouse assault. In D. R. Loseke, R. J. Gelles, & M. M. Cavanaugh (Eds.), *Current controversies on family violence* (2nd ed., pp. 5–18). Thousand Oaks, CA: Sage.

Holtzworth-Munroe, A., & Meehan, J. C. (2004). Typologies of men who are maritally violent: Scientific and clinical implications. *Journal of Interpersonal Violence, 19*, 1369–1389.

Murphy, C. M., & Eckhardt, C. I. (2005). *Treating the abusive partner: An individualized cognitive–behavioral approach.* New York, NY: Guilford Press.

Paradis, A., Reinherz, H., Giaconia, R., Beardslee, W., Ward, K., & Fitzmaurice, G. (2009). Long-term impact of family arguments and physical violence on adult functioning at age 30 years: Findings from the Simmons longitudinal study. *Journal of the American Academy of Child & Adolescent Psychiatry, 48,* 290–298. doi: 10.1097/CHI.0b013e3181948fdd

Yllo, K. (2005). Through a feminist lens: Gender, diversity, and violence. In D. R. Loseke, R. J. Gelles, & M. M. Cavanaugh (Eds.), *Current controversies on family violence* (2nd ed., pp. 19–34). Thousand Oaks, CA: Sage.

chapter 5

Female-on-Male Intimacy Violence: Descriptions, Consequences, and Counseling Implications

As noted in Chapter 1, identifying, studying, and providing treatment for women who have physically abused their male partners is controversial. In an early NFVS (Straus & Gelles, 1988) of 6,000 couples, 12.4% of husbands and 12.1% of wives reported being a victim of spouse violence, apparently indicating gender symmetry of IPV. Furthermore, a U.S. DOJ NCVS found in 2004 that 1.3 per 1,000 men and 3.8 per 1,000 women experienced IPV (Catalona, 2007), highlighting 3 times more IPV toward women than men (gender asymmetry). A recent Centers for Disease Control (CDC) study found that one out of seven men (13.8%) and one out of four women (24.3%) have experienced severe IPV (M. C. Black et al., 2011), with result rates between the NFVS and NCVS rates. These results exemplify the divergent views often taken on the issue of female-on-male IPV as well as the differences between community samples (e.g., NFVS) and crime/agency samples (e.g., NCVS). Scholars seem to line up based on conclusions of either gender symmetry (approximately equal rates between genders; NFVS) or gender asymmetry (significantly more male-initiated IPV; NCVS) on the issue of IPV (e.g., DeKeseredy, 2011; D. G. Dutton, 2006).

This chapter presents information on sources and kinds of data collected on female-on-male IPV, descriptions of female partner-abusers, consequences of IPV,

Note. This chapter was coauthored with Jeanette Madkins. She is currently the assistant director of the Student Counseling Services at Texas A&M University. She received her PhD and master's in counseling psychology from Texas A&M University. She is a licensed psychologist in the state of Texas and a board certified counseling psychologist. Her interests include anger concerns, women's issues, sexual assault, trauma, eating disorders, spirituality, interpersonal dynamics, academic/career issues, diversity issues, training and supervision, and outreach and consultation.

71

and possible treatment implications. In addition, the chapter examines the controversial nature of female-on-male IPV, such as using violence as self-defense, initiating IPV, understanding the context for IPV, and assessing IPV with the CTS.

Gender Symmetry Controversy

Currently, the gender symmetry controversy is far from resolved, and it has created an enormous amount of debate and in some cases much animosity. Some have accused feminist writers of ignoring the empirical data (D. G. Dutton & Corvo, 2006) and suppressing research results that validate female IPV (Straus, 2007). Feminist writers respond stating that "research portraying women as 'equally violent' as men reduces public sympathy for women victims" (Loseke & Kurz, 2005, p. 91) and that such research is used to excuse male IPV against females. Furthermore, some suggest that critics of the feminist view of IPV are not only unfamiliar with feminist research and scholarly works but simply have an axe to grind against feminism as a movement (DeKeseredy, 2011). Others suggest that a failure to acknowledge female-to-male IPV is disingenuous and avoids the issue of reducing IPV regardless of the source (Straus, 2009). Finally, some hold that limiting the study of IPV to only males is "sexist" (J. M. Ross & Babcock, 2010). This issue is fraught with conflict and political debate that can be distracting for providers, and yet it is important to understand the debate and identify relevant research to enhance treatment regardless of political debate.

Several barriers have made it difficult to obtain a consistent picture of female-on-male IPV. Some studies indicate that both men and women deny and minimize IPV because of relationships dynamics (Heckert & Gondolf, 2000). Women in particular often feel guilt and shame for not leaving their abuser and therefore fail to disclose the abuse (Lindgren & Renck, 2008). Furthermore, society rejects the idea of male victimization because of the long-held stereotype of the strong, tough, invulnerable male (Dowd, 2001). In fact, men are reluctant to report assaults both by women and by other men, even in cases of severe injuries (Henman, 1996). Some evidence indicates that women neglect to report as much as 75% of their use of IPV (Mihalic & Elliott, 1997). Nevertheless, even with what appears to be underreporting of female IPV, research consistently documents its occurrence in national surveys (e.g., Archer, 2000; Straus & Gelles, 1990), community studies (e.g., J. M. Ross & Babcock, 2010), and clinical studies (Cascardi et al., 1992). Obtaining accurate information on the occurrence and frequency of IPV for each client is a process and most likely will emerge over time based on a therapeutic alliance with the client, rather than on a series of questions asked in an initial interview.

Feminist Criticism

Much of the feminist criticism has targeted the NFVS research conducted by Straus and colleagues (Straus & Gelles, 1986; Straus et al., 1980) and the inadequacies of the CTS that was used in these studies. Critics argue that the CTS fails to (a) consider gender differences, such as strength, injuries incurred, and levels of fear (J. W. White et al., 2000); (b) examine IPV beyond the context of conflict, such as unprovoked IPV (Fantuzzo & Lindquist, 1989); and (c) examine issues such as motivation for IPV and emotional abuse (Dasgupta, 2002). The CTS2 improved on these omissions. However, many of these criticisms—especially the criticism that some studies fail to consider the context for IPV—are justified. For example, the NVAW surveys indicated that IPV against women was more often accompanied by psychological abuse, controlling behavior, and fear of injury or death than IPV against men. Thus, some suggest using both quantitative (e.g., CTS) and qualitative (e.g., victims' interviews) assessment methods (DeKeseredy & Schwartz, 2001) for a more balanced and context-based assessment.

With regard to these criticisms, Straus (1999) acknowledged that his research has focused on physical assault and not the context for IPV. Although he supports research that focuses on context and effects of IPV, he argued against including these variables with studies on violent acts (Straus, 1990). He also acknowledged that women, on average, experience more frequent and more severe results of IPV (e.g., physical injury, economic loss, and psychological symptoms) than men (Straus, 2009). In addition, he stated his focus on physical assault is for legal, social policy, and ethical reasons. Even a "minor" defensive assault by women places them and their children in danger of severe retribution by men (Feld & Straus, 1989).

A final criticism is the different results produced by the NCVS research and the family conflict surveys such as NFVS. NCVS indicates significantly more male-to-female IPV than the NFVS. Straus (1999) addressed this issue from an empirical perspective and concluded that national representative studies support both that (a) men and women initiate IPV equally in community samples (e.g., NFVS), and (b) men initiate violence more often than women in samples taken from crime reports and women's shelter (e.g., NCVS). In a similar manner, M. P. Johnson (2006) contended that different types of violence (e.g., IT, situational couple violence) are distinguished by different motives and behaviors. Like Straus, Johnson suggested that each study samples different populations and, therefore, different types of IPV. Failure to make this distinction results in highly questionable conclusions and generalizations. Straus (1999) concluded that both types of data are necessary, and that neither one should be negated by the other; rather, each should be seen as representing different populations (e.g., women's shelter samples vs. community samples). Crime surveys such as NCVS tend to define abuse as criminal acts or injury to the victims, typically resulting in very low rates of violent acts by women. Conversely, community surveys define violence as a broad range of behaviors from mild violence (e.g., pushing, grabbing, slapping) to more severe forms of violence (e.g., sexually assaulting, beating up) that couples use to resolve conflicts. However, this violence is not labeled as a criminal act.

The most important implication of this discussion is that consumers of IPV research must define the particular sample for each study before applying the results to their particular clinical population. One would expect different results from different samples.

Contextual Factors of Female-on-Male Intimacy Violence

Determining motivation for IPV is a difficult undertaking, especially when data are limited to self-report responses. An accurate determination would necessitate knowing specific sequences of couple interaction and other background information that is largely prohibitive with large sample studies and phone interviews (Browne, Salomon, & Bassuk, 1999). Furthermore, couples' reports typically lack reasonable agreement on IPV occurrence and type (Armstrong, Wernke, Medina, & Schafer, 2002). Because men in particular tend to underreport and minimize the severity of their own IPV (Kessler et al., 2001), researchers have developed correction equations to adjust for reporting bias (Heyman & Schlee, 1997).

Bias with female IPV reporting has been studied much less than with males, with the exception of a study by Sarantakos (2004). Sarantakos identified 68 families with alleged wife-on-husband violence and collected data from the wives' mothers and children in addition to both husband and wife. In 64% of the cases, family members indicated there was no husband aggression prior to wives' violence against their husbands. The author concluded that wives' report of their violence was highly questionable and that the self-defense justification for female-on-male violence was unfounded in the majority of cases in the sample. Perhaps partners who engage in IPV, whether male or female, are prone to significant reporting bias.

Self-Defense

One of the most controversial issues related to the context for IPV is women's motivation for hitting their male partners. Some have argued that the violence used by women against men is purely self-defense or a reaction to years of abuse by their partners (Cascardi & Vivian, 1995). Several studies lend support to this position (e.g., Hamberger & Guse, 2002; M. P. Johnson, 2001).

Although self-defense is often the reason given for female IPV with clinical couples (Hamberger & Guse, 2002), a number of studies indicate that self-defense is only one of many reasons for female IPV and not necessarily the most frequent reason (Medeiros & Straus, 2006). In several studies, women reported the primary motivations for using IPV were coercion, anger, attempts to punish a partner for misbehavior, demand for attention, and retaliation/punishment, especially for sexual infidelity (Hettrich & O'Leary, 2007; Stets & Hammons, 2002).

On the basis of these studies, it seems reasonable to conclude that although women use IPV in self-defense, it is not consistently the primary or only motivation in most situations. Women's motivation for using violence covers a wide range of reasons that are based on the particular circumstances, rather than being bound by one particular motivation (S. C. Swan & Snow, 2006). Self-defense is more often a motivation in criminal justice and agency samples than community samples. An awareness of these context factors is especially important when counselors are attempting to develop an accurate picture of the sequence of events that led to a violent episode.

Who Initiates Intimate Partner Violence?

Another controversial contextual issue is who initiates IPV. In the 1985 NFVS study with a community sample, Straus and Gelles (1988) found that in 53.1% of the cases women hit first, whereas in 42.3% of the cases husbands hit first. In addition, the man was the only violent partner in 25.9% of the cases, the women in 25.5% of the cases, and both partners were violent in 48.6% of the cases. In a study of 1,725 young adults, Morse (1995) found that in 29.7% to 37.7% of cases, the IPV was perpetrated only by females, whereas males were the sole perpetrators in 9.9% to 13.9% of the cases. A recent national longitudinal study of 11,370 young adults, ages 18 to 28 years, indicated that approximately 24% reported IPV (Whitaker, Haileyesus, Swahn, & Saltzman, 2007). Of the violent participants, 50.3% were nonreciprocally violent, and of these 70% were women. Men were most likely to cause injury. Furthermore, mutual IPV caused more injuries than nonreciprocal IPV, regardless of who initiated IPV.

Although these studies must *not* be taken as the final word on the motivation for IPV and the initiation of female IPV, it would be indefensible to conclude that women use violence only in self-defense and never or seldom initiate IPV. Female-initiated violence does exist, and with some samples, it is used solely by females. To view females as only victims in IPV would be a great oversight as well as contribute to furthering IPV by omission. Family violence scholars may run the greatest risk of misrepresenting the realities of IPV when they take extreme positions on issues without allowing for exceptions or when they exclude or condemn research that contradicts their own positions. Conversely, caution must be exercised in drawing hard-and-fast conclusions or overgeneralizing these studies to all women who engage in IPV. Motivations and circumstances for IPV vary greatly across samples (e.g., community vs. women's shelter) and types of IPV (e.g., IT vs. CCV; Weston, Marshall, & Coker, 2007).

Consequences of Female-on-Male Intimacy Violence

Context-based studies have focused on consequences of IPV to call attention to the differential effects of IPV on men and women. The majority of studies on physical injuries indicate that overwhelmingly women sustain greater physical injury than men even though both males and females used similar forms of IPV (Rennison & Welchans, 2000; Straus, 2009). Furthermore, men are better able to restrain a violent female partner and thus prevent or lessen their own injury. In a similar manner, although violence is damaging to both men and women psychologically and emotionally, women report greater distress, depression, and PTSD-related symptoms (Straus, 2009). However, less research focuses on the consequences of female IPV against males, even though a considerable amount of research has been conducted comparing abused men to abused women.

Physical Injury to Men

In the NVAW survey, female-on-male IPV accounted for 40% of injuries attributed to IPV, 27% of serious injuries requiring medical care, and 38% of all partners who lost time at work. In a study of male college students, 40% reported being physically abused by girlfriends, with 29% reporting serious abuse (Simonelli & Ingram, 1998). Emergency room reports indicate that males are treated for a variety of injuries inflicted by wives/partners, including ax injuries, burns, hitting with fireplace pokers, gunshots, and burns from boiling liquids (Duminy & Hudson, 1993; McNeely, Cook, & Torres, 2001). Thus, males can sustain injuries from their female partners, and this type of IPV is a problem nationwide. Furthermore, national surveys indicate that men incur one third of all IPV injuries (Catalano, 2006; Rennison & Welchans, 2000).

Victims of Homicide

In addition to sustaining physical injury from female partners, males are also victims of homicide. Although homicide is the least likely outcome of IPV, its occurrence attracts much attention and forms the basis for criminal justice policy (O. Barnett et al., 2011). Several national surveys indicate that females commit one third of the intimate partner homicides (Bachman & Saltzman, 1995; Catalano, 2006; Rennison & Welchans, 2000). Although many women murder their partners in self-defense, current evidence does not support the conclusion that all of these murders are based on self-defense (Hines & Malley-Morrison, 2001; C. R. Mann, 1996).

Psychological and Emotional Consequences

IPV has harmful psychological effects for both men and women, with some studies indicating that women report higher levels of distress and depression than men (Cascardi et al., 1992; Feeny, Zoellner, & Foa, 2000). For both men and women, as the level and severity of IPV increases so does the severity of depression, stress, and psychosomatic symptoms (Stets & Straus, 1990). Compared with nonabused men, abused men report more depression, stress, and psychosomatic symptoms (Cascardi et al., 1992; Stets & Straus, 1990). Simonelli and Ingram (1998) examined emotional and physical abuse with undergraduate males and found that 90% reported experiencing verbal aggression or emotional abuse from a partner. The abused men had significantly greater psychological distress and depression than the nonabused men. Hines and Malley-Morrison (2001) found that the greater the emotional abuse experienced by college males, the greater their risk for PTSD and alcoholism. Overall, between 50% and 90% of men experience some type of psychological aggression from female partners (e.g., being threatened, being insulted or sworn at; Hines & Malley-Morrison, 2001; Hines & Saudino, 2003).

The evidence for the effects of female-on-male violence is much less extensive than for female victims, but the evidence that does exist points to the seriousness of the emotional and psychological effects of IPV on men. This research highlights the importance of being aware of one's biases in working with partner-abused individuals, especially males. IPV against males produces more than physical harm. Such men may be hesitant to discuss their physical or psychological symptoms or at best minimize them (Henman, 1996). Counselors must be willing to address their biases concerning this issue as well as to assess for and treat such symptoms in abused males.

Comparisons Between Men and Women's Use of Violence

Several gender differences pertaining to IPV need to be highlighted. First, although men and women use approximately the same level of violence, the rate of injury is between 2 to 5 times higher for women compared with men across studies (e.g., Archer, 2000; Cascardi & Vivian, 1995). Furthermore, men and women are likely to use different types of violent behavior. Cantos et al. (1994) determined that women were more likely to kick, bite, hit with a fist, hit with a weapon, and threaten with or use a gun or knife, whereas men were more likely to push, grab, shove, choke, strangle, or beat up. Giordano, Millhollin, Cernkovich, Pugh, and Rudolph (1999) found similar results. In these studies, women were found to inflict the greatest injury when they used a weapon, with men inflicting the most injury using their hands. Although females and males perpetrate verbal and physical aggression at equal rates, females are more likely to perpetrate psychological aggression than males (Hines & Saudino, 2003; Straus & Sweet, 1992).

Although both men and women experience negative psychological effects from IPV, a larger percentage of women report greater fear of their partners than do men (Dasgupta, 1999; Lindgren & Renck, 2008). Also, women reported ongoing fear for extended periods of time. Furthermore, women felt more vulnerable with their partners after using IPV. Women's fear is predicated on men's greater size, physical strength, and a history of assaulting the female partner. In addition, only a component of an abuse cycle need be manifested (e.g., loud voice), often without violence, to elicit an intense fear response that is associated with IPV (Pontius, 2002). Men were not fearful of their female partners' use of IPV unless weapons were used.

Although IPV is destructive in intimate relationships regardless of the source, the gender differences are noteworthy for policy and resource allocation. These differences, however, should not pit one ideological camp against the other. The different effects of IPV on men and women should inform the distribution of resources and promote effective intervention for victims and perpetrators whatever the gender, not marginalize one group or the other. It is important to resist the pull to institutionalize a movement or ideology for its own furtherance, as doing so impedes efforts to accurately describe, define, and reduce IPV.

Characteristics of Intimately Violent Females

There is a lack of research that examines characteristics of intimately violent females. This dearth of research is understandable when we realize that until recently, women have been viewed largely as victims of IPV. However, an understanding of female IPV within context is critical for timely prevention and effective intervention. This section examines correlates and predictors of female-on-male IPV, typologies of IPV, and personality typologies based on personality measures.

Several social-structural variables are related to females who use IPV. Related socioeconomic factors include the following: low income (Rennison & Welchans, 2000), unemployment of husband (Newby et al., 2003), and habitation in poverty-stricken neighborhoods (Cunradi, Caetano, Clark, & Schafer, 2000). Studies indicate that young women age 16 to 24 are the most violent, with IPV decreasing with age (Suitor, Pillemer, & Straus, 1990). Up to 40% of females in their teens and early 20s report perpetrating IPV (O'Leary, 1999).

Many women who use IPV suffer with anxiety, depression, anger, and PTSD symptoms (S. C. Swan & Snow, 2003) as well as alcohol and drug problems, mental illness, and childhood trauma (Dowd, Leisring, & Rosenbaum, 2005). Intimately violent females also have an increased risk for suicide, personality dysfunction, and mood disorders (Ehrensaft et al., 2006). It is not surprising that research has found a direct relationship between childhood abuse and the inclination toward later victimizing others (S. C. Swan & Snow, 2006).

Two of the strongest predictors of female IPV are a history of aggression (Giordana et al., 1999; Moffitt et al., 2001) and exposure to violence in the family of origin (S. C. Swan & Snow, 2003). In particular, paternal emotional and physical abuse has been found to predict maltreatment in future intimate relationships (Kaura & Allen, 2004). For example, having an emotionally abusive father often results in higher levels of hostility by the adult daughter toward her intimate partners. In addition, having a mother who is aggressive toward a daughter significantly contributes to the daughter's later use of dating aggression (Kaura & Allen, 2004; Riggs & O'Leary, 1996.) Thus, a childhood history of being exposed to, experiencing, and engaging in violent behavior by either parent strongly predicts IPV for women.

Typologies of Partner-Violent Females

Typology research with males who abuse their female partners has been extensive (see Dixon & Browne, 2003). Much of this research suggests between two and four types of partner-abusive men. However, typology research with female partner-abusers is less well-developed.

Advocacy Typologies

The existing typologies often reflect the various reasons females use IPV. For example, advocacy views of female IPV present typologies that imply a reactive or self-defense explanation for using IPV (Malloy et al., 2003). Worcester (2001) enumerated a three-category typology: (a) self-defense and/or escape from a violent partner, (b) reaction to attempts to limit autonomy, and (c) reaction to power and control. House (2001) proposed a similar typology of female IPV: (a) using IPV in self-defense to avoid injury, (b) using IPV in an attempt to stop a violent partner from using IPV, (c) provoking an assault in order to gain control over one's partner when an assault occurs, (d) retaliating against a partner for a previous assault, and (e) using violence to prevent being abused. These typologies assume a lack of culpability for female IPV. Violence is a reaction to either the direct oppression by the male partner or the indirect oppression of a gender-biased society.

Academic Typologies

Another typology of female partner violence is what Malloy et al. (2003) referred to as "the academic view" of female IPV. M. P. Johnson and Ferraro (2000) typify the academic perspective with a four-category typology: (a) situational couple violence that occurs from either husband or wife without coercion or attempt to control by either partner, (b) violent resistance based on self-defense, (c) IT in which only one partner is violent and controlling, and (d) mutual violent control in which partners are involved in using violence to control the other. Johnson emphasized that mutual IPV focuses on control, rather than on a gendered paradigm that views women as victims, regardless of the circumstances. IT and situational couple violence have received the most support (M. P. Johnson, 2006).

S. C. Swan and Snow (2002, 2003) identified a three-category typology: (a) women as victims, (b) women as aggressors, and (c) mixed relationships. A final typology model based only on bidirectional IPV borrows from M. P. Johnson (2006), Holtzworth-Munroe and Stuart (1994), and Langhinrichsen-Rohling (2005) and conceptualizes three types: (a) dynamic domination in which both partners use IPV to control and coerce the other; (b) dyadic dis-regulation in which both partners have difficulty regulating their emotions and behaviors, resulting in mutual violence; and (c) dyadic reciprocal couple violence (Langhinrichsen-Rohling (2010).

As with the advocacy typologies, the academic typologies hold that men initiate IPV and often for reasons of control and/or coercion. Unlike the advocacy view, the academic view also accepts that females and males can engage in mutual violence without motivation to control and that females can initiate unprovoked IPV to control, coerce, and punish. The academic view also holds that males and females likely differ on their reasons for using IPV.

Conclusions

Female IPV typology research has received much less attention than similar typology research on partner-violent males, in part because of the different agendas of the feminist advocacy and of academic views regarding female IPV. Perhaps the best conclusion to draw from typology studies is that intimately violent men and women differ somewhat on issues related to motivation, severity of violence used, and psychopathology. The bidirectional and control-based models appear to have the most support and flexibility for counselors. However, the challenge for counselors is to obtain enough accurate information to first determine whether the IPV is bidirectional or unidirectional and then to determine the type of bidirectional IPV. Recent research indicates that control accounts for sizable variance across all subtypes (Graham-Kevan & Archer, 2008), and that men and women differ *not* on the amount of controlling behavior but the type of controlling behavior used (Felson & Outlaw, 2007). Control may be less a gendered issue and more a relationships issue, with the exception of IT.

Why Do Abused Men Stay?

Although a significant amount of research has looked at why women stay with abusive men, there has been very little research examining why men stay with abusive women. This paucity of empirical research is exacerbated both by the difficulty in recruiting adequate numbers of victimized males and by the feminist view of patriarchy as the sole cause of partner abuse

(Hines & Malley-Morrison, 2005). There is evidence that men stay in relationships with abusive females to fulfill psychological needs. Many men value the relationship commitment and have a genuine love for their wife (Pagelow, 1984). Furthermore, some men endure the violence to satisfy dependency needs. These men rely on the relationship and often attribute the violence to circumstantial causes. Finally, many males may feel emasculated by the prospect of publicly admitting that their relationship does not fit with societal expectations and gender role stereotypes; acknowledging being abused by his female partner may bring in to question his manhood (Hines & Malley-Morrison, 2005; Langley & Levy, 1977).

Beyond the psychological needs that influence the decision to stay, many men face contextual needs that heavily factor into the process. Lifestyle habits such as maintaining a standard of living and sharing a family home can be jeopardized if a male leaves the abusive relationship (Steinmetz, 1977–1978). In addition, the legal system has not yet identified a means to recognize male victims of female IPV (O. Barnett et al., 2011). Thus, males who leave the abusive relationship face the risk of losing their children because of a legal system that tends to award custody to mothers. This risk is heightened by the possibility that males may not be willing to admit to the victimization. Most important, abused men must weigh the need to protect themselves with the need to protect their children from an abusive mother (Steinmetz, 1977–1978).

Case Example

Treatment Implications for Female-on-Male Violence

Zaida was one of three women arrested in one jurisdiction over a year's period for female-on-male partner violence and diverted into a counseling program. All other members of the group were men. Zaida was 57 years old and had been married for 35 years. She worked in a factory and admitted having a problem with alcohol. She looked haggard and perhaps unwell.

The evening that she completed her 26 sessions in the program, she finally opened up about her reasons for hitting Kumar. He seldom talked to her, she complained, and she was "damned mad about it." When she came home from work and saw Kumar drinking a beer in front of the TV, she often greeted him with a question, such as, "What's for supper?" If she didn't like his answer, she just "bopped him on the head." If she got "really pissed off," she grabbed his beer and threw it on the floor. Kumar never defended himself even once, but if she socked him, he would not speak to her the rest of the evening.

The therapist tactfully pointed out that he "thought he saw a connection" between Zaida's assaults and Kumar's refusal to speak to her. Zaida was stunned into silence, but she listened attentively as men in the group commented. The men told her that Kumar probably would talk to her if he didn't have to worry about getting socked. Zaida was thoughtful but said nothing more until the final good-byes. As she proudly marched off, she told the group members that they would never see her again, and they didn't. (O. Barnett et al., 2005, p. 316)

Counseling Implications for Female Intimate Partner Violence

Compared with research on males, research on female IPV treatment is significantly underdeveloped. As a result, the following discussion reflects more clinical wisdom and supposition that is based on related research than exclusively empirically informed practice. Most treatment programs for females use intervention models similar to those used with male offenders, that is, psychoeducation and cognitive–behavioral anger management interventions to address anger and assertiveness issues (Dowd, 2001). However, many female programs also offer an emphasis on areas that are unique to women, which is the primary focus of this section. See Chapter 9, Assessment and Treatment for Adult Victims of Intimacy Violence, for a more in-depth discussion of general abuser research related to treatment. Unfortunately, to date few outcome studies exist on treatment of female partner abusers, and none include comparison groups or controls (Dowd & Leisring, 2008). The few published pre- to posttreatment studies noted reductions in passive–aggressiveness and propensity to abusiveness (Carney & Buttell, 2004); decreases in passive–aggressiveness, control of partner, and propensity for abusiveness (Carney & Buttell, 2006); and improvement of psychological abuse/coercion, self-esteem, general contentment, and assertiveness (Tutty, Babins-Wagner, & Rothery, 2006). Unfortunately, no direct measures of physical abuse showed significant changes. Most of the treatment information that follows is based on clinical wisdom, research on female offender characteristics, the few single-group nonexperimental studies noted above, and extrapolations from evidence-supported treatments for male offenders.

Some IPV literature characterizes female-on-male violence as "qualitatively and quantitatively different" from that of men (Perilla, Frndak, Lillard, & East, 2003, p. 18). These differences are likely due to the developmentally greater emphasis placed on intimacy and interpersonal relationships for females compared with males. Gilligan (1993) argued that interpersonal relationships take on more importance for females than males because the female identity centers on building relationships. Pollack and Gilligan (1982) posited that the female need for affiliation is composed of two components: fear of isolation and hope for intimacy. Research has found that when women with a high need for affiliation undergo significant stress, they are more likely to become aggressive within their relationships if their internalized inhibition for aggression is low (Mason & Blankenship, 1987). Ben-David (1993) took this concept one step further and argued that relational priorities are the origins for female intimate aggression. According to her model, threat to a female's domain or sphere of relational commitments and loyalties partially accounts for the higher incidence of female IPV as compared with female violence or aggression toward nonintimates. In support of this view, Baumeister and Sommer (1997) found that female aggression against strangers is less likely than for males. It is interesting that Doumas, Pearson, Elgin, and McKinley (2008) found that the intimate partner pairings of females who have anxious attachment with male partners who have avoidant attachment predicted IPV for both men and women. Some females may be more prone to pursue male partners when they experience anxiety or fear of abandonment as males withdraw or avoid intimacy-demanding situations; this situation sets the stage for IPV. Attachment along with previously noted motivators for female IPV (e.g., jealousy, power, self-defense, retaliation for emotional hurt) must be considered when formulating treatments.

The treatment for female IPV as opposed to male IPV must take into account relevant differences in motivation as well as relational and contextual factors. Most important, the issue of safety must remain at the forefront as female perpetration of psychological and physical aggression has been shown to predict future aggression by male partners (Straus, 2009). In addition, given the importance of affiliation needs, same-sex group treatment is preferred over individual treatment in most circumstances (the exceptions being severe psychopathology; Hamel, 2005) to counter social isolation as well as to capitalize on peer influence for change. Interventions emphasizing attachment needs, the therapeutic alliance, anger management, interpersonal skills, and boundaries also should be a part of any treatment regimen for female IPV (Dowd & Leisring, 2008). As well, family interventions focusing on couple relationships (Stith, Rosen, & McCollum, 2003) and relationships with children are critical for stabilizing the home environment (Hamel, 2005). Finally, given that many female offenders have histories as both victims and perpetrators, it is important to include elements of victims and advocacy services either in treatment or as an ancillary service. The following discussion presents several programs for partner abusers who are female; these programs include many of the above-noted issues plus components adapted from models for male partner abusers that emphasize psychoeducation and CBT.

Example Intervention Programs

A Canadian program for female partner abusers, the Responsible Choices for Women program, uses a group format conducted across 15 weeks, with each session lasting 2 hours (Tutty et al., 2006). This program assumes that females who perpetrate IPV may have different motives than males, including self-defense and self-initiated violence for control and revenge. The goals of treatment include the following:

- decreasing abusive behavior,
- accepting personal responsibility for own behavior,
- increasing self-esteem,
- increasing appropriate assertive behavior,
- improving family relationships,
- decreasing stress,
- increasing expressed empathy for those affected by the women's abusive behavior, and
- ending/reducing abuse of their children.

The groups are led by male–female coleaders who use a variety of CBT interventions, such as cognitive restructuring, stress reduction exercises, and role playing. Over the course of treatment, three separate contacts are made with a member's partner to check on the participant's progress and the partner's safety. Evaluation data have indicated improvements in many nonabusive areas but with no significant reduction of physical abuse.

Hamberger and Potente (1994) argued that treatment of female intimate aggressors should have a primary goal of ceasing the violence and ensuring protection of the woman and children. Their 12-week program emphasized safety planning, anger control, other self-management strategies, children's issues, alcohol and drug abuse, and assertiveness and was based on the assumption that the violence was a result of victimization and self-defense. Furthermore, Hamberger suggested that treatment for women who abuse partners should include interventions for specific circumstances, such as: (a) women who also are abuse victims and need support networks and safety plans to avoid and escape further abuse; (b) women who have been conditioned to accept all the blame in relationships should focus on balanced responsibility; and (c) women who are the predominant perpetrators need to focus on anger management, power and control, and accountability. In addition to specific interventions, treatment must include the development of trust, the provision of advocacy and resources, and the establishment of a safe environment. Because many women also were abused, treatment should focus on strengthening self-esteem, assertiveness, and empowerment while exploring and resolving family-of-origin conflicts.

Carney and Buttell (2004, 2006) used a CBT program patterned after treatment programs for male IPV. Their 15-week program includes three phases: (a) orientation and intake, (b) psychoeducation about violence and anger management to change thinking and behaving, and (c) termination. The program assumes females initiate IPV. Program evaluation indicated improvement on indirect variables related to abuse, such as passive–aggressiveness, control of partner, and propensity for abusiveness. However, treatment did not reduce IPV.

On the basis of their own clinical work with IPV, Leisring, Dowd, and Rosenbaum (2003) described a number of treatment differences between men's and women's IPV groups. In addition to including CBT interventions for men such as time-outs, cognitive restructuring, and stress management, they emphasize strong member support, as they believe that women initiate more group cohesion and engage in more support toward one another than males. Also, compared with men, women exhibit less resistance to treatment and use their maternal role as motivation for change. The women also more readily accepted responsibility for their aggression than men.

Leisring et al. (2003) suggested several modifications to traditional male IPV programs in order to provide more effective treatment for female abusers. First, include an emphasis on safety in order to counter the increased risk of retaliation by their male victims. Second, the need for shelter, money, safety, and food must be addressed before treatment can be expected to be effective. Third, because of the increased incidence of PTSD found in female aggressors, treatment must attend more carefully to severity of symptoms and consequences of the disorder. For example, because of increased incidences of suicide and depression among females, treatment should focus on conditions that destabilize mood (Dowd et al., 2005). Fourth, attend to one of the primary motivations for change for female aggressors: their role as a parent. Women frequently maintain the role as primary caregiver during treatment, and as a result they need additional support in this role, such as parenting skills. Finally, treatment should focus on deemphasizing the use of power and control in relationships and developing appropriate assertion and negotiation skills.

Seamans (2003) is one of the few authors who has offered treatment suggestions based on empirically derived data. She proposed a number of treatment recommendations that are based on a qualitative study of thirteen women referred for treatment. First, she recommended that all women entering treatment for IPV should be prescreened for substance abuse problems and psychiatric disorders. Next, women's life circumstances must be continually assessed for safety, and appropriate victim assistance referrals must be provided. Finally, children should also be treated because they are victims of witnessing parental violence and often are victims of physical abuse.

Finally, Dowd and Leisring (2008) provided a summary of best practices. They suggested that treatment providers include the following modules in treating *all* partner-violent women:

- safety plans, safety assessment, and conflict management skills;
- emotional regulation skills, with an emphasis on anger;
- relationship skills;
- stress-management, coping, and relaxation; and
- self-esteem enhancement.

For women who have conditions that compromise emotional and behavioral regulation, treatment modules should include assessment for the following:

- mood disorders,
- hormonal and medical conditions,
- PTSD, and
- substance abuse.

Treatment modules for women in relationships and with families should include the following:

- parenting and nonviolent discipline strategies; and
- couple or family treatment, as appropriate.

The above programs largely emphasize areas of treatment focus unique to female abusers while using interventions similar to male abuser programs. However, no randomly controlled clinical research has been conducted on outcome effectiveness with partner-violent females. Many of the above suggestions are similar issues addressed for females who have been victims of violence, perhaps because of the assumption that most female perpetrators are also victims. The accuracy of this assumption needs to be tested empirically. It is likely that there are different types of female offenders, with different motivations, including some who are offenders only and others who are offenders and victims. If this turns out to be the case, then as with male offenders, different types of female offenders may require different kinds of treatment.

Summary

The issue of female-on-male intimacy violence has generated an enormous amount of debate, accusations, and animosity. Whatever the political implications, the vast majority of studies indicate that women engage in intimacy violence at significant levels and that not all of this violence is from a defensive posture, although more women than men report using violence in self-defense. It seems that a crucial issue in making sense of all the studies on intimacy violence is to consider the sources. DOJ surveys that focus on violence as a reported criminal act tend to indicate that men engage in 3 or more times as much intimacy violence as females, whereas family conflict studies (e.g., Straus) that use representative community samples have found that approximately equal numbers of men and women initiate violence against their partners. Straus has stated that both types of research must be considered for a complete picture of intimacy violence.

Male victims of partner violence report similar consequences of the violence as female victims, such as physical injury, depression, and psychosomatic symptoms, although female victims tend to incur 2 to 6 times as many injuries as male victims.. However, as with male offenders, the strongest predictors of female intimacy violence are a history of aggression and exposure to violence in the family of origin.

Typologies of female partner-abusers have focused almost exclusively on females' reasons for using intimacy violence. More research is needed that goes beyond motivation for using violence and includes personality, relationship, and various violence variables.

Finally, treatment for female partner violence is in its infancy. Virtually no effectiveness studies have been conducted. Most treatment approaches incorporate psychoeducational and cognitive–behavioral interventions from male offender treatments and add elements that clinicians believe are unique to women offenders, such as attention to safety, suicide risk, a woman's role as a parent, PTSD symptoms, and group dynamics and support. Treatment, perhaps more than any other area of female partner abuse, needs extensive research to provide better informed interventions.

Suggested Readings

DeKeseredy, W. S. (2011). Feminist contributions to understanding women abuse: Myths, controversies, and realities. *Aggression and Violent Behavior, 16,* 297–302.

DeKeseredy, W. S., & Dragiewicz, M. (2007). Understanding the complexities of a feminist perspective on women abuse: A commentary on Donald G. Dutton's rethinking domestic violence. *Violence Against Women, 13,* 874–884.

Dowd, L., & Leisring, P. A. (2008). A framework for treating partner aggressive women. *Violence and Victims, 23,* 249–263.

Hines, D. A., & Malley-Morrison, K. (2001). Psychological effects of partner abuse against men: A neglected research area. *Psychology of Men and Masculinity, 2,* 75–85.

Johnson, M. P. (2006). Conflict and control: Gender symmetry and asymmetry in domestic violence. *Violence Against Women, 12,* 1003–1018.

Leisring, P.A., Dowd, L., & Rosenbaum, A. (2003). Treatment of partner aggressive women. *Journal of Aggression, Maltreatment & Trauma, 7,* 257–277.

Malloy, K. A., McCloskey, K. A., Grigsby, N., & Gardner, D. (2003). Women's use of violence within intimate relationships. *Journal of Aggression, Maltreatment & Trauma, 6,* 37–59.

Straus, M. A. (2009). Current controversies and prevalence concerning female offenders of intimate partner violence: Why the overwhelming evidence on parent physical violence by women has not been perceived and is often denied. *Journal of Aggression, Maltreatment, & Trauma, 18,* 552–571.

Swan, S. C., & Snow, D. L. (2006). The development of a theory of women's use of violence in intimate relationships. *Violence Against Women, 12,* 1026–1045.

Tutty, L. M., Babins-Wagner, R., & Rothery, M. A. (2006). Group treatment for aggressive women: An initial evaluation. *Journal of Family Violence, 21,* 341–349.

chapter 6

Same-Sex Intimate Partner Violence

Same-sex IPV has received the least attention of any area in the IPV literature. In part, this lack of attention is due to a segment of society viewing lesbian and gay couples' relationships as unnatural and thus unacceptable, although societal views on gay and lesbian relationships are rapidly changing, as evidenced by legal recognition of same-sex marriages in a number of states and countries. Another impediment has been the position of some feminist scholars that only men can be perpetrators of IPV and only females can be victims of IPV (C. Brown, 2008). Concerning the latter, some feminists have been slow to accept gay and lesbian violence because its occurrence is counter to what feminist theory would predict, that is, that IPV occurs because of unequal power distribution between men and women (Lettellier, 1994). Male-to-male IPV is not perceived as abusive because *all* males are socialized to be aggressive and violent, and therefore neither partner is a victim (Merrill, 1998; Peterman & Dixon, 2003). Many in society view lesbian relationships largely as egalitarian and nonoppressive. They believe that if IPV occurs at all neither partner could or would actually hurt the other (McLaughlin & Rozee, 2001). Furthermore, female-on-female IPV is often viewed as an act of self-defense and to a large degree a result of rage based on victimization in a patriarchal society (Renzetti, 1992). Personal responsibility is greatly diluted, with responsibility largely attributed to societal oppression.

Letellier (1994) argued that denying same-sex violence because it fails to fit the feminist model of IPV is heterosexist and largely hinders further study and effective treatment. Letellier and others (McClennen, 1999) suggested that explanations for IPV should integrate sociopolitical analysis such as feminist theory with psychological analysis to subsume both same-sex and heterosexual IPV.

Also, some hold that lesbian IPV occurs for the same reasons male-on-female violence occurs—emotional reactivity, hierarchy in the relationship, power, and self-defense (McClennen, Summers, & Daley, 2002). Finally, disempowerment theory suggests that individuals who feel less adequate or empowered are more prone to use less conventional means to assert themselves, including IPV. Same-sex couples are particularly vulnerable given their marginalized and often oppressed status in the culture (McKenry, Serovich, Mason, & Mosack, 2006).

A third impediment to more fully examining same-sex IPV has been the gay and lesbian community. They have been reticent to openly examine the issue of gay and lesbian partner violence because it is viewed as adding to the public's general negative view of same-sex relationships (Hines & Malley-Morrison, 2005). Some even deny the possibility of female-on-female IPV (Island & Letellier, 1991). However, a substantial research base supports the occurrence of gay and lesbian IPV, noting prevalence rates equal to or greater than rates in the heterosexual community (Friess, 1997; Renzetti & Miley, 1996). One national survey indicated that women in lesbian relationships experience more IPV than women in heterosexual relationships, and lesbians are abused at higher rates than gay men (Tjaden & Thoennes, 2000). Depending on the study, the rate of same-sex violence has been found to be between 11% and 73% in the gay and lesbian community (Craft & Serovich, 2005; Gunther & Jennings, 1999). These estimates likely are conservative ones given that same-sex couples report IPV much less than heterosexual couples (Hardesty, Oswald, Khaw, & Fonseca, 2011).

This chapter discusses characteristics of IPV in same-sex couples, similarities and differences with heterosexual IPV, predictors and causes of same-sex violence, types of same-sex violence, reasons for staying in same-sex abusive relationships, and treatment implications.

Case Example

Alice, 44

I recently separated from my partner of 11 years. We have a joint bank account and a house together, and I have co-parented my partner's son. What brought things to a head was when my partner forced me to have sex and I was injured during the assault. Over time I have suffered a head injury from being hit with a 2 × 4, numerous other physical assaults and control. I am bipolar and have attempted suicide a few times. I have been hospitalized. My partner leaves notes on my car and at my house, comes to my house whenever she wants, and talks to mutual friends about me. She had the gas turned off at my new place. She got the key to my new place when I gave a copy to our son. Now I've changed the locks. I'm in the process of separating our finances, and I wonder what "winning" I win if I give her everything and get to move on with my life. I'm on disability so my resources aren't that great. Right now I see a doctor, go to support group, and see a therapist, but it's a daily struggle to not hurt myself and to keep my resolve to sever my relationship. (National Coalition of Anti-Violence Programs, 2004, pp. 7–8)

Characteristics and Explanations of Intimately Violent Same-Sex Couples

Childhood Victimization

Few studies have been conducted on characteristics of same-sex IPV. However, research indicates several commonalities across gay and lesbian relationships. The most consistent characteristic is the greater presence of a history of child abuse as compared with heterosexuals (Hershberger & D'Augelli, 2000). National data indicate that as distinct from heterosexual participants, gay and bisexual men experienced more childhood emotional and physical abuse, whereas lesbian and bisexual women reported experiencing harsher physical maltreatment (Corliss, Cochran, & May, 2002). In some samples of lesbians, childhood physical and sexual abuse was reported by a majority of the respondents (Margolies & Leeder, 1995; Stoddard, Dibble, & Fineman, 2009).

Additional research on lesbian and gay IPV supports the notion of childhood violence as a risk factor for later IPV (Craft & Serovich, 2005; Fortunata & Kohn, 2003). These findings are consistent with traumatic stress research that indicates that survivors have a higher incidence of traumatic stress as well as a greater tendency to victimize others than nontraumatized individuals (Classen, Palesh, & Aggarwal, 2005). Revictimization and victimization of others are directly correlated with the severity of childhood abuse (Russell, 1986; Werner, 1989).

Alcohol and Substance Abuse

Alcohol and substance abuse also are risk factors for lesbian and gay IPV. Gays and lesbians have higher rates of alcohol and substance abuse than heterosexuals (Appleby, 2001; Renzetti, 1998). Renzetti (1998) held that between 20% and 35% of gays and lesbians have a problem with alcohol to some degree. Lesbians in particular report using alcohol more frequently and in greater amounts and experiencing greater alcohol-related morbidity than heterosexual women (Cochran, Keenan, Schober, & Mays, 2000). McClennen et al. (2002) found a relationship between substance abuse and IPV for gay males but not for lesbians. Furthermore, some researchers suggest a connection between the high rates of CSA, depression, and suicidal ideation reported by lesbians and an increased risk of alcohol-related problems (Hughes, 2003). Most researchers are cautious about suggesting causality between substance abuse and IPV, but alcohol is often a setting condition (Renzetti, 1992). Also, alcohol is used to control or coerce a partner to have sex (Waldner-Haugrud, Gratch, & Magruder, 1997) or is used to boost one's sense of confidence and assertiveness, both of which may result in IPV (Renzetti, 1998).

Personal and Interpersonal Characteristics

Other characteristics of gay and lesbian IPV include dependency, jealousy, and power imbalance (Barelds & Dijkstra, 2006; McClennen et al., 2002). As in heterosexual IPV, the conflict between dependence and independence of the partners is a consistent factor in same-sex IPV (Renzetti, 1992). As the abused partner moves toward more independence, the less secure and more dependent partner becomes more dependent, which is accompanied by an increase in IPV (D. H. Miller, Greene, Causby, White, & Lockhart, 2001). In support of the dependent–independent dynamic, Margolies and Leeder (1995) found that lesbians who abused their partners described themselves as weak, powerless, vulnerable, unable to express themselves, and engaged in black-and-white thinking. This pattern of violence is often characterized by an ongoing fear of abandonment by a partner, leading to social isolation, followed by IPV to prevent abandonment, and further isolation. Thus, violence was used to manage closeness and distance, and yet it was at the cost of intimacy. Managing a healthy emotional bond between lesbian partners may be even harder to achieve because female socialization emphasizes maintaining connections regardless of the circumstances; in addition, there is often a hostile societal environment, with little support beyond the lesbian community (Peterman & Dixon, 2003).

Landholt and Dutton (1997) found that factors predicting gay IPV were similar to those of male-on-female IPV (D. G. Dutton, 1998), that is, insecure attachment, anger, and poor relationships with parents in childhood. IPV was seen as both an expression of the fear of abandonment as well as a method to prevent the partner from leaving the relationship. In support of this notion, a study found that an insecure attachment mediated the relationship between relationship stressors and IPV with same-sex couples (Craft, Serovich, McKenry, & Lim, 2008).

In a unique qualitative study, Ristock (2003) conducted in-depth interviews with 80 lesbians who had experienced IPV. The women reported various combinations of emotional abuse (e.g., isolation, threats of suicide), verbal abuse (e.g., name calling, insults), stalking, and physical and sexual abuse. Several consistent themes about power emerged. The first revolved around being abused in a first relationship. These women were generally younger than the abusive partner, had not been "out" as long as the abusive partner, and often found out after the relationship ended that their abusive partner had a history of being a "serial abuser" in previous relationships. A second important theme was shifting power relations. Although a few women described a "cycle of violence" as has been applied to abusive heterosexual relationships by L. E. Walker (1979), others described a less predictable, fluctuating power dynamic that resided in the relationship rather than one person. Participants described fighting back to retaliate or in self-defense as the relationship ended. Several women related being abused in one relationship and becoming controlling in another relationship. The authors suggested that lines of perpetrator and victim are not as clear-cut as is seen in some violent heterosexual relationships. Thus, counselors should be cautious of assuming stable perpetrator/victim roles with all lesbian couples.

Macrosystem Factors

C. Brown (2008) posited that societal attitudes like minority stress and heterosexism have an adverse influence on same-sex IPV. Thus, external macrosystem influences first impose a culture of homophobia, heterosexism, and victim blaming on gays and lesbians. Homophobia becomes internalized, resulting in IPV in response to cultural oppression and shame. With little support and with discrimination from the community, gays and lesbians in abusive relationships often see few alternatives but retaliation or isolation and loneliness; consequently, many stay in the abusive relationship (Cruz, 2003). The specter of HIV makes the environment doubly inhospitable for the gay and lesbian community. These factors create a difficult environment for gays and lesbians, and yet cause-and-effect relationships between a hostile environment and IPV in the gay/lesbian community is lacking empirical support. A more prudent position is to view macrosystem stressors as vulnerability factors rather than causal ones.

Although macrosystem conditions such as heterosexism and gender role socialization can create an oppressive atmosphere for gay and lesbian couples, it is important not to dilute personal responsibility for IPV. Certainly, being in a same-sex violent relationship creates unique and complex relational dynamics that can dilute and numb one's sense of self-efficacy. Acknowledging the damaging effects of centuries of male dominance must be considered in any discussion of IPV, but along with societal influence, personal responsibility by victims and perpetrators must be considered—not to blame the victim, but to help elevate, empower, and heal. Societal influence and personal responsibility are not mutually exclusive but complementary.

Mutual Violence

The issue of mutual violence in gay and lesbian relationships has been a controversial one. Some in the gay/lesbian professional community have taken a position that mutual violence among gays and lesbians is a myth (McClennen et al., 2002). They view much same-sex violence as residing in unequal power within the relationship, with a clear perpetrator and victim. Hines and Malley-Morrison (2005) maintained that the basis for dismissing mutual violence largely is theoretical and predicated on the following assumptions: (a) mutual violence minimizes the violence because it equalizes power, (b) because men are socialized to be violent they can never be victims, and (c) lesbians who fight back against their abusive partners are doing so in self-defense or as a result of rage from earlier abuse. Hines and Malley-Morrison suggested that mutual violence and other types of IPV occur in gay and lesbian relationships for reasons similar to heterosexual relationships (e.g., CCV, self-defense, control/power).

Similarities of Gay/Lesbian and Heterosexual Violence Predictors

Many predictors and correlates of same-sex IPV are similar to those of heterosexual IPV. For example, in a sample of 62 lesbians (victims and perpetrators) Marrujo and Kreger (1996) distinguished between three types of IPV participants: (a) primary aggressors, who resembled heterosexual abusers in being pathologically jealous, controlling, and angry; (2) primary victims, who resembled heterosexual partner-violent victims with low self-esteem and depression; and (3) participants, who fought back in self-defense. The similarity of the first two types with heterosexual violent partners is apparent. The last type, defensive IPV, is a motivation for some heterosexual women. Furthermore, some partner-violent gays, lesbians, and heterosexual women are characterized by borderline traits such as fear of abandonment by partners, which triggers anxiety, anger, jealousy, and affective instability (Landholt & Dutton, 1997). Violence is less an issue of dominance and more an issue of intimate anger (D. G. Dutton, 1998).

Although similar, gay/lesbian and heterosexual IPV must also be considered within context. Macrosystem variables such as homophobia, heterosexism, and homonegativity must be considered as environmental stressors and contexts for gays and lesbians not directly applicable to heterosexual IPV. Research has noted several sources of stress unique to gays and lesbians, including stress from the "coming out" process and subsequent stressors related to family adjustment, conflict over one's sexuality within a heterosexist society, the hiding of one's identity, internalized homophobia, and isolation attributable to minority stress (Balsam & Szymanski, 2005; Iwasaki &Ristock, 2007). These stressors are related to lower relationship quality and to aggression in gay and lesbian relationships and are not experienced by heterosexual partners (C. Brown, 2008).

Types of Same-Sex IPV

The type of IPV used in same-sex relationships is similar to IPV in heterosexual relationships. However, little research has been conducted on violence typologies in same-sex relationships. Beyond Marrujo and Kreger's (1996) research, other typology models have been identified. Renzetti (1992) suggested three types of physically abusive lesbian relationships. The first type is situational battering, which is the least frequent and least severe type of violence. This type occurs as a result of a particular situation and is similar to CCV with heterosexual couples. The second type is chronic battering, which occurs consistently over time. Finally, emotional battering involves only verbal and psychological abuse, such as name calling, harsh criticism, humiliation, and threats to leave or harm the partner. Renzetti's model focuses on the type of violence, not the characteristics of the perpetrator. Recently, Hardesty, Oswald, Khaw, Fonseca, and Chung (2008) identified three types of same-sex IPV: IT, situational violence, and mutual violence, which are similar to M. P. Johnson's (2006) typology for heterosexual IPV.

Social Isolation

A particularly intimidating form of abuse is social isolation. This form of abuse is an especially powerful manner to control a same-sex partner because of societal homophobia and same-sex negativity. The abusers often are extremely jealous and possessive of their partners and feel particularly vulnerable when their partners are with other friends and family (Barelds & Barelds-Dijkstra, 2007; Renzetti, 1992). Abusive partners often interrogate their partners about where they have been, what they are thinking about, what phone calls they have made, how long they were on the Internet, and who they contacted or received mail from. The abusive partner may even use tactics to prevent the partners from leaving, such as refusing a partner the use of his or her vehicle or actually moving the partner away from family, friends, and familiar surroundings so the partner will be forced to be more dependent on the abusive partner. As with male-on-female IPV, same-sex abusive partners often attempt to undercut their partner's confidence and sense of self-efficacy by repeatedly emphasizing the abused partner's lack of self-worth and that others will not believe him or her. Research has indicated that younger gays and lesbians who have recently "come out" are at greater risk for this type of abuse (Cruz, 2003; Ristock, 2003).

Staying in Intimately Violent Same-Sex Relationships

A few studies have identified reasons why gay men stay in abusive relationships. Cruz (2003) interviewed 25 men self-identified as gay or bisexual and asked them, "What factors contributed to your staying in the relationship?" These men were generally out of the abusive relationship at the time of the interview. Their responses were as follows in order of most to least mentioned: financial dependence, naiveté/inexperience, love, hope for change, loneliness, commitment, emotional dependence, cycle of violence, fear, guilt, low self-esteem, physical attraction, physical dependence, and trapped. Merrill and Wolfe (2000), with a sample of abused gay and bisexual men, found that the most commonly reported reason for staying was hope for change and love for the partner. Staying for financial reasons was not a major reason. Other reasons for staying included HIV status, lack of knowledge about IPV, and lack of available appropriate support resources. Craft and Serovich (2005) noted additional reasons for staying: poor health, financial concerns, fear of losing a caregiver, and few community resources.

Research indicates that lesbians stay in abusive relationships for many of the same reasons mentioned above. Renzetti (1992) found that love and hope for change were the main reasons for staying in abusive relationships, followed by not wanting their partner to be arrested, embarrassment, financial loss, and fear of more abuse. Patzel (2006) identified the following common reasons heterosexual women and lesbians "held back" from leaving an abusive partner: (a) affection for the abuser; (b) fear of the abuser and fear of being alone; (c) experiences of child abuse that increased their tolerance for abuse; (d) self-blame for partner's abuse; (e) difficulty labeling the abuse; and (f) situational factors, such as child custody, lack of resources, and lack of support from family and friends. As distinct from heterosexual women, lesbians identified (a) fear of homophobic and heterosexist responses from family and agencies, and (b) desire to uphold the feminist ideal of supporting all women as factors that kept them in abusive relationships.

It is important for counselors to be aware of these factors as they assist abused partners consider barriers to leaving an abusive relationship. In particular, counselors must be sensitive to the unique societal barriers faced by gay men and lesbians in leaving an abusive partner. For many, leaving a partner is leaving family. Furthermore, leaving the relationship may be seen as disloyalty to and even betrayal of the gay and lesbian community. As with other culture-based barriers to leaving an abusive relationship, the solution may be seen as worse than the problem.

Paradox of Seeking Help in the Lesbian Community

Oatley (1994) related that many lesbian victims of IPV are in an awkward and vulnerable position if they seek help from the lesbian community. Many victims fear they will receive little support outside the lesbian community and are fearful of alienating or being abandoned by lesbian friends, who in all likelihood know their abusive partners and may feel forced to take sides. They also may see the abusive partner as their sole source of support, particularly if they have been isolated from other support by the abuser. In addition, some lesbians will not leave the abusive relationship for fear of retaliation by the abuser, such as limiting the victim's involvement in the gay/lesbian community (Balsam & Szymanski, 2005). Finally, some lesbians do not report IPV because the lesbian community may accuse her of being a traitor to lesbianism and/or feminism (Patzel, 2006). Better to tolerate IPV and support the community than to expose the lesbian community to more ridicule, harassment, and discrimination. Thus, many partners deny or minimize IPV.

In gay and lesbian relationships where clear abusers and victims can be identified, the decision not to leave an abusive relationship, for whatever the reason, often results in the need to accommodate to the abusive situation and adapt to the abuse. Psychological defenses such as denial, rationalization, and cognitive dissonance may justify staying in the relationship (O. Barnett et al., 2011). These psychological mechanisms may be motivated by some level of love and affection for the abuser, which research indicates is a primary reason that many gays and lesbians remain with abusive partners (Cruz, 2003). This view is consistent with many who view a partner's jealously and abuse as a type of tangible evidence of love (O. Barnett et al., 2011).

Case Example

Alan, 39

I still care deeply for the man who has been abusing me for the past two years. I don't know how much more I can take. I have constant pain from nerve damage in my back and am on crutches. My partner is HIV+, a drug addict, and has another boyfriend. He really only gets abusive when he is using drugs; then its unbearable. I'm very confused because we rely on each other when one of us gets sick, and my partner stays with me at times when he loses his housing. I called the police the last time things got rough, and now he has assault charges pending against him. I really don't want him to get into trouble, and he is also pressuring me to drop the charges. I also took out an order of protection against him, and he retaliated by taking out an injunction against harassment against me. We talk on the phone every day, and we've decided to go to that judge and ask him to dismiss both orders. I'm hoping we can work it out between us. In the meantime, I am facing back surgery and will need help. I feel suicidal every day and don't know if it's worth going on. I need him to help me after the surgery, and he needs a place to stay. He says horrible things to me which make me feel terrible. I was going to the support group for LGBT victims of domestic violence, but after I told him where we met I was asked to leave the group. He never would have come and bothered anybody, but I guess a rule is a rule. Now I just want to die. There doesn't seem to be any end in sight. (National Coalition of Anti-Violence Programs, 2004, pp. 8–9)

Traumatic Bonding

D. G. Dutton and Painter (1981, 1993) described trauma bonding in male-on-female IPV as a form of the Stockholm syndrome in which captives bond with and identify with their captors as a means to survive the life-threatening circumstances in a hostage-taking situation. The power differential alone forges a bond between captor and captive. Applied to IPV, Dutton suggests that two particular elements create the potential for a trauma bond. First, a power imbalance exists in which the abused person perceives himself or herself as dominated by the abuser. The second element is intermittent harassing, beating, threatening, and/or intimidation. The combination of a power imbalance and intermittent abuse along with a pre-existing love bond and periods of relative quiescence and normalcy are extremely effective in producing a strong emotional bond between an abused partner and the abusive partner (D. G. Dutton, 1995).

Although traumatic bonding is not identical to L. E. Walker's (1979) cycle of violence that describes the dynamics that keep abused women in relationships with male partners, the commonality between the two explanations is the intermittent abuse with periods of relative calm. Dutton's trauma bonding concept would seem to apply equally well to some gay and lesbian relationships (D. G. Dutton & Painter, 1981). Descriptions of isolation, fear of abuse, love toward the abuser, dependence, and hope for change attributable to nonabusive periods (Ristock, 2003) are as common in gay and lesbian relationships as in heterosexual relationships. Although trauma bonding research has not been conducted on gays and lesbians, the ingredients are certainly present in these relationships for its occurrence. Table 6.1 provides information pertaining to myths and actual facts of same-sex violence. This information is critical for counselors, the general public, and same-sex couples.

Counseling Implications

There is little research or much of a literature base in general that addresses treatment of victims or perpetrators in gay or lesbian IPV. Perhaps the lack of attention to treatment is attributable both to the reticence of abused gays and lesbians to seek out treatment and to a lack of viable and/or accommodating treatment settings (Balsam, Martell, & Safren, 2006). To varying degrees, the lack of help-seeking behavior may be attributed to the unhelpful or unwelcoming helping professionals who lack knowledge about the gay and lesbian culture and convey a judgmental and unaccepting attitude about the lifestyle as well as the seriousness of the abuse (C. Brown, 2008). Counselors and other professionals first must be willing to examine and address their own biases and limitations regarding GLBT issues and IPV (Walsh, 1996). Furthermore, counselors must communicate an empathic understanding of the societal biases toward gays and lesbians and consider these biases when establishing goals and implementing interventions. Although important in any counseling endeavor, it is particularly important with these clients to develop a therapeutic alliance built on trust, acceptance, and a nonjudgmental attitude. In addition, agencies must have clear policies on dealing with homophobia and homonegativity by staff, volunteers, and heterosexual cli-

Table 6.1
Same Sex Violence: Myths and Facts

Myth	*Fact*
Sexual assault and domestic violence do not occur in same-sex relationships (denial).	Sexual assault and intimacy violence occur in same-sex relationships as frequently and as severely as they do in heterosexual relationships.
The frequency and severity of partner violence is considerably greater with gay men than with lesbians.	Some research indicates greater frequency and severity of intimacy violence with lesbians than with gay men.
Sexual and domestic violence occur in same-sex relationships because there is something inherently unhealthy with these relationships.	People abuse partners in same-sex relationships for the same reasons people abuse each other in heterosexual relationships (e.g., learning, power, insecure attachment).
The bigger, more masculine, or masculine-identified person is always the abusive partner in a domestic violence relationship.	Size, masculinity/femininity, and gender identity are not causes of abuse and do not determine who is the abusive partner.
It is easier for a same-sex person to leave an abusive relationship.	Same-sex individuals have similar difficulties in leaving an abusive relationship as do heterosexuals. Homophobia and heterosexism also contribute to difficulties leaving an abusive relationship.
Mutual violence does not occur with same-sex couples.	Mutual violence occurs in gay and lesbian relationships much as it does in heterosexual relationships.
Male-to-male intimacy violence is not abuse because all males are socialized to be aggressive and violent, and therefore neither partner is a victim.	Key dynamics of intimacy violence are the same in all types of same-sex and heterosexual relationships (power and control, violence occurs in a cycle, violence escalates over time, and so forth).
Rape does not happen in lesbian relationships.	About one third of lesbians report being forced to have sex against their will by a partner.

Note. Information from Cruz (2003); Hines & Malley-Morrison (2005); Letellier (1994); B. Levy & Lobel (1998); Merrill (1998); Oatley (1994); Peterman & Dixon (2003); Renzetti (1992); Renzetti & Miley (1996); Ristock (2003); Tjaden & Thoennes (2000); and Turell (2000).

ents (Renzetti, 1996). In a similar manner, counselors and agencies should identify gay/lesbian-friendly services in the community, including shelters for those individuals attempting to leave abusive relationships.

In treating the abusive partner, most programs have borrowed heavily from treatment programs for heterosexual partner abuse (e.g., Peterman & Dixon, 2003). These treatment programs tend to use CBT in a group format and consist of (a) holding abusers responsible for their violence; (b) training in anger management; (c) training in relaxation techniques; and (d) practicing new, more functional conflict resolution skills but within a culturally sensitive and affirming context (Balsam et al., 2006). In addition, abusers are assisted in recognizing more vulnerable emotions beneath the anger associated with their abuse, such as fear of abandonment, jealousy, low self-esteem, and dependency. Because a large percentage of gays and lesbians have experienced some form of childhood abuse and victimization (Corliss et al., 2002), treatment also must focus on CPTSD and PTSD. Depression, affect dysregulation, emotional numbing, and hypervigilance must be treated along with anger containment.

Attachment Disruptions

As a result of being verbally, physically, and/or sexually abused at the hands of a parent or family member, many gays and lesbians are vulnerable to an especially damaging type of attachment trauma (Kobak, Cassidy, & Zir, 2004). Individuals abused by a parent face the unsolvable dilemma of being traumatized by an attachment figure. Thus, not only is the child left unprotected, but he or she is violated by the primary source of security that is expected to provide protection. Such individuals are highly reactive; are more prone to experience a breakdown in organized coping strategies and loss of coherent, appropriate problem-solving behavior; and are characterized by angry outbursts and, in many cases, aggressive behavior (Briere & Scott, 2006). Treatment for both victims and abusers should include a focus on resolving PTSD symptoms with a variety of exposure interventions within a supportive environment (Briere & Scott, 2006). Abusers with PTSD symptoms may need some resolution with these symptoms before anger management and alternatives to violent behavior can be fruitfully implemented. In addition, psychodynamic treatment should focus on attachment issues and a corrective emotional experience.

For victims of partner abuse, a safe and secure environment must be established first, after which they can learn how to manage symptoms such as depression, anger, and anxiety. As with other victims of IPV, gay and lesbian victims of partner abuse need a supportive network both within and beyond the therapy session. Because gay and lesbian victims may be forced to leave their abuser, they are often placed in the awkward position of seeking support and solace from the same support group who also provide community support for their abusers or from family and acquaintances outside of the gay and lesbian community. Unfortunately, there are no published studies on treatment effectiveness with same-sex violence treatment. As with female-on-male IPV, research is desperately needed to inform and guide treatment with same-sex populations while taking into consideration unique characteristics of the gay/lesbian community.

An Excerpt From a Focus Group of Service Providers

Domestic violence assumes marriage, assumes spousal relationships, assumes a lot of things that do not apply to lesbians . . . so there is a problem with using that paradigm of domestic violence [in treatment]. The whole issue of heterosexism and homophobia in the relationship and sort of projecting maleness onto a partner or projection issues around an abusive mother onto a partner with a same-sex abuse—So I think those are issues—how those issues play out in the relationship—I think they are different than they are when I'm working with heterosexuals. But a fist is a fist. So the other part is entirely the same. Violence is violence and trauma is trauma. (*Murmurs of agreement from the group.*) (Ristock, 2003, p. 338)

Finally, battered women's shelters and other organizations often provide ongoing support groups for victims of IPV. Unfortunately there are many fewer such organizations that openly welcome gays and lesbians (C. Brown, 2008; Merrill & Wolfe, 2000). When gays and lesbians do seek help from victim agencies, their abuse is often met with disbelief or minimization (Peterman & Dixon, 2003). Some have been told that their abuse experience does not constitute domestic violence and are turned away (Renzetti, 1989). Often private therapists have been found to be more supportive and helpful to abused gays and lesbians (Merrill & Wolfe, 2000).

There is much work to be done in the area of same-sex IPV. Current research has barely scratched the surface in identifying, defining, and treating same-sex IPV. Future research and development needs to establish empirically supported treatments, further develop community organizations to support victims of same-sex intimacy violence, and develop more relevant data bases on various characteristics and dimensions of same-sex IPV.

Summary

Same-sex intimacy violence research and scholarly writing have lagged behind that of heterosexual intimacy violence. This dearth is attributed by some to a homophobic society, feminist advocacy, and the gay and lesbian community. Existing research indicates that rates of same-sex intimacy violence are equal to or exceed heterosexual intimacy violence. Furthermore, the strongest predictor of aggressing against a same-sex partner is having been abused as a child—the same predictor for partner violence by adult males. Other correlates with same-sex violence perpetration include alcohol and substance abuse, excessive dependency, and borderlines traits.

Gay and lesbians report staying in abusive relationships for many of the same reasons abused partners stay in heterosexual relationships: fear, love, economics, hope for change, and low self-esteem. In fact, many scholars see more similarities than differences between gay/lesbian and heterosexuals intimacy violence characteristics and dynamics. Dutton suggested that in many instances, intimacy violence may be less an issue of dominance and more an issue of intimacy anger. However, unlike heterosexual intimacy violence, same-sex violence occurs within a societal context of homophobia and heterosexism. Finally, in treating same-sex intimacy violence, counselors must consider societal context factors such as isolation, fear of alienation from the gay and lesbian community, and homophobia along with PTSD symptoms, insecure attachment, depression, and anger. Treatment models most often use interventions from cognitive–behavioral and psychoeducational programs.

Same-sex intimacy violence as a field of study is in its infancy, although a few scholarly and research endeavors are beginning to emerge. However, given the frequency and dire consequences of same-sex intimacy violence, domestic violence scholars and researchers must give a higher priority to this topic in the future.

Suggested Readings

Jackson, N. A. (2007). Same-sex domestic violence: Myths, facts, correlates, treatment, and prevention strategies. In A. R. Roberts (Ed.), *Battered women and their families: Intervention strategies and treatment programs* (3rd ed., Springer series on family violence; pp. 451–470). New York, NY: Springer.

Letellier, P. (1994). Gay and bisexual domestic violence victimization: Challenges to feminist theory and response to violence. *Violence and Victims, 9,* 95–106.

Leventhal, B., & Lundy, S. E. (Eds.). (1999). *Same-sex domestic violence: Strategies for change*. Thousand Oaks, CA: Sage.

McClennen, J. C. (2005). Domestic violence between same-gender partners. *Journal of Interpersonal Violence, 20,* 149–154.

Merrill, G. S., & Wolfe, V. A. (2000). Battered gay men: An exploration of abuse, help seeking, and why they stay. *Journal of Homosexuality, 39,* 1–30.

Peterman, L. M., & Dixon, C. G. (2003). Domestic violence between same-sex partners: Implications for counseling. *Journal of Counseling & Development, 81,* 40–47.

Renzetti, C. M., & Miley, C. H. (Eds.). (1996). *Violence in gay and lesbian domestic partnerships*. Binghamton, NY: Harrington Park Press.

chapter 7

Assessment of Intimate Violent Offenders

Counselors need a thorough understanding of the context when assessing for IPV. However, the fact that IPV occurs within a relationship dynamic often makes gathering accurate information about IPV in the relationship difficult to obtain and challenging to interpret. Victims' level of commitment to the relationship and expectation about staying or leaving the relationship can bias responses. Understanding the effects that couple dynamics has on both victims and perpetrators of IPV is critical for conducting a functional assessment of IPV.

This chapter addresses how to assess intimate-partner-violent offenders with regard to the relationship context, individual characteristics of offenders, frequency and severity of violence, couple versus individual or group treatment, and self-report measures. The following discussion begins with the assumption that IPV first emerges in conjoint couple therapy. However, a large portion of offenders begin treatment in same-gender group treatment programs because of legal mandates, without clinicians having had any initial contact with the victims. This circumstance is addressed in the discussion here as well as in Chapter 8.

Research Related to Practice

Developmental Course of Violence

Once IPV begins, it is likely to continue. Previous IPV by a partner has been found to predict a 46% to 72% probability of violence at 30 months based on IPV at premarriage and at 18 months after marriage (O'Leary et al., 1989). Quigley and Leonard (1996) similarly found that 76% of men who had engaged in IPV during their first year of marriage continued to use IPV in the second and third

101

years of marriage. Initial severity was the best predictor of continued IPV, with the risk factor increasing to 86% with men who used severe violence. Developmentally, IPV often increases from age 15 to 25 and then decreases from the late 20s through the 30s, followed by gradual decreases to age 70 (O'Leary, 1999).

Taken together, these studies suggest that severity of IPV and age of abuser must be considered in predicting the developmental trajectory of IPV. It is especially important to consider these factors in clinical settings when considering risk management issues for client safety and appropriate treatment matching (e.g., gender-specific groups vs. couple therapy).

Psychological Abuse

Psychological abuse often is viewed as less critical than physical abuse because most often it is not an arrestable offense. However, psychological abuse both precedes and accompanies physical abuse (O'Leary, 1999). Psychological abuse includes demeaning verbal attacks, isolation, intimidation, suspiciousness, and monitoring, and it negatively affects partners' emotions, self-esteem, mental health, and physical health (Follingstad, 2009). Assessment for psychological abuse should be included in assessing for IPV.

Underreporting Violence

Women's Report

Despite its prevalence, IPV often goes undetected in couple counseling. Research indicates that approximately 67% of couples who attend couple counseling (not for IPV) report having experienced at least one incident of IPV when they are asked about it (O'Leary, Vivian, & Malone, 1992). Yet initial intake reports indicated that only 6% of the wives reported that IPV was a problem (O'Leary et al., 1992). When these same women were directly questioned about IPV, 44% acknowledged that husband-to-wife IPV was a problem. And when they completed the CTS, 53% acknowledged husband-to-wife IPV as a problem. Ehrensaft and Vivian (1996) found similar results, with one half of female partners reporting mild IPV on the CTS but not in the interview and one fourth reporting severe IPV on the CTS but not in the interview. When questioned about this discrepancy, the most often stated reasons for not reporting were as follows: (a) IPV was not viewed as a problem, (b) IPV occurred infrequently, and (c) IPV was viewed as a secondary problem that would resolve itself once the primary problem was solved. Thus, women in couple therapy often do not report IPV without prompting.

Men's Report

Men, even more than women, fail to report their violent behavior, and if they do, it tends to be greatly underreported and minimized, especially severe violence (G. Brown, 2004; Lawrence, Heyman, & O'Leary, 1995). However, even with reported couple violence many counselors fail to adequately assess for IPV or intervene when violence is clearly a significant problem in the relationship (M. Hansen, Harway, & Cervantes, 1991). A national survey of psychologists indicated that 95% agreed it was their responsibility to assist IPV victims, but less than

19% routinely screened for IPV (Samuelson & Campbell, 2005). Furthermore, many couple and family counselors fail to view IPV as a problem or do not use appropriate interventions when they identify IPV (M. Hansen et al., 1991). As a result of these data, some organizations have recommended that specific standards and guidelines for evaluation and treatment be established by all professional disciplines concerned with family violence (see APA, 1996a, 1996b).

Assessing Couple Violence

As noted earlier, with 67% of couples in counseling, at least one member of the couple reported one or more incidents of IPV after being prompted. However, counselors often fail to assess for IPV or intervene even when IPV is apparent (O'Leary, 1995). Given this state of affairs, counselors should assess for the possibility of IPV with every couple, regardless of the presenting problem. To ensure a proper assessment for IPV, counselors can incorporate several procedures to conduct a thorough yet reasonable length assessment.

Assess Both Partners

Even with the awareness of female IPV, domestic violence treatment programs have placed significantly greater emphasis on male-to-female violence than female-to-male violence, largely because males are more likely than females to inflict severe injuries (Straus, 2009). However, with research indicating that a significant percentage of women initiate and perpetuate IPV (Straus, 2009), counselors must not avoid or minimize this possibility in the assessment process. Even if it is determined that female violence was in self-defense, a behavior that occurs often enough and is rewarded in some manner can become a repeatable option in conflict (D. G. Dutton, 1988) as well as put the woman in greater danger (Straus, 2009).

There is little doubt that large numbers of women are victims of IPV, but this description does not fit all cases. As Gottman (1999) stated, "We need to realize that the helpless battered women's syndrome Lenore Walker (1984) described is not typical at all" (p. 62). However, a fact-based, balanced view would necessitate the awareness that males inflict more harm and tend to use violence to control and intimidate more than do females. Safety and cessation of violence should be the first priorities in the assessment and treatment process, regardless of the source of violence.

Initial Interview Process

Couple Conjoint and/or Individual Interviews

The initial contact with couples is crucial in making informed decisions about the course of treatment. Given that *most* couples do not make an appointment for treatment with IPV presented as the major concern, counselors need to make the assessment for IPV a part of their general intake assessment process. As noted above, initially it is often difficult to obtain accurate information about IPV even when seeing women individually; however, an individual session will likely increase the chances of such information being disclosed, as direct pressure from the partner to withhold information is absent. Individual and conjoint interviews provide an opportunity to gain information pertaining to the context, extent, patterns, and consequences of violence and give each partner an opportunity to divulge information about IPV.

Also, partners must be apprised of confidentiality and its limits. Assuming that IPV emerges as a problem and (a) both partners are committed to nonviolence, (b) both partners feel safe in the relationship, and (c) the violence was mild to moderate, the following assessment format can be used as a general guide in the assessment process.

General Guidelines in Assessment Process

Specific questions need to be asked in both conjoint and individual sessions regarding where, when, how, and how often physical abuse takes place as well as any exceptions to physical abuse. Also, detailed descriptions of violent incidents and violent patterns should be obtained from both partners. To obtain this information, it is often beneficial to schedule at least a 2-hour block of time to allow for a conjoint interview followed by individual interviews with each partner. The exception to this sequence would be if the counselor were aware prior to the session that one of the partners was in immediate danger because of IPV, in which case individual meetings with each partner should occur first to determine the next step in the treatment process. For example, if the victim was clearly the female and she reported intense fear of further violence, the counselor should consider forgoing a conjoint meeting until safety is addressed.

Regardless of whether counselors are conducting an individual or conjoint interview, they will need information pertaining to the following:

1. Counselors should ascertain the context for IPV, including situational triggers, aggressive language, patterns of interaction preceding and following abusive episodes, frequency and severity of abuse, and times when triggers and abusive patterns occurred but did not result in IPV.
2. The cognitive and affective experiences preceding and following abuse episode should be determined.
3. Counselors should discover the consequences of abuse on the individual, partner, family, couple, occupation, and physical and mental health, including the desirability of these consequences.
4. Counselors should carefully attend to individuals' and couples' responses to inquiries and the degree to which they take or fail to take responsibility for their actions, especially the alleged perpetrator. (Adapted from Murphy & Eckhardt, 2005)

Therapeutic Alliance

The therapeutic alliance is one of the most consistent predictors of treatment outcome (Castonguay, Constantino, & Holtforth, 2006) and is critical throughout the treatment process. Development of the alliance includes agreeing on counseling tasks and goals and establishing a therapeutic bond (Bordin, 1979). The alliance is particularly critical with those treatment issues that are often associated with resistance and alliance ruptures, such as IPV, especially if treatment is legally mandated or coerced by a partner. These individuals often expect reprisal, criticism, negative evaluation, and lack of understanding and empathy (Rathus & Feindler, 2004). Throughout the treatment process, counselors should attend to the therapeutic alliance and provide high levels of empathy, acceptance of the client(s), active listening, and attentiveness to resistance and disruption in the alliance. Some general indicators of resistance and alliance disruption include the following: (a) directly expressing negative sentiment toward the counselor; (b) indirectly expressing negative sentiments, such as through sarcasm or withdrawal behavior; (c) continually disagreeing on goals and tasks of counseling; (d) being overly compliant, (e) using avoidance maneuvers, such as expressing confusion, skipping from topic to topic, and cancelling appoints; (f) using self-justification for problem behaviors and placing an emphasis on creating a positive impression; and (g) being nonresponsive to intervention (Safran, Crocker, McCain, & Murry, 1990). Furthermore, Murphy and Eckhardt (2005) identified several other indicators of resistance specifically germane to partner abusers: (a) directly or indirectly implying that counselors do not truly understand their situation; (b) if the partner abuser is on probation, lumping the counselor with those whom he or she feels victimized by, such as the probation office and criminal justice system; and (c) expressing concern that the counselor will use in-session information against the client.

Dealing With Resistance and Therapeutic Alliance Repair

The primary tack for dealing with resistance and alliance disruption is directly addressing what is presently occurring in the interview process between the counselor and client(s). Safran and colleagues (Safran et al., 1990; Safran, Muran, & Eubanks-Carter, 2011) suggested the following steps for alliance repairing:

1. Attend to ruptures in the alliance.
2. Be aware of feelings toward the client(s), most notably, a lack of empathy.
3. Be aware of one's own role in the therapeutic interaction and alliance.
4. Identify and explore the issue needing repair, allowing clients to express their negative experience, consequences, and solution. This step may include direct talk about the client's and counselor's relationship, such as issues of trust.
5. Validate the client's experience and overtly express one's own role in the disruption.

Depending on clients' responses, the counselor also may use one or several of the following specific rupture/repair strategies:

1. Repeat the therapeutic rationale. With partner abusers, this step likely includes the counselor's intent to help the client eliminate abusive behavior.
2. Adjust tasks or goals of counseling.
3. Clarify misunderstandings.
4. Examine relationship themes related to the rupture.
5. Link the rupture to a pattern of interaction in-session and/or in the client's life.

The repair process is particularly important as many clients have long histories of unsuccessful repair strategies, such as anger, intimidation, violence, and avoidance. The repair process focuses on counselors staying engaged with clients in a manner that is optimal for maintaining clients' engagement rather than disengagement. Hence, the process will necessitate counselors' ability to modulate the intensity of the interaction on a moment-by-moment basis to provide clients with a different and, it is hoped, more positive repair experience.

Individual Interviews

Individual interviews, especially for female victims, are particularly important and should be presented as a routine part of the assessment process whether or not abuse is suspected. Understandably, many victims of violence feel threatened discussing violence in their partner's presence. In the initial conjoint interview, counselors must be attuned to and sensitive of the female partner's level of comfort and nonverbal messages when inquiring about conflict resolution, especially if the counselor has no previous knowledge about the couple's violence. For example, if when addressing conflict resolution conjointly, a partner does not elaborate or provide detail, exhibits verbal or nonverbal discomfort, and/or is frequently verbally or nonverbally checking with partner on details, then counselors should consider reducing the conjoint interview time and moving to individual sessions, starting with the female partner. At this point, the counselor can assess for risk of lethal violence and/or risk of recidivism and whether or not an immediate plan for safety should be constructed and implemented. Likewise, it is important to be aware of male partners' presentation as well, as they may feel threatened by their female partner. Again, the issue of IPV from both perpetrators' and victims' perspective should be addressed in individual sessions with both men and women partners because mutual situational couple violence is the most common type of IPV (M. P. Johnson, 2006).

Defining Violence

Another important assessment issue is defining IPV. Many men and women do not consider pushing or slapping with an open hand abusive. In these situations, counselors need to clearly define verbal, psychological, and physical abuse. Providing specific examples of abuse rather than simply asking if either has ever been abused by the other will often result in more accurate information. Answers to questions such as the following may provide a clearer context for assessing the violent pattern: "Specifically, how do you two resolve conflicts?" "Have you ever slapped, pushed, restrained, etc. or had these done to you?" "Do you ever personally feel threatened by your partner's behavior?" or "Have you ever been forced to engage in sexual activity against your will?" Administering instruments such as the CTS prior to the interview often achieves this end or begins the consciousness-raising process in redefining and accentuating physical abuse (see the section titled Assessment Instruments in this chapter).

Severity, Frequency, and Context

Once IPV is identified, questions should focus on severity, frequency, and the context of IPV; IPV patterns and consequences; and risk levels for the target(s) of the IPV. In mild to moderate cases of CCV and/or mutual violence, it is not uncommon for both partners to minimize the significance of IPV and even become irritated with the counselor for emphasizing IPV over other issues (Holtz-worth-Munroe, Beatty, & Anglin, 1995). In all cases of IPV, it is important for the counselor to emphasize the dangerousness of and destructive nature of IPV both physically and psychologically. This emphasis would also include stressing personal responsibility for the abusive partner(s). The ever-present specter of IPV creates an almost impossible atmosphere for building trust and a mutually satisfy-ing couple relationship (S. M. Johnson, 2002).

After the issue of physical violence has been addressed, the counselor should also explore any type of sexual abuse and psychological abuse. These issues often do not come up during discussions of physical violence. Basile (2002) conducted a national survey and found that 34% of women were victims of sexual coer-cion or aggression by a partner. Two instruments that are discussed later can help counselors assess for these two types of abuse: the CTS2 (Straus et al., 1995) and the PMWI (Tolman, 1989). Langhinrichsen-Rohling, Huss, and Rohling (2006) provided a detailed but flexible assessment process for aggression that considers these multiple levels of violence.

Severity: A Predictor of Reoccurring Violence

When IPV has been identified, it is important that the counselor begin to assess for risk of reoccurrence in order to create a safe environment for the partner at risk and for treatment. The higher the risk of reoccurrence, particularly severe violence, the more likely it is that same-gender group treatment will be the initial treatment of choice and the greater the need to focus on the safety of the at-risk partner.

Offenders on Probation for Domestic Violence

Offenders are often more prone to underreport and/or distort information about their offense. If one of the partners is mandated to treatment because of a domestic violence charge, the counselor should obtain a copy of the arrest report and other relevant documentation as well as obtain consent to talk to his or her probation of-ficer about the offense. Counselors should be open with clients as to what informa-tion about the offense they obtained from the probation office. In cases of severe violence and/or repeated offenses, it may be appropriate to meet together with the offender and his or her probation officers in the initial stage of treatment to ensure that all relevant information is available at the beginning of treatment. This tack often reduces the offender's distortion of facts as the assessment process proceeds. Conversely, caution should be exercised in sharing with the offenders information obtained from partners unless such information emerges from a conjoint session.

Common Couple Violence

As stated earlier, severity of IPV is one of the best predictors of its reoccurrence. A starting point in assessing severity is distinguishing between physical abuse as an act or acts and IT as a pattern of control and intimidation. Different types of abuse typically are indicative of different types of abusers and thus necessitate different types of treatment. Physical abuse is the act or acts of inflicting physical harm, and it occurs at about equal rates for both men and women (Straus, 2009). The highest percentage of IPV is an expression of emotion, characterized by mild and often reciprocal violence (i.e., CCV).

Terroristic Violence

Terroristic violence is often perpetrated by men and is most often an effort to control and/or punish. It is usually accompanied not only by physical abuse, but also by psychological/emotional abuse (e.g., threats, humiliating and degrading remarks; M. P. Johnson, 2006). Psychological/emotional abuse may occur without physical abuse, but terroristic violence typically includes psychological/emotional abuse. Men who engage in terroristic violence have higher rates of personality disorders (e.g., antisocial and borderline) than men who engage in situational violence. Terroristic violence tends to be highly stable and therefore should be distinguished from CCV in considering treatment matching. Same-gender groups are most likely the initial treatment modality of choice for terroristic violence.

Predictors of Violence Reoccurrence

Although severity of violence is an important predictive factor of IPV, other factors should also be included in this process. Female survivors' prediction of the risk for abuse has been found to be one of the most accurate predictors of risk level. Weisz, Tolman, and Saunders (2000) used female violence survivors' predictions based on Time 1 focal violent incidents and the possibility of reoccurrences of violence after a 4-month period (Time 2). They identified 11 out of 26 items as significant predictors of IPV: he kicked her, bit her, or hit her with his fist; he forced her to have sex; he choked or strangled her; she obtained a protective order before the focal violent incident; she was treated for injuries from a dispute before the focal violent incident; there were more violent disputes between the focal incident and the court date; he threatened her to get her to drop charges; he told her she could not leave or see certain people; he restricted her use of phone or car; he accused her of an affair; and she predicted more violence from a dispute would occur within the next year (highest correlation).

It is noteworthy that 4% of the women predicted a low risk of severe violence and yet experienced severe abuse within the 4-month period. Although survivors' predictions are critical in anticipating future violence, some women may report some of the above factors and still predict, inaccurately, a low risk of severe violence in the future. The less accurate predictions may be a result of trauma that decreases their ability to make more accurate risk assessment of dangerous behaviors (J. C. Campbell, 1995) and adversely impairs a victim's memory of the previous dangerous behaviors (Browne, 1987). Other mitigating factors are the victim doubting her own judgment because of repeated criticism by the abuser and the determination that her children would be better off if she remains with the abuser (M. A. Dutton & Dionne, 1991).

On the basis of the above information, counselors should both identify contexts that predict IPV as well as consider the survivor's prediction of subsequent violence. In particular, counselors should take seriously the survivor's prediction even if other more salient risk factors are absent. For women who report risk factors but fail to predict violence, counselors are advised to take more time discussing and processing their perceptions of the risk factors as well as assessing for trauma.

In severe cases, survivors, who often are female partners, may suffer from some degree of trauma, which can result in mistrust of the counselor, denial, minimization of the abuse, and a sense of hopelessness and shame (T. W. Miller & Veltkamp,

1996). On the basis of the Trauma Accommodation Syndrome stages (i.e., victimization; cognitive disorganization and confusion denial, avoidance, and conscious inhibition; reevaluation; and coping and/or resolution; T. W. Miller & Veltkamp, 1996), L. E. Walker's (1979) cycle of violence (see Table 7.1), and trauma bonding theory (D. G. Dutton & Painter, 1981), it might be expected that individuals who stay with their abusive partners, especially during times of apparent reduction or cessation of violence, would have a greater tendency to minimize and thus underreport partners' violent behaviors. Thus, an adequate alliance is essential. In addition, these individuals may need individual counseling focusing on the trauma before they can productively consider the relationship with the abuser (see Chapter 8).

If mutual violence is occurring, counselors should not condone abuse from either partner but, rather, should clearly determine who is at greatest risk (males tend to inflict more harm) and address this issue first in terms of danger, trust, and cessation. Questions pertaining to violence patterns, contexts, and severity will help the counselor make this determination.

Safety Plans for Victims

If during the individual interview it becomes clear that moderate to severe violence is occurring, safety options should be explored, such as staying with family

Table 7.1
Cycle of Violence

Phase	Partner–perpetrator may . . .	Partner may . . .
Phase 1: Tension building	Pick fights Act jealous and possessive Criticize, threaten Drink, use drugs Be moody, unpredictable Humiliate the partner	Feel like he/she is walking on eggshells Try to reason with partner Try to calm the partner Try to appease the partner Keep silent, try to keep children quiet Feel afraid or anxious
Phase 2: Acute violence incidence	Verbal abuse Sexual assault Physical abuse Increase control over money Restrain partner Destroy property, phone Emotionally assault	Experience fear, shock Protect self and children Use self-defense Call for help Try to flee, leave Pray for it to stop Do what is necessary to survive
Phase 3: Remorse/make-up	Ask for forgiveness Promise it won't happen again Stop drinking, using drugs Go to counseling Be affectionate Initiate intimacy Minimize or deny abuse	Forgive Return home Arrange for counseling Feel hopeful Feel manipulated Blame self Minimize or deny abuse

Note. Information from L. E. Walker (1979).

members, going to a local shelter, and/or involving police. However, for many women, these options initially are not viewed as viable ones (e.g., because of culture constraints). It is a standard policy, based on codes of ethics, that counselors will attempt to protect survivors of IPV by encouraging them to find a safe haven, yet counselors often make this attempt without considering the multiple and convoluted forces that influence the survivor's decision to stay or leave. Unfortunately, some women's shelters provide assistance only when an abused woman has left her partner. Counselors need to be sensitive and responsive to each woman's situation and help her protect herself (and her children) to the degree that she is willing and able at any given time. The struggle of staying or leaving a dangerous abusive relationship is difficult for many women, and it is often based on factors other than physical violence alone (e.g., emotional abuse, financial resources; Gortner, Berns, Jacobson, & Gottman, 1997). These other factors should be acknowledged by the counselor. Hence, the counselor may provide a woman with information about women's shelters but also continue providing support and help her develop a safety plan if she chooses to stay with her partner.

Safety plans generally include the following:

1. Identify risk patterns and behaviors of the abuser.
2. Identify individuals to call in a crisis.
3. Familiarize oneself with procedures used by self and others to contact law enforcement.
4. Plan escape routes and identify safe havens.
5. Identifying safe and less safe places in the home.
6. Obtain extra house and car keys.
7. Put together an escape kit (e.g., money, checks, important papers, valuables, and so forth). (Harway & Hansen, 1994)

Alcohol and Drugs

Alcohol and drug abuse are associated with 60% to 70% of men who abuse their partners (Conner & Ackerly, 1994; Foran & O'Leary, 2008). Heavy and binge users are 2 to 3 times more likely than moderate users to abuse female partners. A thorough assessment of alcohol and drug consumption is necessary to ascertain the role these substances play in the violence pattern. Substance abuse treatment may be necessary prior to IPV treatment.

Assessment Instruments

Specific Violence and Related Instruments

Assessment instruments can provide information about IPV that may not come up in the initial interview process. The most widely used inventories for assessing partner violence are the CTS, composed of 19 items, and the CTS2 , composed of 78 items. Compared with the CTS, the CTS2 provides more detailed coverage of five areas of abuse: injury to others, physical aggression, physical assault, negotiation skills, and sexual coercion. O'Leary, Heyman, and Neidig (1999) modified the 19-item CTS by adding six additional items that assess psychological abuse.

Respondents provide answers in reference to their behavior toward their partner and their partner's behaviors toward them. Although the CTS has been criticized for failing to address contextual issues, it provides useful information on frequency and types of IPV.

The PMWI is composed of 58 items that are based on an extensive list of emotional abuse items. It is used to obtain contextual information from abused women regarding verbal emotional abuse and dominance/isolation by their male partners. Respondents can provide answers in reference to their behaviors toward their partners and their partners' behaviors toward them. The Spousal Assault Risk Assessment Guide (Kropp, Hart, Webster, & Eaves, 1995) is a useful instrument to assess for spouse violence risk. Other instruments that address violence-related symptoms are the Multidimensional Measure of Emotional Abuse (MMEA; Murphy & Hoover, 1999), the Fear of Spouse Scale (O'Leary & Curley, 1986), and Beliefs About Woman Abuse (D. G. Saunders, Lynch, Grayson, & Linz, 1987). Both partners should complete the instruments. This practice is particularly important given that partner agreement is typically low on self-reports. Many scholars suggest erring on the side of safety and viewing any endorsement of violence on instruments as valid (Murphy & Eckhart, 2005). Furthermore, they suggest that in cases of disagreement on responses, go with the highest frequency reported. The interested reader is referred to Feindler, Rathus, and Silver (2002) and Rathus and Feindler (2004) for in-depth discussions of family and partner violence assessment instruments and methods.

The major drawback for many of these instruments is they address frequency of psychological, sexual, and physical abusive behavior but provide less information on context. Therefore, counselors must obtain information from individuals about immediate and long-term precursors and patterns leading up to an abusive incident(s). The following are example questions that address context information.

Background Distal Factors
- What was going on in your life prior to the most recent violent incident? Were there any particular stressors during this time? What were they?
- On a scale of 1 to 10 with 10 being the relationship could not get any better and 1 indicating the relationship could not get any worse, how would you rate the relationship with your partner prior to the most recent violence incident? Explain.
- How often and under what circumstances do the violent episodes occur?
- Did you witness any violence in your home growing up? Please explain.

Proximal Situational Triggers
- What was happening right before the violent incident?
- Specifically, what were you doing?
- Specifically, what was your partner doing?
- Was something said or done that triggered the incident?
- What would your partner likely say triggered the incident?
- What made the episode get worse? Better?
- How did you feel during the incident?
- How did the violent episode end?

- How did you and your partner try to repair your relationship following the incident? (Murphy & Eckhart, 2005)

Counselors should also ask about the types of violence used as another means to cross-check responses on the instruments noted above.

Other Useful Instruments

A useful instrument to obtain information about the couple relationship is the Marital Satisfaction Inventory–Revised (MSI-R; Snyder, 1997). This inventory is composed of 150 items and provides information regarding various aspects of a couple's relationship (e.g., problem-solving communication, affective communication, and family history of distress) as well as a Global Distress scale and an Aggression scale. Elevated scores on the Global Distress and Aggression scales in particular would suggest a need for further assessment for violence. Because the MSI-R Aggression scale items are integrated with other scale items and the emphasis of item content is on aggression experienced by the respondent (rather than committed by the respondent), response sets to answer in a socially desirable manner are greatly reduced (Snyder & Snow, 1996). Therapists might consider using the MSI-R initially and then using other instruments as needed to obtain greater clarity on specific forms of violence. Additional instruments relevant for assessing couple violence and related issues include the following: symptom checklists, such as the Brief Symptom Inventory (Derogatis, 1993), for identifying symptoms such as depression, suicidality, and anxiety; the Michigan Alcoholism Screening Test (Selzer, 1971); the Danger Assessment Scale (J. C. Campbell, 1995), which predicts violence recidivism based on the survivor's report; the Trauma Symptom Checklist–40 (TSC-40; D. M. Elliott & Briere, 1992); Psychopathy Checklist–Revised (PCR; Hart, Hare, & Harpur, 1992); and in some cases a personality measure such as the Minnesota Multiphasic Personality Disorder (2nd ed.; MMPI-2; Butcher, Dahlstrom, Graham, Tellegen, & Kaemmer, 1989) or the Million Clinical Multiaxial Inventory III (MCMI-III; Millon & Davis, 1997).

Assessing for Characterological Disorders

Another assessment consideration is the severity of violence and related characterological disorders. This issue is particularly important because as the level and severity of physical aggression increases, so does the likelihood of personality disorder (O'Leary, 1993).

At least one half of men who are court ordered for IPV treatment possess distinct personality disorder traits (Dixon & Browne, 2003), with some studies reporting rates as high as 80% to 90% in both court-referred and self-referred men (D. G. Dutton & Starzomski, 1993; Hamberger & Hastings, 1986; D. G. Saunders, 1992). Assessing for level and severity of violence along with using personality measures can help at this point in the assessment process. The MCMI currently is the most widely used measure of personality in IPV studies.

Finally, semi-structured interviews offer a different method of diagnosing personality disorders as defined by the *Diagnostic and Statistical Manual of Mental Disorders* (4th ed.; *DSM-IV*, American Psychiatric Association, 1994). They require considerable practice and experience by the interviewer and are more time intensive to administer than group-administered paper-and-pencil instruments. However, they hold greater potential for obtaining more accurate diagnosis with some abusers, such as individuals with borderline and/or antisocial features. One such instrument is the Structured Interview for *DSM-IV* Personality (B. Pfohl, Blum, & Zimmerman, 1997).

Counseling Modalities

An important decision is whether or not to see a couple conjointly or refer one or both to group or individual counseling. Although there are ideological issues related to this topic, currently there are no firm guidelines to make this determination. Some evidence indicates that either gender-specific groups or couple therapy significantly reduces physical and psychological aggression with mild to moderate abuse (O'Leary, 1995). Some couple treatment programs require same-sex group treatment (e.g., men's batterers' groups, women's survivors' groups) prior to couple treatment (e.g., Gondolf, 2002; Stith, 2000). However, some hold that in many cases of situational reciprocal couple violence treating men without the involvement of their partners does not stop the IPV (Stith, McCollum, Rosen, Locke, & Goldberg, 2005) because the underlying relational dynamics that fuel the IPV are not directly addressed. With these couples, counselors must target relationship dynamics to stop the IPV. Conversely, couple therapy with a terroristic violent partner may in fact increase IPV. A reasonable position seems to be that conjoint therapy is recommended if (a) violence is situational and mild to moderate in severity, (b) both partners are committed to the relationship, (c) neither partner is in any immediate danger, and (d) the abuser(s) takes responsibility for the violence and commits to nonviolence (Holtzworth-Munroe et al., 1995; Stith, Rosen, McCollum, & Thomsen, 2004).

In the case of terroristic violence, both partners should first complete gender-specific treatment, and then the counselor can evaluate them for the possibility of couple work. Ensuring safety for victims is of utmost importance with all IPV treatment but especially for cases involving terroristic violence. Thus, treatment for this type of violence likely includes seeing the victim separately and exploring safety options, including finding a safe place to reside for a period of time away from the abuser in some instances.

Biology or Environment?

There are critical neurological and genetic factors that may provide setting conditions for aggressive behavior (Hines & Saudino, 2009). However, environmental and developmental factors have an even greater influence on the expression of IPV in particular contexts with a particular person (Hines & Saudino, 2009). This position represents the view of most scholars and researchers in the field (Ehrensaft et al., 2003; Hines & Malley-Morrison, 2005). On the basis of these assumptions of IPV—especially the influence of social cognitive theory (Gelles & Cornell, 1990) and sociocultural theories (Moore & Stuart, 2005)—cognitive–behavioral/feminist group approaches to treatment predominate in the field. Recently there has been a growing interest in psychodyanamic approaches either in place of or adjunctive to the cognitive–behavioral/ feminist approaches (Lawson, 2010; Sonkin & Dutton, 2003).

Although this chapter has presented the assessment process largely as occurring in the initial stage of counseling, assessment is an ongoing process throughout the course of treatment. In fact, counseling should involve weekly mini-assessments of weekly progress or relapse. Inquiries should focus on how couples handled conflicts, distress, and successes.

Summary

Providing effective counseling services to IPV offenders necessitates a thorough assessment of the context and relationship dynamics in which the IPV occurs. However, the historical and current relationship dynamics often make accurate information about IPV difficult to obtain and challenging to interpret. Victims' emotional states often are highly variable; thus, their position on staying or leaving the abusive relationship may vary from moment to moment, greatly biasing responses. Research indicates a strong bias for underreporting both from victims and especially from perpetrators. Failure to consider IPV within such a context greatly hampers functional assessment and, thus, effective treatment.

Others factors to include in a comprehensive assessment include severity of IPV (common vs. terroristic violence), age of abuser, presence of psychological abuse, use of drugs and alcohol and relationship to IPV, individual's and couple's patterns of behavior and thinking leading to violent episodes, exceptions to IPV even when violent escalation occurs, and protective factors. Given that up to 67% of couples in counseling report at least one incident of IPV, counselors must routinely assess for IPV with all couples in counseling, regardless of the presenting concern. Furthermore, with research indicating that a significant percentage of women initiate and perpetuate IPV, counselors must consider this possibility in the assessment process.

A critical issue in the assessment process is choice of counseling modality, that is, conjoint couple counseling or same-gender groups. This choice is a critical consideration as in many cases of CCV the violence is reciprocal and treating men without the involvement of their partners does not stop the IPV. The underlying relational dynamics fuel the IPV and must be addressed to stem the violence. Counselors must target relationship dynamics to stop the IPV.

A common metric used by some IPV scholars and clinicians is that conjoint couple counseling is reasonable if the following conditions are met: (a) violence is situational and mild to moderate in severity, (b) both partners are committed to the relationship, (c) neither partner is in any immediate danger, and (d) the abuser(s) takes responsibility for the violence and commits to nonviolence. Conversely, couple therapy with a terroristic violent partner may in fact increase IPV.

Finally, the assessment process should include standard assessment tools such as the CTS and CTS2, the PMWI, and the MMEA. These instruments often provide information about IPV that may not emerge during the interview process.

Suggested Readings

Feindler, E. L., Rathus, J. H., & Silver, L. B. (2002). *Assessment of family violence: A handbook for researchers and practitioners*. Washington, DC: American Psychological Association.

McCloskey, K., & Grigsby, N. (2005). The ubiquitous clinical problem of adult intimate partner violence: The need for routine assessment. *Professional Psychology: Research and Practice, 30,* 264–275.

Murphy, C. M., & Eckhardt, C. I. (2005). *Treating the abusive partner: An individualized cognitive–behavioral approach*. New York, NY: Guilford Press.

Otto, R. K., & Douglas, K. S. (Eds.). (2010). *Handbook of violence risk assessment: International perspectives on forensic mental health*. New York, NY: Routledge/Taylor & Francis Group.

Rathus, J. H., & Feindler, E. L. (2004). *Assessment of partner violence: A handbook for researchers and practitioners*. Washington, DC: American Psychological Association.

Stith, S. M., McCollum, E. E., & Rosen, K. H. (2011). *Couples therapy for domestic violence: Finding safe solutions.* Washington, DC: American Psychological Association.

Thompson M. P., Basile K. C., Hertz, M. F., & Sitteler, D. (2006). *Measuring intimate partner violence victimization and perpetration: A compendium of assessment tools*. Atlanta, GA: CDC, National Center for Injury Prevention and Control.

chapter 8

Treatment for Intimate Violent Offenders

Until recently, the literature on treatment for IPV offenders largely has focused on male partner-abusers (see reviews in Aldarondo & Castro-Fernandez, 2011; Kamphuis & Emmelkamp, 2005). In fact, suggesting a need for treating female partner-abusers has been referred to as victim blaming (Kurz, 1993). Thus, few studies have been conducted on treatment effectiveness with female IPV. As a result, much of discussion below focuses on the treatments that have been developed for male partner-abusers and then adapted for females and same-sex couples. CBT and feminist-based psychoeducation approaches are addressed first, followed by psychodynamic and interpersonal models of treatment, and more recent integrated approaches that include motivational approaches such as motivational interviewing. Couples treatment versus group treatment also is addressed.

It is important to note that treatments will vary for groups, couples, and individuals on the basis of offenders' experiences with issues such as oppression, racism, and prior victimization. For example, evidence indicates that many male and female partner-abusers have histories of exposure to parent violence or physical and/or sexual abuse in childhood (Trull, 2001; Widom & Maxfield, 2001). In such cases, childhood abuse may need to be included in the treatment of IPV.

Cognitive–Behavioral/Feminist Counseling Models

CBT/feminist models of treatment emphasize psychoeducation, anger management, conflict containment, communication training, stress management, and patriarchal power and control resocialization (D. G. Dutton, 2007). An initial task in treatment is to assist participants in gaining skills to prevent or slow anger and/or conflict escalation. Of particular focus are the precipitants to and sequel of the escalation process. Therefore, teaching anger management skills is a major thrust of treatment in which the participants learn to recognize physical, behavioral, and situational cues to anger buildup (e.g., becoming more or less agitated, physically active, or angry; being aware of tension in the neck and so forth; having an awareness of conflict-related topics; and knowing couple style of interaction). Once cues are identified, some type of time-out strategy is implemented in a manner that includes but does not punish the partner. Participants are also taught physical relaxation and cognitive refocusing skills to defuse the buildup of tension, distress, and anger. Table 8.1 presents examples of interventions counselors might use with different types of stressors experienced by partner abusers who are struggling with anger.

Identify Abuse-Related Emotions and Thoughts

Partner abusers often misinterpret their partners' behavior (Marshall & Holtz-worth-Munroe, 2010). Thus, they are taught to identify and examine emotions and thoughts related to abusive behavior and to use self-talk that emphasizes rational, realistic self-statements to defuse the anger. This process is followed by learning

Table 8.1
Anger Management Strategies by Types of Stressors

Type of Stressor	*Strategy*
Internal	Focused breathing
	Learning cognitive view of emotional arousal
	Thought-stopping technique
	Identifying and replacing inaccurate beliefs about violence
	Self-calming self-talk
	Calming imagery
	Physical activity
	Mindfulness training
External	
Interpersonal	Assertiveness training
	Communication training
	Conflict management
	Time-out
	Grounding activities
General	Stress-inoculation training
	Focused breathing
	Self-calming self-talk
	Calming imagery
	Selective avoidance
Unalterable circumstances	Relaxation training
	Self-calming self-talk
	Identifying and replacing inaccurate beliefs about violence
	Mindfulness
	Seeking social support
	Selective avoidance

Note. Information from Neidig & Friedman (1984), Hamberger (1997), Holtzworth-Munroe et al. (2002), and Murphy & Eckhardt (2005).

appropriate assertiveness and communication skills. Other interventions focus on abusers accepting responsibility for their IPV, developing a functional level of empathy, learning nonviolent means of conflict resolution, dealing with extreme affective arousal, and learning to understand the negative effects of IPV on themselves and their loved ones.

Socialization Issues

Resocialization focuses on men's use of IPV and is based on the assumption that women are oppressed in society (Pence & Paymar, 1993). Men are educated about the power differential between genders, the importance of equality in relationships, and respect for partners. The primary goal is for men to change their attitudes, which are supported by a society that values women less than men and holds that men have a right to impose their views on women using whatever strategy necessary, including IPV. Furthermore, responsibility for the violence is placed on the perpetrator, not the victim. Based on feminist theory, this element of treatment is often highly confrontational and challenging. However, the literature is mixed on its effectiveness in changing attitudes and behaviors. Research indicates that the need for resocialization does not apply to all men or to all men equally (D. G. Dutton, 2006).

As is apparent from the above discussion, the primary focus of CBT and feminist models has been on aggressive behavior and male socialization, with little or no consideration of "indirect targets such as self-esteem, dependency, personality disorders, or marital dissatisfaction" (Feldman & Ridley, 1995, p. 331). The same treatment is considered appropriate for all abusers, regardless of the levels of violence or the patterns of abuse. However, reviews (e.g., Babcock et al., 2004; Feder & Wilson, 2005) have indicated that group treatment of abusers has a modest effect on reducing IPV and fails to meet the same level of effectiveness reached with general counseling populations. Given this state of affairs, it is critical to consider elements of treatment beyond the typical CBT and feminist approaches.

Psychodynamic/Interpersonal Counseling Models

Variables that are often overlooked in many published treatment models are the so-called indirect targets (i.e., self-esteem, dependency, personality disorders; Feldman & Ridley, 1995). And yet their importance has been supported in recent research indicating that violent men report more insecure, preoccupied, and fearful attachment styles than nonviolent men (D. G. Dutton et al., 1994; Holtzworth-Munroe, Meehan, et al., 2003). In addition, violent men report higher levels of jealously, dependency, and preoccupation with their wives and less trust in marriage (Holtzworth-Munroe et al., 1997; Murphy, Meyer, & O'Leary, 1994). These factors appear to be important elements in accessing and changing life-long poor attachments that provide the setting conditions for IPV (D. G. Dutton, 2007; Jennings & Murphy, 2000).

Some suggest that modification of attachment styles and internal working models of relationships is most directly accomplished with psychodynamic models of therapy (Lawson, 2010). With this focus, counselors use themselves as a therapeutic lever for change by entering clients' typical interactional pattern of relating and then interdicting and restructuring this pattern. From this perspective, the goals of treatment are to accomplish the following:

- Create an optimal trusting atmosphere for the enactment of the client's working model of relating;
- allow the client's typical interactional pattern to be enacted (within limits);
- assist clients in being aware of what they are doing while they are doing it; and
- interdict their typical enactment of complementary roles that are based on working models, thereby forcing clients to rethink, modify, and correct the assumptions underlying their working model. (Strupp & Binder, 1984)

The focus of the counseling process is the *current* relationship between the counselor, group members, and, if deemed appropriate in later conjoint treatment, the abuser's significant other(s) rather than past relationships with caregivers (e.g., parents). Levenson (1995) held that changing the relationship between the client and therapist (as well as between other group members) generalizes to relationships with current people in a client's life beyond the group.

A psychodynamic model provides a necessary adjunct to feminist and CBT models, given the interpersonal nature of abuse and the characterological features of many abusers (Lawson et al., 2001). By integrating these models, the more overt and identifiable links to battering (e.g., intimidation and physical abuse) are addressed with CBT/feminist methods while the early maladaptive relational models and trauma are addressed with psychodynamic models. Recent research provides some support for an integrated model of treatment. Lawson (2010) found that an integrated CBT/psychodyanmic approach was more effective in reducing IPV, improving attachment bonds, and reducing interpersonal problems than CBT alone.

Group Treatment Modality

Group therapy is the most widely used modality in treating IPV. Single-gender treatment groups provide an opportunity for group members (a) to receive support and challenge from other members who have similar problems; (b) to be exposed to role models with whom they can identify; (c) to decrease their social isolation; and (d) to obtain, practice, and refine interpersonal skills (Babcock et al., 2004).

Pregroup Interview

It is difficult to obtain detailed information on issues related to each participant's personal/family relationship history, including violence (witnessing, being victimized, and perpetrating), criminal background, and physical and mental health during group treatment sessions because of time limitations and initial defensiveness by participants. Nevertheless, this information is critical for gauging treatment planning, deciding on inclusion or exclusion from the group, and assessing for level of danger to partners (frequency, severity, and duration of IPV). In addition, if the group therapy is court-ordered, it is important to address court documents about the abuse with the client. Other information would include drug and alcohol use, which predicts recidivism (Fals-Stewart, Kashdan, O'Farrell, & Birchler, 2002), and acting out behavior (e.g., probation violations, resisting arrest), which predicts premature treatment termination (Scott, 2004).

Establishing a Therapeutic Milieu

A pregroup interview with each participant is important to create an initial therapeutic milieu for treatment. This process initiates a collaborative relationship before the group begins. Hence, it is particularly important when working with involuntary or reluctant clients, such as men on probation or when partner reconciliation is made contingent on group attendance. Successful outcome is related to a collaborative relationship in which the client and counselor agree on goals and tasks and establish clear expectations for treatment. In a similar manner, discussion of termination expectations also predicts successful outcomes (Quintana & Holahan, 1992). Furthermore, a supportive alliance with group members enhances session attendance (Taft, Murphy, Elliott, & Morrel, 2001) and is associated with lower levels of psychological and physical abuse (Taft, Murphy, King, Musser, & DeDeyn, 2003). Many view the therapeutic alliance as holding more promise for lasting change than feminist models that emphasize confrontation at the expense of relationships (Taft et al., 2003).

Motivational Interviewing

Recent research using motivational interviewing (MI; W. R. Miller & Rollnick, 2002) as a pregroup intervention has noted significant improvements in attitudes and receptiveness to treatment for partner-violent men compared with control groups (Kistenmacher & Weiss, 2008; Musser, Semiatin, Taft, & Murphy, 2008). MI is also effective with minority clients (Taft, Murphy, Elliott, & Keaser, 2001). Proponents of MI view resistance as at least a two-person dynamic, rather than a client trait. This conceptualization implies that resistance can be increased or decreased based on a counselor's manner of interacting with a client—a concept that is particularly critical when working with clients who are referred by the courts or who attend largely because of pressure from a partner. Clients lacking a commitment to change are not likely to be motivated by direct confrontation of their denial or rationalization (Murphy & Eckhardt, 2005). In fact, confrontation is more likely to strengthen a client's resolve NOT to change, with great effort exerted to prove the counselor wrong. MI combines basic concepts of client-centered therapy and strategic responses to elicit change talk and commitment to change. Basic MI principles of change include the following:

- Express empathy—Acceptance promotes change.
- Develop discrepancy—Motivate change by highlighting the gap between the client's goals and values versus present behavior.
- Roll with resistance—Join clients in exploring their apprehension to change as well as inviting new perspectives.

- Support self-efficacy—Enhance clients' confidence that they are capable of change.
- Avoid confrontation—Avoid arguing or challenging client.

Furthermore, MI includes five general methods for facilitating client change.

- Ask open-ended questions.
- Listen reflectively.
- Affirm by appropriate compliments and statements of appreciation.
- Summarize.
- Elicit change talk by helping the client to
  a. appreciate disadvantages of the present state of affairs,
  b. appreciate advantages of change,
  c. convey optimism about change, and
  d. convey intention to change.

Murphy and Eckhardt (2005) summarized the following basic principles of MI applied to treating partner-violent men in the early stages of change:

- Use a high level of empathy and reflective listening.
- Clarify your role vis-à-vis the referral source and partner.
- Let the client "own" the change process.
- Elicit a detailed description of the client's relationship experiences and problematic behaviors in a blame-free fashion.
- Pay attention to any potential signs of a client's motivation to change, and facilitate the client's verbalization and elaboration of these motivations (p. 149).

MI enables counselors to address a "no excuses for violence" philosophy in a manner that increases the chances of obtaining a commitment to no IPV. MI is often used in conjunction with other theories of counseling, such as CBT, typically in the initial stages of counseling to enhance motivation early on and then in subsequent stages when motivation to change wanes.

For those clients who are attending treatment by court order, it important for counselors to share with the offender their knowledge of the offense as based on the arrest report or on other collateral information but to do so in a nonjudgmental manner. Furthermore, counselors can assess for clients' current stage of change (see section titled Transtheoretical Model of Change, pp. 129–131).

Male–Female Group Coleaders

Many abuser groups use a male–female group coleader team. This arrangement provides a model of cooperation, an example of an egalitarian couple relationship, and it also enhances the modification of poor attachment patterns (Rosenbaum & Kunkel, 2009). Furthermore, participants receive feedback from a credible, opposite-sex counselor on gender stereotypes, power/control issues, and related issues. Also, the group provides an opportunity for participants to learn how to nurture one another, experience and develop empathy, grieve childhood traumas, and express shame within a context that previously triggered guardedness and competition. As a result of these experiences, participants decrease their isolation and increase their emotional investment in relationships with group members, resulting in less pressure on their partners to meet all their intimacy needs (Jennings & Murphy, 2000). Female offender groups provide similar opportunities for support and challenging. Some view the group arrangement as a much more natural and necessary arrangement for females than it is for males.

Contact Victim

Early in the treatment process, the counselor needs to contact the abuser's partner to obtain his or her perception of the violence in order to develop a safety plan, to inform him or her about services for victims, and to provide information about the treatment program (Stith, Rosen, et al., 2004). Because partners who stay with abusive partners may also minimize or deny the violence, the counselor should stress three points during safety planning (Hamberger, 1997): (a) The partner is responsible for his or her safety and the safety of the children, (b) safety planning requires work and strategizing, and (c) safety plans must be reevaluated and updated.

Treatment Match Considerations

The above treatment concepts are applicable across group treatments. However, different types of group treatment may be considered for different types of partner abusers. L. E. Walker (1995) suggested that those men who exhibit power and control needs and who physically abuse only in the home may benefit from psychoeducational interventions focusing on anger management and gender resocialization. Treatment for abusers with serious psychological problems would vary depending on the diagnosis. For example, on the basis of partners' reports of IPV, D. G. Saunders (1996) found that men with dependent personality disorders responded best to process/psychodynamic group approaches whereas men with antisocial personality disorders had better outcomes with feminist/CBT group approaches.

Although there presently is no research supporting differential treatment for female partner abusers, it is likely that women, like men, would be more responsive to different treatments depending on personality characteristics. That is, for more dependent women who experience anxiety about partner separation, a process/psychodynamic approach similar to that outlined by D. G. Saunders (1996) might prove most effective. Conversely, those who use terroristic violence might be more responsive to a treatment program that includes a strong CBT component. Partner-abusive women may have different needs than partner-abusive men; therefore, the structure and content of sessions would be different in some areas, such as parent education, child care, and housing resources (Dowd & Leisring, 2008).

Culturally Competent Interventions

Studies suggest that men who are cultural minorities are more likely to drop out of treatment than are Caucasian men (Gondolf & Williams, 2001; D. G. Saunders & Parker, 1989). Although no research supports the superiority of same-race group treatment over mixed-race groups, culturally sensitive approaches have been developed for African Americans, Asians, Native Americans, and Latinos (Aldarodno & Mederos, 2002; D. A. Donnelly, Smith, & Williams, 2002). Although there are differences between these programs, common suggestions include the following: using less confrontational approaches, such as MI; acknowledging discrimination in the justice system and society; using same-race counselors; using language similar to the target group; and obtaining target groups' community support.

As previously stated in Chapter 6, there have been no studies conducted examining treatment for same-sex couple violence. Much of what is discussed below regarding couples counseling also is applicable to same-sex couples. The particular challenge for counselors is to be aware of not only IPV dynamics of power, but also the unique dynamics for many victims of same-sex IPV, the primary one being a fear that reporting IPV and/or seeking help outside the lesbian/gay community will result in retaliation by the community. If lesbian and gay couples are good candidates for conjoint sessions (e.g., both are committed to nonviolence, violence was mild to moderate, and so forth), such sessions may be the best context for treating same-sex IPV because the treatment seeks to preserve the relationship rather than end it and thus poses little or no threat to the participants' sense of community loyalty. Another consideration is that counselors should be cautious about adhering to a stable perpetrator/victim characterization. Counselors must conduct a thorough assessment of IPV patterns and the participants' roles and triggers for IPV for each couple.

Couple Counseling

General Issues

Benefits of Couple Counseling

Couple counseling for IPV has been criticized for blaming the victim (Bograd, 1988), encouraging the underlying inequity of power between the partners (L. E. Walker, 1993), and colluding with the abuser in perpetuating a fear of retribution for honest expression of thoughts and feelings by the victim (L. E. Walker, 1995). Furthermore, many states mandate group treatment as a term of probation (Rosenbaum & Kunkel, 2009). Consequently, many partner abuse treatment programs give little credence to couple work following completion of same-gender group treatment for men (Stith & McCollum, 2009). Although the option of couple work must be considered cautiously, if couples desire to reconcile, group work alone will be inadequate to address the relational patterns that have supported IPV (Stith & McMonigle, 2009). This notion is especially critical as 50% to 70% of women remain with or return to an abusive partner (Feazelle, Mayers, & Deschner, 1984). Group treatment may assist in reducing and ending IPV, but interactive patterns of controlling behaviors, emotional abuse, and emotional anticipation of abuse and/ or intimidation by one or both partners may remain unchanged, thus maintaining a viable context for future violence. These recursive, interpersonal dynamics often continue in the absence of violence and yet are key variables that predict later violence by both men and women (Murphy & O'Leary, 1989). If conjoint treatment is safe—and particularly in cases of situational as opposed to terroristic IPV—then this context may be the most effective setting in which couples can challenge old patterns of interaction and implement more effective ones not associated with violence (Stith et al., 2005). In addition, because discordant couple relationships are related to IPV and couples treatment improves marital satisfaction (Pan et al., 1994), a reduction in marital discord will likely contribute to a reduction in IPV.

Individual Couple or Couple Group Treatment

Couple counseling may be conducted with an individual couple or with a group of couples. Some research suggests that multiple-couple group counseling, as compared with individual-couple counseling, may result in less recidivism for male partner-abusers (Stith, Rosen, et al., 2004). Benefits of multiple-couple groups over individual-couple counseling include the following: (a) peer support both in and outside the group, (b) multiple male and female perspectives, (c) member confrontations of each other; and (d) universalization of IPV (Stith, McCollum, Rosen, & Locke, 2002).

Safety Issues

When working with couples, the initial tasks of counseling are to (a) acknowledge issues of responsibility for the IPV, (b) commit to a nonviolence contract, and (c) implement a safety plan to reduce the threat of future IPV. Another safeguard used by some programs is an individual pre- and postsession interview with each partner to assess for reoccurring or potential violence and to process intense feeling generated in the session (Stith, 2000).

Therapeutic Alliance With Each Partner

A particular challenge for counselors is developing and maintaining a solid therapeutic alliance with each partner while simultaneously structuring the session for safety and progress. Counselors must exhibit a clear, confident presence in the session along with a willingness to use their influence to maintain control of the session but with a genuine attitude of caring for both partners. For example, counselors must set clear limits about expressing negative affect, interrupting, talking over the counselor or partner, and making veiled or overt threats. Counselors can help minimize interruptions and intense affect by attending to each partner in a balanced fashion. The counselor's position in this process will obviously vary from couple to couple depending on the circumstances. It is best to discuss the issue of session structure in the assessment phase. All issues discussed regarding the therapeutic alliance with individuals apply equally to couples.

Cognitive–Behavioral Aspects of Couple Therapy

The predominant orientation for couple counseling is CBT and feminist-based therapy, which largely extends and elaborates the interventions and goals used in men's groups. Couples are assisted in identifying precursors to violence, including individual emotional states (e.g., anger, depression, anxiety), physical states (e.g., tired, physical pain/discomfort, under- or overstimulation), interactional patterns (e.g., discussion of conflict issues, criticism, pursue–withdrawal patterns), and thoughts and beliefs. Once these patterns have been identified, appropriate interventions can be considered, such as using time-outs, enhancing self-awareness, using rational self-talk, learning stress management techniques, establishing rules for fair fighting, practicing anger control, using behavioral exchanges, and practicing self- and other-validation (Holtzworth-Munroe, Meehan, Rehman, & Marshall, 2002; Neidig & Friedman, 1984). Couples are taught to identify and interdict (e.g., time-outs) these precursors to IPV well before they reach a point of no return. In addition, it is important for couples to establish a daily debriefing time to provide a predictable and conducive atmosphere for productive communication. These strategies provide the essential structure for implementing and maintaining effective communication and problem-solving skills and, particularly, ending IPV. These ideas and strategies would be most useful once the abusive partner has experienced a significant degree of mastery over the violence and the partner's fear of violence is greatly reduced.

Acceptance

An important skill for couples to learn and use in *later stages* of treatment is emotional acceptance (Dimidjian, Martell, & Christiansen, 2002). However, a focus on acceptance should *not* be implemented if IPV is still a threat or if only low levels of trust are present. Acceptance is an attitude of collaboration with the partner while rejecting unacceptable behavior such as IPV. Acceptance includes developing (a) couple empathic joining around the problem, (b) emotional detachment from the problem, and (c) increased ability to take care of oneself when confronted with the partner's aversive actions. These goals are accomplished through reframing the problem, disclosing soft feelings (e.g., "I felt alone when you said that.") as opposed to hard feelings (e.g., "You're such a jerk for saying that!"), and active listening. Because emotional acceptance often requires couples to be emotionally vulnerable, the more tangible behavioral skills (e.g., time-outs, anger management) should be mastered first in the treatment program, and a sufficient level of trust should be present. As trust builds, the counselor can shift back and forth from change interventions (e.g., CBT) to acceptance interventions as is necessary to maintain momentum in the counseling process.

Self-Care

Acceptance through self-care (e.g., time alone to read, time with friends or family without the partner) serves to build couple acceptance by an alternative method of need fulfillment and promotes greater individuation and self-reliance (Jacobson & Christensen, 1996) that are often lacking in violent relationships. However, these strategies must be developed and implemented in a manner that does not distance or punish the partner or exacerbate the conflict.

Repair Strategies

A final consideration for couple treatment is teaching couples to repair conflicts rather than responding to conflict by avoidance, contempt, defensiveness, stonewalling, criticism (Gottman, Driver, & Tabares, 2002), or violence. Gottman and associates suggested that to repair conflict couples must be able to create positive affect in nonconflict contexts, which in layman terms is friendship. Helping couples know each others' inner psychological world, express mutual fondness and admiration, and turn toward the other rather than away (emotional bank account) all contribute to blunting negative affect and repairing conflict. With a backlog of positive and soothing couple interactions, successful repair during conflicts can be almost anything, but more obvious strategies include practicing self- and other-soothing, taking a time-out, using humor, and accepting part of the responsibility for the problem (Gottman, 1999).

As in men's group treatment, feminist concepts of power and equality are integrated with the CBT interventions (Stith, Rosen, et al., 2004). These issues become even more prominent in couple work because of the tension created by immediacy of the conjoint sessions. The behaviors and emotions associated with rigid sex roles can be explored and redefined in session. However, the counselor should not assume that all male-to-female violence reflects a lack of equality or an oppressive environment. These issues need to be considered on a case-by-case basis.

Solution-Oriented Aspects of Couple Counseling

Another more recent model for treating couple violence is solution-oriented therapy (Stith, Rosen, et al., 2004). As is the hallmark of solution-focused therapies, the emphasis is on identifying and accentuating strengths and exceptions to the problem rather than the problem's occurrence. For example, counselors might ask questions to identify times when the typical interactional pattern or the abuser's mood cycle leading to violence occurred but did not result in IPV. Counseling would then revolve around ferreting out the particulars of the pattern's occurrence without the IPV and how they can build on this pattern minus the violence. Less focus is placed on maladaptive behaviors or their consequences.

The dropout rate with solution-oriented therapy is one half that of traditional group treatments (Stith, 2000), which have consistently reported a 40% to 60% dropout rate within the first 3 months (Gondolf, 1997). Counselors using a solution-oriented approach must be careful that a focus on solutions rather than deficits does not dilute the importance of partner-abusers' accepting personal responsibility for the violence or the need to rethink and change attitudes that would maintain a victim status but without IPV. To achieve this balance, Stith, Rosen, et al. (2004) used solution-focused therapy as their primary conceptual model but also drew heavily from cognitive–behavioral, feminist, narrative, and Bowen theories in working with couples.

Emotionally Focused Couple Therapy

A final couple approach for later stages in treatment is emotionally focused couple therapy (EFT; S. M. Johnson, 2004). EFT generally is not a mainstay in domestic violence programs and is not recommended for all couple violence cases. At least a moderate level of trust, low to no probability of violence, and investment in the relationship by both partners would be necessary for this approach to be effective. EFT would be most appropriate for higher functioning, nonviolent couples who continue to struggle with rigid interaction patterns that block emotional engagement, but who no longer engage in violence or use the threat of violence to control or problem solve. EFT would be *contraindicated* for severe cases of IPV and terroristic violence. Therefore, it would be critical for couples first to have completed treatment that successfully eliminated violence from the relationships.

Healthy Attachment

The primary contribution of EFT is its emphasis on a healthy attachment between partners. Bowlby (1988) viewed a secure attachment as an essential and adaptive element of healthy human functioning that is accompanied by a sense of security, trust, dependence, and safety. With previously violent couples, partners typically have developed protective emotional strategies, such as withdrawal or stonewalling, because of attachment injuries; thus, their emotional accessibility, responsiveness, and trust are greatly restricted. Bowlby (1988) held that many partner abusers are predisposed to anxious and ambivalent attachment styles that result both in desiring closeness and yet also the competing experience of fearing closeness. Consequently, the relationship often revolves around reciprocal negative interaction patterns characterized by hostility, blaming, criticism, and negative affect.

Because of prior violence, it is not unusual that when previously abusive partners take responsibility for their violence and no longer use violence, any attempt they make to repair or reassure their partner is rejected by the partner. This response is understandable given the history and possible long-term trauma that was inflicted; yet, until the injured partner can allow his or her partner to soothe and reassure him or her, the withdrawal, anger, and negative interaction pattern will continue, even if violence is no longer present. Failure in these reparative attempts breeds more failure. EFT focuses on helping couples bridge this gap by restructuring the couple interaction to allow the injured partner to accept the previously abusive partner's support and reassurance (S. M. Johnson, 2002). The possibility of a reparative interaction can happen only if violence is eliminated and the injured spouse is no longer fearful of the partner.

Restructuring of Emotions

In EFT, expressing and restructuring emotions is the means for changing dysfunctional interaction patterns and increasing accessibility and responsiveness (S. M. Johnson, 2004). The context of counseling revolves around themes of closeness–distance, abandonment, isolation, and interdependence. The counselor first attempts to access primary emotions related to the relationship, such as fear, anger, or sadness. Next, counselors help couples maintain emotional contact while experiencing these emotions without either partner verbally attacking or withdrawing; thus, the couple can reprocess and change their experience with one another. This experience counters the expectation of abandonment, fear, or vulnerability. It is this new emotional experience between partners, rather than insight, that leads to a new relationship meaning and more functional interaction patterns. Successful counseling occurs when animosity and distancing are replaced with reassuring emotional engagement and intimacy.

Individualized Treatment

The majority of treatments for IPV involve groups with individuals and couples. However, Murphy and Eckhardt (2005) contended that because of the heterogeneous nature of abusers, an individual approach allows for tailoring to the specific needs of the client, which although related to the abusive behavior, often go beyond it, such as trauma symptoms, personality disorders, and immense resistance. In particular, issues related to CSA most often are avoided in group settings with partner-abusive men. Murphy and Eckhardt outlined a four-phase model of CBT for partner-abusive men.

- *Phase 1:* Stimulating and consolidating motivation to change, with goals related to decreasing resistance, increasing change talk, alliance building, and goal setting. Techniques include MI, reflective listening, and affirming.
- *Phase 2:* Promoting safety and stabilization, with goals related to ending IPV, stabilizing, and dealing with blocks to effective treatment. Techniques include CBT interventions, acquisition of problem-solving skills, and interventions related to drug abuse.
- *Phase 3:* Enhancing relationship functioning, with goals focusing on changing problematic cognitions, improving communication skills and problem-solving skills, and reinforcing effective parenting skills. Techniques include cognitive restructuring of maladaptive cognitions, psychoeducation about healthy relationships, and attainment of parenting skills.
- *Phase 4:* Promoting trauma recovery and preventing relapse by promoting goals related to reducing trauma symptoms, supporting self-efficacy in decision making, and preventing relapse. Techniques include trauma processing, relapse prevention, and booster sessions.

Integrating Treatment Orientations

No single treatment addresses all dimensions of IPV (Babcock & La Taillade, 2000). Carden (1994) suggested an approach that is both developmental (successively incorporating CBT, psychodynamic, and systemic concepts) and stratified (individual, group, couple). At the developmental level, the transtheoretical model (Prochaska & DiClemente, 1992), which is discussed below, can be incorporated to inform counselors about the stages of change and possible counseling models to implement at each stage. At the stratification level, choices would be based on the type of abuser and the severity of IPV. For example, individual counseling may be suggested for men who exhibit strong antisocial behavior, engage in the most severe types of IPV, and are strongly opposed to treatment. The majority of cases would begin with same-sex group treatment, although mild to moderate IPV cases may begin with couple therapy.

Transtheoretical Model of Change

Process models of counseling have been applied to male abusers' groups (Daniels & Murphy, 1997). In particular, Prochaska and DiClemente's (1992) transtheoretical model has shown promise in working with the resistance and denial so often characteristic of this population (Daniels & Murphy, 1997). Typically, CBT and feminist models of treatment attempt to motivate change directly by confronting abusers' defenses and rationalizations. Although confrontation is a necessary part of treatment, if it is the primary means of motivating change, it may not be effective with all participants (Babcock & La Taillade, 2000). The transtheoretical model views change as progressing through a series of five stages (i.e., pre-contemplation, contemplation, preparation, action, and maintenance), with each stage focusing on different levels of readiness for change and different methods of intervention for each stage. Personal responsibility receives progressively more emphasis as men move through succeeding stages.

Several studies have provided support for the transtheoretical model's assumptions that men in the precontemplation stage show less change (Scott & Wolfe, 2003) and are at a significantly greater risk of premature termination of treatment than men in advanced stages of change (Scott, 2004). Conversely, men in advanced stages of change use more behavior change processes than men in earlier change stages (Eckhardt, Babcock, & Homack, 2004).

The first two stages (i.e., precontemplation and contemplation) are particularly relevant in working with partner abusers. The primary goal during early sessions is to increase consideration of change and motivation to change. This goal is accomplished by providing a supportive and empathic environment in which counselors explore participants' ambivalence and motivation to change as well as the consequences of their violent behavior. Therefore, in most instances, strong confrontation is minimized in these early stages. The intention is to assist the men in exploring and proceeding to the preparation-for-change stage and not simply to impose a particular view on them. As the men progress through each stage, it is common for them to be in different stages of change with different issues. For example, they may be operating in the precontemplation stage with their acceptance of responsibility for violence and yet be operating in the preparation-for-change stage as they plan how to communicate more clearly with their partners without angrily withdrawing from an interaction. The transtheoretical model incorporates the integration of levels of change (i.e., behavioral symptoms, cognitions, interpersonal issues, family issues, and personality), stages of change processes (e.g., shifting across levels of change), and theories of counseling (Prochaska & DiClemente, 1992). This model is particularly useful when resources prevent implementing separate treatment groups for each type of abuser.

Especially in the precontemplative stage, counselors refrain from direct challenges and focus on reflective listening (e.g., "You can't understand why she left this time, because you've been a lot angrier than this before."), open-ended questions (e.g., "What do you think will happen in this relationship if it continues on as is without change?"), and reframes (e.g., "Another way to think about that is that even though you say she was asking for it, you made a choice to slap her after she questioned you."). Taft, Murphy, Elliott, and Morrel (2001) found that MI responses greatly improved retention rates in domestic violence men's groups. These responses address what is important to the men at the time, not what is central to a particular model of treatment (e.g., challenging thoughts that underlie their violence).

More focused cognitive interventions are added to these interventions as the men move into the contemplation and preparation-for-change stages. Counselors help group members examine how they think in polarities (e.g., "If I don't have control, I'm not a man."), how they selectively attend to partners' negative behavior, the pros and cons of change, and the long-term effects of IPV. It is also important to encourage the group members to express their feelings about change, such as how it feels to talk about change in the presence of the group and how they think other group members and leaders might feel or think about them. During the preparation-for-change stage, once the client has made a commitment to change, the counselor uses more focused behavioral-oriented interventions, such as renewing commitment to nonviolence, setting realistic goals to ending the abuse, and constructing strategies to reach goals. During the action and maintenance stages, specific skills are taught and practiced in and out of session. Issues related to relapse prevention and maintenance of new thoughts and behaviors are addressed. Psychodynamic interventions are interspersed throughout the treatment, especially at points of resistance where alliance repair is important.

When to Use Couple Therapy

Successful completion of group or individual counseling provides the option for couple counseling if deemed appropriate. Under these circumstances, the couple may be expected to enter counseling at the contemplation or preparation-for-change stage. A developmental framework suggests that skill building should be the initial focus for treatment (Lawson, 2003). However, even before teaching new skills from a CBT perspective, counselors might use solution-oriented therapy to identify times in a couple's relationship when violence and intimidation were minimal or nonexistent. After amplifying the exceptions to the rule of conflict/violence, counselors can use CBT to add other skills to the existing solutions.

As trust increases and the risk of violence decreases, other more affective-oriented interventions can be considered, such as developing emotional acceptance and, in some cases, using EFT. Because EFT assumes a deeper level of work than the CBT/feminist and the solution-oriented approaches, some individuals may again begin at the precontemplation stage. Finally, systemic concepts are used throughout treatment phases. Counselors are aware of and intervene in patterns of communication and interaction that function as setting conditions for abuse (e.g., pursue–withdrawal). These patterns often extend into family-of-origin relationships (e.g., cross-generational coalitions). Working with children in the family may also occur at this time because exposure to parent violence increases the risk of children later using IPV and developing trauma symptoms.

Relapse Prevention

Relapse prevention is particularly critical in partner abuse given the high recidivism rates (Babcock & La Tallaide, 2000). These high rates may indicate problems in maintaining changes achieved in counseling (Daniels & Murphy, 1997). In particular, it is important to differentiate between incidences of lapse (temporary slip back to use of IPV) versus relapse (complete return to use of IPV); the goal is for the partner abuser to view a lapse as a signal to engage in active intervention to avoid a relapse (Murphy & Eckhardt, 2005). Factors that increase the risk of relapse include separations/divorces, loss of a family member or job, partner affairs, financial difficulties, serious illness, problems with children, pregnancy, and childbirth, to name a few (Murphy & Eckhardt, 2005). Two particularly stressful events are use and abuse of substances and unresolved relationship conflicts. Most people in treatment for IPV will experience many of these stressors; therefore, treatment must focus on more than violence cessation. From the beginning of treatment, counselors should be thinking of preparing clients for termination. A large part of this process is obtaining greater and greater buy-in and personal responsibility for change by clients by having them be increasingly more involved in setting goals, determining homework assignments, and anticipating blocks to change and maintenance. Finally, depending on safety and commitment, involvement of significant others in treatment is critical (e.g., parents, siblings, or friends). These people can help or hinder progress and maintenance of gains.

In-session activities can be included from the beginning, such as exploring context issues for IPV and warning signs that lapse may be in the offing. Questions might include the following: "What might you be thinking, feeling, or doing that indicates you may be sliding back to old habits?" "What might be going on at home, work, etc. that could make you vulnerable to sliding back?" and "How will respond these lapses?" Another issue that should be addressed is how to deal with the inevitable lapse or relapse after it occurs. It is the exception when a lapse or relapse does not occur. In particular, it is important to address the importance of taking personal responsibility rather than blaming self or others for the slip. Personal responsibility is more present and future oriented, whereas blame tends to get people stuck in the past, which often leads to depression—only increasing the probability of more lapses and relapses. Finally, two to four booster sessions spread over several months provide support and accountability beyond the end of formal treatment. These sessions should revolve around clients' needs and agendas, with a focus on prompting clients for strategies and perspectives, rather than being counselor focused (Murphy & Eckhardt, 2005).

Treatment Effectiveness

Male Group Therapy

Effectiveness research has been conducted almost exclusively on heterosexual male partner abusers; thus, the following discussion reflects this research. A major weakness with many studies is the high dropout rate (40% to 60% within 3 months) and short-term follow-up (cf. Gondolf, 1997). The dropouts appear to be the men who most need treatment. These men committed the most severe violence, had the greatest psychopathology, and were the most likely to reoffend (Gondolf, 1997). Recidivism rates for completers have ranged from 24% to 40% within 6 to 24 months of termination (Feldman & Ridely, 1995; Hamberger & Hastings, 1993).

Babcock et al. (2004) conducted a meta-analysis comparing several treatments (e.g., feminist psychoeducational and CBT). The authors found small effects of treatment on recidivism and no difference between treatment models. However, treatment is considered superior to no treatment. Finally, in a study of court-ordered male partner-abusers, Feder and Wilson (2005) found a small treatment effect when they examined police reports of recidivism. These and similar studies have led many in the IPV field to conclude that current treatments for male partner-abusers, though somewhat effective (small effect), still leave much to be desired (e.g., Holtzworth-Munroe & Meehan, 2004), particularly when compared with psychotherapy with general clinical populations, which produce medium to large effects (Lambert & Ogles, 2004).

From another perspective, a study by Jones, D'Agostino, Gondolf, and Heckert (2004) challenged the conclusion that treatment has little or no impact on recidivism rates of male abusers. They assessed multisite intervention programs involving 633 male abusers and their partners using propensity score analysis with a quasi-experimental design. On the basis of a 15-month follow-up with participant partners, the authors found that completion of treatment reduced the probability of reassault by 33% with the full sample and almost 50% with court-ordered men.

Some suggest that degree of psychopathology is a critical issue when considering treatment effectiveness. D. G. Dutton, Bodnarchuk, Kropp, Hart, and Ogloff (1997) found that male partner-abusers who scored high on measures of borderline, avoidant, and antisocial personality had the poorest treatment outcomes compared with those men with less severe or no pathology. In a similar manner, Langhinrichsen-Rohling, Huss, and Ramsey (2000) found that antisocial abusers were least likely to complete treatment, and if they did, their counselors predicted they would be least likely to remain violence free following treatment. Other studies have found that as psychopathology increases so does the rate of reassault, dropout and failure to begin treatment, and rearrest for partner violence (Clements, Holtzworth-Munroe, Gondolf, & Meehan, 2002; Eckhardt et al., 2003). These results are not unique to partner-abusive males but characterize most individuals in treatment with more severe psychopathology (Butcher & Williams, 2000).

On the basis of the above-mentioned reviews, it is accurate to conclude that group treatment for male partner-abusers is more effective than no treatment, but that factors such as psychopathology, differences between completers and drop-outs (e.g., education, employment, criminal record; Babcock & Steiner, 1999), and substance abuse (Gondolf & White, 2001) may be important moderators that influence successful treatment. Furthermore, no particular treatment approach appears to be significantly more effective than any other approach (Babcock et al., 2004).

Couple Therapy

Although IPV is very common in relationships, few studies have examined couple treatment effectiveness. In the most recent review of the research on this topic, Stith et al. (2003) identified six studies that used an experimental design and nine studies that used quasi-experimental designs. The six studies varied on the type of comparison group and treatment used. Five of the studies included a multi-couple group with various types of comparison groups (e.g., individual abuser sessions, individual couple therapy, or men's group). CBT was the most common intervention model, and one study used a solution-focused approach. A final study compared individual treatment versus behavioral couple therapy for substance abusers and examined the impact of each on domestic violence (Fals-Stewart et al., 2002). Overall, results indicated that partner-abusive men who were treated with their female partners in either individual-couple groups or multi-couple groups significantly reduced IPV. Fals-Stewart et al.'s study (2002) found that couples therapy was more effective than individual therapy in reducing IPV. A study by Brannen and Rubin (1996) similarly found multi-couple therapy to be more effective than men's group treatment in reducing IPV. The remaining four studies found no significant difference between the various comparison groups in reducing IPV. Stith et al. concluded that women were no more at risk when they attended conjoint couple treatment than if their male partner attended group or individual treatment.

The nine quasi-experimental studies (i.e., studies that lacked control groups or had no random assignment to comparison group) examining couples treatment were more varied in their results than the experimental studies. The primary intervention for all but one study was some derivation of psychoeducational therapy and CBT. In considering experimental and quasi-experimental studies, the reviewers concluded that conjoint couples therapy was at least as effective as gender-specific treatment. Finally, there was no evidence to support the feminist criticism that conjoint treatment is more dangerous for female partners than gender-specific treatment.

A final IPV study not included in the most recent reviews used an experimental design to compare 42 couples randomly assigned to one of two groups: individual-couple therapy or multi-couple treatment (Stith, Rosen, et al., 2004). Nine couples served as a no-treatment comparison group. Participant violence was mild to moderate. The treatment model for both individual-couple and multi-couple groups was an integration of solution-focused therapy, narrative therapy, Bowen therapy, and CBT. Conjoint treatment was preceded by 6 weeks of gender-specific group treatment for each partner. The multi-couple group reported significantly positive changes on marital satisfaction, attitudes about wife abuse, and levels of IPV. Neither the individual-couple nor the untreated comparison groups reported significant changes on these variables. On the basis of clients' report, the authors attributed "group process factors" as critical variables distinguishing the more successful multi-couple group from the other two groups.

The above-mentioned studies suggest that couple and multi-couple group therapies with multiple approaches are at least as effective, and in many cases more effective, in reducing IPV as same-gender group therapy using CBT/feminist treatment approaches with mild to moderate IPV. No evidence supports the view that couple therapy is more dangerous than group treatment for men.

Critique of Intervention Models

Most treatments use feminist psychoeducational and/or CBT for groups or couple therapy (Babcock et al., 2004). However, each approach has been criticized on several levels. Feminist psychoeducational models have been found (a) to have little or no impact on recidivism after 5 years (Healy, Smith, & O'Sullivan, 1998); (b) to place too little emphasis on a supportive therapeutic alliance while emphasizing confrontation, often with clients who have low motivation to change (Murphy & Eckhardt, 2005); (c) to emphasize personal responsibility as a primary intervention, which leads to shame and large dropout rates (Harway & Evans, 1996); and (d) to view partner abuse by males almost exclusively as criminal behavior, with little distinction between abusers on the basis of psychopathology or skill deficits (D. G. Dutton & Corvo, 2006). The CBT approaches primarily have been criticized by feminists and those supporting feminist treatments for (a) focusing on anger, stress, and the inability to express emotions, which avoids the most important issue of patriarchy and oppression of women and thus amounts to collusion with the abuser (Pence & Paymar, 1993); (b) teaching anger management without resocialization, resulting in greater skill in controlling their partners (Gondolf & Russell, 1986); and (c) placing an overemphasis on cognitions, with little attention to emotion (Babcock & LaTaillade, 2000). As previously stated, integrated models likely will prove to be the most effective treatments. But to date, only one such treatment has been examined (Stith, Rosen, et al., 2004).

Criminal Justice Involvement

Beyond counseling interventions, abusers should be held accountable for their violence through the legal system. This matter is related more to the issues of fairness and justice than rehabilitation alone (McClennen, 2010). Victims' advocates through women's shelters and probation offices can be helpful in obtaining protective orders or restraining orders against abusers. Mandatory arrest and no-drop policies (pursuing a charge against abusers whether or not victims wanted to pursue arrest) have been instituted in recent years (Eitle, 2005; Worrall, Ross, & McCord, 2006). Protective orders, mandatory arrest, and no-drop policies have shown mixed results in effectively protecting women (McClennen, 2010). Follow-through by law enforcement and victims was critical in the effectiveness of these policies.

Phil and Susan

Phil and Susan sought couple therapy because of Phil's long history of IPV toward Susan. They were separated at the time they sought treatment. Both had graduate degrees and worked in professional occupations. Susan had a 14-year-old son from a previous relationship, and the couple had an infant daughter from their 8-year marriage. They had been in couple treatment previously, and Phil had attended same-gender IPV group treatment. He also had been hospitalized twice for depression. Furthermore, Phil had a history of aggression toward members of his family of origin. Susan had left Phil and returned three times over the last 5 years.

After individual interviews with each partner, the counselor recommended that Phil attend a men's group for IPV before starting couple therapy; however, Phil stated that the group had not been particularly helpful in the past. He stated a commitment to nonviolence and to improving the relationship with Susan. In the individual interview with Susan, the counselor addressed the issue of safety and her commitment to the relationship. Susan currently felt safe around Phil but said she would end the relationship if he were violent again. She also stated a preference for conjoint couple sessions rather than same-gender group treatment as the previous group treatment did not address their interpersonal concerns. In the initial conjoint session, the counselor discussed the issue of couple treatment with regard to nonviolence, safety for Susan and the kids, and the couple's commitment to improving the relationship. Because of Phil's history of violence, periodic individual sessions were scheduled with each partner to monitor safety issues.

Treatment spanned 7 months of weekly conjoint sessions, with occasional individual sessions for each partner to address safety issues, Phil's depression and sense of entitlement, and Susan's posttraumatic symptoms. Conjoint sessions focused on Phil recognizing his anger and sense of entitlement and taking responsibility for his violent behavior, increasing the couple's skill in resolving disagreements nonviolently, identifying and interdicting escalating arguments, learning repair strategies, increasing nonsexual intimacy, and using collaborative time-outs. Middle and later sessions added increasing trust and collaboration, improving Phil's relationship with Susan's son, and addressing parenting issues. Phil also began taking an antidepressant for his depression.

The couple agreed that Phil could return to the couple's home after 2 months of successful treatment. One month after Phil returned to living at home, he pushed Susan during an argument. Susan chose not to leave or to ask him to leave although it was strongly suggested by the counselor. Susan expressed a strong desire to make the relationship work and was willing to risk another violent outburst. Phil expressed genuine remorse for his actions and worked more diligently to stop the violence. Safety issues became focal along with time-out procedures and individual self-care. Another violent outburst did not occur after this incident. The therapist expressed concern about Phil's ability to maintain a nonviolent and nonintimidating style of interacting with Susan, but both partners stated a determination to stay together and "make it work." The frequency of individual sessions with Phil increased, focusing on his sense of entitlement and often contemptuous attitude toward Susan during disagreements. Phil was able to reduce but not totally eliminate these two elements of his personal style. Two booster sessions were conducted at 3 months and 6 months posttreatment. At 3-, 6-, and 12-month follow-ups, each partner was interviewed individually, and each reported that violence had not occurred again, although Susan felt uneasy on occasion because of Phil's intimidating style of talking. Although the counselor was not in agreement with termination after the final booster session, Phil and Susan stated they were happy with the progress that they had made.

This case provides an example of the difficulty in rigidly holding to prescribed treatment parameters (e.g., beginning with same-gender group treatment) even when it seems appropriate. Although the counselor disagreed with many of the decisions made by the couple pertaining to living arrangements and safety, the concern about them dropping out of counseling if they didn't receive the treatment they wanted was seen as an even greater risk factor. Although treatment outcome was less than hoped for and ended before the counselor believed it should, results were moderately positive. However, the long-term prognosis for IPV was not considered positive. Unfortunately, these results are not unusual with perpetrators who have a long history of IPV and violence. Some counselors might insist on counseling being conducted within the constraints of certain parameters if the couple wants to work with that particular counselor. Each counselor must consider the violence risk probability, ethical obligations, and safety issues as well as his or her own level of comfort with a particular couple in deciding about the parameters for treatment. Different counselors may make different treatment decisions with similar cases.

Summary

Treatment models for intimacy violence offenders are largely underdeveloped, even those for male partner-abusers on whom most research has been conducted. Treatments for female and same-sex partner-abusers largely have been adapted from those models developed for male offenders but with few studies to indicate their level of effectiveness with these populations. Some have criticized the influence of feminism for the lack of treatment model development for all types of IPV offenders.

The majority of treatment models use psychoeducational and cognitive–behavioral interventions and largely have focused on resocialization for male patriarchy and development of anger management skills—within a group treatment modality. Research on male offender treatment has been shown to be better than no treatment but not as effective as psychotherapy intervention with general populations. Treatment drop-out rates for male offenders have tended to be high (40% to 60% within 3 months) as is the reoffending rate for completers (24% to 40%). Many in the field suggest using integrated approaches that include cognitive–behavioral, psychoeducational, and psychodynamic approaches to address anger, patriarchy, and personality/attachment issues. In addition, some research has suggested that different types of offenders should receive different treatments (e.g., cognitive–behavioral treatment for antisocial, psychodynamic/affective treatment for borderline, and psychoeducation for nonpathological CCV).

More recent research has found couple therapy to be at least as effective and sometimes superior to same-gender group treatments with CCV, especially in multi-couple group therapy. These results have led some to suggest using multiphase treatment that includes same-gender groups and conjoint treatment that is based on severity of violence and psychopathology. However, little research has been conducted on multiphase and integrated model treatments. These are challenges for researchers in the futures.

Suggested Readings

Babcock, J. C., Green, C. E., & Robie, C. (2004). Does batterers' treatment work? A meta-analytic review of domestic violence treatment. *Clinical Psychology Review, 23*, 1023–1053.

Holtzworth-Munroe, A., Meehan, J. C., Rehman, U., & Marshall, A. D. (2002). Intimate partner violence: An introduction for couple therapists. In A. S. Gurman & N. S. Jacobson (Eds.), *Clinical handbook of couple therapy* (3rd ed.; pp. 441–465). New York, NY: Guilford Press.

Lawson, D. M., Kellam, M., Quinn, J., & Malnar, S. G. (2012). Integrated cognitive behavioral therapy and psychodynamic psychotherapy for intimate partner violent men. *Psychotherapy, 49,* 190–201.

Murphy, C. M., & Maiuro, R. D. (Eds.). (2009). *Motivational interviewing and stages of change in intimate partner violence.* New York, NY: Springer.

O'Leary, K. D., & Woodin, E. M. (Eds.). (2009). *Psychological and physical aggression in couples: Causes and intervention.* Washington, DC: American Psychological Association

Stith, S. M., McCollum, E. E., & Rosen, K. H. (2011). *Couples therapy for domestic violence: Finding safe solutions.* Washington, DC: American Psychological Association.

Whitaker, D. J., Baker, C. K., Pratt, C., Reed, E., Suri, S., Pavlos, C., . . . Silverman, J. (2007). A network model for providing culturally competent services for intimate partner violence and sexual violence. *Violence Against Women, 13,* 190–209.

Whitaker, D. J., & Lutzker, J. R. (Eds.). (2009). *Preventing partner violence: Research and evidence-based intervention strategies.* Washington, DC: American Psychological Association.

chapter 9

Assessment and Treatment for Adult Victims of Intimacy Violence

Assessing and treating survivors of physical, sexual, and psychological abuse requires training and skills beyond general training in counseling. Providing treatment for victims of abuse requires not only a high level of specialized conceptual and therapeutic skill but also a high level of emotional and physical health. Counselors who lack both can adversely affect treatment and are at an increased risk of burnout. Burnout is an ongoing risk with this population; thus, counselors must be mindful of their sense of self, appropriate boundaries with their clients, and caseload. Most graduate training programs are lacking in appropriate training to enable their graduates to diagnose and treat victims of trauma and interpersonal victimization (Courtois & Gold, 2009). Consequently, many counselors provide treatment for victims of IPV having received little or no graduate training with this population. Even worse, many counselors are unaware they are treating such clients because of a lack of relevant assessment skills and/or reticence of clients to reveal IPV (O'Leary et al., 1992). This practice is not only unethical—however well-intentioned—but also potentially harmful (Courtois, 2002).

Counselors treating victims of partner abuse should seek additional training through workshops and independent readings and should receive direct supervision of their work from a counselor experienced with this population. Specialized training in trauma-based interventions is particularly important because recent clinical literature conceptualizes many of the psychological and physical symptoms of partner abuse as being some degree of a posttraumatic response (Briere & Jordon, 2004; Courtois, 2008). Because of the high rate of diagnosed PTSD with women who have been abused by their partner (mean prevalence of 63.8%; Kessler, Sonnega, Bromet, Hughes, & Nelson, 1995), counselors must be mindful of this possibility with each client. Failing to do so may result in long-term negative effects for victims, as research indicates that abused women with PTSD continue to experience symptoms up to 9 years following the last abuse incident (Woods, 2000). Furthermore, the controversy suggesting that many methods used in treating trauma are suggestive and coercive (Courtois, 1999; Loftus, 1993) should cause clinicians to be conscientious and thorough in their assessment with these cases.

Because most traumatic stress literature indicates that the most severe and frequent trauma symptoms from interpersonal trauma are associated with being female (Breslau, Chilcoat, Kessler, & Davis, 1999; Leskin & Sheikh, 2002), the focus of this chapter largely is on women. The following discussion reviews current models of treatment, which are primarily integrated models that focus on cognitions, behaviors, emotions, and the therapeutic alliance. These models typically include three stages of treatment: (a) stabilizing the situation, building the therapeutic alliance, skill building, and promoting self-care; (b) trauma processing; and (c) integrating learnings from previous stages.

Conceptual Models for Treatment

Currently, the development and validation of treatment models for victims of interpersonal trauma and IPV are in their infancy. However, several methods of treating trauma symptoms (e.g., exposure therapy and CBT) have shown preliminary promise. The predominant models of treatment are integrated (e.g., CBT and psychodynamic therapies) and multimodal (e.g., develop a safety plan, build a therapeutic alliance, treat depression, and advocate for the victim with the police), drawing from a wide range of theories and methods (Briere & Scott, 2006). The following discussion provides an overview of concepts and procedures used in integrated and multimodal treatment models for treating females who have been abused by partners (cf. Courtois & Ford, 2009; Cloitre, Stovall-McClough, Miranda, & Chemtob, 2004).

Trauma-Focused Models

Trauma-focused models emphasize the treatment of trauma symptoms, although many of the interventions would be appropriate for victims with or without trauma histories. They build on the earlier work of J. L. Herman (1992) and van der Kolk, McFarlane, and van der Hart (1996) in the use of treatment stages. The only two experimental treatment studies conducted with partner-abused women have used CBT and exposure therapy interventions (D. M. Johnson, Zlotnick, & Perez, 2011; Kubany et al., 2004). Only Kubany et al. (2004) reported a reduction in PTSD symptoms, which was attributed to exposure therapy plus CBT.

Flexible Treatment Structure

In keeping with the multimodal perspective, treatment is to be applied flexibly to identify and respect the individual needs of each client, including the unique developmental phase of recovery. For example, a greater focus will be placed on safety and security with victims still in an actively abusive relationship. However, for clients in a relationship that was previously abusive but is no longer threatening, a greater focus will be placed on symptoms and trauma-related material.

Courtois and Ford (2009) suggested that treatment of trauma symptoms include the following general stages and substages:

- Safety and stabilization, including education and identification of feelings through verbalizing somatic states and learning skills to manage trauma symptoms.
- Deconditioning of traumatic memories and responses and memory reconstruction.
- Integration of learning and increased adaptive living.

In addition to direct treatment, interventions also should include advocacy and direct services for victims, such as use of IPV shelters, involvement of law enforcement, information on housing, and involvement of child services.

Influences on the Expression of Trauma

Trauma literature indicates that the level of posttraumatic symptomatology is a function of four variables: (a) victim variables, which increase the likelihood that a stressor will produce posttraumatic symptoms (PTS), such as being female (Leskin & Sheikh, 2002), being younger or older in age (Koenen et al., 2002), having a lower SES (Rosenman, 2002), having a previous psychological disorder (Brady, Killeen, Brewerton, & Lucerini, 2000), and possessing a genetic predisposition (Stein, Jang, Taylor, Vernon, & Livesley, 2002); (b) variables that increase stressor intensity, such as intentional acts of violence (Briere & Elliott, 2000), life-threatening circumstances (Ullman & Filipas, 2001), physical injury (Briere & Elliott, 2003), witnessing death (Selley et al., 1997), and sexual victimization (Briere, Woo, McRae, Foltz, & Sitzman, 1997); (c) subjective response to stressors—for instance, clients who interpret the trauma more negatively (e.g., horror or helplessness) are at an increased risk for posttraumatic reactions (Brewin, Andrews, & Rose, 2000); and (d) response to victim, such that the intensity of PTS varies according to the level of poststressor support and acceptance by people (Coker et al., 2002).

These four variables do not function independently from one another but interact in a multivariate fashion to influence victims' unique response to trauma (Briere, 2004). However, this view does not minimize or ignore the inherent impact of the traumatic event(s) regardless of the contextual factors. Consequently, counselors should consider the severity, duration, and frequency of trauma stressors along with the range of victim variables that function as relative risk factors for PTS. The interaction of these factors is further moderated by pre-, peri-, and poststressor variables, such as social support, cultural beliefs, and genetic influences (Briere, 2004). Counselors must modulate their expectations and treatment plans with these variables in mind. This process is one of the greatest challenges faced by counselors working with trauma clients.

Therapeutic Relationship and Related Issues

Many victims of IPV experience an intense sense of helplessness, loss of control, and diffuse personal boundaries as a result of their abuse. They often mistrust other people, including their counselors. The more severe, frequent, chronic, and prolonged the abuse the greater the psychological distress and challenge for the counselor. With these clients, counselors must strike a balance between cooperation, acceptance, and equality on the one hand and professionalism, appropriate leadership, and meaningful direction on the other hand (Enns, Campbell, & Courtois, 1997).

In her work with clients with borderline personality disorder, Linehan (1993) described a series of dichotomous factors that function best in synthesis to one another: (a) oriented to change versus oriented to acceptance,; (b) unwavering centeredness versus compassionate flexibility, and (c) benevolent demanding versus nurturing. Balancing these characteristics is a moment-to-moment and a session-to-session process that varies in accord to each client's need. For example, with women who have a long history of abuse, providing intense and excessive kindness and warmth without providing appropriate structure may trigger strong reactions of distrust and anger (Linehan, 1993). Abused individuals often struggle with seeing themselves as acceptable and worthy; therefore, expressions of warmth, kindness, and caring are often incongruent with their perception of what they deserve, which results in suspicion of the provider.

Noncondemning Attitude Toward Abuser

A particularly important balance for counselors to maintain is providing appropriate support for clients as they relate their stories of abuse without being critical or harsh about their partners or their choice to stay in an abusive relationship. Counselors must assume a balance between not condemning the abuser and yet not accepting the abuser's behavior as presented by the victim. This posture may be one of the most challenging for the counselor given the often gut-wrenching stories shared by victims about their abuse. A client's relationship with an abusive partner is often complicated and multilayered because abuse and intimidation are often coupled with abuser remorse and sorrow as well as acts of caring and provision (L. E. Walker, 1979). It is important for a counselor to realize that regardless of the warmth and trustworthiness he or she, the counselor, provides, the client has had a longer-term and more intimate attachment and relationship history with the abuser than the counselor. Thus, if a counselor vilifies the abuser or pressures the victim to leave the abuser, the client may prematurely terminate treatment or have difficulty establishing and maintaining an alliance with the counselor. This situation is particularly true if the victim is still living with the abuser. Rather, the counselor can help clients process their feelings and thoughts about the abuser and the circumstances in a noncondemning manner. However, there is no guarantee that clients will seek safety or even remain in treatment. The case below illustrates the level of conflict that victims of abuse often experience in making reasoned judgments about an abusive partner.

Case Example

Janet

Janet came to see me as a private client. She was in an abusive relationship with a man fifteen years younger than herself and wanted help to leave. She was a lawyer and had used her knowledge of law to get charges against her partner dropped or reduced on prior occasions. She claimed that she wanted him out but couldn't get rid of him as he had a key. I suggested she change her locks, but she said that wouldn't work as he would just break in.

The next time I saw her, her tone, memory, and attitude toward the relationship had changed. She was considering getting back with her partner. "Why shouldn't I?" she asked. I went over, in detail, the descriptions of his abusiveness that she had reported to me in the prior session: choking her, insulting her, threatening her life, putting a gun to her head and pulling the trigger (the barrel was empty). She agreed, but I could see the emotional undercurrent pulling her back. She missed her next appointment. One month later she came to see me again but was disheveled and barely sober. She seemed in a dissociative state. She told me she was back with her partner but it was all right. I again reminded her of his abuse potential.

Three months later I found out that the police had been called back to her residence twenty-three times but that she either refused to charge her partner whenever they arrived or else dropped the charges the next day. And when the police said they would insist on taking him to court, she told them she would show up in court and say she made the whole thing up. Eventually, the police stopped responding. (D. G. Dutton, 1995, p. 170)

As a result of previous and current trauma experiences, it is not uncommon for a victim's feelings to cycle between anger and even hatred to love and understanding of her partner. If the counselor aligns inflexibly with the victim against the abusive partner, when the client's feelings shift toward caring and understanding of the abuser, the client is likely to view the counselor as the opposition. Therefore, it is important to help clients explore and process these conflicted experiences in a safe, accepting, and nonpartisan atmosphere. Clients may consider choices that are at odds with those of their counselors and the accompanying agency, but counselors must maintain support of the client's autonomy and choice potential in exploring these options. Factors such as custody of children, financial demands, fear of retaliation, and attachment to the abuser can create ambivalence for clients about how they should handle the abusive relationship. A client's fear of retaliation is often justified given that approximately 70% of IPV occurs after a women leaves the relationship (APA, 1996a; Stahly, 1996). Furthermore, the risk of femicide is highest when females attempt to leave their abusive partners (H. Johnson & Bunge, 2001). Likewise, counselors and clients may become targets of threat and intimidation by the abuser as the abuser's sense of control and security is challenged by their partner's involvement in treatment (APA, 1996a).

Institutional Alliance

An important treatment context issue that is often overlooked in the literature is the importance of a supportive therapeutic environment beyond the counselor (e.g., receptionists and other support staff), sometimes referred to as the *institutional alliance* (Pinsof, 1995). Pinsof suggested that an initially weak counselor–client bond can be strengthened by a stronger bond with the service institution. Conversely, a lack of a consistent institutional alliance with many of the more severe victims may contribute to their premature termination and/or even slower therapeutic progress. It is difficult to rebuild the client's trust for others when only one or a few institutional staff convey an atmosphere of trustworthiness and safety. This situation is particularly relevant in clinics and larger social service organizations that have multiple counselors and support personnel. People who have initial and ongoing contact with victims, such as receptionists, have an important role in creating a warm, safe, accepting, and therapeutic environment for victims.

Staff Splitting

Many victims with severe and prolonged abuse histories can present formidable challenges to all with whom they have contact, including the support staff. Therefore, it is important to train the staff about how to provide appropriate structure but in a flexible and warm manner that maintains a therapeutic environment for victims. In particular, Linehan (1993) pointed out the need for staff to be aware of "staff splitting," which occurs when the staff disagrees over treatment issues of a victim or when the client creates dysfunctional triangles by siding with one staff member against another member. These dynamics often occur because of the intractability of the client's symptoms and a lack of flexibility by counselors and staff in their perceptions of a client. A counselor's well-intentioned motivation to be helpful to clients may be thwarted by a lack of progress or equally well-meaning colleagues who have a different view on treatment, resulting in conflict and blaming. For example, staff/counselors and clients may be seen as either a "good guy" or "bad guy" because of disagreement on treatment issues.

Another dichotomy is viewing clients as either too fragile, which lowers therapeutic expectations, or believing that clients need to work harder, which gives rise to a more demanding approach. These dynamics can split the staff or split the staff and clients, thus interfering with successful treatment. Linehan suggested the importance of counselors and staff working as a team and addressing these issues in a timely manner, beginning by acknowledging the different views of the team. It is important to move toward synthesis by accepting that both sides of the split (e.g., the client is fragile vs. the client is not working hard enough) typically have some validity.

Finally, staff should discuss how they will deal with such splits before they occur, as staff splitting is very common in treating difficult client cases. Bowen (1978) suggested that dyads tend to be unstable when stressed and as a result tend to triangle in a third party to stabilize the dyad. The ability of one person in the triad to remain emotionally less reactive while remaining connected with the other members can help lessen the emotional reactivity of the situation and move the participants toward more productive, nonblaming problem solving. Bowen's view of individuation with involvement and Linehan's idea of recognizing the synthesis between dichotomies (i.e., good or bad) together can help manage the staff splits. Ignoring these dynamics can serve to revictimize clients and contribute to counselor burnout and, in turn, ineffective treatment.

Assessment

Creating a Therapeutic Context

As previously stated, trauma history provides important information for placing each victim's experience and symptoms in a coherent context in preparation for treatment. Research indicates that clinicians often do not assess directly for current abuse, and those that do often fail to assess for traumatic experiences such as having suffered from child abuse, being stalked, or having witnessed abuse (Briere & Zaidi, 1989). The assessment interview should be developed and paced on the basis of clients' presentation style, degree of psychological mindedness, and current abuse situation (Briere & Scott, 2006). For clients in crisis, safety, crisis management, and stabilization should be the priority in the assessment process. The more formal assessment process that follows might have to wait until clients are stabilized and safe.

Client Readiness

Regardless of emotional state, counselors should first determine clients' readiness to engage in the counseling. Even stabilized clients may not be disposed to elaborate in great detail about the abuse until they feel safe and a minimal but solid therapeutic alliance has been developed with the counselor. Developing and maintaining a therapeutic relationship with a traumatized client can be challenging. The challenge arises because the interpersonal aspects of trauma, such as mistrust, betrayal, dependency, love, hate, and fear, are often recreated in the relationship with the counselor (Ford, Courtois, Steele, van der Hart, & Nijenhuis, 2005). Furthermore, shame, denial/minimization, avoidance of immediate emotional pain, and limited memory of traumatic events add to the reluctance of many clients to explore relationship-related trauma (Kinsler, Courtois, & Frankel, 2009). The assessment should be viewed as an open-ended process, not a one-time event, as new information likely will emerge as the alliance develops. Ongoing assessment is necessary to inform and adjust treatment interventions and expectations.

Greater detail and different facts may emerge as clients develop a more stable sense of themselves and the therapeutic environment. On the other hand, some clients may be *too* forthcoming in the initial interview, feel extremely vulnerable after their disclosure, and either pull back in subsequent sessions or drop out of treatment. Clients should be engaged in such a way as to enhance their sense of choice. Courtois (2008) suggested addressing next steps of treatment within an informed consent and educational context. Thus, clients should be informed and educated about the goals of treatment as well as the caveats at each stage. For example, during the first session, counselors should inform clients about the drawbacks of sharing too much too soon and should later process clients' readiness at each step of treatment.

Assessment Process

The assessment should begin with a thorough developmental history, including the family and significant extra-family relationships as well as current relationships, current and past medical history, mental health history, and trauma and abuse history, which should include physical and psychological abuse from childhood on. Other important issues are occupational history and cultural and religious beliefs. Counselors should explore the client's feelings and thoughts about the abuse history and should obtain information on the severity, extent, frequency, and duration of the abuse. Counselors must be mindful of the tendency of traumatized clients to compulsively reexpose themselves to similar past traumas (Ford et al., 2005). This information may become evident in the interview process, especially with regard to leaving a current abusive partner. See Wilson and Keane (2004) and Briere (2004) for in-depth coverage of assessment.

Assessing for Strengths

The developmental history should include exploring areas of strengths and resources that clients possess and utilize. These resources, along with external relationship support, can be used as a platform for rebuilding and recovery. Once strengths and resources have been identified, the counselor can interweave them throughout the treatment process for encouragement and as a base on which to build other more functional behaviors.

Prior Trauma

The assessment should address any type of violence (physical, sexual, or both) beyond current IPV. Victims of physical violence have high incidences of partner rape (33% to 59%; J. C. Campbell & Alford, 1989; Monnier, Resnick, Kilpatrick, & Seals, 2002) and childhood abuse (50%; McCauley et al., 1997). Women abused both as children and as adults report greater symptoms and distress than those who did not experience child abuse (Briere, 2004). Also, the greater the severity, frequency, and duration of the violence, the greater and more severe are the symptoms. In addition, the counselor should assess the pattern and context for the abuse, such as where and how the violence cycle began and what methods of control were used—for example, intimidation, threats, isolation, and jealousy. It is important to note that assessing for prior trauma is not intended as a time to thoroughly process the trauma experience. Rather, this is an opportunity for the client to share general information about past traumas without going into great detail or reexperiencing strong trauma emotions. The counselor can explain that greater detail will be obtained at a later date.

PTSD

The assessment process should also include assessment for specific PTSD symptoms. PTSD symptoms include the following: (a) intrusive reexperiencing, such as flashbacks, affective states, somatic sensations, nightmares, interpersonal reenactments, and emotional distance from the traumatic experience (e.g., ranging from not knowing to presenting the experience as a witnessed narrative); (b) autonomic hyperarousal toward reminders of the trauma; and (c) numbing of responsiveness by avoiding distressing internal sensations and previously satisfying experiences. Other symptoms that often co-occur with PTSD include (a) intense emotional reactions and emotional dysregulation; (b) interference with ability to concentrate and learn from experience; (c) memory disturbances and dissociation, such as amnesia, depersonalization, and derealization; (d) aggression against self and others; and (e) inability to convert physical sensations into basic feelings such as anger, fear, and happiness, resulting in the experience of emotions as physical problems (Friedman, Resick, & Keane, 2007).

CPTSD

Table 9.1 lists the symptoms most often associated with CPTSD. These symptoms go beyond PTSD symptoms and may or may not include significant PTSD symp-

Table 9.1
Complex Posttraumatic Stress Disorder Symptoms

1. Complex trauma results from exposure to severe stressors (e.g., emotional abuse, physical abuse, sexual abuse, neglect, witnessing violence/torture, domestic violence, and organized sexual exploitation). These stressors most often begin in childhood or adolescence, occur repeatedly over an extended time period (months and years), and are perpetrated within the caregiving system or by other adults, who typically are expected to be the source of security, protection, and stability (e.g., parents, teachers, spouse/partners; Courtois & Ford, 2009).
2. Change in emotional regulation
   • depression
   • sudden shifts in mood without apparent external triggers
   • modulation and containment of anger/rage
   • emotional numbing
   • difficulty identifying, labeling, and expressing emotions
   • preoccupation with self-harm and chronic suicidal preoccupation
3. Change in consciousness and concentration
   • memory (amnesia)
   • various dissociative states, such as depersonalization and derealization
   • separate states of consciousness
4. Change in self-perception
   • disruption in a continuous sense of self
   • excessive and often unwarranted sense of shame and guilt
   • diminished self-esteem
   • low sense of self-efficacy
   • distorted sense of separateness, including diffuse boundaries with others
5. Change in perception of the perpetrator
   • uncritical incorporation of perpetrator's belief system
   • inordinate focus on the relationship with the perpetrator
   • ascribing unrealistic control to the perpetrator
6. Cognitive functioning
   • diminished curiosity
   • diminished planning and anticipatory skills
   • disrupted orientation to time and place
   • diminished executive functioning
   • impaired problem-solving skills
7. Changes in relations with others
   • disruption in attachments
   • social withdrawal
   • mistrustful of others' intentions
   • interpersonal problems
8. Biological and medical problems
   • somatization
   • increased medical and physical problems
   • analgesia
9. Behavior problems
   • poor impulse control
   • aggressiveness
   • eating disorders
   • sleep problems
   • extremes, such as undue compliance or oppositional behavior
10. Change in systems meanings
   • sense of despair
   • lack of confidence for a hopeful future

Note. Information from Cook et al. (2005, p. 392), Courtois (2008, p. 88), and J. L. Herman (1992).

toms. CPTSD is most often a result of ongoing abuse by a significant other over a long period of time.

Tension-reduction activities such as self-mutilation, binging–purging, excessive or impulsive sexual behavior, and compulsive stealing also may be present with some trauma experiences such as childhood abuse. In addition, depression is highly correlated with victims of IPV, regardless of the severity, as are panic disorder, intense anxiety, and alcohol use (J. C. Campbell, Sullivan, & Davidson, 1995). Because of the intensity of these symptoms, clients may also be at risk for suicide (Ullman & Brecklin, 2002). A limited number of open-ended questions such as "Tell me about recent (or past) incidences of violence and how they have affected you" can elicit detail about trauma symptoms without asking questions about every symptom.

Assessment Instruments

In addition to gaining information by conducting clinical interviews and observing the client and his or her style, counselors can obtain information from various instruments. Standardized instruments add an objective dimension to the assessment process that cannot be obtained through the interview process. For example, clients may provide information on standardized instruments that they may not provide in interviews.

Standard instruments such as the MMPI-2 and the MCMI provide information on general symptoms and personality style; however, these instruments fail to adequately assess for PTSD and dissociative symptoms and should be supplemented with more specialized instruments (Courtois, 2008). Counselors can choose specialized trauma symptom instruments on the basis of the initial assessment interview and the results from standard psychological instruments (e.g., MMPI-2 and MCMI-III). Several instruments are available that specifically assess for trauma symptoms.

Courtois (2008) recommended the following instruments for identifying trauma symptoms and PTSD: Clinician-Administered PTSD Scale (Blake et al., 1996), Impact of Event Scale–Revised (Weiss & Marmar, 1997), and the Detailed Assessment of Posttraumatic Stress Diagnostic Scale (Briere, 2001). Specific CPTSD symptoms can be assessed with the Trauma Symptom Inventory (Briere, 1995), the Structured Interview for Disorders of Extreme Stress (Pelcovitz et al., 1997), the Inventory of Altered Self Capacities (Briere, 2000), the Trauma and Attachment Belief Scale (Pearlman, 2003), and the Dissociative Experiences Scale (Bernstein & Putnam, 1986).

Because dissociative symptoms often pose a particular challenge to identify, a structured interview format may elicit information that inventories do not. The following interview systems were developed expressly for this purpose: the Structured Clinical Interview for *DSM-IV* Dissociation Disorders (Steinberg, 1994), the Office Mental Status Examination for Complex Chronic Dissociative Symptoms and Multiple Personality Disorder (Loewenstein, 1991), and the Dissociative Disorder Interview Schedule (C. A. Ross et al., 1989).

Instruments such as the CTS and the CTS-2 can assess for frequency and severity of violent acts. The CTS-2 provides attention to sexual assault as well as physical and psychological abuse. The PMWI provides counselors with information on psychological and emotional abuse.

Providing Feedback

The results of this evaluation can provide a comprehensive picture of clients' trauma history and help guide the treatment process. In addition, feedback to clients can further educate them on symptoms and provide perspective on their circumstances. Counselors must take care not to overwhelm clients with pathology when providing feedback. The feedback should strike a balance between providing accurate assessment information and identifying the client's strengths and resources. For example, if dissociation and/or avoidance are prominent symptoms, counselors can discuss them as the body's initial solution for surviving negative effects of the trauma. In addition, counselors can point out clients' behaviors that attempt to improve their quality of life, which will encourage growth and an identity based on functionality rather than debility (Courtois, 1999). Counselors need to nurture appropriate dependency and provide a source of secure attachment as a foundation for the therapeutic process (Dalenberg, 2004; Kinsler et al., 2009).

Finally, even after the formal assessment, informal assessment is an ongoing process. Often new material or different perspectives of the traumatic event(s) emerge after clients become more committed to and involved in the counseling process. However, counselors must be careful about assuming new material is present and then intensely probing for the assumed material. Considerable criticism has arisen concerning counselors who engage in this type of forced or coercive style of inquiry (Loftus, 2003; Saywitz, Goodman, & Lyon, 2002). The notion of "planting" or encouraging clients to consider additional abuse episodes largely on the basis of general victim profiles is not only unethical but also countertherapeutic. A discussion of the integration of standard psychological measures and specialized trauma instruments in evaluating trauma can be found in Briere (2004) and Wilson & Keane (2004).

Assessment Implications for Counseling

Once counselors have conducted the initial assessment they can begin to piece together a functional profile for beginning to work with the client. The assessment can provide an understanding of the client's self- and other schemas, defense mechanisms, ability to self-regulate emotions, functional competence, and relational functioning. It is also important to identify clients' resources and strengths. These elements—not a sense of weakness or incapacity—should be the basis for building clients' capacity for growth and self-efficacy.

Treatment Pacing

As a general rule, counselors' initial expectations for interventions and the pace of the counseling process can be based on the severity, frequency, and duration of the abuse along with the client's relationship to the abuser and reaction to the abuse. For example, a recent single abuse episode by a stranger would tend to result in less chronic and severe symptoms than chronic, frequent, and severe sexual and/

or physical abuse by a partner or significant person who holds some type of influence or power over the victim. With the latter, the victimization process would involve significant accommodation to the continuing abuse, which tends to have more negative characterological effects on the victim, particularly if abuse began in childhood and extended into adolescence or beyond (complex trauma; Briere, 2004). Treatment for the former may involve more focused CBT addressing the acute traumatic event along with emotional supportive interventions.

Severe Abuse

More severe and long-term abuse (e.g., CSA, IPV) likely will require longer term treatment that focuses on the counselor–client relationship, dissociation, safety planning, self-harm, and advocacy work (Courtois, 2008). These individuals will likely struggle with trusting anyone; thus, trust will be a critical issue throughout treatment regardless of other issues. Treatment also will focus on individual symptoms (e.g., depression, self-mutilation) and component parts of the trauma response (e.g., self-blame, avoidance) while maintaining a perspective of the larger picture of trauma as a disorder with many symptoms (Briere & Jordon, 2004). The counselor–client relationship provides an opportunity for clients to learn to trust someone else and themselves. It is through this relationship that clients are able to reestablish a sense of personal integrity and control (Pearlman & Courtois, 2005).

Treatment

Research indicates the importance of integrating several approaches and techniques to deal with the many symptoms and problems associated with partner abuse and trauma (Friedman et al., 2007). Of these approaches, CBT and exposure therapy have received the most support in the clinical and research literature (Cloitre et al., 2004; Ford et al., 2005). However, these approaches cannot be applied in a blanket fashion without consideration of the dosage for individual clients' differences, trauma histories, and stage of treatment as this could exacerbate (i.e., retraumatize) rather than ameliorate symptoms (Briere & Scott, 2006). Clients must first achieve some sense of safety and control over strong emotions before addressing their trauma histories. This consideration is particularly relevant to clients with more extensive and prolonged trauma histories associated with CPTSD (Courtois, 2008).

Treatment Stages

The following discussion revolves around three general stages of treatment (Courtois, 2008). The initial stage focuses on development of a working alliance, improvement of affect regulation, trauma education, attention to personal safety, stabilization, skill building, and self-care. Some suggest further subdividing this stage into separate stabilization and affect-regulation stages (van der Kolk, 1996). Transition to the middle stage typically occurs when clients experience greater stability, coping skills, and affect regulation. The middle stage focuses on processing the traumatic experience(s). The final stage emphasizes integrating learnings from previous stages and normalizing issues related to relationships, sexuality, social life, and occupation.

Although these stages are presented in a linear fashion, clients may proceed through the process in a series of starts and stops on the basis of their readiness to proceed, with varying periods of time between the stages; in addition, the next stage may overlap in a cyclical manner with the previous stage. Many clients seek services only for the first stage of stabilization, enhancement of safety, education, and affect regulation and never move beyond this stage (Courtois, 2008). For some, the first stage is adequate for their level of trauma, and further treatment is unnecessary.

Psychopharmacology

Psychopharmacological treatment is also recommended in conjunction with psychotherapy (Briere & Scott, 2006). Appropriate medications can help in the stabilization process by reducing (a) the tendency to interpret incoming stimuli as reoccurring trauma, (b) hyperarousal, (c) avoidance behavior as a result of hyperarousal reduction, (d) impulsive aggression, and (e) depression and numbing (J. R. T. Davidson & van der Kolk, 1996). Drug therapy often makes it possible for clients to participate productively in counseling. However, medications most often are not curative of themselves but need to be used adjunctive to psychotherapy (Briere & Scott, 2006). Research reviews indicate that the degree of symptom reduction attributable to counseling is significantly greater than that of medications (Foa, Keane, & Friedman, 2000; Friedman, Davidson, Mellman, & Southwick, 2000). Medications are most useful with severe trauma to reduce symptoms in order to conduct counseling (Briere & Scott, 2006).

Stage 1

The initial activities in the first stage of treatment include continuing and deepening the working alliance that was begun in the assessment process, obtaining informed consent, determining the client's needs and goals, discussing the treatment process, and increasing and focusing motivation for treatment. The working alliance is the context in which clients modify their perception of self and others regarding the trauma.

Client Safety

Client safety is critical in this initial stage of treatment. It encompasses both real and imagined threatening situations. Many clients are still living with or associate with their abusers and need prolonged support to enable them to assertively pursue a safe environment for themselves and their children (Courtois, 2008). The tendency to be drawn back into situations similar to their trauma often challenges the counselor's patience and logic. For clients with long histories of abuse and trauma, the idea of safety is foreign, with many expressing a sense of "leaned helplessness" (L. E. Walker, 1979) with regard to their ability to ever achieve a comfortable level of safety. To a great degree, successful counseling is predicated on client safety; however, its achievement may proceed in starts and stops. In this process, counselors help clients step back and evaluate their situation (e.g., living with an actively abusive partner) to determine safe and unsafe situations. This position is often difficult for some clients to assume. Those with a long abuse history often function in a partially dissociative, narrow-focused state while in an abusive context and therefore fail to see beyond a survival perspective; they often mistrust others, even those who are trying to help them (Briere & Scott, 2006). Some of these clients avoid social situations because of shame and fear of reprisal by their abuser. They struggle seeing themselves as having options or being able to remove themselves from the unsafe circumstance. Thus, counselors must be cautious about making passionate appeals to clients' sense of safety and quality of life. This tack often will have the opposite effect and push clients away, with many dropping out of treatment. Providing acceptance and support, moving at the client's pace, and working within their framework are critical. To the degree clients are willing, they are helped to develop safety plans that include identifying early warning signs of danger, making specific plans for escape, looking for warning signals from children, and finding preestablished safe locations and support. For some clients, a safety plan may begin with becoming more comfortable in a social setting beyond the abusive context. Major goals in this stage are preventing injury and retraumatization.

Noncompliance

Managing clients' noncompliance is crucial in achieving some degree of enhanced safety and meeting counseling goals. Given the high rate of noncompliance with trauma clients (Dalenberg, 2004), counselors must monitor their own emotions toward clients' noncompliance and clients' tolerance for change. Addressing responsibilities, goals, and tasks in a flexible manner that is consistent with clients' values and goals can help prevent the re-creation of trauma-related interpersonal dynamics (e.g., confrontation, loss of choice) with clients. Counselors can invite clients to share their emotions and thoughts about their apprehension to change. Counselors also may choose to discuss the issue of noncompliance with clients as an understandable self-protection mode that has served a purpose but that can be reexamined. Thus, noncompliance may be reframed as a resource. MI also may be useful. Finally noncompliance may be related to a lack of trust between counselor and client; therefore, shifting focus to the therapeutic alliance and repair may increase compliance.

Distress Reduction and Anxiety Management Training

Anxiety and dissociation are a result of and a defense against danger and personal threat. Distress reduction and anxiety management training includes interventions such as deep muscle progressive relaxation, controlled breathing, thought stopping, cognitive restructuring, covert modeling, and role play to reduce and control anxiety (Briere & Scott, 2006). The cognitive techniques are also effective with depression. Box 9.1 is an abbreviated version of the protocol used in the trauma treatment program at Los Angeles County's University of Southern California Medical Center.

However, there are some clients who experience an increase in anxiety, rather than a decrease, when using either deep muscle progressive relaxation or diaphragm breathing. Clinical experience indicates that for some clients who experience chronic flashbacks and use intense avoidance behaviors and hypervigilance,

Box 9.1 Focused Breathing/Mindfulness Instructions

Initial Information

- Clarify that attending to breathing and learning to breathe deeply and slowly can reduce anxiety and increase calm and relaxation.
- Some people may become light-headed when starting deep breathing; therefore, it should be performed while seated.
- Note that they will be asked to breathe into the belly, which may take some practice at first if they have not done it before.

Practice Sessions

- Encourage clients to assume a comfortable sitting position. It is best to put feet flat on floor and not cross their legs in order not to restrict blood flow.
- Practice in the order presented below. Depending on how quickly or slowly the client proceeds, the process will take from 10 to 15 minutes.

  1. Ask clients to close their eyes during the process if they are comfortable doing so as this will reduce external stimuli. Otherwise they may keep them open if they are more comfortable. For some clients, closing their eyes may lead to dissociation.
  2. Invite the client to focus on being in the present moment and the experience of slow, controlled breathing.
  3. Encourage clients to slowly inhale through the nose, hold their breath for a brief moment at the top of inhalation, and then slowly exhale through pursed lips as if gently and slowly blowing on a spoonful of hot food. Suggest that they inhale to the count of 3 to 5 seconds and exhale to the count of 3 to 5 seconds.
  4. Suggest that they place one hand on their abdomen at about navel height so they can feel the belly rise and fall with each breathe. Sometimes imagining that the belly is a balloon that inflates and deflates with each breath helps clients engage in the process more fully.
  5. Once clients have practiced the above for 8–10 times, ask them to add a relaxing word at the end of the exhalation, such as *calm, peace, safety,* or a word of their choosing.
  6. Ask clients to observe and examine but not to judge any thoughts that enter their mind. Such thoughts will likely reduce with practice. This is rudimentary mindfulness practice.

- Ask clients to practice this sequence at home for 5 to 10 minutes twice a day.
- Eventually, encourage clients to practice breathing throughout the day as needed to manage anxiety and distress.

Note. Information is from Briere & Scott (2006, pp. 279–280) and J. A. Cohen, A. P. Mannarino, & E. Deblinger (2006, pp. 76–78).

any degree of relaxation may be a trigger for more symptoms (Briere & Scott, 2006). For these clients, the deep muscle relaxation may prove more effective than diaphragm breathing, as the progressive tensing and relaxing of muscles allows the client to remain in a relaxed state for relatively short periods of time.

Finally, the use of either relaxation technique alone will likely not be adequate to markedly reduce trauma symptoms (Rothbaum, Meadows, Resick, & Foy, 2000). Relaxation techniques must be used as a part of the total treatment regime.

Dissociation

Dissociation is a more challenging symptom to address and, like anxiety, will be a factor to manage throughout the counseling process, especially in the middle stage of treatment that addresses traumatic memories. The goal is to assist clients in gaining control over their reactions to intense emotional reminders of the trauma, as these experiences precipitate the transition to dissociative states (Steele & van der Hart, 2009). Dissociated experiences such as feelings of detachment or emotional numbing, decreased awareness of surroundings, derealization, and depersonalization buffer and protect clients from overwhelming feelings created by a trauma experience, but they also prevent clients from being fully aware and present in the moment. They may report being somewhere else or being nowhere (Cloitre, Cohen, & Koenen, 2006). Paradoxically, a reliance on avoidance provides only temporary relief and actually exacerbates symptoms such as intrusive experiences, emotional numbing, and low frustration tolerance for daily activities (Courtois, 2008; Liotti, 2004). As a result, these clients lose touch with a sense of continuous time and self-awareness. It is important, therefore, to establish structure in daily activities, such as defining problems, setting goals, maintaining regular appointments, establishing routine in eating and sleeping, identifying emotional experiences and sensations, and grounding themselves in the physical world through conscious and purposeful engagement with tangible aspects of their environment. Although the specific manner of intervention varies based on the severity of dissociation (i.e., from mild, such as emotional numbing, to severe, such as dissociative identity disorder), the overall goal in treatment is to manage and eventually eliminate the avoidance response of dissociation. In sessions, counselors and clients can agree on a prearranged signal from clients—such as raising their hand—that indicates a need to reduce the emotional intensity of a specific part of the trauma discussion (Cloitre et al., 2006). The main intervention is helping clients to gradually tolerate more and more intense trauma memories without avoidance. Furthermore, counselors can remind clients that they are in a safe place and that the trauma happened in the past. Conversely, if a client is still in contact with the abuser, and especially if the client is still being abused, intervening effectively with more severe dissociation will be difficult or impossible until the client's living arrangements are stable and safe.

Grounding

Another intervention to deal with dissociation is helping clients become grounded in the present. Physical touching of predetermined familiar objects and visual focus on objects associated with the present are often the most useful grounding modalities for clients (Briere & Scott, 2006; see Box 9.2). Appropriate touch between the helper and client (e.g., shoulder or hand) can also enhance this process once the alliance is established, but it must be discussed and prearranged signals established, especially with sexually abused clients, who may be prone to misinterpret touch. In

| Box 9.2 | Grounding Techniques |

1. Grounding helps clients actively focus on their outside world. Therefore, they always keep their eyes open and attempt to become acutely aware of things in their environment, one visual, auditory, or olfactory stimuli at a time (e.g., clock face, picture on the wall, sound of the air conditioner, and so forth). Grounding will assist clients to gain control over negative feelings and to feel safe in the present. During the teaching process, it is important for therapists to position themselves in the client's visual field and to engage the client in a supportive and clearly present manner to draw attention to the therapist's presence.
2. Ask clients to identify their negative internal experience (e.g., anger, dissociation, and so forth) and rate the experience from 0 to 10, with 10 being the most intense and 0 being the least intense. It is not necessary for clients to describe their experience in great detail as doing so may intensify the experience. Make note of their rating before the grounding exercise.
3. Have clients reorient their attention externally to their environment and clearly identify their location. Emphasize that they are in control of this experience, they are safe, and they are in the present. Ask the client to slowly describe individual articles in their immediate environment, including details such as color, specific article (e.g., desk, chair, curtains), location (e.g., on the wall or door), and time of day. Descriptions of visual stimuli can be followed by physical grounding, such as awareness of posture, texture of material on the arms of the chair, the texture of their own skin, movement of toes and fingers, and the feeling of their feet on the ground. Next, have clients name a safe place, going into detail about its location, what it looks like, and how they feel when they are there. Obtain as much detail as possible about the safe place. Throughout this discussion use the client's name and your name.
4. For clients who have learned focused breathing, they can take a few breaths with eyes open to further relax and associate the experience with feeling calm and in control.
5. Have clients again rate their level of distress/anxiety after the exercise and compare it with the pre-grounding rating. If negative experiences have decreased in intensity, talk about the differences and how they reduced the distress. Give clients credit for successes. If the distress did not decrease, process the experience and ask clients what they think might improve the experience.

Note. Information from Briere & Scott (2006, pp. 97–98).

addition, as these clients often act impulsively, counselors need to help them think through consequences of their actions, including the type of people they associate with and the places they frequent. Physical exercise and mindfulness exercises also contribute to a sense of control and mastery over their body and emotions.

Self-Harm Behaviors

In an attempt to regain a sense of control, avert emotional flooding, and contain emotional dysregulation, many trauma victims engage in self-harm behaviors such as cutting, using drugs and alcohol, and having suicidal thoughts and behavior; the incidence of self-harm behavior can range from infrequent to daily, particularly for those with long abuse histories (Cloitre et al., 2006). Histories of sexual abuse and severe neglect in childhood tend to predict self-destructive behaviors, and the absence of a secure, predictable, and prolonged attachment figure maintains the abuse (Cloitre et al., 2006). The lack of a secure and prolonged attachment contributes to individuals' difficulty in identifying and utilizing personal assets to control self-destructive behavior. Such behaviors often occur following feelings of disappointment and/or abandonment, and clients report feelings of numbness and disconnection following these episodes.

Van der Kolk (1996) suggested that dissociation is learned as a means of dealing with the abuse and may account for the urge to self-mutilate. These clients often develop a type of analgesic response to the abuse that produces a sense of numbness. The numbness and dissociation that served as a buffer from pain during the abuse becomes a barrier to feeling alive and connected to the present moment. These individuals often report that not only is self-mutilation *not* painful, but that it provides a sense of relief and well-being (van der Kolk, 1996). However, emotional numbness can result in abused clients becoming more susceptible to revictimization as it reduces awareness of their environment and signs of danger.

Developmentally Arrested

Some believe that traumatized individuals become emotionally stuck at the developmental cognitive level at which they were abused (van der Kolk, Hostetler, Herron, & Fisler, 1994). If this theory is accurate, it is even more important for clinicians to provide a safe, supportive, and predictable therapeutic environment, as this is the context in which clients learn to self-regulate their emotions (Briere & Scott, 2006). To achieve this type of therapeutic environment, counselors must focus on the process of client validation and support and must resist reenacting the traumatic cycle by unwittingly becoming a rescuer, victim, or victimizer. Instead, they can help clients move from "speechless terror" (van der Kolk, 1996) to identifying triggers and putting their experiences into words. This process helps dissipate some of the terror related to their trauma.

Education

Another important component of treatment is educating clients about trauma and its effects. This process helps demystify the confusion, fear, and lack of control that many clients experience (Briere & Scott, 2006; Najavits, 2002). The education process helps clients gain an understanding of symptoms such as intrusive thoughts and avoidance tendencies in an effort to increase emotional distance from the trauma experience. Furthermore, clients can be made aware that symptoms such as intrusive thoughts and dreams are the mind and body's first attempts to heal the trauma memory by extinction or desensitization and cognitive adjustment to the traumatic event (Briere & Scott, 2006). However, some traumas are too intense to respond to the body's natural attempts to heal and need additional focused emotional processing. Then, clients are better able to put the trauma experience into a sequence of a beginning, middle, and end as well as identify triggers for memories, emotions, behaviors, responses, and autonomic responses (J. A. Cohen, Mannarino, & Deblinger, 2006). Furthermore, clients are taught how to identify and associate emotional states as meaningful signals rather than as a threatening experience from which to escape or as a trigger to aggress against self or others. Identifying and naming their feelings gives them a greater sense of mastery. Finally, clients are taught specific skills, such as coping skills (e.g., self-soothing self-talk), self-care, and problem-solving skills.

Mindfulness

Mindfulness-based cognitive therapy (Teasdale et al., 2000) focuses on teaching clients to reflect on their thoughts and experiences by means of passive engagement. For example, Linehan's (1993) work with females with borderline organization focused on teaching how to observe, describe, and participate by taking a nonjudgmental stance, focusing on one thing in the moment, and being effective rather than "right." Research has been conducted primarily with individuals suffering from depression or anxiety (e.g., Orsillo, Roemer, & Barlow, 2003), although some research has found preliminary effectiveness with affect dysregulation for women with histories of CSA (Wolfsdorf, 2001). Mindfulness is effective both as a primary invention to reduce symptoms and as a relapse-prevention method.

Stage 2

The first stage of treatment can begin to transition into the middle stage when clients are able to stabilize their emotions, begin to feel safe, and establish a greater sense of personal control (Courtois, 2008). Although clients have experienced some of the trauma material through education and stabilizing interventions, focused trauma processing and resolution occurs primarily in Stage 2. Progressing to this stage may be a smooth and natural continuation of Stage 1 or a more distinct and delineating process. Because of the intense nature of the work in the middle stage of treatment, counselors would be wise to obtain additional consent (beyond that obtained in the intake session) from clients before embarking on this stage (Courtois, 2008).

The overall goal of this stage is to activate conditioned emotional and cognitive responses associated with the traumatic event(s)—that is, exposure interventions—in a safe, supportive, and controlled environment and to engage a traumatic memory/image with reduced associated emotions (van der Kolk et al., 1996). Research indicates that once this total traumatic experience has been deeply experienced and reprocessed emotionally and cognitively, successful resolution will take place (Cloitre et al., 2004; Rothbaum et al., 2000). However, exposure interventions are not appropriate for all trauma cases.

Contraindications for Processing Trauma Experiences

Processing trauma experiences may be contraindicated when the client has the following:

- very high anxiety,
- severe depression,
- acute psychosis,
- high risk of suicide and other self-harm behaviors,
- overwhelming guilt or shame associated with trauma experience,
- inadequate affect regulation capacity,
- recent and significant trauma exposure, or
- intoxication or significant substance dependence. (Briere & Scott, 2006; Cloitre, Koenen, Cohen, & Han, 2002; Najavits, 2002)

When these contraindications are present, counselors are advised to continue developing anxiety management skills introduced in Stage 1, such as deep muscle relaxation, thought stopping, cognitive restructuring, preparation for a stressful event, and so forth. Continue to assist clients in stabilizing their environment and themselves emotionally and relationally. In most cases, continued skills development will provide a basis for doing the necessary exposure interventions.

Exposure Therapy

The primary work of this stage is reexposure to traumatic material. This material includes the objective information about where, when, who, how often, severity, and so forth as well as the subjective interpretation and reactions to the experience (Briere & Scott, 2006). In less severe and uncomplicated cases in which traumatic memories are near the surface, counselors often can simply provide a safe and attentive atmosphere in which clients discuss their experiences. Clients can be encouraged to relate their recollections of the trauma via pictures, diaries, or written narratives. This process can result in rapid resolution of the traumatic event (van der Kolk et al., 1996).

Severe cases involve a more gradual, controlled, and predictable trajectory in working with traumatic material (Briere & Scott, 2006). Reexperiencing the trauma material in fragments, such as momentary intrusive thoughts, flashbacks, or nightmares, fails to provide resolution because it precludes the formation of an integrated memory (D. J. Siegel, 2003). Trauma memories tend to be stored as perceptual, affective, and somatic states and often lack verbal symbolization (van der Kolk, 1996). The reexperiencing process facilitates the symbolization of the trauma into words and in turn allows the reprocessing of the experience from the emotional and visceral/somatic to a continuous narrative or autobiographical memory with a beginning and end.

Once the trauma memory is processed, it is more easily seen as a distinct experience of the past rather than a representation of the client's entire world. This practice enables the client to discriminate between danger and safety (Rothbaum & Foa, 1996). Processed traumatic memories become more like everyday memories that have a context and a meaningful narrative. The reexperiencing also reduces intrusion and avoidance. The processing of these memories should be viewed as a natural, gradual unfolding process that occurs as the client feels more secure, less guarded and has less need to avoid. Hence, the process is often called *controlled* or *graduated exposure*.

Readiness for the Trauma Narrative

Before engaging the client in the narrative process, counselors should examine clients' readiness to proceed. Cloitre et al. (2006) posed the following questions counselors can think about to determine whether clients are ready to proceed with the trauma narrative:

- Is the client committed to the treatment? This does not mean that clients have no reservations but that they are aware of and committed to the work to be done.
- Is the client relatively stable at the present time? This means that clients are at least minimally effective in addressing stressors in their lives; it does not mean an absence of stressors. However, clients who are dealing with life-changing stressors such as deaths, medical/health issues, or unexpected relationship losses may be too vulnerable to effectively process trauma and should delay this stage.
- Has the client demonstrated some capacity for an alliance with the therapist? Building an alliance is a challenge for many clients who have an interpersonal trauma background. However, clients who do not give and receive feedback to the counselor or are hesitant to communicate about their level of distress may not be ready to commence trauma work. In addition, clients need to believe that the counselor has their best interest in mind and is capable of helping them.
- Has the client been able to learn and use the skills presented in Stage 1? It is important that clients have developed at least a minimal level of competence in managing their anxiety and possess the capacity to implement these skills during the trauma narrative process. (Cloitre et al., 2006, pp. 343–345)

Processing Trauma Memories

To successfully reprocess a trauma experience, new information must be introduced that is counter to the traumatic memory (Rothbaum & Foa, 1996). This information is both emotional (e.g., secure attachment, low anxiety) and cognitive (e.g., "I am safe now," "I will be OK") and must occur within the context of a strong therapeutic alliance. Clients are exposed to the original trauma material through imaginal exposure and telling the trauma story. In addition to retelling their story, clients may write a trauma narrative or record their stories in order to reread and replay the narrative numerous times between sessions. Exposure is interspersed with periods of reduced distress (e.g., shift focus to a relaxing, nonthreatening scene and use progressive muscle relaxation) at a pace and intensity level that matches the client's ability to metabolize the traumatic events. It is a controlled process that modulates the intensity of the reexperiencing by gradually and repeatedly refocusing on the trauma. Too much intensity, too soon could overwhelm clients, especially chronic trauma survivors, resulting in even more powerful avoidance responses (Briere & Scott, 2006). Clients are assisted in retelling the traumatic story with a beginning, middle, and end to reexperience the trauma situation at a moderately high level of emotional intensity without being overwhelmed. A moderately high level of conditioned emotional activation is necessary for clients to be able to process the trauma experience through desensitization and reorganization of the traumatic memories. However, the level of emotional intensity and trauma memory are titrated based on each client's capacity to tolerate the exposure (i.e., therapeutic window; Briere & Scott, 2006). Clients who express little or no emotional activation—or who experience emotional numbing or dissociation—as they tell their trauma story may have insufficient emotional activation to trigger trauma memories and adequately process the trauma. Briere and Scott (2006) suggested controlling the level of intensity in each trauma-processing session so that emotional intensity is lowest at the beginning and end of a session, with the highest level of emotional intensity occurring around the mid-point of the session. Thus, clients regain their emotional composure before leaving the session.

By creating an autobiography of the trauma with a beginning, middle, and end, the client can reorganize the traumatic memory or experience as a historical event rather than a continual, uncontrolled experience in the present. The fragments of images, sensory stimuli, and thoughts that are experienced as intrusive and uncontrollable become organized, stable experiences placed within the bigger picture of life before, during, and after the trauma. In fact, some experts suggest beginning the narrative with descriptions of clients' lives prior to the trauma(s) and then working forward to the trauma to clearly delineate a time without trauma (Cloitre et al., 2006). This course is difficult to implement with clients who were abused as young children who have little or no recollection of life without trauma. Developing a verbal representation of the trauma event(s) creates a more balanced, historically organized memory of the trauma and provides some distance from the original sensory–perceptual representation of the trauma memory, helping clients better modulate their emotions (Cloitre et al., 2006). Following exposure work, clients experience an extinction or reduction of trauma symptoms and gain more control of their emotions and memories associated with the trauma. Also, clients are better able to make new interpretations of the trauma and issues related to fear, shame, and guilt.

In addition, it also is important for clients to feel in control of the process. For example, clients are encouraged to decide how much detail to provide before they recount the trauma event. Subsequent sessions should involve the client describing greater detail of the focal trauma experience with each successive session. This process would include bringing a greater focus to emotions and physiological responses related to the trauma (Rothbaum & Foa, 1996). Experiencing the feelings and physiological response and describing them verbally provides greater clarity of clients' experiences of the traumatic event(s) as well as a greater sense of control over the traumatic experience. Also, clients can reread and replay audio recordings of the trauma story between sessions to strengthen and accelerate the extinction process. However, arousal beyond the client's tolerance level interferes with the accommodation of new information and fosters greater sensitization rather than habituation to the trauma memories (Briere & Scott, 2006).

Following exposure episodes, counselors can assist clients in discussing their reactions to reexperiencing the trauma. These discussions may include not only clients' view of the trauma-processing experience, but also clients' view of the counselor during the process as well as issues related to shame, loss, and grief (Courtois, 2008). The counselor and client also can identify cognitive distortions and themes resulting from the trauma, such as "It's all my fault. If I wouldn't have gotten drunk, the rape wouldn't have happened," or "All men are dangerous. I will never trust men again," or "I am too weak and fragile to be able to make it in this world." Counselors can help clients begin to examine such beliefs and help them come to more accurate conclusions. For example, "Getting drunk greatly reduced my ability to make good decisions and protect myself, but my boyfriend chose to rape me and he is responsible for this behavior."

It is particularly important to contrast the past trauma and accompanying experiences with the present. Distinguishing between these two time-frames highlights the functionality of clients' responses and feelings of fear and helplessness when the abuse was occurring in the past and yet also the present circumstances in which these same responses and fears may not logically fit the circumstances; that is, the past is not the present. In order to accomplish this realization, clients must be in a stable, safe setting and able to logically and empirically draw a distinction between past and present.

Preparation to End Session

Before the client leaves the session, counselors should check on his or her level of anxiety and distress associated with the exposure. If the client's distress levels have not subsided to a manageable degree, some form of systematic relaxation (e.g., controlled, focused breathing; progressive muscle relaxation) can most likely achieve this end. In addition, counselors need to help clients assess whether they have adequate support from family and friends. This support is critical for reinforcing the client's emerging sense of safety and reconceptualization of the traumatic event within a distinct context. For those clients who have little social support, counselors and other professionals may need to help them develop a social support system through local organizations, churches, survivor groups, and so forth. Counselors should be closely assessing the effects of these interventions both formally (e.g., symptom inventories) and informally through observation and client reports and should make necessary intervention adjustments as needed. Less severe cases may be resolved after relating the traumatic event(s) only a few times. The trauma-related emotions may resolve and be reintegrated into autobiographical memory fairly quickly.

Outcomes for Stage 2

If Stage 2 has been successful, clients' symptoms will have lessened and they will be better able to consider issues related to safety, self-esteem, relationships, and trust on a continuum rather than on an all-or-nothing basis. In addition, clients can begin to make distinctions between current life experiences and the past trauma. Furthermore, clients should be more capable of identifying, examining, and replacing inaccurate beliefs about themselves, others, and safe/unsafe circumstances. Clients are in a position to begin exploring more proactive activities. Group counseling can provide a support community that decreases isolation, shame, and loneliness. In a group, clients are provided with an opportunity to explore and validate their perceptions and emotions from group members with whom they identify. The sense of identification with others who have had traumatic experiences enhances the capacity for trust, hope, interpersonal efficacy, and increased self-esteem (Enns et al., 1997).

Stage 3

This final stage is an opportunity for clients to consolidate their learnings and changes from the previous stages and begin to establish a different type of normalcy. This stage may include reworking or establishing closure with previous relationships associated with their abuse. Clients can refine and practice boundary setting in various contexts and fine-tune their evolved self-regulatory skills (Courtois, 2008). In addition, clients can begin to engage in more enjoyable and pleasant activities. Especially for victims of long-term, chronic trauma, many individuals have known little pleasure or positive activities in their lives and expect the negative and unpleasant in most situations. Life oftentimes seems like drudgery and an unhappy existence. Counselors can help these clients identify, plan, and engage in activities that create a sense of enjoyment, peace, and spontaneity. This process may take place slowly for some victims who have long histories of abuse.

Although their symptoms may have subsided significantly, remnants of the trauma experience are likely to be present for many years, especially for those individuals with extensive trauma backgrounds. As their lives develop greater and more meaningful continuity, issues related to close intimate relationships, friendships, careers/occupations, parenting, and leisure activities may become more focal in treatment. Counselors need to help clients become more aware of and develop their feelings of mastery and pleasure. Some clients may also develop an interest in generative activities, such as helping other survivors, promoting social justice issues, and working on prevention. These activities often symbolize their overcoming victim status and acquiring a personal sense of empowerment and self-efficacy.

Cognitive Processing Therapy

Cognitive processing therapy (CPT) is similar to the above-mentioned model of treating traumatic events but is based on information processing theory and has a primary focus on processing beliefs and the accompanying emotions related to a traumatic event, rather than a focus on exposure to traumatic memories and emotions for the purpose of extinction, although extinction occurs as a part of the repeated cognitive processing. Major components of CPT include the following: (a) clients may write an impact statement regarding the trauma; (b) clients may identify stuck points in beliefs about the trauma; and (c) clients may challenge and balance overaccomodated beliefs related to the trauma, including how the traumatic event affects beliefs related to safety, intimacy, self-esteem, power/control, and trust. CPT is effective with survivors of CSA and sexual assault (Chard, 2005; Nishith, Resick, & Griffin, 2002) and those who have military-related PTSD (Monson et al., 2006).

Countertransference

The aftermath of trauma is often accompanied by clients' extreme reactions to others, including their counselors. Extreme client emotions such as anger often are difficult for counselors to deal with therapeutically even when they are experienced in working with trauma victims. In particular, sustained client hostility presents a formidable challenge for counselors in their attempts to maintain a balance between appropriate structure to teach anger and self-management and emotional tracking to maintain the therapeutic alliance. Early psychoanalytic views on counselor countertransference were that it was something to be eliminated or at least tightly controlled. However, current views on countertransference perceive it as inevitable (although not necessarily therapeutic) and potentially offering an opportunity for a therapeutic interaction between client and counselor (Levenson, 1995). Currently, the issue has become when and how to disclose countertransferential material and what to disclose to clients rather than how to suppress or master such feelings. Particularly relevant material to disclose includes the impact of the client on the counselor, the counselor's hopes for the client, and the counselor's hopeful feelings about the client. Timing and consideration of the client's ability to use this information productively are critical. Such responses should also be used sparingly.

Revictimization in Treatment

Dalenberg (2004) suggested that countertransference by counselors can revictimize traumatized clients by recreating earlier experiences with attachment figures that were invalidating, degrading, and berating. Counselors' responses such as anger may confirm a client's self-concept that he or she is unworthy of the counselor's time or that there is no hope for improvement. Clients in Dalenberg's (2004) study reported that when counselors expressed anger at them, a genuine apology was most effective in repairing the relationship.

Although interpersonal trauma literature tends to focus on women and children, the above-mentioned model is equally effective with men who report trauma symptoms. The stages and principles apply to most traumatic events.

Summary

Counselors who treat survivors of physical, sexual, and psychological abuse typically need training and skill sets beyond what most graduate counseling programs offer. Furthermore, working with survivors requires a high level of emotional and physical health. Counselors who lack both can adversely affect treatment and are at an increased risk of burnout. Unfortunately, many counselors provide treatment for survivors of abuse despite a lack of training.

The most severe and frequent trauma symptoms from interpersonal trauma are associated with being female. In addition, women who experience IPV are diagnosed with high rates of PTSD (mean prevalence of 63.8%). Abused women with PTSD continue to experience symptoms up to 9 years following the last abuse incident (Woods, 2000). Furthermore, these women are more likely than nontraumatized women to have experienced childhood sexual and physical abuse. Therefore, a large portion of the treatment research focuses on women.

Clinical research with victims of physical abuse has a relatively short history. Current models of treatment largely are integrated models that focus on cognitions, behaviors, emotions, and the therapeutic alliance. The most common models of treatment involve three stages: (a) building a working alliance, improving affect regulation, enhancing personal safety, stabilizing, skill building, and self-care; (b) processing the traumatic experience(s); and (c) integrating learnings from previous stages and normalizing issues related to relationships, sexuality, social life, and occupation.

Research has largely shown success with various components of the model, with preliminary research indicating at least moderate effectiveness with the complete model. Severe cases of abuse often are treated episodically over a long period of time to allow clients time for consolidation of changes and acclimation to new thoughts, feelings, and behaviors. These cases often prove exceedingly challenging for counselors and support staff. There is more research for uncomplicated (single incident) than complicated trauma such as complex PTSD.

Suggested Readings

Briere, J., & Scott, C. (2006). *Principles of trauma therapy: A guide to symptoms, evaluations, and treatment*. Thousand Oaks, CA: Sage.

Cognitive therapy processing: A web based learning course. Retrieved on March 20, 2010, from https://cpt.musc.edu/index

Cloitre, M., Cohen, L. R., & Koenen, K. C. (2006). *Treating survivors of childhood abuse: Psychotherapy for the interrupted life*. New York, NY: Guilford Press.

Cloitre, M., Koenen, K. C., Cohen, L. R., & Han, H. (2002). Skills training in affective and interpersonal regulation followed by exposure: A phase-based treatment for PTSD related to childhood abuse. *Journal of Consulting and Clinical Psychology, 70*, 1067–1074.

Courtois, C. A. (2004). Complex trauma, complex reactions: Assessment and treatment. *Psychotherapy: Theory, Research, Practice, Training, 41*, 412–425.

Courtois, C. A., & Ford, J. D. (2009). *Treating complex traumatic stress disorders: An evidence-based guide*. New York, NY: Guilford Press.

Friedman, M. J., Keane, T. M., & Resick, P. A. (2007). *Handbook of PTSD: Science and practice*. New York, NY: Guilford Press.

Kubany, E. S., & Ralston, T. C. (2008). *Treating PTSD in battered women: A step-by-step manual for therapists and counselors*. Oakland, CA: New Harbinger.

Kubany, E. S., & Watson, S. B. (2002). Cognitive trauma therapy for formerly battered women with PTSD: Conceptual bases and treatment outlines. *Cognitive and Behavioral Practice, 9*, 111–127.

chapter 10

Dating Violence, Sexual Assault, and Stalking

Case Example

Joe and Ashley

Joe was a big, good-looking guy. All of Ashley's friends were envious when she and Joe started going out her freshman year. He seemed so cool and self-assured. Ashley really felt swept off her feet. Joe was three years older than she and he always seemed to know just what he wanted. Ashley often doubted herself and she could hardly believe that Joe really wanted to be with her. At first, she loved the way he made decisions for both of them and seemed so protective of her. She felt pressured when he wanted them to start having sex, and she didn't think she was ready, but she couldn't risk losing him. And Joe had a temper. Ashley was surprised and hurt the first time he yelled at her, and it scared her. Joe blamed her for making him mad; Ashley blamed herself, too. "If you'd just quit nagging me, I wouldn't get so angry," he said.

Since his friends thought he was an easygoing guy, Ashley began to believe it was her fault that Joe got angry. After a while, it seemed that Ashley was always wrong. Joe's comments turned ugly: "You're so stupid you don't know what you are saying." He got mad if she talked to another guy. He kept tabs on her whereabouts, calling her at all hours and questioning her about what she was doing or who she was with. He told her she was getting fat and no other guy would want her. He made fun of her. Ashley cried a lot, but whenever she got close to wanting to break up, Joe would turn around and start being the sweet, loving boyfriend she wanted him to be.

During one of their arguments, Ashley was upset and turned to leave the room. Joe grabbed her and shook her. She pulled away, and he pushed her to the floor. She was terrified by the look in his eyes. The next day he showed up with flowers and an apology. He told her that it was just that he loved her so much, she made him crazy. She told herself he didn't really mean it.

During the next few months, things got worse. Joe hit Ashley several times. Once, when he had a few beers, he just kept hitting and hitting and wouldn't stop. Ashley wore heavy makeup and long-sleeved shirts a lot. A friend tried to talk to her about what was going on, but Ashley made excuses: "I fell down the stairs." "I walked into a door—I'm so clumsy." (J. Y. Levy, 2004)

This chapter focuses on dating violence (DV), including sexual assault (SA) and stalking (ST). Some might reason that these behaviors are not appropriate in a text dealing largely with family violence; however, there are several reasons for this inclusion. First, abuse that occurs within an unmarried but intimate relationship is distinct from abuse or assault from a stranger or known but nonromantic relationship. Although a dating relationship is likely less stable than a partner/marital relationship, it typically occurs within a context of emotional commitment and trust. A violation of this trust by DV and/or SA has further-reaching consequences than assault from a stranger (O. Barnett et al., 2011). Second, DV and SA typically begin no later than junior high school (Foshee, Linder, MacDougall, & Bangdiwala, 2001), and they increase in prevalence over time (Wolitzky-Taylor et al., 2008), are remarkably stable (O'Leary & Slep, 2003), and predict later IPV in marriage (O'Leary et al., 1989). Third, almost 75% of female ST victims knew their stalkers, with 30.3% of the stalkers being a current or former intimate partner (Baum, Catalano, Rand, & Rose, 2009). Thus, ST of females largely occurs within a relationship context. Knowledge of DV, SA, and ST is important for anyone working with relationship violence because of the immediate physical and psychological damage and the fact that they predict later IPV in longer-term relationships.

What Is Dating Violence and Sexual Assault?

Dating Violence

A limited definition of DV includes physical and emotional abuse and/or the threat of abuse committed by at least one member of an unmarried, dating couple regardless of sexual orientation. Broader definitions include SA. SA is distinguished from DV in this chapter to reflect different consequences for victims. For both, the dating relationship may be intimate or casual (Gosselin, 2003). Although DV research often refers to junior or senior high school students and college students, it can refer to any age participants who are dating.

Sexual Assault

SA refers to unwanted or forced sexual relations (e.g., intercourse, oral sex, or anal sex), including attempted SA, by force or threat of force independent of sexual orientation. It includes unwanted sexual contact, such as fondling or other types of sexual touching. As distinct from DV, the issue of consent typically is associated with SA. How to define consent is a highly charged issue and varies along gender lines. Determining what is and is not consent for a sexual encounter is highly variable. The point at which unwanted sexual behavior is perceived to be an SA is influenced by age, sex, race, SES, and the relationship to the perpetrator (Banyard et al., 2007). Victims romantically involved with their perpetrators are less likely to report SA.

Prevalence and Extent of Dating Violence and Sexual Assault

Conclusive research is lacking on DV and SA. For example, literature reviews indicated that DV rates ranged from 9% to 65% (Close, 2005; S. F. Lewis & Fremouw, 2001), with SA ranging from 5.4% to 11% in a national survey (Youth Risk Behavior Surveillance, 2004). The range of prevalence rates for DV raises concerns about actual rates. Some suggest that many teens want to keep the abuse confidential, which thus undermined response candor (Hickman, Jaycox, & Aronoff, 2004).

Estimates of Dating Violence by Age Groups

Junior and Senior High School Students

A nationally representative sample ($n = 14,041$) of 7th through 12th grade found an overall rate of 9.9% for DV (8.8% of females and 11% of males; Lobach, 2008). Furthermore, 8.4% of Euro Americans, 14.2% of African Americans, and 11.1% of Hispanics reported DV. The Youth Risk Behavior Surveillance System survey (YRBSS survey; CDC, 2011) of 9th- through 12th-graders found DV rates ranging from 6.1% to 13.8% ($Mdn = 10.2\%$). Urban youths reported more DV than suburban or rural youths (Rennison & Welchans, 2000).

As with IPV, bidirectional violence is the most frequent type of DV (Spencer & Bryant, 2000). Also, DV is highly stable for individuals in a relationship for at least 3 months (O'Leary & Slep, 2003) and predicts IPV in young adulthood (Williams, Craig, Connolly, Pepler, & Laporte, 2008).

College Students and Adults

College students have reported varying percentages of DV. Luthra and Gidycz (2006) found the incidence of self-reported use of DV to be 25% for women and 10% for men. A large representative study of college students from 32 nations ($n = 13,601$) found that nearly one third of men and one third of women physically assaulted their dating partners in the previous 12 months. Bidirectional DV was the most prevalent type of violence, followed by female-only violence, with male-only violence being the least frequent (Straus, 2008).

Prevalence and Extent of Sexual Assault

Junior and Senior High School Students
The YRBS survey (CDC, 2011) found that combined male and female rates of forced sex ranged from 9.6% to 15.3%, with rates for females ranging from 9.2% to 13.1%. Black youths and Hispanic youths reported slightly higher rates than

White youths. Another national sample of high school students found that 8% of students reported unwanted sexual intercourse or rape (Howard, Wang, & Yan, 2007a).

College Students

The National College Women's Sexual Victimization (Bureau of Justice Statistics, 2002) surveyed 4,000 women and found that rape occurred at a rate of 35.3 per 1,000 women. The women knew their perpetrators in 47% of cases. A recent NCVS (Rand, 2009) estimated that 9.1% of males and 21.4% of females were sexually assaulted by an intimate partner, and 33.6% of males and 44.3% of females were sexually assaulted by a friend or acquaintance. Women are 5 times more likely to be raped by a date than by a stranger (DeKeseredy & Schwartz, 1998). One study noted that 64% of female college students who were raped did not acknowledge or report the rape (Bondurant, 2001).

Summary of Research

Combining all studies, physical and sexual victimization for males and females is approximately equal, with lower rates for those ages 12 to 15 than those ages 16 to 20. DV is most likely to be bidirectional with dating couples (Straus, 2008). Females are more likely than males to initiate DV (Hines & Saudino, 2003; Straus, 2008). However, most studies indicate that females are victims of SA much more frequently than males. Furthermore, there is a growing prevalence and a downward trend in age onset of DV and SA (McFee, Turano, & Roberts, 2001). This trend is consistent even with younger females, as middle-school-age females initiate more mild, moderate, and severe DV than do same-age males when controlled for self-defense (Foshee et al., 2001). However, violence by males caused more physical injury and psychological damage.

Stalking

Definition and Specific Behaviors

ST is defined as "the willful or intentional commission of a series of acts that would cause a reasonable person to fear death or serious bodily injury and that, in fact, does place the victim in fear of death or serious bodily injury" (Office for Victims of Crime, 2002, p. 1). The most common elements of ST are following, harassing, and threatening. Following occurs with 82% of female and 72% of male victims. Harassing includes making unwanted phone calls (61% of female and 42% of male victims), sending unwanted letters or items (33% of female and 27% of male victims), and vandalizing property (30% of male and 29% of female victims). A credible threat, although often difficult to determine, includes both overt/verbal and nonverbal threats that instill fear of serious harm. Although these behaviors define ST, it is their repetition, duration, escalation over time, and the elicitation of fear and intimidation from victims that often leads to its identification. In 9% of the cases for female victims and 6% for male victims, stalkers threaten to kill or actually do kill the victim's pets (National Institute of Justice [NIJ], 1998). This behavior portends more serious behavior toward the victim, as stalkers are violent toward their victims 25% to 35% of the time. ST is highly correlated with DV and SA (Melton, 2007).

Cyberstalking

A recent extension of ST is cyberstalking. Cyberstalking is using a broad range of technologies (e.g., cell phones, e-mail, spy ware, and so forth) to threaten and harass that makes a reasonable person afraid and fear for his or her safety (Southworth, Finn, Dawson, Fraser, & Tucker, 2007). Examples include sending viruses to someone's e-mail address, disrupting someone's e-mail, and compiling considerable information about someone through the Internet.

Extent of Stalking

On the basis of the NVAW survey (Tjaden & Thoennes, 1998) of 8,000 men and 8,000 women, 8% of women and 2% of men reported having been stalked at some point in their lives, with estimates suggesting 1 million women and 400,000 men are stalked each year. An NIJ survey (Fisher, Cullen, & Turner, 2000) of 4,432 college women found that 13.1% reported being stalked in the prior 7 months. Of these 13.1% of women who were stalked, 42.5% were stalked by a boyfriend or ex-boyfriend. A similar survey found that almost 75% of victims knew their stalker, 40% of victims received threats of harm, 30% of stalkers intended to seek revenge or retaliation, 85% of victims received unwelcomed e-mails, 11% of victims were stalked for 5 or more years, and nearly half of the victims were stalked one or more times a week (Baum et al., 2009).

Homicides

The vast majority of the victims of intimate partner homicide are females, with women in cohabiting relationships with males being 9 times more likely to be killed by their partner than married women (Shackelford & Mouzos, 2005). Approximately 30% to 50% of women who are murdered in the United States are murdered by intimate male partners or ex-partners (Fox, 2005). Approximately 20% of all femicides are females between 15 and 24 years of age (Paulozzi, Saltzman, Thompson, & Holmgreen, 2001). One out of every three femicides is committed by the victim's husband or boyfriend. In 75% of femicide cases by males partners, there were prior histories of DV (J. C. Campbell et al., 2003). Furthermore, perpetrators who followed their victims were more than twice as likely to attempt to murder or actually murder their victims. Also, when a male threatens to harm the woman's children, the risk of attempted or actual murder increases by 9 times (McFarlane, Campbell, & Watson, 2002). ST behavior is not simply intimidating; in some cases it is a strong predictor of homicide. It tends to occur over a long period of time (average 2 years; Spitzberg, 2002) and escalates in intensity over time (Emerson, Ferris, & Gardner, 1998).

Stalking Laws

ST has been a crime only since 1990, with California being the first state to pass an antistalking law. There are now antistalking laws in all 50 states (Rosenfeld,

2000). Two states, Maine and Arizona, use harassment and terrorizing statutes to deal with ST. Because many ST laws are broadly defined, states have been challenged on the lack of specificity on the one hand and encroachment on freedom of speech on the other. For ST laws to endure challenges to free speech, they must be based on clearly defined behavior (Wallace, 2005).

There are federal and state antistalking laws in place to protect those being stalked. Under these laws, perpetrators can be charged with stalking for repeatedly engaging in the following:

- following or appearing within the sight of another,
- approaching or confronting another individual in a public or private place,
- appearing at the workplace or residence of another,
- entering or remaining on an individual's property,
- contacting a person by telephone, and
- sending unwelcomed postal mail or e-mail to another. (NIJ, 1998).

Regardless of the law, stalkers violate restraining orders 40% of the time (Spitzberg, 2002).

Gay and Lesbian Dating Violence and Sexual Assault

Same-sex DV for adolescents has been reported to be as high as 22% in national samples (Halpern, Young, Waller, Martin, & Kupper, 2004). A YRBSS survey (CDC, 2011) found that between 19.1% and 29.2% (*Mdn* = 27.5%) of lesbian or gay youths and 17.7% to 28% (*Mdn* = 23.3%) of bisexual youths reported experiencing DV. Furthermore, between 14.1% to 31% (*Mdn* = 23.7%) of lesbian or gay youths and 16.6% to 32.1% (*Mdn* = 22.6) of bisexual youths reported being forced to have sexual intercourse. Freedner, Freed, Yang, and Austin (2002) found that DV rates for the males were as follows: gays, 44.6%; bisexuals, 57.1%; and heterosexuals, 28.6%. DV rates for the female were as follows: lesbians, 43.4%; bisexuals, 38.3%; and heterosexuals, 32.4%.

Race and Cultural Factors

Race

Little research has been conducted on racial or ethnic differences and DV and SA. Most national surveys either fail to disaggregate race and ethnicity or too few diverse subjects are included in samples for meaningful comparisons. However, a few studies have provided some preliminary data. A sample of 318 Latino adolescents in Los Angeles high schools reported that 25% of boys and 21% of girls experienced DV, and 15% of boys and 14% girls reported experiencing SA (Jaycox, 2004, in Hickman et al., 2004). In a large study (*n* = 4,525) of Hispanic or Latino ninth-grade students, greater acculturation and ethnic discrimination were associated with greater DV victimization of females (Sanderson, Coker, Roberts, Tortolero, & Reininger, 2004). This finding may have implications for prevention issues in the Latino culture.

Cross-Cultural Samples

Few studies have been conducted with cross-cultural samples. The most comprehensive survey was conducted by Straus (2008) with university students from 32 nations. One third of female students and one third of male students engaged in DV with a dating partner in the previous year. Bidirectional violence was the most frequent pattern of violence, followed by female-only violence. Dominance by either partner was associated with increased probability of DV.

Overall, DV and SA rates from other countries are similar to those in the United States (O. Barnett et al., 2011). As with many U.S. studies, these studies show variation across samples both within and across cultures. Straus's (2008) study is perhaps the most dramatic, indicating the significant amount of DV perpetrated by females across several countries when compared with males. It is important to emphasize the problematic nature of DV regardless of who initiates it and not to downplay female-initiated DV simply because it causes less injury than male-initiated DV.

Risk Markers and Predictors for Perpetration of Dating Violence, Sexual Assault, and Stalking

Family-of-Origin Environment

Research consistently finds that family-of-origin experience has the strongest influence on the perpetration of DV and SA. High correlations have been found between negative attitudes about women learned in the family and male sexual promiscuity and SA (Reitzel-Jaffe & Wolfe, 2001); antisocial behavior of males, inadequate parenting, and DV (Capaldi & Clark, 1998); and childhood abuse and DV (Wolfe, Scott, Wekerle, & Pittman, 2001). Adolescent boys exposed to parental violence are more likely to view DV as acceptable in romantic relationships (Kinsfogel & Grych, 2004). Interparental violence was not linked to girl's use of DV with this sample.

Multiple Influences

Other research has found that witnessing parental violence alone is not always sufficient to explain later DV. Males who witnessed parental violence and viewed DV as acceptable were more likely to engage in DV (O'Keefe, 1998). For females, witnessing parental violence and experiencing child abuse were associated with later DV.

Some studies have found multiple influences within and outside the family. For example, a 5-year longitudinal study of eighth- and ninth-graders ($n = 1291$) identified several risk markers for DV (Foshee, Benefield, Ennett, Bauman, & Suchindran, 2004). Males who (a) had been hit by an adult with the intention to harm, (b) had low self-esteem, and (c) had been in a physical fight with a peer were more likely to commit serious DV. Furthermore, having a friend who was a victim of DV and using alcohol both predicted chronic perpetration of DV. The relationship between drug and alcohol use and DV is particularly strong for males

(Magdol et al., 1997). Models for predicting male DV and SA are stronger than those for females (Molidor, Tolman, & Kober, 2000).

Stalking

Most often ST is included with DV and SA variables, largely because all three behaviors are highly correlated (Melton, 2007). The largest category of stalkers, called *relational stalkers*, is composed of former or current partners of victims (L. P. Sheridan, Gillett, Blaauw, Davies, & Patel, 2003) who have engaged in DV prior to ST (Gosselin, 2003).

Attachment Pattern

Attachment has been proposed as an influencing factor for perpetrators of DV and ST. Research suggests that DV and ST are related to experiencing a loss or abandonment by an attachment figure in childhood (McCann, 2003) and extreme jealousy and dependency in close relationships (Wigman, Graham-Kevan, & Archer, 2008). Partner loss or abandonment may precipitate DV or ST as an attempt to maintain contact with the partner (Chapple, 2003). This is similar to D. G. Dutton's (2007) model that associates IPV with insecure attachment.

Gender Socialization

Families that support a negative or devalued opinion of women contribute to DV, SA, and ST (Senn, Desmarais, Verberg, & Wood, 2000). Some women accept the position that they have no right to refuse a sexual advancement or require protection against pregnancy, especially racial/ethnic minorities (Rickert, Sanghvi, & Wiemann, 2002). Some suggest that this view comes from an ingrained societal belief that men have the right to demand sex from their partners and to take it by force if necessary. Furthermore, some women in abusive relationships believe that their self-worth is contingent on the relationship, which makes it difficult to leave the relationship (Power, Koch, Kralik, & Jackson, 2006). They often misinterpret the man's jealousy as love rather than as danger. Table 10.1 identifies a number of context factors that predict DV, SA, and ST. A large number of these are related to experiences in the family of origin.

Effects of Dating Violence, Sexual Assault, and Stalking

The outcomes of DV, SA, and ST tend to exact a higher price from females than males, although both experience similar symptoms as victims. In addition, as compared with victims who do not have a history of maltreatment, victims who do have a history of maltreatment as children tend to exhibit more and greater intensity of symptoms, such as depression, anxiety, suicidal ideation, and drug and alcohol abuse (Wolfe, Scott, Wekerle, & Pittman, 2001). These factors increase their risk of being both perpetrators and victims of DV, SA, and ST. Furthermore, DV both exacerbates existing emotional wounds from childhood maltreatment and increases the risk of even more complex psychological and physical sequelae (Jouriles, Platt, & McDonald, 2009). Female victims experience confusion, on-

Table 10.1
Predictors of Perpetrators of Dating Violence, Sexual Assault, and Stalking

Family-of-origin environment
  Negative attitudes about women[a]
  Destructive anger expression styles
  Witnessing interparental violence[a]
  Acceptability of violence[a]
  Inadequate parenting
  Childhood abuse
  Gender-specific influences from opposite-sex parent
  History of family distress and violence
  Loss of a significant attachment figure
  Parent divorce[a]
Other factors
  Being hit by an adult with the intention to harm[a]
  Low self-esteem[a]
  Physical fight with peer[a]
  Alcohol use[a]
  Peers
  Media (television and video game violence)[a]
  Being White
  Trauma-related symptoms
  Being a victim of a dating violence[b]
  Major mental disorders[a]

Note. Information from Bushman & Anderson (2009); Capaldi & Clark (1998); Connolly & Friedlander (2009); Kaura & Allen (2004); Kinsfogel & Grych (2004); O'Keefe (1998); Reitzel-Jaffe & Wolfe (2001); Sappington et al. (1997); Wolfe, Scott, Wekerle, & Pittman (2001); and Wolfe, Wekerle, et al. (2003).
[a]Applies primarily to males. [b]Applies primarily to females.

going depression, feelings of paranoia, and PTSD (Harris & Valentiner, 2002) as well as chronic headaches, unhealthy weight control, risky sexual behavior, pregnancy, and suicide (Olshen, McVeigh, Wunsch-Hitzig, & Rickert, 2007). Individuals with a history of childhood abuse who continue to experience DV are at a greater risk for CPTSD symptoms (e.g., mistrust of self or others, dissociative symptoms, and emotional dysregulation; Courtois, 2008).

Characteristics of Perpetrators and Victims

It is important to identify characteristics of perpetrators and victims in order to target at-risk populations for prevention and treatment. However, research on DV, SA, and ST is less well developed than research on IPV with married couples and partners. What research exists is similar to the more established research on IPV. The research on ST is the exception. For example, several stalker typologies exist, with some focusing on obsession with the love object (Cox & Speziale, 2009) whereas others focus on the stalker–victim relationship and the context of the stalking (Mohandie, Meloy, McGowan, & Williams, 2006). Several patterns are associated with stalkers, including a high incidence of the following: (a) psychological disorders, including severe mental illness (30%; e.g., schizophrenia); (b) personality disorders (50% to 60%; especially borderline, antisocial, and narcissistic); and (c) substance abuse disorders (30 to 50%; Rosenfeld, 2004).

Perpetrator Descriptions

Common Criminals

A study of 346 male stalkers found that 27.4% were "common criminals" with criminal histories of drug use, resisting arrest, and other antisocial behaviors (Jordon, Logan, Walker, & Nigoff, 2003). They are similar to antisocial IPV males (D. G. Dutton, 2007). These men engage in more severe DV, SA, and ST and often are described as controlling, intimidating, impulsive, and manipulative (Abbey, McAuslan, Zawacki, Clinton, & Buck, 2001).

Low Self-Esteem

Low self-esteem typically has been associated with victims of IPV (Hotaling & Sugarman, 1986), but in more recent DV research self-esteem also has been associated with male perpetrators of DV and SA (Magdol et al., 1997). Low self-esteem is often manifested through hypersensitivity to rejection. These individuals become aggressive in anticipation of rejection by a romantic partner. They may use violence with a partner to compensate for feelings of powerlessness (Berns et al., 1999).

Interpersonal Control

Perpetrators of DV and SV report a high need to control their partners by means of physical abuse, threats of harm, and threats to leave the relationship (K. E. Davis, Ace, & Anda, 2000). Aggression may serve to enforce control in order to maintain a sense of dominance and is often related to hypermasculinity. Although they use such tactics less frequently than males, females also do use control tactics with partners (M. P. Johnson & Ferraro, 2000).

Traditional Attitudes and Anger

Traditional male attitudes are associated with DV, SA, and ST (Hill & Fischer, 2001). E. H. Thompson (1991) found that both males and females who engaged in DV exhibited more masculine and less feminine gender orientation. Perhaps the degree to which one subscribes to stereotypic male attitudes of aggressiveness is related to DV.

Victims

Identifying victim characteristics is as important as identifying perpetrator characteristics. Some victim characteristics are similar to the perpetrators, but there are distinct effects separating victims from perpetrators (S. F. Lewis & Fremouw, 2001). Victims of DV, SA, and ST report higher levels of PTSD, depression, and anxiety and lower self-esteem than nonabused partners (Howard, Wang, & Yan, 2007a, 2007b). ST victims report levels of PTS similar to that of victims of other types of traumatization, including affective instability, fear, shame, decreased trust, increased alienation, and self-blame (Kamphuis, Emmelkamp, & Bartak, 2003).

Self-Esteem

Self-esteem has been addressed extensively in the IPV literature, and a negative correlation has been found between self-esteem and frequency and use of severe violence (Cascardi & O'Leary, 1992). In a similar manner, females who experienced DV reported significantly lower self-esteem than females who were not abused by their partners (Cupach & Spitzberg, 2000). Most important, low self-esteem makes it harder for these women to leave abusive relationships.

Disengaging From the Abuser

Another topic of victim research is the motivation for remaining in an abusive dating relationship. A study of high school students found that only 37% of abused dating partners decided to break up or threatened to break up with their abusive partners (Watson, Cascardi, Avery-Leaf, & O'Leary, 2001). Furthermore, women in abusive relationships with a history of CSA versus non-CSA victims reported a greater number of separations and returns (Griffing et al., 2005). CSA victims were more likely to return to their abusers because of their attachment to the abuser, which highlights the negative effect of CSA in later abusive relationships. Thus, treatment should include addressing any CSA along with the current abusive relationship.

Treatment

Levels of Intervention

Research indicates that without remedial action, DV often continues into longer-term relationships (Ehrensaft et al., 2003; O'Leary, 1999). Particularly for those with long histories of abuse, some form of treatment is necessary to lessen the long-term adverse effects of victimization (Wekerle & Avgoustis, 2003) and to prevent carryover into marriage and other long-term relationships (Carr & Van-Deusen, 2002; Frias-Armenta, 2002). Such individuals are at a 3.5 times greater risk of being in a partner-violent relationship as an adult (Coid et al., 2001).

Wolfe and Jaffe (1999) suggested a three-level model of prevention and intervention: (a) primary prevention to preempt DV, SA, and ST before they occur; (b) secondary prevention to reduce prevalence at the early stages of development; and (c) tertiary prevention/intervention following their full expression. Primary followed by secondary prevention are the preferred order of interventions. These programs emphasize education about gender stereotyping, self-esteem, violence awareness, avoidance of date-rape drugs and alcohol, anger management, role of power and control in relationships, changing attitudes about DV, and problem-solving and communication skills (Foshee, Reyes, & Wyckoff, 2009). Research has focused on primary and secondary prevention.

Junior and High School Programs

Research on school-age programs is promising though limited. The five randomized studies have found some degree of improvement in knowledge and, to a lesser degree, an improvement in attitudes about aggression (Foshee & Reyes, 2009).

Only two studies examined whether treatment reduced psychological abuse, physical abuse, and sexual abuse (Foshee et al., 2004; Wolfe, Werkerle et al., 2003). Both studies noted reductions in DV and SA. The curricula were of similar content and used an educational and skills-development format. These two studies are discussed more fully below (i.e., in the sections titled Safe Dates Program and Youth Relationship Project).

Safe Dates Program

Foshee et al. (1996, 1998, 2000, 2004) conducted a large study (*n* = 1,886) for eighth and ninth-graders. The study included 14 different public schools with subjects randomly assigned to either a control or a treatment group to test the Safe Dates program. The group-based treatment program included specific activities at school, including a school play on DV, a nine-session curriculum presented by classroom teachers, and a student poster contest. The control group was involved in the community activities only. Safe Dates was aimed at changing attitudes that condone partner violence and at promoting gender equity, developing conflict management skills, and increasing knowledge about community resources. DV was specified as psychological abuse, sexual abuse, and physical violence. Effectiveness measures were administered at pretest, 1 month following completion of the program, and yearly after that for 4 years, including a booster session for half of the treated students between the 2nd- and 3rd-year follow-ups.

Results of the Safe Dates program varied at each follow-up point of data collection. Overall, and particularly 4 years posttreatment, compared with controls, students who participated in the Safe Dates program reported significantly less physical, serious physical, and sexual violence perpetration. The booster session did not improve the effectiveness of the program. In addition, at the 1-month follow-up, a primary prevention sample (no violence at baseline) that received the treatment reported less initiation of psychological abuse than the control group. At the same time, a secondary prevention sample (DV at baseline) that received the treatment reported less psychological abuse and sexual violence perpetration at follow-up than the control group. The results of this study provide strong evidence for both the effectiveness of a preventative dating program as well as the longstanding impact that such a program can have on reducing various types of DV even 4 years posttreatment.

Safe Dates Program Sessions Overview

The program is composed of nine 45-minute sessions, a play, and a poster contest (Foshee & Langwick, 2004). Safe Dates includes school and community interventions for eighth- and ninth-grade students. Goals of the program consist of changing attitudes related to relationship abuse, reducing gender stereotyping, developing conflict management and communication skills, and enhancing help-seeking behavior. In addition, the program was designed to serve both as a prevention program and as an intervention program for those involved in DV. Furthermore, the program assumes that both boys and girls can be both perpetrators and victims, and it includes activities for both victims and perpetrators. Finally, materials are provided for parents. Each session provides educational materials but also includes group discussions and exercises. The nine educational sessions cover the following topics:

1. *Defining Caring Relationships.* This session introduces the program and discusses how youths want to be treated in dating relationships.
2. *Defining Dating Abuse.* The various types of DV are addressed in this session, with examples and statistics.
3. *Why Do People Abuse?* This session identifies the causes and results of dating abuse.
4. *How to Help Friends.* The difficulties in leaving an abusive relationship are discussed in this session along with information on how to help friends in such relationships.
5. *Helping Friends.* This session continues with the previous session topic and uses role-plays to develop skills to help friends in abusive relationships.
6. *Overcoming Gender Stereotypes.* Discussions and small-group exercises pertaining to stereotypes and their effects on dating relationships are included in this sixth session.
7. *Equal Power Through Communication.* This session includes learning and practicing eight skills for effective communication.
8. *How We Feel, How We Deal.* As the name of this session implies, the topic is to help students learn to recognize and deal with problematic feelings, such as anger, that can lead to dating abuse.
9. *Preventing Sexual Assault.* The final session teaches about SA and how to deal with it.

Finally, students participate in the *There's No Excuse for Dating Abuse* play and a poster contest related to healthy relationships (see manual; Foshee & Langwick, 2010).

The curriculum was developed to be used by teachers in junior and senior high schools in order to affect both students and the community. This program is an effective and efficient prevention and intervention program for counselors working in and/or with school districts (see website for more information: http://www.hazelden.org/web/public/safedates.page).

Youth Relationship Project

A second study by Wolfe and colleagues (Wolfe et al., 1996; Wolfe, Scott, Wekerle, & Pittman., 2001; Wolfe, Wekerle, et al., 2003) was conducted with community youths (ages 14–16) referred by Child Protective Services (CPS) who had histories of maltreatment. They were assigned to either a treatment group ($n = 96$) or a control group ($n = 62$). The Youth Relationship Project (YRP) is an 18-week group-based treatment program group that is divided into four sections and includes education about healthy and abusive relationships, gender-based role expectations, conflict resolution and communication skills, and social action activities. The material is presented in three parts: (a) abuse and power dynamics in close relationships, (b) skill development, and (c) social action. In the study, each session lasted 2 hours and was led by two coleaders: one male and one female. The control group received the usual CPS services of bimonthly visits from a social worker and basic shelter and care as necessary. Measures were administered at pretest, posttest, and periodic follow-ups over 16 months posttreatment (assessed an average of 4.7 times after treatment).

Results indicated significant reductions in perpetration of physical and emotional abuse over the length of treatment and follow-up as well as monthly decreases for the treatment group. In both the treatment and control groups, girls reported perpetrating higher initial levels of physical abuse and experienced greater reductions in physical abuse over time than boys. Girls also reported greater emotional abuse perpetration and threatening behaviors initially than boys. Girls reported greater decreases in their threatening behavior over time than boys. As compared with the control group, the treatment group reported greater reduction in all forms of victimization over time. The format of the program is as follows.

YRP Sessions Overview

Section A: Violence in Close Relationships:
It's All About Power
1. Introduction to Group: Summary
2. Power in Relationships: Explosions and Assertions
3. Defining Relationship Violence: Power Abuses

Section B: Breaking the Cycle of Violence:
What We Can Choose
4. Defining Powerful Relationships: Equality, Empathy, and Emotional Expressiveness
5. Defining Powerful Relationships: Assertiveness Rather Than Aggressiveness
6. Date Rape: Being Clear, Being Safe

Section C: The Context of Relationship Violence
7. Date Rape and Learning How to Handle Dating Pressure
8. Gender Socialization and Societal Pressure
9. Choosing Partners and Sex Role Stereotypes
10. Sexism
11. Media and Sexism

Section D: Making a Difference:
Working Toward Breaking the Cycle of Violence
12. Confronting Sexism and Violence Against Women
13. Getting to Know Community Helpers for Relationship Violence
14. Getting Out and About in the Community: Visiting Social Service Agencies
15. Getting Out and About in the Community: Experience at Social Service Agencies
16. Getting Out and About in the Community: Planning for Social Action to End Relationship Violence

17. Getting Out and About in the Community: Visiting Social Service Agencies
18. End of Group Celebration (see manual; Wolfe et al., 1996)

More recently, Wolfe and colleagues expanded YRP to include 8th- through 12th-graders as a comprehensive school-based program to include all youths in promoting healthy relationships and preventing DV (Wolfe, Crooks, Hughes, & Jaffe, 2009). The program, titled the Fourth R, consists of a 21-lesson skill-based program taught by teachers; it targets violence, high-risk sexual behavior, and substance use among adolescents. Study results indicate that youths who participated in the program showed significantly less physical DV than control groups (see website for more information: http://youthrelationships.org/index.html).

Foshee and Langwick's and Wolfe et al.'s studies were not the only studies to conduct follow-up evaluations, but their follow-ups spanned the longest period after treatment (4 years and 16 months, respectively). More research is needed to provide greater refinement for treatment and treatment tailoring to gender, but this research strongly supports the positive effects of preventative intervention on various types of DV. Furthermore, this research suggests that both trained mental health workers (Wolfe, Crooks, et al., 2003) and classroom teachers (Foshee et al., 1996) can provide effective intervention for DV. Safe Dates and YRP/Fourth R focus on changing both the individual and the sociocultural context in which relationship abuse occurs.

University Programs

University programs designed to reduce rates of DV, SA, and ST are more numerous than high school programs (Marcus & Swett, 2003); however, with a few exceptions (e.g., Schwartz, Magge, Griffin, & Dupuis, 2004; Woodin & O'Leary, 2010), program evaluations are rare. Schwartz et al. (2004) conducted a randomly controlled study with male college students using four 90-minute didactic and skills-development sessions addressing the following issues: gender-role stereotypes and conflicts, healthy and nonhealthy entitlement attitudes, and communication and anger management skills. Results indicated that compared with the control group ($n = 30$), participants in the experimental group ($n = 28$) were significantly less accepting of stereotypical and traditional gender roles, were more confident in communicating needs and emotions, had healthier entitlement attitudes, and had better anger management skills at posttreatment. Abusive behavior was not assessed.

In the only other study with young adults, Woodin and O'Leary (2010) conducted an assessment and one 2-hour session of MI as an intervention to reduce couple violence with a group of college students who had experienced mild physical violence with their partners. Couples were assessed at 3, 6, and 9 months posttreatment. Compared with a control group ($n = 25$ couples), participants in the experimental group ($n = 25$ couples) had a greater reduction in physical violence and harmful alcohol use and had less acceptance of female psychological aggression and male psychological aggression (with women only).

Although samples sizes were small, these studies suggest that brief interventions can have an impact on changing attitudes and behaviors related to DV as well as reduce physical violence and problem alcohol use. Future studies should examine the combination of the psychoeducational and communication interventions with the MI interventions. Combining these two programs into a four- or five-session program could result in an efficient and cost-effective program to reduce DV with young adults.

O. Barnett et al. (2011) offered a number of suggestions for improving prevention of DV: (a) Offer clinics for victims of childhood abuse and at-risk daters; (b) alert women to the dangers of interpersonal control; (c) provide guidance about avoiding date-rape drugs; (d) address sexist attitudes and problems of peer-group support for aggression; (e) teach anger management, conflict resolution skills, and stress-reduction skills; (f) present antidrug messages and alcohol misuse awareness programs; and (g) discuss attachment, commitment, and stress (pp. 318–319).

Unfortunately, long-term follow-up studies with large samples of young adults like those conducted with high school students are nonexistent. A large percentage of university programs primarily focus on strategies for women to prevent rape (O'Donohue, Yeater, & Fanetti, 2003).

Rape Prevention for Men

Rape prevention programs for men target attitudes toward DV and SA such as rape myths ("Women who get raped while hitchhiking get what they deserve"), lack of empathy, and gender differences. Some studies have indicated greater changes in attitudes about SA and DV (e.g., O'Donohue et al., 2003), whereas others have not (Gidycz et al., 2001).

A review of prevention programs suggests that programs aimed at all-male groups are more successful than those focused on mixed-gender groups (Foubert & Marriott, 1997). The greatest weakness of the current rape prevention programs is that research has shown that they have little or no impact on the incidence of rape (L. A. Anderson & Whiston, 2005). However, even with inconclusive research results, most experts suggest the benefits of prevention programs and the need for universities to take a stronger leadership role in providing prevention programs. In response, the American College Health Association produced a toolkit titled Shifting the Paradigm: Primary Prevention of Sexual Violence (available at http://www.acha.org/SexualViolence/docs/ACHA_PSV_toolkit.pdf). It provides facts, concepts, strategies, and resources to those on campuses who are interested in the prevention of SA.

In addition, 50% to 70% of all SAs involve alcohol (Abbey, 2002). Several websites provide suggestions for those working with college students to reduce the use of alcohol (see http://www.collegedrinkingprevention.gov/StatsSummaries/4tier. aspx). Furthermore, Larimer and Cronce (2007) provided a thorough literature review of prevention and treatment of college drinking. Abbey (2002) suggested several actions that can be taken by colleges and universities: (a) Examine and revise campus policies regarding alcohol and violence; (b) seek the support and involvement of organized social groups such as Greeks and athletes to oppose high-risk drinking and/or forced sex; (c) encourage collaboration between those on campus who are responsible for alcohol programming and for SA prevention; and (d) make inquiries about SA and alcohol in all health, counseling, and judicial affairs visits.

Finally, on the basis of a review of the research, Foshee et al. (2009) suggested the following strategies to prevent dating abuse:

- Intervene with parents to decrease the likelihood that children will be exposed to parental and family-based risk factors for adolescent dating abuse and adult partner abuse.
- Prevent and reduce behavioral precursors to dating and partner abuse, such as bullying and aggression toward peers.
- Intervene with children who have been exposed to family violence and are at increased risk for dating abuse by altering factors that mediate and moderate the association between exposure to family violence and dating abuse (e.g., gender stereotypes).
- Deliver dating abuse prevention programs to adolescents.
- Offer to young couples premarital education and counseling programs designed to improve couple communication, problem-solving skills, and marital satisfaction and to decrease marital distress and conflict.
- Offer SA prevention programs on college campuses, because many of the cognitions, attitudes, and behaviors altered by these programs have been associated with the use of sexual violence against partners. (p. 178)

The authors suggested that the influences on DV and later IPV have their origins in the home (e.g., witnessing violence); thus, intervening early with parents who create at-risk contexts for their children and adolescents is critical in preventing DV. The importance of including homes, schools, and communities in the prevention process cannot be overstated.

Tertiary Prevention

Tertiary prevention for victims of DV, SA, and ST is identical to treatment programs for IPV (Chapters 5 and 9 of this text). In many cases, intervention occurs only after a victim has experienced varying degrees of abuse from a dating partner, typically after more severe abuse has occurred and/or after an extended period of abuse (Watson et al., 2001).

Goals of intervention include developing a safety plan, gaining a perspective on the abusive situation, stabilizing the victim's environment, addressing trust issues and emotional symptoms, processing trauma experiences, developing appropriate boundaries between self and abusive partner, and marshalling social support (Dowd & Leisring, 2008). Other important issues include addressing the minimization or denial of abuse, exploring whether or not to stay in the relationship, and developing alternative support systems. As opposed to IPV, dating couples are seldom cohabitating, which makes the issue of leaving the abuser or financial dependence on the abuser less of an issue in treatment. However, leaving an abusive dating relationship is oftentimes no less dangerous than in a domestic violence context (Rosen & Stith, 1995).

DV and SA victims often report low self-esteem and insecure romantic attachment. As a result, they would benefit from a treatment focus on individuation. This focus is often a long-term process and requires on-going support, education, and interaction with like-minded peers. Prevention programs can enhance this process following individual and/or group treatment.

Treatment for SA would likely include all of the above goals and strategies plus additional considerations that would not be included in treating only DV. For example, medical examination/rape kits and treatment should always be a consideration along with legal counsel (Ahrens et al., 2000). Rape crisis centers are often best equipped to provide comprehensive intervention in the initial stages of intervention following the SA. Victims who are also survivors of childhood abuse benefit from ongoing, long-term support groups (Courtois, 2008).

ST victims, who may have experienced DV and SA before a breakup with the stalker, greatly benefit from treatment and advocacy that decreases their vulnerability (Blaauw, Winkel, Arensman, Sheridan, & Freeve, 2002). Protective orders are often used to achieve this end, and yet stalkers violate these orders 40% of the time (Spitzberg, 2002). Furthermore, laws protecting women who have been abused or stalked have been unevenly enforced or nonexistent until recently. Many see a distinct antivictim bias in the criminal justice system, particularly when the victim is acquainted with the perpetrator (Spohn & Holleran, 2001). A more recent stalking threat is cyberstalking (Merschman, 2001). Anticyberstalking legislation is needed.

Treating Perpetrators

Treatment for perpetrators of DV, SA, and ST beyond primary and secondary treatment is indistinguishable from the treatment of IPV perpetrators for adult males. Interventions include both educational and skill-building modules and focus on power and control (O'Leary, 1999), communication and problem-solving skills (Wolfe, Wekerle, Scott, Straatman, & Grasley, 2004), and anger management skills (Schwartz et al., 2004).

Summary

Research pertaining to DV, SA, or ST is scant compared with that of adult IPV. However, existing prevalence rates indicate DV and SA are quite common, with lifetime rates ranging from 12%–40% for DV and 2%–20% for SA. ST prevalence rates are somewhat less at 0.6%–4.8%. Other research indicates that approximately one in ten to one in five high school students report DV. Victims of dating abuse incur significant injury, poor health outcomes, and psychological/emotional problems such as depression, anxiety, and PTSD. DV in middle adolescence tends to be more mutual between genders, with some research indicating that older adolescents and college-age students report that men more frequently perpetrate violence and perpetrate more severe forms of violence than females. However, girls report initiating DV more often than males, whereas males perpetrate more SA and cause more injury than females.

DV, SA, and ST are thought to be related to a variety of factors, including patriarchal attitudes, peer support of violence, hostility, childhood abuse and exposure to violence, and low self-esteem. However, research consistently finds that family-of-origin experiences have the greatest influence on the perpetration of DV, SA, and ST.

Finally, treatment programs are less prevalent than prevention programs. Research indicates that primary and secondary programs are consistently effective in changing negative attitudes about partner violence, although with somewhat less success in reducing or preventing actual dating violence. These programs tend to include educational, skill-building, and experiential components.

Suggested Readings

Brewster, M. P. (2003). *Stalking: Psychology, risk factors, interventions, and law*. Kingston, NJ: Civic Research Institute.

Close, S. M. (2005). Dating violence prevention in middle school and high school youth. *Journal of Child and Adolescent Psychiatric Nursing, 18*, 2–9.

Foshee, V. A., Benefield, T. S., Ennett, S. T., Bauman, K. E., & Suchindran, C. (2004). Longitudinal predictors of serious physical and sexual dating violence victimization during adolescence. *Preventive Medicine: An International Journal Devoted to Practice and Theory, 39*, 1007–1016.

Foshee, V. A., & Langwick, S. (2010). *Safe Dates: An adolescent dating abuse prevention curriculum* (2nd ed.; Program manual). Center City, MN: Hazelden Publishing and Educational Services.

Hickman, L. J., Jaycox, L. H., & Aronoff, J. (2004). Dating violence among adolescents: Prevalence, gender distribution, and prevention program effectiveness. *Trauma, Violence, & Abuse, 5*, 123–142.

Wolfe, D. A., Crooks, C., Jaffe, P., Chiodo, D., Hughes, R., Ellis, W., . . . Donner, A. (2009). A school-based program to prevent adolescent dating violence: A cluster randomized trial. *Archives of Pediatrics and Adolescent Medicine, 163*, 692–699.

Wolfe, D. A., Wekerle, C., Gough, R., Reitzel-Jaffe, D., Grasley, C, Pittman, A., . . . Stumpf, J. (1996). *The Youth Relationships Manual: A group approach with adolescents for the prevention of woman abuse and the promotion of healthy relationships*. Thousand Oaks, CA: Sage.

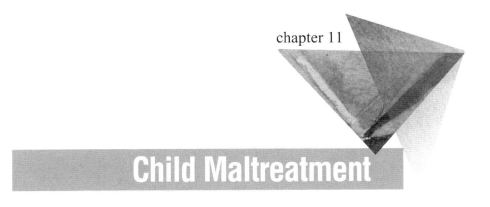

chapter 11

Child Maltreatment

As with wife abuse, child maltreatment (CM) was seldom addressed by the judicial system until the late 1970s and early 1980s, except in extreme cases or death. The attitude was that issues related to child abuse are a "family problem" and require little if any outside legal interference. However, every state now has specific laws protecting children against abuse; such laws are based on the Child Abuse Prevention and Treatment Act of 1974 (National Clearinghouse on Child Abuse and Neglect Information, 2004). This act defines child abuse, mandates reporting of suspected CM, and requires states to establish requirements for mandatory reporting. Nonetheless, CM continues to have a major impact on families and society. For example, CM is the primary cause of death among children under the age of 4 (U. S. DHHS, 2010).

This chapter includes a discussion of CM as related to definitions, types, predictors, prevalence rates, and consequences. Additional discussion addresses perpetrator characteristics.

Defining Child Maltreatment

On the basis of the federal Child Abuse Prevention and Treatment Act (CAPTA) as amended by the Keeping Children and Families Safe Act 2003, CM at minimum is defined as

- any act or failure to act on the part of a parent or caretaker which results in death, serious physical or emotional harm, sexual abuse or exploitation; or
- an act or failure to act which presents an imminent risk of serious harm.

Box 11.1   A Child's Abuse Stories

I was 12 years old when my uncle, whom I was quite fond of, put his hands inside my pants and sweater on three different occasions. We would often play fight, which I felt was okay, until he started making advances. I tried to tell my parents on the way home that I didn't feel good about what my uncle was doing. Although my parents were there when it happened, my dad was quick to reply, "You got what you asked for." How could I tell them that I'd been sexually abused by four others?

One evening while both of my parents were away, my brothers and a neighbor boy made a hiding place from extra large boxes and blankets in my brother's basement bedroom. They told my sister and myself to come with them—they wanted to show us something. We went along. They told us to take off our clothes. We didn't want to. After being called names and humiliated, we did as we were told. We lay down and let them do what they wanted. My brothers said, "If you tell, we'll get you into trouble."

Another day, the same neighbor boy attacked me in broad daylight while I was going for a walk. I thought he was running to catch up with me but when he reached me he caught me from behind and grabbed my breasts. He pulled me down into the grass, saying he wanted to make love to me. I struggled to get away while he mauled at my body. Finally I was able to free myself. I hid behind a nearby church while my attacker looked for me. After he left, I went home feeling numb and dirty.

Situations like these happened to me about 10 times for 2 years.

—Anonymous

Unfortunately, this example of child abuse is all too common. Such cases often go unreported, with many victims living out their lives dealing with the consequences of abuse either without ever seeking professional help or waiting well into adulthood before seeking help.

Most states acknowledge four types of CM: neglect, physical abuse, sexual abuse, and emotional/psychological abuse. Although they are defined as separate acts, they often co-occur.

Harm and Endangerment

The National Center on Child Abuse and Neglect (Child Welfare Information Gateway, 2008) established two standards for defining abuse and neglect. The *Harm Standard* requires demonstrable evidence of harm to a child as a result of an act or omission of care (National Incidence Study [NIS-1]; U. S. DHHS, Administration for Children and Families, 1981). Evidence refers to credible information, such as the perpetrator acknowledging his or her actions and/or a verifiable injury. However, critics argue that this definition excludes CM cases that have been substantiated but not to the level required by the Harm Standard. Therefore, the *Endangerment Standard* was added (NIS-2; Sedlack, 1991). Children who have experienced maltreatment but have not been harmed fall under the Endangerment Standard. Endangerment includes all children who fall under the Harm Standard.

Child Neglect

Child neglect is the failure to provide for a child's basic needs in the following areas: physical (e.g., lack of food, shelter, appropriate supervision), medical (e.g., failure to obtain medical or mental health treatment), educational (e.g., complicit with child's truancy), and emotional (e.g., demeaning, withholding affection, or ridiculing; Sedlak et al., 2010). The occurrence of any of these examples does not always mean a child is being neglected. Other factors such as cultural values, differing standards within a community, and poverty may result in some or all the above factors not being viewed as neglect. However, once families are informed of these standards, the continuation of such acts may constitute neglect.

Neglect is viewed as an act of *omission* (O. Barnett et al., 2011) and is often referred to as the most forgotten form of CM. The "act of omission" concept is misleading, with some concluding that neglect is less serious, especially when compared with physical or sexual abuse (Dubowitz, 1994). However, neglect is the most-often reported form of CM and results in the highest number of fatalities (35.8%) of all types of CM (U.S. DHHS, 2010).

The following are examples of neglect, some of which people would not view as neglect:

- parents leaving their 6-year-old child to care for a 3-year-old child,
- failure to provide medication for a child with a serious heart condition,
- failure to provide consistent meals for children,
- failure to provide adequate supervision,
- allowing school truancy, and
- failure to provide adequate hygiene. (McClennen, 2010)

Physical Abuse

Physical abuse refers to any type of physical injury (from minor bruising to severe fractures and death) occurring as a result of hitting, kicking, shaking, choking, throwing, burning, or any other acts that harm a child, whether intended or not. This definition focuses on acts of violence that cause some form of observable *harm*. The Endangerment Standard includes risk or fear of injury to a child, such as a parent not having a child wear a seat belt.

States allow some leeway for reasonable corporal punishment, such as spanking on the buttocks without physical injury (Myers, 1992). However, corporal punishment as an acceptable means of discipline is controversial and viewed by some as child abuse (Straus, 2005).

Corporal Punishment

Some scholars are critical of using any type of physical violence toward children. Straus and Donnelly (2008) have argued that spankings legitimize violence as a means of conflict resolution and contribute to major social and interpersonal problems. Research provides some support for Straus's concerns. In three of Straus's

(2004) studies, comparisons of children who were spanked with those who were not spanked found that the spanked children had (a) slower rates of cognitive development, (b) lower scores on tests of educational achievement, and (c) increased probability of crime as an adult. Conversely, other research (Baumrind, 1996; Larzelere, 2000) has failed to support the notion that spanking per se is harmful and has suggested that a blanket condemnation of spanking is unwarranted.

Child Sexual Abuse

Child sexual abuse (CSA) is defined by CAPTA as follows:

> The employment, use, persuasion, inducement, enticement, or coercion of any child by an adult or to engage in, or assist any other person to engage in, any sexually explicit conduct or simulation of such conduct for the purpose of producing a visual depiction of such conduct; or the rape, and in cases of caretaker or inter-familial relationships, statutory rape, molestation, prostitution, or other forms of sexual exploitation of children, or incest with children. (CAPTA, 2003)

This definition includes the actions by a parent, caregiver, or other persons to fondle a child's genitals, penetration, sodomy, indecent exposure, and exploitation through enticement by pornographic materials. In many states, CSA can also be committed by a person under the age of 18 when the age difference is 2 or more years between perpetrator and victim (e.g., Statutory Rape Act, 2010) or when the abuser is in a position of authority over another child (Browne & Finkelhor, 1986). Most states have specified ages at which one is capable of consenting to sexual relationships, which most often fall between ages 14 and 18 (Myers, 2002).

O. Barnett et al. (2005) proposed that most definitions of CSA include four key components: (a) the possibility of abuse occurring both in and out of the family, (b) the abuse includes both physical contact and noncontact activities, (c) the adult's abuse of power and authority to achieve sexual gratification, and (d) there are age or maturational differences between the abuser and the victim. The last two components warrant further comment. Both involve the abuse of power by the abuser. In component c, children are viewed as incapable of providing legitimate informed consent to any kind of sexual activity with an adult. Regardless of how sexually provocative a child's behavior may be, it is unquestionably the adult's responsibility *not* to respond to it. In component d, under certain circumstances, a child who is abused by another child may be exploited by virtue of the perpetrator's size, age, sex, or status, regardless of the age differences between children, such as an 8-year-old brother sexually abusing his 7-year-old sister.

CSA is the least prevalent of the three major identified areas of CM, and yet it has received the most attention in the research (K. Elliott & Urquiza, 2006). National representative surveys (e.g., U.S. DHHS, 2010) largely include reports from state and federal CPS agencies but often underreport actual incidents of CSA. However, retrospective reports from the general population indicate that 20% to 25% of females and 5% to 15% of males reported CSA (Finkelhor, 1994). One meta-analysis of 22 American studies of CSA suggested much higher prevalence rates for girls (30% to 40%), with comparable rates for boys (13%; Bolen & Scannapieco, 1999). Parents and relatives are the perpetrators 50% to 90% of the time. Girls are at least 3 times more likely to be sexually abused than boys, but researchers suggest CSA of boys is much higher than reported because of the social stigma of males being sex abuse victims; thus, much abuse is not reported.

Emotional/Psychological Abuse

Emotional/psychological abuse is defined by CAPTA as a pattern of behavior that impairs a child's emotional development or sense of self-worth. This abuse may include constant criticism, threats, or rejection as well as withholding love, support, or guidance.

The American Professional Society on the Abuse of Children (APSAC) provides a set of guidelines (numbered 1–5 below) for identifying emotional abuse (EA), enumerated in their publication *Guidelines for the Psychosocial Evaluation of Suspected Psychological Maltreatment in Children and Adolescents* (APSAC, 1995). Furthermore, Numbers 6 through 9 represent behaviors identified earlier by other experts as indicators of EA (Hart, Brassard, & Karlson, 1996). If the following behaviors are severe and ongoing, they are likely indicative of EA.

Guidelines for Identifying Emotional Abuse of Children

1. Spurning: belittling, degrading, shaming, or ridiculing a child; singling out a child to criticize or punish; and humiliating a child in public.
2. Terrorizing: committing life-threatening acts; making a child feel unsafe; setting unrealistic expectations with threat of loss, harm, or danger if they are not met; and threatening or perpetrating violence against a child or child's loved ones or object.
3. Exploiting or corrupting that encourages a child to develop inappropriate behaviors: modeling, permitting, or encouraging antisocial or developmentally inappropriate autonomy; restricting or interfering with cognitive development.
4. Denying emotional responsiveness: ignoring a child or failing to express affection, caring, and love for a child.
5. Neglecting mental health, medical, and educational needs: ignoring, preventing, or failing to provide treatments or services for emotional, behavioral, physical, or educational needs or problems.
6. Rejecting: avoiding or pushing away.
7. Isolating: confining, placing unreasonable limitations on freedom of movement or social interactions.
8. Unreliable or inconsistent parenting: contradictory and ambivalent demands.
9. Witnessing IPV (domestic violence). (APSAC, 1995)

Some of these behaviors, such as derogatory name calling or threatening a child, can have long-term consequences (Kairys, Johnson, & Committee on Child Abuse and Neglect, 2002), and yet they are often the most difficult type of CM to prove and prosecute legally.

EA and Other Forms of CM

EA is almost always present when other forms of CM emerge, thus making it hard to distinguish EA from other forms of CM. EA is a component of most forms of CM and the strongest predictor of the persistence of CM (Binggeli, Hart, & Brassard, 2001). However, EA can occur by itself, such as in a contentious divorce.

Prevalence Rates of Child Maltreatment and Fatalities

On the basis of the *Child Maltreatment 2009* report (U.S. DHHS, 2010), approximately 3.6 million children were the subject of at least one CPS report in the United States. Following investigations, approximately 720,000 children were determined to be victims of child abuse or neglect. The victimization rate in 2009 was 10.1 per 1,000 children, a decrease from 12.4 per 1,000 in 2003. As distinct from the *Child Maltreatment* reports, the National Incidence Studies (NIS-4; Sedlak et al., 2010) include reports from other professionals in such settings as public schools, day care centers, hospitals, voluntary social service agencies, mental health agencies, county juvenile probation and public health departments, public housing, and shelters for runaway and homeless youths and for victims of domestic violence in addition to CPS reports. The NIS-4 study included both the Harm Standard and the slightly more lenient Endangerment Standard. Table 11.1 identifies types and incidences of CM in the NIS-4 report.

As with the *Child Maltreatment 2009* report, the NIS-4 report represents an overall reduction in CM from previous studies (i.e., 19% reduction from the NIS-3 report in 1993). This reduction is consistent with a steady decline in CM since 1990. Finkelhor and Jones (2006) offered four factors that may account for this reduction: (a) improved economic conditions, (b) increased agents of social change (e.g., more police), (c) pharmacological advances in treating anxiety and depression in children and adults, and (d) an increase in offenders incarcerated for CM.

Other surveys have been conducted on lifetime prevalence rates, with adults providing reports that were based on their recollections of childhood experiences. A meta-analysis of 22 studies found lifetime prevalence rates (i.e., over the course of childhood) of sexual abuse to be 30% to 40% for girls and 13% for boys (Bolen & Scannapieco, 1999)—much higher than NIS-4 reports.

Table 11.1
Types and Incidences of Child Maltreatment (CM)

Type of CM	Harm Standard	Endangerment Standard
All children maltreated	1,256,600 (17.1)	2,905,800 (39.5)
Neglected	771,700 (61%; 10.5)	2,251,600 (77%; 30.6)
Physically abused	323,000 (58%; 4.4)	476,600 (57%; 6.5)
Sexually abused	135,300 (24%; 1.8)	180,500 (22%; 2.4)
Emotionally abused	148,500 (27%; 2.0)	302,600 (36%; 4.1)

Note. Numbers in parentheses are the percentage of children abused in the total sample for each type of abuse followed by the incidence rate per 1,000 children. Percentages add up to over 100% as many children were victims of several kinds of abuse. Information from Sedlack et al. (2010).

Fatalities

Approximately 1,777 children died in 2009 as a result of injury from abuse, neglect, or both (U.S. DHHS, 2010). This number was an increase of 50 deaths from 2008 and translates to a rate of 2.34 children per 100,000 children, with the following age range breakdown:

- 46.2% of the deaths occurred with children younger than 1 year,
- 80.8% were under 4 years of age,
- 9.5% were 4 to 7 years old,
- 4.2% were 8 to 11 years old,
- 4.0% were 12 to 15 years old, and
- 1.4% were 16 to 17 years old.

Infant boys had the highest fatality rate, with almost 2.36 deaths per 100,000 boys of the same age. Infant girls had a fatality rate of 2.12 deaths per 100,000. Neglect alone or in combination with another type of CM accounted for the highest number of deaths (66.7%), followed by physical abuse alone or in combination (44.8%), emotional/psychological abuse (1.2%), and sexual abuse (1.9%). Perpetrators in 75.8% of the cases were one or both parents.

Victim Characteristics

An important issue in both preventing and treating CM is the identification of victim characteristics and risk factors. Such information provides a context for determining where to focus resources and informs treatment planning and interventions.

Age

Some have suggested that child abusers are no respecters of age or gender (Gosselin, 2003); however, there are certain trends with regard to ages of the victims (U.S. DHHS, 2010):

- 33.4% were under 4 years of age (<1 year accounted for 12.6%),
- 23.3% were 4 to 7 years of age,
- 18.8% were 8 to 11 years of age,
- 17.8% were 12 to 15 years of age, and
- 6.3% were 16 to 17 years of age.

Children under the age of 1 had the highest victimization rate at 20.6 per 1,000 children of the same age, followed by 11.9 for age 1, 11.3 for age 2, and 10.6 for age 3. As age increases, the rate and percentage of victimization decreases.

There are moderate differences in the age of greatest risk of abuse between the four types of maltreatment. Nearly half of all physical abuse cases occur with children under the age of 8, with 32% occurring with children between ages 12 and 17. Data indicate little variability of sexual abuse from birth to age 17 in frequency (U.S. DHHS, 2010). However, neglect was highest for children age 3 and younger. Finally, older children are more likely to experience EA than younger children. Serious injury as a result of neglect is more likely with young children.

Gender

In previous national surveys, boys had a higher rate of physical abuse and girls had a higher rate of sexual abuse. In the most recent surveys, there were no significant gender differences on physical abuse. However, gender rates are different on other categories of abuse (NIS-4; per 1,000 children based on the Harm Standard):

	Boys	*Girls*
All abuse	6.5	8.5
Sexual abuse	0.6	3.0
Severity of harm	0.6	1.4

Note. All differences significant at $p < .05$.

Girls were sexually abused more than boys under both the Harm Standard (5 times) and the Endangerment Standard (almost 4 times). This higher rate likely accounts for the greater severity-of-harm rate. The higher sexual abuse rate for girls accounts for the overall higher abuse rate for girls versus boys.

Neglect

Gender rates for neglect are similar to physical abuse, with boys accounting for 48.3% of cases and girls for 51.3%. Girls are more likely than boys to experience emotional neglect.

Race/Ethnicity

The following results are from the Child Maltreatment survey (U.S. DHHS, 2010). This survey provided a larger number of race/ethnic categories than the NIS-4 survey.

	% of the Total Combined CM	*Rate per 1,000 per Category*
African Americans	22.0	15.1
American Indian/Alaska Natives	1.1	11.6
Asian	0.9	2.0
Hispanic	20.7	8.7
Multiple Race	3.2	12.4
Pacific Islander	0.2	11.3
Caucasian	44.0	7.8

The CM rate for African American, American Indian or Alaska Native, and multiple races had the highest rates of victimization. The NIS-4 found similar results for both the Harm and Endangerment Standards on overall CM, overall abuse and neglect, and physical abuse; it also found similar results for sexual abuse for the Endangerment Standard for Caucasians, African Americans, and Hispanics.

Socioeconomic Factors

Children of low SES status had significantly higher rates of maltreatment in all categories and across both Harm and Endangerment Standards.

In the NIS-4 survey, low SES was defined by any of the following indicators:

- household income below $15,000 a year;
- parents' highest education level less than high school; or
- any household member participating in a poverty-related program, such as food stamps, public housing, or subsidized school meals.

These children experienced some type of CM at more than 5 times the rate of children not in low SES families (i.e., 22.5 vs. 4.4 incidences/1,000); they were more than 3 times as likely to be abused (physical, sexual, and emotional) and about 7 times as likely to be neglected. Furthermore, the severity of CM in low-SES families was 5.8 times higher than for children not in low-SES families. Also, compared with children who had employed parents, children who had unemployed parents experienced 2 to 3 times more overall maltreatment, 2 times more abuse, and more than 3 times the rate of neglect.

There are several problems associated with poverty that increase the likelihood of CM, such as more transient residences, poorer education, and higher rates of substance abuse and mental disorders (Sedlak & Broadhusrt, 1996). These factors combine with less social support to increase the likelihood of CM compared with families without these same problems. Furthermore, poverty increases parent distress and depression, which results in more punitive and hostile parenting, which in turn results in a less engaged and nurturing parenting style (Zielinski & Bradshaw, 2006).

Personal Characteristics

In addition to the above-mentioned factors, children at risk for CM often have more behavioral, medical, and developmental problems, such as prematurity, attention deficit and hyperactivity disorder, low birth weight, low IQ or mental retardation, and physical disability (U.S. DHHS, 2010). These children are more difficult to control and manage than other children, putting them at a higher risk for CM. However, unlike the NIS-3 survey, the NIS-4 survey indicated that children with a disability (e.g., mental retardation, hearing and visually impaired) compared with nondisabled children had lower rates of physical abuse under both standards and lower rates of sexual abuse under the Endangerment Standard. The decreases from NIS-3 to NIS-4 may be attributed to closer oversight of these children in schools and additional assistance programs for at-risk children, such as early child intervention programs that focus on educating and supporting parents who have at-risk children.

Family Characteristics

There are a number of family factors that are highly related to CM in general and CSA in particular. Families with a high risk for CM tend to be isolated, with few external support networks (Zielinski & Bradshaw, 2006). In addition, high-risk parents tend to have poor relationships with their children. These parents tend to interact with their children in a hostile and nonnurturing manner (Coohey, 1995) and tend to use more corporal punishment than parents who do not abuse their children (Straus & Donnelly, 2008). It is not surprising that family conflict and lack of positive family interaction patterns are strongly related to child abuse potential.

Children residing with their married biological parents generally had the lowest rate of maltreatment overall (NIS-4; Sedlak et al., 2010). Conversely, children who lived with a single parent and his or her cohabiting partner experienced the highest rate of maltreatment in all categories. The differences are quite dramatic. For example, children living with a single parent and live-in partner as compared with children living with married biological parents had over 8 times the overall rate of maltreatment, over 10 times the rate of physical abuse, almost 20 times the rate of sexual abuse, and almost 8 times the rate of neglect. Children in father-only homes are twice as likely to be maltreated compared with children in mother-only homes (Sedlak et al., 2010).

Community Factors

Four community factors are related to CM: low economic and resource level, high resident turnover, single parents with multiple children, and residence in close proximity to high poverty (Coulton, Crampton, Irwin, Spilsbury, & Korbin, 2007). Families of maltreated children tend to move twice as frequently as nonmaltreating families. As a result, they experience more frequent disruptions in caregivers and school attendance. These factors create more instability with children and caregivers, causing a breakdown in community organization and control; thus, there is a greater risk of harm for these children who have the least power.

Child Sexual Abuse Risk

There are several risk factors unique to CSA. A stepdaughter is 5 to 7 times more likely to be a victim of CSA than a biological child (Finkelhor, 1984). Girls who have lived without their biological mothers are 3 times more likely to be sexually abused than girls who have lived with their biological mothers. Furthermore, girls who perceive their mothers as unavailable physically or emotionally are at greater risk for CSA (Finkelhor, Moore, Hamby, & Straus, 1997). Also, girls whose mothers who were sexually abused were 3.6 times more likely to be sexually abused. Finally, girls whose mothers had a history of sexual abuse and drug use were at the highest risk for CSA (McCloskey & Bailey, 2000). The importance of the mother–daughter relationship in both contributing to and protecting against female sexual abuse cannot be overemphasized. *This relationship should be central in any effort at prevention or remediation.*

Additional risk factors for both girls and boys are as follows: (a) having a mother who works outside the home or who has a disability, (b) living in a home in which there is consistent parental conflict, (c) living in a home in which parents have alcohol or drug abuse problems, and (d) living without both parents for long periods of time (J. Brown, Cohen, Johnson, & Salzinger, 1998; McCloskey & Bailey, 2000).

Sibling Abuse

A difficulty in identifying sibling abuse is that aggression between siblings is so pervasive and universal that it has rarely been viewed as abusive, and in fact more often it is viewed as normative (Gelles & Cornell, 1990). However, research indicates that sibling aggression is the *most prevalent type of family violence,* with 80% of siblings between the ages of 3 and 17 reporting they were physically violent against a sibling at least once (Straus & Gelles, 1990). Furthermore, a national survey indicated that 14% of siblings between 3 and 17 years of age reported using severe violence, such as beating up or using a gun or knife against a sibling (Eriksen & Jensen, 2009). Males reported perpetrating higher rates of sibling violence, and females reported higher rates of victimization by other siblings (Button & Gealt, 2010). In addition, sibling sexual abuse is the most prevalent type of family incest (K. M. Thompson, 2009), with over twice as many females than males being victims (Krienert & Walsh, 2011). Finkelhor (1980) found that 15% of female and 10% of male undergraduate students ($n = 796$) reported some type of sexual activity with a sibling, with fondling and touching of genitals being the most often reported type. In a large sample ($n = 13,013$) from the National Incident-Based Reporting System of individuals who experienced sibling sexual abuse, males and females reported the following as the most frequent type of sexual abuse: forcible fondling of genitals (54.9% vs. 54.9%, respectively), followed by forcible rape (30% vs. 4.1% respectively), and forcible sodomy (9.2% vs. 36.9%, respectively; Krienert & Walsh, 2011). Males were more likely to be victimized by other males (87%).

The most common consequences of any type of sibling abuse are depression, anxiety, fear, anger, and guilt (Mackey, Fromuth, & Kelly, 2009). Other consequences associated with sibling sexual abuse include eating disorders, substance abuse, low self-esteem, suicide, and long-term problems with future intimate relationships (McVeigh, 2003; K. M. Thompson, 2009). The issue of sibling abuse is often ignored or minimized by society. Counselors cannot ignore the seriousness of sibling abuse and must assess for it when working with children and adolescents.

Exposure to Parental Violence

A recent nationally representative survey estimated that 15.5 million children live in homes where IPV occurs, with 7 million of these children exposed to severe IPV (McDonald, Jouriles, Ramisetty-Mikler, Caetano, & Green, 2006). Furthermore, in 35% to 70% of homes in which IPV occurs, perpetrators also abuse their children (Edleson, 1999). The exposure of children to interparental abuse results in severe consequences for children. Kitzmann, Gaylord, Holt, and Kenny (2003) conducted a meta-analysis of 118 studies that examined psychosocial outcomes of children exposed to interparental violence. Results indicated the following: (a) There was a strong association between witnessing IPV and significant disruptions in children's psychosocial functioning, (b) witnesses had significantly worse outcomes than nonwitnesses, and (c) witnesses' outcomes were not significantly different from children who had been verbally or physically abused. Another review found that 13% to 50% of children and adolescents exposed to interparental violence were diagnosed with PTSD (Rossman & Ho, 2000).

The effects of witnessing IPV on children and adolescents rises with increasing distress of the mother and frequency of IPV (Edleson, Mbilinyi, Beeman, & Hagemeister, 2003). As these factors increase in intensity, children and adolescents are more prone to exhibit behavioral problems and also to show a decrease in social competence (Onyskiw, 2003). Furthermore, preschool and school-age children often blame themselves for the violence (McClennen, 2010), which increases their aggressive behavior, anxiety, and depression (Margolin & Vickerman, 2011). These children are placed in an irresolvable bind in which both the source of security and the source of trauma are the same person(s); hence, these children often have insecure attachments responses (Hesse & Main, 2006).

In addition, Straus, Gelles, and Steinmetz (1980) and Kalmuss (1984) suggested that children who witness parental violence are at greater risk of using severe physical violence than those who were victims of physical abuse. In particular, men who witnessed interparental violence had 3 times the rate of using physical abuse than nonwitnessing men (Straus et al., 1980). D. G. Dutton (1998) contended that the combination of being exposed to interparental violence, being shamed by a parent, and having insecure attachment sets the eventual course of IPV.

Table 11.2 summarizes risk factors for CM.

Perpetrator Characteristics

Relationship to Abused Child

Most adults who perpetrate CM are caregivers.

- In 81% of all CM cases, perpetrators were the birth parents.
- In 12.4% of the cases, perpetrators were nonbiological parents and parents' partners.
- In 6.4% of cases, perpetrators were other family members and unrelated adults.
- Birth parents were the primary perpetrators in three types of CM: physical abuse (72%), emotional abuse (73%), and neglect (92%).
- In 63% of the cases of sexual abuse, the perpetrator was someone other than the biological parent (Sedlak et al., 2010).

Alcohol Use, Drug Use, and Mental Illness

The following issues were deemed as factors related to CM: alcohol use (13%), drug use (10%), and mental illness (7%). These factors were most often implicated in CM when perpetrators were parents (Sedlak et al., 2010).

Child's Race and the Perpetrator

Finally, when considering all types of maltreatment, the child's race had no correlation to his or her relationship with the perpetrator, except in cases of physical neglect (Sedlak et al., 2010). The majority of children physically neglected by their biological parents were White (58%), whereas the majority of those neglected by a nonbiological parent or parent's partner were Black (53%).

Table 11.2
Risk Factor Characteristics Associated With Child Maltreatment

Risk Factor or Condition	Example/Characteristic
Individual pathogy of perpetrator	Self-expressed anger and anger control problem
	Depression
	Low frustration tolerance
	Low self-esteem
	Rigidity
	Deficits in empathy
	Substance abuse/dependence
	Physical health problems
	Physiological reactivity
Parent–child relationship	
Child factor	Difficult child behaviors
	Young age
	Physical and mental disabilities
Adult factor	Deficits in parenting skills
	Unrealistic expectations of children
	Parenting role is perceived as stressful
	Negative bias/perceptions regarding children
Family environment	Current abusive family practice (e.g., spouse abuse)
	Intergenerational abuse family practices (e.g., child abuse)
	Marital discord
	Few positive family interactions
Situational conditions	Low socioeconomic status
	Single-parent household
	Public assistance
	Blue-collar employment
	Unemployment or part-time work
	Situational stress (e.g., large family size)
	Social isolation and lack of social capital
Societal conditions	Cultural approval of violence in society
	Cultural approval of corporal punishment
	Power differentials in society and family

Note. Adapted from *Child Maltreatment: An Introduction* (2nd ed., p. 58) by C. L. Miller-Perrin and R. D. Perrin, 2007, Thousand Oaks, CA: Sage. Copyright 2007 Sage Publications. Adapted with permission. A representative but not exhaustive list of sources for information displayed in this table includes the following: D. A. Black et al. (2001a); Cappell & Heiner (1990); Caselles & Milner (2000); Coohey (2000); Finkelhor (1984); Gelles & Cornell (1990); McCloskey & Bailey (2000); Milner and Chilamkurti (1991); Sedlak & Broadhurst (1996); Whipple & Webster-Stratton (1991).

Gender

In the NIS-4 survey, 68% of the children were maltreated by a female and 48% were maltreated by a male; proportionally similar figures were found in the U.S. DHHS (2010) study: 53.8% by a female and 44.4% by a male. When the perpetrator was a birth parent, 75% were mothers and 43% were fathers (many were maltreated by both parents). Children who were maltreated by nonbiological parents or parents' partners were maltreated by males 64% of the time (Sedlak et al., 2010).

Furthermore, the NIS-4 survey found that different types of CM were associated with different patterns based on the sex of the offender.

- Child neglect was most often perpetrated by females (86% vs. 38% by males).
- Children were more likely to be sexually abused by males (87% vs. 11% by females).
- Fathers were more likely to physically abuse than mothers (62% and 41%, respectively).

Age

Across the majority of CM categories, the most common age groups for perpetrators were ages 26–35 and 35 years and up (Sedlak et al, 2010). The exceptions were perpetrators under 26 years of age who were not parents, were nonbiological parents, or were partners of parents.

Risk Factors

Perpetrators of CM are characterized by a number of factors that can assist in preventative and remedial interventions. Some of these characteristics differ across types of CM. However, several characteristics are present across all four types of CM when compared with nonabusive parents: depression, general interpersonal problems, low expression of positive behavior, stressed/low frustration tolerance, anxiety, history of child abuse, drug and substance abuse, and isolation (D. A. Black, Heyman, & Slep, 2001a, 2001b; Wolfe, 2006). These studies indicated that female perpetrators more often than male perpetrators tended to be depressed, anxious, and isolated. Having a history of child abuse and violence was consistently a strong predictor of CM for males. Substance use and abuse seems to be a problem with approximately equal numbers of men and women who maltreat their children and accounts for almost two thirds of child fatalities in the United States. For both men and women, stress and negative emotional arousal associated with low frustration tolerance interfered with rational problem solving (Mammen, Kolko, & Pilkonis, 2002). Parents who maltreat their children often have significant deficits in knowledge of normal child development, which results in unrealistic expectations for children (C. M. Rodriquez, 2010); in addition, these parents lack significant empathy and perspective-taking regarding their children (Francis & Wolfe, 2008).

Predominately Male Offenders

Of the four types of CM, CSA is perpetrated predominately by males (93%) and usually by someone other than biological parents (63%)—most often a person other than the nonbiological parent or partner of a parent (Sedlack et al., 2010). These offenders differ from other types of CM offenders in a number of ways but especially the predatory nature of their offense. Some suggest this predatory nature may be due to the fact that the majority of child sexual offenders begin developing a deviant interest and sexual preoccupation with children in childhood or adolescence (J. Sullivan & Beech, 2004). Many propose that this early interest is a result of being sexually abused as a child (Peter, 2009; Widom, 1995).

Other personal characteristics associated with male child sex offenders include poor impulse control (Cohen et al., 2002), intimacy and relationship deficits (Malamuth, 2003), and antisocial orientation (Hanson & Morton-Bourgon, 2005). Juvenile offenders also have the following characteristics: low self-esteem, social isolation, poor social skills, and poor family environment (Barbaree, Marshall, & McCormick, 1998). Hanson and Morton-Bourgon (2005) found that repeat male sex offenders had "(a) negative family background; (b) problems forming affectionate bonds with friends and lovers, and (c) attitudes tolerant of sexual assault" (p. 1155). Poor family environments and relationship deficits were common characteristics found in all studies.

Predominately Female Offenders

National studies indicate that females are more likely than males to neglect their children (Sedlak et al., 2010). This finding is most likely related to the fact that mothers and mother-substitutes most often are the primary caregivers of children as well as the person most likely to be held accountable for any deficits in child care or child rearing.

Other research found that physically abusive and neglectful parents tend to interact less positively with their children than nonneglecting parents (Crittenden, 1998). These parents are also less likely to talk and play with their children, to demonstrate warmth and caring, to show concern, or to exhibit nonverbal affection (Azar & Wolfe, 2006). Compared with nonabusive mothers, mothers who neglect and/or physically abuse their children have greater difficulty being physically and emotionally available to their children or engaging them in a positive manner. This difficulty may be related to a lack of these experiences in their own relationship histories (Garbarino & Collins, 1999) and to depression, low self-esteem, low social support, quality of current relationship, and poor impulse control (J. Brown et al., 1998).

There is growing concern that female perpetration of CSA may be more prevalent than the 7% (vs. 93% for males) attributed to females (Sedlack et al., 2010). Some research indicates that prevalence of female perpetration of CSA may reach as high as 20% (Peter, 2009). Many believe that the cultural expectation of male-only child sexual perpetrators has limited societies' ability to seriously consider females as child sexual abusers, especially if the victim is a male teenager (Boroughs, 2004; Peter, 2009).

On the basis of interviews with Canadian police officers and psychiatrists, Denov (2001) found that the gender of the offender is critical in defining sexual offense. The pervasive denial of women as sexual aggressors likely accounts for underrecognition and, thus, underreporting of the offense. In cases in which females have been identified as the perpetrator, some suggest that these women most often engage in CSA with a male coperpetrator (Davin, 1999); however, other research suggests that the majority of female perpetrators do not molest with a coperpetrator (Peter, 2005). As a result of societal denial, many female offenders reject that their sexual offenses are abusive or harmful to the children they victimize (Cloud,

1998; Fromuth & Conn, 1997). An example of this distortion is the Mary Kay Letourneau case. As a 35-year-old elementary school teacher, she had an ongoing sexual relationship with her 13-year-old male student that eventually resulted in the birth of two children (Cloud, 1998). She expressed little regret and repeatedly justified her actions as being based on mutual love between the couple.

More current examples of teachers who sexually abused their students include Pamela Turner, Kathy Denise White, and Debra Lafave (NBC, 2005). Turner and Lafave in particular received considerable media coverage because they are "attractive women." "I think people can't quite fathom why somebody so attractive wouldn't go for somebody who has more status and power," said Miriam Ehrenber, a psychology professor at John Jay College (NBC, 2005). Furthermore, female offenders often are treated more leniently by the criminal justice system than males. "In some ways, males are likely to be seen as more predatory and females more likely to be seen as having a mental health issue," said Dale Bespalec, child psychologist at the Milwaukee Secure Detention Facility (NBC, 2005).

A majority of female child sex offenders are in caretaking roles for their victims, such as parents, teachers, and child care workers (Roe-Sepowitz & Krysik, 2008; Vandiver & Kercher, 2004). They tend to sexually abuse younger children than do male offenders, although the severity of abuse does not differ between male and female offenders (Peter, 2009).

Finally, because of traditional sexual scripts of females as sexually passive, harmless, and innocent, some scholars portray female offenders as victims or accomplices to male perpetrators (M. Elliott, 1993; McCarty, 1986). More recently, some scholars have stated that female offenders should be viewed as perpetrators— and in some cases as pedophiles (Bunting, 2007)—not simply as victims (Denov, 2003; Nathan & Ward, 2002).

Internet Exploitation of Children

The problem of Internet exploitation has grown exponentially in recent years with the main-streaming of computers and the Internet. Research has found unintentional exposure to Internet pornography for 15- to 17-year-olds runs as high as 70% (Kanuga & Rosenfeld, 2004). In a national survey, Finkelhor and colleagues (Finkelhor, Mitchell, & Wolak, 2000; Wolak, Mitchel, & Finkelhor, 2003) conducted a phone interview with a random sample of 1,501 youths ages 10 to 17. Results found that 19% of the youths were regular targets of unwanted sexual solicitation, 25% received unwanted exposure to sexually explicit pictures, and 6% reported being harassed online. At greatest risk were girls, older teens, troubled youths, frequent Internet users, chat room participants, and those who communicated online with strangers.

A recent 2007 U.S. House staff report prepared for the Committee of Energy and Commerce, *Sexual Exploitation of Children Over the Internet,* noted key findings. Several of these include:

- The number of sexually exploitative images of children over the Internet is increasing, the victims are becoming younger, and the images are growing more violent.

- Estimates indicate that on any given day there may be more than 100,000 sites with commercially available child pornography, and this is likely a multi-billion dollar-a-year industry.
- The Federal Bureau of Investigation estimates that 50,000 child predators are online at any time searching for potential victims.
- Child predators who obtain sexually oriented images of children typically use them not only for self-gratification but also as a means to target potential victims for contact.

The Internet has provided more immediate access to potential victims and likely only will increase in sophistication for identifying and enticing vulnerable children and adolescents into participating in online child pornography or, worse, arranging meetings with sexual predators.

Known Offenders

More disturbing is research concerning the use of the Internet by family and acquaintances to perpetrate sexual crimes against family members who are minors. Mitchell, Finkelhor, and Wolak (2003) examined a national sample of law enforcement agencies' arrests for Internet-related sex crimes against minors. Results indicated that almost as many family members and acquaintance offenders as stranger offenders used the Internet to meet victims online. As do stranger offenders, family members and acquaintances used the Internet to seduce or groom, arrange meetings, reward victims, or advertise or sell victims (Wolak, Finkelhor, Mitchell, & Ybarra, 2008). Victims are vulnerable because of age and immaturity as well as because of the lure, familiarity, and easy access of the Internet.

Explanation for Child Sexual Abuse

Current typologies and explanations for child sex offenders are based almost exclusively on male offenders (O. Barnett et al., 2011). Early models suggested hormones and severe mental disorders such as psychosis, brain damage, and mental retardation as mediators of CSA (Money, 1961; Weinberg, 1955). More recent research suggests other mechanisms that contribute to CSA. O. Barnett et al. (2011) conducted a review of risk factors associated with CSA for both victims and perpetrators. Perpetrators' risk factors included the following:

- childhood physical and sexual abuse,
- antisocial behavior,
- poor impulse control,
- deviant sexual arousal arise by pairing sexual fantasies of children with masturbation,
- sensitive about sexual performance,
- feelings of inadequacy and powerlessness,
- cognitive distortions to justify behavior (e.g., sex with children is harmless or children provoke adults into sexual activities; R. Mann, Webster, Wakeling, & William, 2007),

- neurobiological deficits,
- lack of victim empathy, and
- insecure attachment with parents/caregivers.

Integrated Models

Other models include multiple contributors to explain CSA. Barbaree et al. (1998) proposed a model to explain the development of sexually deviant behavior in adolescence. The catalyst in this model is an abusive family experience that leads to a "syndrome of social disability." The syndrome includes the following factors that set the stage for the development of deviant sexual behavior: lack of attachment to parents, low self-esteem, impaired abilities to develop intimate relationships and empathy, and some degree of antisocial behavior.

A second model suggests that because of a poor parent–child relationship, a child may rely on sexual fantasies and sexualized behavior to deal with stressors in the environment that typically parents buffer (Starzyk & Marshall, 2003). Masturbation and other sexualized behaviors along with sexual fantasies about children include dimensions of power and control. These behaviors become deviant, leading to sexual offenses when the opportunity arises.

Covell and Scalora (2002) based their model on limited empathy, deficits in interpersonal and cognitive development, and sexual abuse. These factors contribute to a lack of interpersonal empathy and ultimately sex offenses.

Finkelhor (1984) proposed a process model emphasizing preconditions for sexual abuse (see Ferrara, 2002). The first precondition is the perpetrator's motivation to sexually abuse a child, which is based on such influences as early childhood conditioning, internalized modeled behavior, and/or some biological factors. In the second precondition, the perpetrator must override previously internalized restrictions on sexually abusive behavior. Substance use and/or mental disorders are two common factors that contribute to overriding these restrictions. A third precondition, overcoming external inhibitors, includes opportunities to abuse a child resulting from ineffective parenting, lack of adequate supervision, and/or an opportunity to be alone with a child. The fourth precondition is overcoming a child victim's resistance. As such, perpetrators seek child victims who are emotionally insecure, deprived, and powerless.

A poor parent–child relationship is the common factor across models. Poor attachment with parents may result in a child's failure to develop critical interpersonal skills, healthy self-soothing skills, cognitive coping skills, and self-regulation skills. Finally, being a CSA victim is one of the strongest contributors to becoming a CSA perpetrator (Whitaker et al., 2008).

Protective/Resiliency Factors and Mediators of the Effects of Child Maltreatment

Children do not all react the same to abuse and neglect, with some experiencing long-term consequences while others experience little or no apparent ill effects. Their response to stressful situations largely can be attributed to two broad categories of factors: (a) a child's internal capacities, such as temperament, age, and developmental skills; and (b) external and contextual factors, such as severity of stress, family support skills, and family stability (Masten & Coatsworth, 1998). The interplay of these factors often determines the effects of trauma and the child's ability to adapt to it. For example, a young child's response to a moderate to severe trauma is more dependent on the parent's response than an adolescent exposed to the same trauma. In the former case, if the parents cope well with the traumatic event then the child likely will not develop serious or extended symptoms. Conversely, a young child who is exposed to ongoing trauma related to parents' behavior (e.g., exposure to interparental violence or CSA by parent/ caregiver) will be more likely to develop more severe and longer-term symptoms. Thus, individual factors must be considered within particular contexts, such as degree of family support.

A child's ability to recover and cope with abuse (i.e., resilience) is moderated by several protective factors. Individual characteristics include optimism, self-esteem, intelligence, creativity, humor, and independence. Protective family factors are related to social support, especially from close relatives. For example, research has identified the following protective factors related to social support: a history of a secure parent–child relationship, parents' coping skills, emotional regulation (e.g., frustration tolerance) in relationships, self-efficacy, positive school experiences, and good peer relationships (Alink, Cicchetti, Kim, & Rogosch, 2009; Luthar, Cicchetti, & Becker, 2000). Specific family resiliency factors include authoritative parenting style, family cohesion, family expressiveness, and marital satisfaction. One study found three family factors associated with children's resiliency and exposure to IPV: healthy parenting, mother's mental health, and less exposure to severe IPV (Howell, Graham-Bermann, Czyz, & Lilly, 2010). In addition, peer support reduces negative consequences such as depression and anxiety for physically abused adolescents (Ezzell, Swenson, & Brondino, 2000).

In addition to distinguishing protective factors, researchers have also identified several mediators of the effects of child abuse. Sexual abuse by mothers to sons is more damaging to males than sexual abuse by the father (R. J. Kelly, Wood, Gonzalez, MacDonald, & Waterman, 2002). Also, the younger the child and the greater the duration of the abuse, the more severe the symptoms (Keiley, Howe, Dodge, Bates, & Pettit, 2001). One finding that is not surprising is that more frequent, severe, and chronic abuse is associated with more severe outcomes (van der Kolk et al., 2005). Furthermore, the more types of abuse experienced by the child, the greater the negative outcomes (Cook et al., 2005). When risk factors outweigh protective factors, the child's coping resources will deteriorate.

The following discussion focuses on the consequences of CM. Research does not always consider the unique context for CM; therefore, in reading the following it is important to note that not all maltreated children will experience the same short- or long-term consequences of CM. Individual cases vary on the basis of the following issues: (a) the child's age and developmental status when CM occurred; (b) the type of CM; (c) frequency, duration, and severity of CM; (d) social support; and (d) the relationship of the victim to the perpetrator (Chalk et al., 2002).

Consequences of Child Abuse and Neglect

Child abuse and neglect have broad-ranging physical, psychological, behavioral, and societal consequences (U.S. DHHS, 2010). These effects are often interrelated. For example, damage to a child's developing brain and nervous system because of physical injury, exposure to parental violence, or sexual abuse can result in psychological consequences such as cognitive delays, impulse control problems, or emotional problems. These psychological problems in turn often lead to high-risk behaviors, such as criminal behavior, both as a juvenile and as an adult (Classen et al., 2005). For example, CSA victims are 28 times more likely than nonabused children to be arrested for prostitution as adults (Widom & Ames, 1994). Furthermore, CSA victims have a 2 to 3 times greater risk of revictimization than nonabused children (Arata, 2002). Recurrence of CM takes place with up to 50% of children within 5 years after the first incident, with first-time victims being over 90% more likely to reexperience CM within 6 months than nonvictims (U.S. DHHS, 2010). Furthermore, if children experience one type of abuse, they are more likely to experience other types of co-occurring abuse (Finklehor et al., 2005). In addition, resulting depression and anxiety increase the risk of abusing alcohol or drugs, smoking, and overeating. Together, these influences can lead to long-term health problems, such as heart disease, obesity, cancer, and sexually transmitted diseases (U.S. DHHS, 2010).

Physical Health Consequences

Physical consequences of child abuse and neglect vary from minors cuts and bruises to severe injuries such as broken bones, extensive wounds, and even death. The following are some of the major health problems associated with child abuse and neglect.

Shaken Baby Syndrome

Shaken baby syndrome is a common type of injury to infants. The force of shaking an infant can result in severe whiplash, causing the tearing of the blood vessels and nerves in the head and neck as well as subdural hemorrhaging and long-term neurological problems (Watts-English, Fortson, Gibler, Hooper, & De Bellis, 2006). The immediate results of this syndrome include vomiting, concussion, failure to thrive, respiratory distress, seizures, and death. Even though not always immediately evident, longer term problems include blindness, learning disabilities, mental retardation, cerebral palsy, and paralysis (Conway, 1998).

Neurological Impairment

Neurological impairment is often a result of child abuse and neglect, particularly long-term (Perry, 2002). Normal brain and neurological–biological development are arrested, resulting in mental, physical, and emotional impairment (Ford, 2009). Children are particularly vulnerable to distress and trauma during the first 5 years of life because of rapid brain and neurological development. Chronic distress caused by CM can create persistent hyperarousal, resulting in problems in regulating emotions and behaviors, hyperactivity, anxiety, sleep disturbances, and increased susceptibility to PTSD (Perry, 2001). Also, physically and sexually abused children were found to have certain brain areas (e.g., cerebral, prefrontal cortex, and hippocampus) that were significantly smaller than nonabused children (Villarreal & King, 2004).

Physical Injuries and Health Problems

Extensive physical injuries and health problems are also associated with CM. The most common type of injury is skin lesions, followed by fractures (Kocher & Kasser, 2000). Thoraco-abdominal injuries are commonly caused by kicks and blows to the chest and abdomen (Myers, 1992). Burns are often associated with scalding hot water and hot objects. Abused children tend to have long-term physical and mental problems beyond the abuse (Perry, 2002), such as sexually transmitted diseases, heart disease, cancer, chronic lung disease, skeletal fractures, and liver disease (Hillis, Anda, Felitti, Nordenberg, & Marchbanks, 2000; Wang & Holton, 2007). Health problems often result from high-risk practices by parents or caregivers associated with abuse and neglect, such as promiscuous sex, smoking, illicit drug use, and poor health habits.

Psychological, Behavioral, and Interpersonal Consequences

Psychological Consequences

Child abuse and neglect have both immediate effects (e.g., fear, anger, and diminished ability to trust) and long-term effects (e.g., anxiety, depression, PTSD, and emotional regulation problems; Wang & Holton, 2007). Victims have been found to be more aggressive, defiant, and noncompliant (Cicchetti & Toth, 2005), even after controlling for poverty, family instability, and interparental violence (Fantuzzo, 1990). These effects are pervasive, with research indicating that up to 80% of young adults who were abused and neglected as children had diagnosable psychiatric disorders by age 21 (Silverman, Reinherz, & Giaconia, 1996). Such individuals experience high rates of depression, anxiety, eating disorders, self-harm behavior, and drug/alcohol abuse (Mahoney, Donnelly, Boxer, & Lewis, 2003). Research found that 81% of abused children exhibited either clinical or subclinical levels of PTSD (Runyon, Deblinger, & Schroeder, 2009).

Cognitive Difficulties

Cognitive difficulties are pervasive, with CM victims scoring lower than the general population on most measures of cognitive functioning, language development, memory, communication ability, and problem-solving skills (Cicchetti, & Toth, 2005). These children tend to perform poorly in school, with lower grades, lower standardized test scores, more learning disabilities, and greater retention than nonabused children (Stroufe, Egeland, Carlson, & Collins, 2005). Neglected children often perform more poorly than abused children (Kendall-Tackett & Eckenrode, 1996).

Behavioral Problems

Maltreated children have at least a 25% greater likelihood of being arrested for delinquency, adult criminal activity, and violent criminal behavior than nonabused children (Mallett, Dare, & Seck, 2009). They also have higher rates of drug and alcohol abuse than nonabused children (Swan, 1998). Furthermore, having been abused or neglected as a child increases the likelihood of being arrested as a juvenile by 59% and increases the likelihood of adult criminal behavior by 28% (Widom & Maxfield, 2001). Antisocial behavior and violence are the two most consistent results of child abuse and neglect (Yates, Carlson, & Egeland, 2008).

Interpersonal Difficulties

Abused and neglected children often exhibit significant social and interpersonal difficulties. They have difficulty forming friendships, exhibiting prosocial behavior with peers, and developing empathy and perspective taking (Burack et al., 2006). Poorly developed social skills and prosocial behavior may partially account for the tendency of these children to be rated as the most unpopular in their classes (Dodge, Pettit, & Bates, 1994) and to have great difficulty in making friends (K. P. Smith & Christakis, 2008). Research suggests that poor interpersonal relationships may be accounted for by difficulty discriminating emotional expressions of peers (Pollak, Cicchetti, Hornung, & Reed, 2000). Neglected children had greater difficulty discriminating emotions than did physically abused children. In a related manner, these children used limited social problem-solving skills, had difficulty identifying nonaggressive social solutions, and felt less concern for another child's distress. These patterns greatly impede stable and healthy attachments with peer, caregiver, and, later, romantic relationships (Cicchetti & Toth, 2005). As adults, these individuals often react to intimacy-demanding situations by withdrawal and avoidance (D. Barnett, Ganiban, & Cicchetti, 1999) and IPV (D. G. Dutton, 2007).

Early identification and intervention are critical to prevent or blunt the effects of CM. The longer these symptoms and problems go unaddressed, the greater the likelihood of long-term symptoms continuing into adulthood and the next generation of children (Cook et al., 2005). Table 11.3 provides the associated effects for the various types of CM.

Economic Consequences

The total economic burden of CM is over $124 billion per year in the United States—a figure based on CPS reports of 772,000 identified victims in 2008 (Fang, Brown, Florence, & Mercy, 2012). Retrospective studies note CM incidence totals 3 to 5 times this number, with the authors suggesting that actual costs may run as high as $585 billion per year. This estimate includes juvenile and adult criminal activity, mental health services, IPV, alcohol and substance abuse, child welfare services, special education services in schools, health care, school failure, lost productivity, and unemployment. This figure fails to account for the emotional and psychological consequences exacted from family members and significant others who are involved with people who have a history of child abuse or neglect.

Summary

CM has a long history in human culture. However, it was only in the early part of the 1900s that a few U.S. states enacted child protective statutes, and it was not until the 1960s that every state enacted mandated reporting by professionals for

Table 11.3

Effects Associated With Child Maltreatment

Type of Maltreatment	Physical/ Medical Effects	Emotional/Behavioral Effects	Social/Interpersonal Effects	Cognitive Effects
Physical	Bruises; head, chest, and abdominal injuries; burns; fractures; diminished brain development; compromised body stress system	Major depression; oppositional defiant disorder; conduct disorder; attention deficit/hyperactivity disorder; PTSD; suicidality; low self-esteem; aggression; fighting, noncompliance; defiance; violation of rights of others; arrests	Delayed play skills; infant attachment problems; poor social interaction skills; peer rejection; deficits in social competence with peers; avoidance of adults; difficulty making friends; deficits in prosocial behavior; hopelessness	Decreased intellectual and cognitive functioning; deficits in verbal skills, memory, problem-solving, and perceptual–motor skills; decreased reading and math skills; poor academic achievement
Sexual	Bruises; genital bleeding; genital pain; genital itching; problems walking and sitting; sleep disturbance; eating disturbance; enuresis; encopresis; stomachache; headache	Anxiety; clinging; nightmares; fears; depression; guilt; hostility/anger; tantrums; aggression; phobias; obsessions; suicidality; difficulty recognizing and discriminating emotions; low self-esteem; CPTSD; PTSD; sexual victimization of others; delinquency; substance abuse; stealing; dropping out of school	Violation of rights of others; poor peer relationships; problems trusting others; social isolation; feelings of alienation; difficulty forming relationships; sexual victimization of others; sexual and physical revictimization	Learning problems; poor concentration; poor attention; declining grades; negative perceptions
Neglect	Death; failure to thrive	Apathy; withdrawal; low self-esteem; poor coping skills; negative affect; physical and verbal aggression; attention problems; conduct problems; anxiety; depression	Disrupted parent–child attachment and interactions; lacking in prosocial behavior; social withdrawal; few friendships	Deficits in receptive and expressive language; overall poor academic performance; deficits in overall intelligence, creativity, and malleability in problem solving; low performance in language comprehension and verbal abilities

(Continued)

207

Table 11.3 (Continued)
Effects Associated With Child Maltreatment

Type of Maltreatment	Physical/Medical Effects	Emotional/Behavioral Effects	Social/Interpersonal Effects	Cognitive Effects
Psychological	Physical symptoms; somatic complaints; hypertension; metabolic syndrome	Aggression; hostility; disruptive classroom behavior; lack of impulse control; self-abusive behavior; low self-esteem; anxiety and PTSD; shame and guilt; conduct disorder; hyperactivity; self-abusive behavior; distractibility; juvenile delinquency; negative outlook; suicidal behavior; interpersonal sensitivity; dissociation; sexual problems; eating disorders	Disturbed parent–child attachment; low social competence and adjustment; difficulty making and maintaining friendships; difficulty with peers	Academic problems; deficits in problem solving; lack of creativity; difficulty learning; declines in intellectual ability and low educational achievement
Exposure to interparental violence	Obesity; somatic symptoms; failure to thrive	Anxiety; depression; posttraumatic symptoms; low self-esteem; aggressive behaviors; poor academic performance; eating disorders	Deficits in interpersonal skills; aggressive behaviors; hostility in interpersonal relationships; reduced empathy	Poor academic performance; impaired problem-solving skills and conflict resolution skills; cognitive deficits; hypervigilance; impaired memory

Note. CPTSD = complex posttraumatic stress disorder; PTSD = posttraumatic stress disorder. Information from Brassard & Donovan (2006); Cicchetti & Barnett (1991); Conron et al. (2009); Crittenden et al. (1994); De Bellis (2001); de Paul & Arruabarrena (1995); Dubowitz et al. (1993); Edleson et al. (2003); Erickson & Egeland (2010); Finkelhor et al. (2005); Gibb et al. (2007); R. Gilbert et al. (2008); Hildyard & Wolfe (2002); Kaufman & Widom (1999); Manly et al. (2001); Putnam (2003); Pollak et al. (2000); Schneider et al. (2005); Sedlak et al. (2010); Rogosch et al. (1995); and Widom (1989).

cases of child abuse. Currently, the various types of CM (physical abuse, sexual abuse, psychological abuse, and neglect) have been specifically defined, but there is still disagreement on those definitions. However, psychological abuse is often the most difficult type of child abuse to prove, and identifying enforceable child neglect is often more challenging because of mitigating factors such as culture, poverty, and community standards.

Prevalence rates of CM vary somewhat because of sampling methods (e.g., CPS-reported abuse vs. adult retrospective reports of abuse), and yet across studies, statistics indicate that CM has remained stable or has declined. For example, DHHS studies report that between 1992 and 1999, sexual abuse decreased by 31%. However, some CM experts are skeptical about these reported reductions and attribute the decreases to a reduction in reporting of actual cases rather than a reduction in abuse cases. These same researchers suggest a greater need for studies to examine reporting practices. Finkelhor et al. (1997) suggested that self-reports by adults who were abused as children are the most accurate results and provide the highest estimates of CM. Estimates by social service organizations and mandated reporting (e.g., DHHS) are viewed as the most plagued by underreporting.

Several trends have emerged from victim characteristics. Younger children under age 8 are the most vulnerable and account for nearly 50% of the maltreatment cases, whereas children ages 6–11 are the age group with the highest risk of CM. In addition, females are at the greatest risk of sexual maltreatment, whereas males are at greatest risk for physical abuse and the most severe forms of physical abuse. Some studies have reported differences in CM rates on the basis of race and ethnicity (e.g., DHHS) whereas other have not (e.g., NIS). Factors most frequently associated with all forms of CM include low SES, social isolation, single-parent families, poor parent–child relationship, and harsh disciplinary actions. Conversely, protective factors against CM include family cohesion, family expressiveness, and marital satisfaction.

Perpetrators tend to be a parent or relative, are more likely to be female than male, are likely to report various psychological and interpersonal problems, and are more liable to have abused substances. However, males are more likely to engage in child sexual maltreatment, whereas females are more liable to engage in child neglect.

A recently emerging context for CSA is the Internet. Existing research indicates that family members and acquaintances are as likely as strangers to use the Internet to abuse children. In addition, it appears the Internet has likely contributed to an increase in child pornography.

Finally, the various forms of CM have extensive and long-term effects on child victims that often extend into adulthood. In addition to neurological impairment and physical injury, compared with nonmaltreated children, maltreated children have significantly more and longer-term psychological, behavioral, and interpersonal problems.

Future research must include greater focus on CM and the Internet. Such research should include identifying perpetrator and victim characteristics as well as promoting new legislation and prevention strategies to protect children and adolescents. Furthermore, until recently, the issue of males suffering from sexual maltreatment and females being sexual perpetrators has been obfuscated by societal biases about women and young males. Future research must obtain more accurate information about the prevalence of sexual maltreatment of males and female sexual perpetrators as well as the characteristics of female perpetrators and male victims.

Suggested Readings

Barnett, O., Miller-Perrin, C. L., & Perrin, R. D. (2011). *Family violence across the lifespan: An introduction* (2nd ed.). Thousand Oaks, CA: Sage.

Black, D. A., Heyman, R. E., & Slep, A, M. S. (2001a). Risk factors for child physical abuse. *Aggression and Violent Behavior, 6,* 121–188.

Black, D. A., Heyman, R. E., & Slep, A, M. S. (2001b). Risk factors for child sexual abuse. *Aggression and Violent Behavior, 6,* 203–229.

Cook, A., Spinazzola, J., Ford, J., Lanktree, C., Blaustein, M., Cloitre, M., . . . van der Kolk, B. (2005). Complex trauma in children and adolescents. *Psychiatric Annals, 35,* 390–398.

Finkelhor, D., Ormrod, R., Turner, H., & Hamby, S. L. (2005). The victimization of children and youth: A comprehensive, national survey. *Child Maltreatment: Journal of the American Professional Society on the Abuse of Children, 10,* 2–5.

Kanuga, M., & Rosenfeld, W. D. (2004). Adolescent sexuality and the Internet: The good, the bad, and the URL. *Journal of Pediatric and Adolescent Gynecology, 17,* 117–124.

McClennen, J. C. (2010). *Social work and family violence: Theories, assessment, and intervention.* New York, NY: Springer.

Miller-Perrin, C. L., & Perrin, R. L. (2007). *Child maltreatment: An introduction.* Thousand Oaks, CA: Sage.

chapter 12

Assessment and Treatment for Child Maltreatment

CM victims, including those exposed to interparental violence, are at risk for significant psychological and physical symptoms. Common symptoms include PTSD, anxiety, depression, interpersonal problems, intrusive thoughts, hyper-arousal, and a host of personality-related problems (Finkelhor et al., 2005). This chapter reviews the treatment process for CM and addresses issues related to assessment, diagnosis (especially for PTSD), and individual and family inter-ventions. Particular emphasis is placed on phase-based treatments that typically include the following phases: stabilizing the client, processing the traumatic experience, cognitive processing, and consolidating learning and enhancing re-siliency.

PTSD symptoms can be especially difficult to identify and treat without a thorough knowledge of the disorder and appropriate training. The plastic-ity of the brain and nervous system make children particularly vulnerable to PTSD as compared with adults. Children are 1.5 to 2 times more likely than adults to be diagnosed with PTSD following a traumatic experience (Fletcher, 1996). However, youths often are underdiagnosed when standard diagnostic protocols are used. Miele and O'Brien (2010) found that general assessment procedures found baseline PTSD diagnoses in residential and outpatient agen-cies to be 2.3% and 5.4%, respectively, whereas trauma-focused interviews in the same settings identified PTSD in 47.7% and 44.6% of these cases, re-spectively. Children and adolescents often are not forthcoming with pertinent diagnostic information about symptoms unless asked about specific trauma-based symptoms. The therapeutic alliance is especially critical for obtaining accurate information about PTSD.

PTSD Risk Factors

Several characteristics are associated with increased risk of PTSD after exposure to traumatic stress (see Table 12.1).

Failure to treat victims of CM may result in more pronounced and chronic problems that continue into adulthood (van der Kolk et al., 2005). A longitudinal study following abused and neglected youths found that only one fifth had successful employment, less than half graduated from high school, and over half had psychiatric symptoms (McGloin & Widom, 2001).

Historically, two primary methods have been used in dealing with CM: removal and rehabilitation (Faller, 2011). In 2009, approximately one fifth (124,000) of CM victims were removed from their homes (U.S. DHHS, 2010). Approximately two thirds of these children were placed in foster care while one third of the children were placed with a relative. Sadly, for many of these children, placements are a long-term way of life and entail multiple moves (Faller, 2011). Many of these children receive counseling services as part of the placement plan.

Counseling Effectiveness

In addition to empirically based interventions (see section below titled Empirically Supported Treatments), there are several interventions that are based on theory and clinical wisdom; though these interventions generally have only preliminary empirical support, they do appeal to logic and common sense. Two such programs are Homebuilders (Littell, 2001) and Minding the Baby (Slade, Sadler, & Mayes, 2005). Homebuilders provide intense, short-term treatment (4–6 weeks) for children 0–17 years of age who are at risk for placement in foster care or other out-of-home placements. The goal of treatment is to reduce child abuse and neglect, family conflict, and severe child behavior problems through teaching parents and family members conflict-resolution and relationship-building skills

Table 12.1
Factors Associated With Increased Risk for PTSD

- Being female
- Being a younger or older individual (vs. an individual in middle adulthood)
- Being African American or Hispanic (vs. European American)
- Having a low socioeconomic status
- Having previous psychological problems and dysfunction
- Possessing subfunctional coping skills
- Having a history of family dysfunction
- Having a genetic predisposition
- Having a prior history of trauma
- Experiencing greater distress at the time of the traumatic experience or immediately following

Note. PTSD = posttraumatic stress disorder. Information from Brady et al. (2000); Breslau et al. (2004); Brewin et al. (2000); Briere & Scott (2006); Fauerbach et al. (2002); Feiring et al. (2002); Hamby & Skupien (1998); Koenen et al. (2002); Leskin & Sheikh (2002); Ozer et al. (2003); Putnam (2003); Rosenman (2002); and Stein et al. (2002).

in-home. The clinical staff is available 24 hours a day, 7 days a week for in-home visits and phone consultation. The program has some evidence-based research supporting its effectiveness. Minding the Baby (MTB; Slade et al., 2005) is an 18-month prenatal program that uses weekly community-based home visits for high-risk first-time mothers living in urban poverty. Most of the mothers have histories of trauma, abandonment, and loss. The goal of treatment is to enhance physical/medical and mental health. The nurse visitation component has a long history of success and empirical support in working with medically at-risk mothers and children. The mental health component focuses on developing a healthy attachment between infant, mother, and the extended family. The home visitation team is composed of a mental health worker and a pediatric nurse. Weekly visits typically are 60–90 minutes in length and alternate between visits by the nurse and mental health worker. Preliminary evidence of effectiveness is encouraging. Another program, Parents Anonymous (2008), has been active since the 1960s and provides group interventions for parents who physically abuse their children. These programs try to rehabilitate or prevent physical abuse, emotional abuse, and neglect.

Empirically Supported Treatments

Current evidence-based interventions to treat CM and traumatized children have been adapted from models used to treat abused and traumatized adults (e.g., Skills Training in Affective and Interpersonal Regulation/Narrative Story Telling; Cloitre et al., 2002). The following discussion centers on evidenced-based treatments for CM for children who meet partial or full criteria for PTSD. Comparable treatments often are used with acute stress disorder clients (Briere & Scott, 2006). Children who experience a single case of mild to moderate maltreatment may experience low or negligible symptoms. These children often benefit from adapted and abbreviated forms of the treatments discussed below.

The National Child Traumatic Stress Network (NCTSN, 2012) currently lists 40 acceptable trauma-focused interventions with accompanying descriptions of the treatment model components, research evidence and outcomes, target population, cultural sensitivity, training materials, contact information, and references. Well over one half of the listed intervention models are still in development and have little evidence of effectiveness. Those approaches with the strongest evidence are emphasized here, the majority of which have a strong family systems and CBT base. Approaches such as play therapy, although widely used with abused children, have little supporting evidence; nevertheless, the Office of Victims of Crime considers it a "promising and acceptable treatment" (B. E. Saunders, Berliner, & Hanson, 2004). The NCTSN does not include play therapy in their list of acceptable treatments but does include parent–child interaction therapy (PCIT), which includes play therapy as a treatment component.

In a thorough evaluation of effective psychosocial treatments for children and adolescents who have experienced traumatic conditions, W. K. Silverman, Pina, and Viswesvaran (2008) examined 21 psychosocial treatment studies involving children who had been exposed to traumatic events. These researchers examined the studies' methodological rigor and level of evidence for effectiveness. Trauma-focused cognitive–behavioral therapy (TF-CBT) was the only treatment determined to be a well-established treatment, and school-based group CBT was determined to be a probably efficacious treatment. Examples of those psychosocial treatments that were determined to be possibly efficacious were as follows: cognitive processing therapy, eye movement desensitization reprocessing, client-centered therapy, family therapy, parent–child psychotherapy, and CBT for PTSD. The authors also conducted a meta-analysis and determined that CBT approaches were more effective than non-CBT approaches (e.g., client-centered child therapy). However, both CBT and non-CBT approaches were more effective than no treatment. Other studies identified TF-CBT, abuse-focused CBT (AF-CBT; now called alternatives for families: CBT), and PCIT as meeting the criteria for best practices with abused children and adolescents (Faller, 2011).

An exception to the above-mentioned findings came from a meta-analytic study conducted by Skowron and Reinemann (2005). They found that nonbehavioral treatment approaches ($n = 3$; $d = .87$) produced larger treatment effects than did the behavioral treatment approaches ($n = 12$, $d = .40$). They encouraged caution in interpreting these results because of the small number of nonbehavioral studies and the difference in length of treatment between the two types of approaches. The nonbehavioral approaches averaged 1 year of treatment compared with 3 months for the behavioral treatments. Treatment length is particularly relevant given that a number of CM studies have found CBT to be superior to nondirective supportive or child-centered therapies with relatively brief duration (12–16 weeks; J. A. Cohen et al., 2005; W. K. Silverman et al., 2008).

Effectiveness of Cognitive–Behavioral and Family Interventions

Notwithstanding Skowron and Reinemann (2005), comparison studies support CBT models that include parent/family-based components over nonbehavioral ones for treating CM (W. K. Silverman et al., 2008). J. A. Cohen, Mannarino, and Deblinger's (2006) TF-CBT is the only treatment model—of nine that were rated—for CM to receive the top ranking of 1 (well-supported, efficacious treatment) by the National Crime Victims Research and Treatment Center (B. F. Saunders et al., 2004).

On the basis of an evaluation of existing trauma-focused interventions, NCTSN (2012) listed several common components across treatments:

- using screening and triage;
- using systematic assessment, case conceptualization, and treatment planning;
- providing psychoeducation about trauma and related symptoms;
- addressing children's and families' traumatic stress reactions and experiences;
- using trauma narration and organization;
- enhancing emotional regulation and anxiety management skills;
- facilitating adaptive coping and maintaining adaptive routines;
- teaching parenting skills and behavior management;
- promoting adaptive developmental progression;

- addressing grief and loss;
- promoting safety skills;
- using relapse prevention techniques;
- evaluating treatment response and effectiveness; and
- engaging and addressing barriers to service-seeking.

The Intervention section below largely draws from TF-CBT, AF-CBT, and PCIT. Each approach has unique components that distinguish it from the other two, and yet all three address many of the above components. For example, AF-CBT is most appropriate for physical abuse with school-age children, whereas PCIT can also be used with children as young as 2. Conversely, TF-CBT has been shown to be most effective with children who have been sexually abused, although it has been used effectively with physical abuse and other trauma circumstances.

TF-CBT

TF-CBT is a short-term approach (12–16 sessions) for treating preschool children, school-age children, and adolescents with any type of trauma, including multiple traumas, who exhibit PTSD symptoms, depression, behavior problems, and other problems related to trauma (J. A. Cohen, Mannarino, & Deblinger, 2006). TF-CBT is informed by theories based on attachment, CBT, humanistic psychology, and family therapy. The authors also developed a similar model for treating child traumatic grief. TF-CBT is composed of several core treatment components that are intended to be implemented in a flexible manner tailored to the unique needs of each child and family:

- psychoeducation about childhood trauma and PTSD;
- parenting component, including parent management skills;
- relaxation skills individualized to the child and parent;
- affective modulation skills adapted to the child, family, and culture;
- cognitive coping: connecting thoughts, feelings, and behaviors related to the trauma;
- trauma narrative: assisting the child in sharing a verbal, written, or artistic narrative about the trauma(s) and related experiences, and cognitive and affective processing of the trauma experiences; in vivo exposure and mastery of trauma reminders if appropriate;
- conjoint parent–child sessions to practice skills and enhance trauma-related discussions; and
- improvement of personal safety and enhancement of optimal developmental trajectory through providing safety and social skills training as needed. (NCTSN, 2012, p. 2)

AF-CBT

AF-CBT is a short-term therapy (3–6 months) focused on addressing child physical abuse for school-age children (Koklo & Swenson, 2002). The approach is based on CBT, family therapy, and developmental victimology. Goals of treatment include the following: reducing parental anger and violence, teaching nonaggressive parenting skills, eliminating or reducing physical violence, enhancing children's and parents' coping skills, and enhancing prosocial problem solving and communication in the family. AF-CBT includes three phases: (a) psychoeducation and engagement, (b) individual and family skills training, and (c) application of skills in real-world situations. Treatment interventions focus on changing cognitions, behavior, and emotions and include the following:

- training in techniques to identify, express, and manage emotions appropriately (e.g., anxiety management, anger control);
- training in interpersonal skills to enhance social competence;
- identifying child's exposure to and views of family hostility, coercion, and violence; and
- identifying views on violence, physical punishment, and sources of stress.

Interventions for parents include the following:

- understanding the role of parental and family stressors that may contribute to conflict;
- identifying and managing reactions to abuse-specific triggers, heightened anger, anxiety, and depression to promote self-control; and
- training in effective discipline strategies (e.g., time-out, attention reinforcement).

Interventions for families include the following:

- discussing a no-violence agreement;
- clarifying attributions of responsibility for the abuse and developing safety plans;
- training in communication skills to encourage constructive interactions;
- training in nonaggressive problem-solving skills, with home practice applications;
- involving community and social systems; and
- training in nonaggressive problem-solving skills, with home practice applications. (Child Welfare Information Gateway, 2007)

PCIT

PCIT is a short-term therapy (12–20 sessions) that focuses on changing the negative interactions between parents and children. PCIT was originally developed for severe externalizing behavior with children ages 2–7. It is currently being used with children up to age 12 for whom physical violence occurs within the context of child discipline (Chaffin et al., 2004). PCIT is unique among child intervention models in that the therapist coaches the parent while the parent is interacting with the child. The therapist observes from behind a one-way mirror using a live audio device and guides the parent to interact in positive and effective ways with the child. Parents are provided with real-time, ongoing feedback, including corrections, throughout the 30- to 45-minute coaching sessions. PCIT is composed of two primary phases. In the child-directed interaction phase, parents are coached in filial play therapy with their child not to direct, ask questions, criticize, or use negative statements (e.g., "no," "don't," "quit," or "stop") and to ignore annoying behavior (unless it's dangerous or destructive); the intent is to enhance a nurturing and positive attachment with the child. Parents are taught skills represented by the acronym PRIDE:

- Praise,
- Reflection,
- Imitation,
- Description, and
- Enthusiasm.

In the parent-directed interaction phase, parents are taught to give clear, simple commands and to provide consistent consequences for positive and negative behavior. When children obey a command, they are given a labeled praise (e.g., "Thank you for putting the crayon in the box"). When they fail to obey, they are given a warning and a choice, such as "If you don't put the crayon in the box you will go to time-out." Failure to obey after the warning results in the child going to a time-out chair. Children who refuse to stay in time-out chairs are placed in a safe time-out room. The ultimate goal is to obtain compliance from the child, not to punish the child. Parents are taught to spend more time reinforcing positive behavior and less time disciplining the child. Termination is contingent on the parents' ability to demonstrate appropriate child-directed and parent-directed interaction skills along with the child's compliance (McNeil & Hembree-Kigin, 2010).

In addition to the above approaches, most clinical researchers believe that these trauma-based treatments are most effective when presented in a phase-based manner (Ford, 2009). Major phases include the creation of a safe and caring environment for the child and family, followed by treatment phases focusing on skill development, emotional regulation, trauma process, and integration (see discussion of treatment phases later in this chapter).

The following discussion focuses on the above-mentioned interventions as well as important context factors for successful treatment. Many of the concepts and interventions are similar to the treatment of adult victims of IPV and sexual assault (see Chapters 9 and 10). Adjustments in treatment must be made to accommodate different developmental levels of children and adolescents (E. J. Brown, Albrecht, McQuaid, Munoz-Silva, & Silva, 2004).

Creating a Context for Treatment

Faust and Katchen (2004) suggested the importance of the following four real-world factors in treating children exposed to traumatic situations:

1. *Safe environment/survival.* Has the child or the threat of perpetration been removed from the threatening environment? Without a safe environment,

the child is constantly exposed to traumatizing circumstances, which not only exacerbates the child's symptoms but also renders any type of treatment less effective. Such a situation may necessitate the involvement of CPS, law enforcement, and the court system. Even when counselors have been assured that appropriate safety steps have been taken, they must remain vigilant to make sure that the child is not being exposed to the perpetrator surreptitiously or accidentally. An indicator of this possibility is a lack of therapeutic progress during treatment, regardless of the intervention. In some circumstances, counselors may have few options other than to provide treatment to children who experience on-going traumas (J. A. Cohen, Mannarino, & Murray, 2011).

2. *Safe relocation.* It is not uncommon for maltreated children to experience one or several changes of residence during their involvement in treatment. Foster home placement can be particularly trying as it often entails living with a family previously unknown to the child. Relocation may also result in the child losing personal property, such as clothing, toys, and other valued mementos. In addition, whether real or imagined, relocation may cause a child to worry about his or her safety and general welfare. Counselors must be sensitive to these issues and be prepared to address them if they hope for some degree of success in treatment.

3. *Grief reaction.* In more complex trauma circumstances, children may experience significant loss because (a) the child is removed from the family home, (b) a significant relative is removed from the home, or (c) a caregiver dies or a significant relationship ends. These losses may trigger strong grief reactions that tap into survival impulses for the child. These experiences must be addressed prior to focal work on the traumatic stress and throughout treatment if they reemerge. (Cohen, Mannarino, & Deblinger, 2006)

4. *Risk and protective factors.* Many of the protective factors and issues associated with risk were noted in Chapter 11, and yet a few warrant further discussion. The age of the child must be taken into account in planning treatment. Very young children may be incapable of participating in cognitive–behavioral interventions. Other treatment interventions such as the child-directed interaction phase of PCIT may be more effective initially, although TF-CBT has been used successfully with children as young as 3, with a few adaptations to age (Scheeringa, Weems, Cohen, Amaya-Jackson, & Guthrie, 2011). The child's emotional and cognitive development level must be factored into the treatment plan. Disorganized and chaotic families do not foster the stable, predictable, and safe environment that is necessary for successful treatment of the child (Faust & Katchen, 2004); therefore, treatment may include conjoint family sessions using family approaches such as structural and/or strategic family therapy to create a more stable home/family environment for focused trauma work.

Several resilience factors are particularly relevant to target in treatment: (a) a secure attachment and connection with emotionally supportive adults, (b) cognitive and self-regulation skills, (c) positive self-concept, (d) internal and external motivation to behave efficaciously, and (e) parenting warmth and structure and high expectations for the child (Masten, 2001; Wyman, Sandler, Wolchik, & Nelson, 2000).

Optimal levels of these factors tend to protect and temper the effects of the trauma. Treatment problems increase in the absence or insufficiency of these factors.

Therapeutic Alliance

A fifth critical factor is the working alliance and trust between the child and counselor and the counselor and family. A warm and supportive environment is essential for the child to feel safe enough to deal with trauma material. A strong alliance in the initial phase of treatment predicts success in the middle phase— trauma exposure processing (Cloitre et al., 2002)—whereas a weak alliance is associated with less positive treatment outcomes (Dalenberg, 2004). In addition, a trusting counselor–child relationship is a singular component of healing of itself (Courtois, 2008). Although less research exists about the therapeutic alliance than the more directive and structured interventions, children and counselors rate the therapeutic relationship as more important than specific techniques (Kazdin, Siegel, & Bass, 1990).

The therapeutic relationship with children must be developed on the basis of their specific needs and history. Building an alliance with a child who has experienced extensive and longstanding maltreatment in an unstable environment will be different from building an alliance with a child from a stable family who experienced a single episode of abuse. In the former situation, the child will likely be more mistrustful, cautious, and anxious if he or she initially receives strong expressions of warmth and kindness from the counselor. Instead, the counselor should provide measured warmth and a predictable environment with appropriate structure to match the child's level of trust. It is unreasonable to expect a severely traumatized child to quickly trust the counselor simply because he or she presents as a trustworthy and caring person (Cook et al., 2005).

The therapeutic alliance is central to treatment regardless of the approach and interventions used. It is the substrate for all treatment interventions. The overt focus of the alliance will ebb and flow throughout treatment. At times counselors will directly address their relationship with the child and parents, particularly at sticking points such as feelings of shame or ambivalence about continuing treatment or when the counselor may have challenged clients beyond their level of tolerance. At other times when trust is adequate, greater focus will be placed on skill building or facilitating interaction between parents and child.

Attention to Attachment Style

Some attachment researchers suggest that anger is commonly associated with insecurely attached children (Klohnen & John, 1998). These children engage in demand–withdraw reactions when they encounter disruption in a significant relationship or intimacy-demanding relationship (Hesse & Main, 2000; Schore, 2003). They may reject a counselor's attempts of closeness by avoidance and distrust. Failing to understand the child's rejecting response, the counselor might respond with anxiety or even anger and thus validate the child's expectation of abandonment (Dalenberg, 2004).

With these insecurely attached children, counselors should provide nondemanding warmth and appropriate structure without reacting to the child's rejection and anger. This type of response is more likely to initiate a relationship substrate for developing a therapeutic alliance with the child. It is best exemplified by Winnicott's (1965) concept of providing a "holding environment" for a child in the face of their protest. The counselor provides consistent warmth and structure that is moderated on the basis of the child's ability to trust and to be increasingly more emotionally vulnerable. With more severe CM, developing even a minimal alliance may take more time and effort than with children and adolescents who have less severe maltreatment histories.

Strengths and Solution Behaviors

The child's strengths and solution behaviors can be easily overlooked when dealing with trauma experiences because of the magnitude of the trauma symptoms. However, identifying and exploring these aspects can aid both in developing the therapeutic alliance and in developing a scaffolding upon which to build and expand coping skills. Such a focus also enhances the client's hope and self-esteem (Cryder, Kilmer, Tedeschi, & Calhoun, 2006). A child's awareness that he or she has "done some things right" can be used at a later point in treatment to challenge distorted thoughts that emphasize self-blame, lack of efficacy, and discouragement.

The opportunity for posttraumatic growth (PTG) has been noted in studies with adults and children (Milam, Ritt-Olson, & Unger, 2004; Tedeschi & Calhoun, 2004), although no study currently exists with CM. PTG is a constructive change experienced as a result of struggle with major loss or trauma and is related to (a) the ability to cognitively process negative events to derive positive appraisals, (b) the availability and use of positive support, and (c) positive appraisals of a person's ability to manage and adjust to a stressful situation (Cryder et al., 2006).

For children who have a history of maltreatment, the idea of possessing strengths, finding existing solutions, and experiencing PTG may be totally foreign. Counselors may begin by planting the seeds of strength and existing solutions in the initial interview and may return to them at later points in the counseling process as the child can accommodate this new information. Counselors should strive to balance treatment focus on existing strengths, resources, and other protective factors with external-focused interventions. To the degree clients recognize their preexisting resources as vehicles for change beyond treatment, they will enhance their sense of self-efficacy rather than viewing themselves as weak and totally dependent on others for change.

Counseling Process

The majority of CM treatment models focus on trauma symptoms, particularly posttrauma symptoms and related symptoms such as depression, anxiety, reexperiencing/intrusive thoughts, hyperarousal, and avoidance behaviors (J. A. Cohen, Mannarino, Berliner, & Deblinger, 2000). These models address symptom reduction with abuse-specific cognitive behavioral techniques, such as psychoeducational interventions, anxiety management skills training, and coping-skills training as well as conjoint parent–child work. Regardless of which treatment model is used, interventions must be adjusted for type of maltreatment (i.e., sexual, physical, neglect, psychological, or emotional), the severity and frequency of the abuse, comorbidity, and the relationship of the perpetrator to the victim. Multimodal treatment (individual, family, and group) and integration of a limited number of empirical approaches (e.g., CBT, psychoeducation, and family therapy) are often required with more severe cases. Treatment may occur in different settings, such as inpatient, outpatient, or partial inpatient. Pharmacological treatments may also be appropriate with some children.

Assessment

Before beginning the assessment process it is important to determine whether CPS and law enforcement have completed their forensic investigations. A forensic investigation has the primary intent of determining whether the child was maltreated and, if so, identifying the perpetrator. Forensic interviewers use special kinds of techniques that are not leading or suggesting to ensure that information is admissible in court. Clinical interviews, on the other hand, may use leading questions to examine the impact of the CM (Pearce & Pezzot-Pearce, 2007). Conducting a clinical interview prior to a forensic interview can contaminate the forensic interview and possibly render information obtained in the interview inadmissible in court.

History of the Presenting Problem
Effective treatment must be preceded by a thorough assessment to determine the level of posttraumatic stress symptoms and other context variables. This information will influence the choice of treatment interventions. Counselors should gather information about the reason for the referral, specific concerns and symptoms, and a thorough history of the problem. Cook, Blaustein, Spinazzalo, and van der Kolk (2003) suggested that a history of the problems include the following:

- a developmental history of the child, family, and trauma;
- attachment relationships with the child and primary caregivers;
- involvement of CPS and any placements;
- illnesses, losses, separation/abandonment by parents;
- parent/family mental illness;
- substance abuse;
- legal history;
- strengths and coping skills of child and family; and
- extra-family stressors (e.g., community violence, economic issues, employment).

In addition, it is important to identify any preexisting symptoms and disorders and determine how they may interact with maltreatment symptoms.

Trauma Assessment

To assess for traumatic experiences, Pynoos, Steinberg, and Goenjian (1996) suggested that at minimum assessments should include the following: (a) a clear description of objective and subjective features of the traumatic episode(s); (b) a determination of type and frequency of trauma reminders and their expected future occurrence; and (c) an in-depth enumeration of current and potential secondary stressors, such as resulting medical care, surgery, relocation, change of financial status, or change in school functioning. Also, counselors should investigate the circumstances under which the trauma was disclosed, responses of the family and other relevant people, safety issues, and the child's feelings about the traumatic experience.

Victim's Subjective Experience of Trauma

During the assessment process it is important for counselors, parents, and other support persons to appreciate the child's subjective experience and response in the aftermath of trauma. Factors that are predictive of overall severity of PTSD include experiencing an increased level of fear of dying, being upset over one's reactions to the trauma, and feeling guilt over dangerous behavior (Andrews, Brewin, Rose, & Kirk, 2000). Particular themes are limited only by the child's experience and creativity. Some of these experiences will be easily identified in an initial interview, whereas many will emerge over time.

Caregivers' Responses

Caregivers must learn to be aware of their child's stress reactions and how to help the child process them without smothering or hovering over the child. Appropriate caregiver behavior is a major challenge in treating a traumatized child, as parents may be secondarily traumatized by the continual awareness of the child's trauma or they may be simultaneously dealing with their own trauma, such as a case of IPV against a parent.

Objective Aspects of Trauma Assessment

In addition to assessing a victim's subjective experience of a trauma, certain identifiable circumstances beyond the child have been shown to be associated with PTSD symptoms in children. The following is a list of objective aspects of trauma that are associated with the onset and continuation of PTSD symptoms with children:

- exposure to a direct life-threatening event;
- injury to self;
- witnessing a mutilating injury or grotesque death, especially to family members or friends;
- perpetrating violent acts against others;
- hearing unanswered screams for help and cries of distress or smelling noxious odors;
- being trapped or without assistance;
- proximity to violent threat;
- unexpectedness and duration of the experience(s);
- extent of violent force and the use of a weapon or injurious object;
- number and nature of threats during a violent episode;

- witnessing of atrocities;
- a relationship to the assailant and victims;
- use of physical coercion;
- violation of physical integrity of the child; and
- degree of brutality and malevolence. (Briere & Elliott, 2003; Ullman & Filipas, 2001)

Counselors can assess for the presence of these factors as one element in gauging the severity of the traumatic experience.

Interviews

Interviews are the most widely used method to gather relevant information in diagnosing and treating traumatic stress. A multimethod (e.g., clinical interview, structured interview, assessment instruments), multiple-source (e.g., child, parents, teachers, and medical records) approach is recommended (Pearce & Pezzot-Pearce, 2007). A semi-structured interview can be used to obtain both objective and subjective information from the children and parents. The interview/assessment process is likely to require two to three separate interviews.

Interviewing Parents

Parents often provide more objective information than a child on the trauma incident, any injuries incurred, and the collateral effects of the trauma at home, at school, and in other settings. The counselor should also inquire about the effects of the trauma on the parents, as their emotional and mental state has a great influence on the child's progress. The parents' perspective is particularly important for younger children under the age of 6, who may lack understanding of the interview questions and/or lack the verbal skills to clearly describe their symptoms and the trauma circumstances (Pearce & Pezzot-Pearce, 2007). Parents' reports may take on ever-greater significance because traumatized children may underreport or deny the abuse as an attempt to avoid the aversive aspects of traumatic events (D. M. Elliott & Briere, 1994).

Specific questions counselors can use with parents about their child's or adolescent's presenting problems as a result of maltreatment include the following:

- Can you please provide a behavioral description of the problem/symptom?
- Can you please describe the onset, particularly as related to onset of maltreatment?
- In what contexts are the problems manifested?
- How frequently do the problems occur?
- What are the antecedents of the problem?
- What circumstances make the problems better or worse?
- How do the problems create difficulties for other people, and for whom?
- Can you please describe the child's and the family's feelings about the problems and what caused them?
- What solutions regarding the problems have been attempted, and how effective were they?
- What are the hopes in seeking help now? (Pearce & Pezzot-Pearce, 2007, p. 83)

Interviewing the Child

Presence of Caregiver

The counselor–child relationship begins with the first contact and continues throughout the assessment process on into specific treatment stages. For some children/adolescents, the assessment process can be hampered by their tendency to avoid traumatic material and to mistrust unfamiliar people. As such, it is counselors' responsibility to adjust their interview style and intensity to match the client's motivational level. An often helpful step in this process is to have the primary caregiver present initially to facilitate the transition in meeting the counselor. However, the caregiver should not be present during the whole interview process as children and especially adolescents may be hesitant about sharing personal material about the trauma in the caregiver's presence. This hesitancy is particularly relevant in instances of sexual abuse and when the perpetrator is known by the caregiver (Saigh, 2004).

Adjust Interview Style

The counselor must strike a balance between appropriate empathy and pacing of the assessment process on one hand and adequate interview structure on the other. Younger children and those who were victims of multiple, severe, and prolonged abuse histories likely will take longer to complete the assessment than older, less severely abused children who experienced a single abuse episode. The manner by which counselors handle the assessment process typically sets the stage for later treatment effectiveness. With more severely abused children, counselors will also need to take occasional breaks from the interview to process the child's discomfort with the interview process. The interview provides an opportunity to begin building the therapeutic alliance and creating a safe, predictable environment for the child (van der Kolk, 1996).

Also, it is important to be flexible in the manner that trauma information is obtained. For example, it is critical to obtain the child's perspective on the traumatic event(s) while also helping them manage their emotions in relating their story. Hence, the counselor may need to modulate the intensity of the discussion by starting with more general and less anxiety-producing material and progressing over several sessions toward more specific, threatening material as the child is able to tolerate it. With moderate to severely traumatized individuals, detailed and highly distressing trauma information is delayed until the client has developed a strong therapeutic alliance with the counselor and adequate anxiety management skills are in place.

Provide Treatment Overview

Early in the interview process, the counselor should provide the child and family with an overview of the interview process, including the goals, an age-appropriate explanation of the effects of a traumatic event and symptoms, and how the interview information will be used to help them in the treatment process. Allow clients to ask questions about any phase of assessment and treatment. However, it may not be advisable to go into great detail at this point, particularly about the trauma narrative and emotional processing components. Providing an overview shows respect for parents and children and may help allay some anxiety.

Goal of Assessment

The goal of the initial assessment is to obtain a general picture of the traumatic event and specific symptoms and their context but not to begin processing the child's emotional experience. These two issues cannot always be kept separate, as they intertwine to some degree throughout the assessment and treatment process. However, emotional processing should be central only after the child has acquired adequate emotion-regulation skills.

Formal Diagnosis

When a formal diagnosis is required, a portion of the interview will focus on the *DSM-IV-TR* criteria for PTSD. With this focus, counselors will be most interested in an identifiable traumatic event and the accompanying symptoms of reexperiencing of the trauma, avoidance of aversive aspects of the trauma, emotional numbing, and arousal symptoms.

A diagnosis of developmental trauma disorder has been proposed for the upcoming *DSM-5* for children. This diagnosis would address the symptoms that are not included in the current PTSD diagnosis for children who have experienced multiple, chronic traumas, typically within the context of a relationship (van der Kolk, 2005). As a result of repeated and severe interpersonal victimization, these children experience significant dysregulation (emotions, behavior, relationships, and self-attributions), negative attributions and expectations, and functional impairment. The etiology and symptoms are similar to those discussed earlier regarding CPTSD with female victims of intimacy violence (see Chapter 9).

Child and Parent/Caregiver Instruments

Several instruments are available to administer to parents, children, and other relevant sources. This section reviews instruments that assess trauma and related symptoms and that have acceptable degrees of psychometric data support. Structured data collection should be used in conjunction with less structured clinical interviews rather than as a stand-alone means of data collection. These instruments often elicit information that less structured interviews do not. After the initial assessment, selected measures from below should be administered at least every 4–6 weeks to inform clinical decision making as well as at termination and 3- to 6-month follow-ups.

The Child Behavioral Checklist (CBCL; Achenbach, 1991, 2002) is widely used for assessing general psychological distress with children ages 2 to 18 (116 items). Several forms have been developed that provide the perspectives of the caretaker or teacher; there is also a self-administered version for children ages 11 and older and an observational form used by clinicians to record their direct observations of the child. Scales measure psychopathology and competencies. The CBCL can discriminate between abused and nonabused children as well as between sexually abused and nonabused children. The author has reported acceptable reliability and validity. A similar instrument is the Basic Assessment System for Children–2 (BASC-2; Reynolds & Kamphaus, 2006).

The Trauma Symptom Checklist for Children (TSCC; Briere, 1996) is a 54-item self-report inventory that assesses trauma-related symptoms for children between the ages of 8 and 16. The TSCC specifically evaluates for child abuse (sexual, physical, and psychological), neglect, other interpersonal violence, whether the child has witnessed others' trauma, major accidents, and disasters as well as six clinical scales (Anxiety, Depression, Posttraumatic Stress, Sexual Concerns, Dissociation, and Anger). Other forms of the TSCC include a parent-report version for younger children ages 3 to 12 (Trauma Symptom Checklist for Young Children; TSCYC; Briere, 2005) and a 44-item form that does not contain items related to sexual concerns. The TSCC has two validity scales: Underresponse and Hyperresponse. It has good reliability and validity.

The Child Sexual Behavior Inventory (CSBI; Friedrich, 1998) is a 38-item instrument to describe a child's sexual behaviors (ages 2–12) observed by a caregiver. The caregiver describes the sexual behavior, and the results are a total score, a Developmentally Related Sexual Behavior score (age and gender appropriate sexual behaviors), and Sexual Abuse Specific Items score (empirically related to history of sexual abuse), which is based on nine areas: boundary problems, exhibitionism, gender-role behavior, self-stimulation, sexual anxiety, sexual interest, sexual intrusiveness, sexual knowledge, and voyeuristic behavior. The CSBI has demonstrated good reliability and validity.

The UCLA PTSD Index for *DSM-IV* (Pynoos, Rodriguez, Steinberg, Studer, & Fredrick, 1998) is a 49-item self-report instrument that determines whether or not a child meets criteria for a *DSM-IV* diagnosis of PTSD. Children identify and rate the severity of each traumatic event they have experienced and select the one that was most upsetting to them. This event is used as the index trauma for rating trauma-related symptoms. On the basis of symptom severity, the child's scores can be classified as mild, moderate, or very severe PTSD.

The Children's PTSD Inventory (CPTSDI; Saigh et al., 2000) is composed of 47 questions that are administered by a clinician to determine whether or not a child meets the criteria for a *DSM-IV* diagnosis of PTSD. The CPTSDI consists of questions that parallel the five symptom clusters of the *DSM-IV* PTSD disorder: exposure to traumatic event and situational reactivity (8 items), presence of reexperiencing symptoms (11 items), avoidance and numbing symptoms (16 items), increased arousal (7 items), and significant impairment (5 items). The authors have reported acceptable reliability and validity.

The Childhood PTSD Interview–Parent Form (Fletcher, 1996) is administered to a child's parents and addresses the following PTSD symptoms: stress-exposure, reexperiencing, avoidance and numbing, and increased arousal.

Finally, it may be necessary to obtain more detailed information about the presence and severity of depression and anxiety. Self-report instruments for depression include the Children's Depression Inventory (Kovacs, 1985; for ages 7–16), the Beck Youth Depression Inventory (J. S. Beck, Beck, & Jolly, 2001), and the Beck Depression Inventory–II for children age 13 and older (A. T. Beck, Steer, & Brown, 1996). Self-report measures for anxiety include State–Trait Anxiety Inventory for Children (Spielberger, Edwards, Montuori, & Lushene, 1973) and the Manifest Anxiety Scale for Children (March, Parker, Sullivan, Stallings, & Conners, 1997).

An initial combination of instruments might be the CBCL for general symptoms and the TSCC or the TSCYC for specific trauma symptoms. More specific measures can be added as needed (e.g., depression and/or anxiety). It is also important to assess multiple areas of functioning from multiple sources (i.e., parents, teacher, and child; Cook et al., 2003).

Psychopharmacological Treatment

A final assessment consideration is whether or not to include psychopharmacological treatment along with counseling. Research on this issue is just now emerging for CM. Some suggest using medications only after counseling has proven ineffective (C. L. Donnelly & Amaya-Jackson, 2002). Research provides some support for the effectiveness of medications in treating trauma symptoms such as nightmares, reexperiencing of traumatic events, hyperarousal, and comorbid depression (for a review, see Brown et al., 2004). It would be particularly important to consult with a child and adolescent psychiatrist who appreciates both psychopharmacological treatment and counseling, especially with children and adolescents who were exposed to severe trauma and have severe symptoms.

Integrating the Assessment Process

All these means of assessment must be used in conjunction with each other rather than exclusive use of only one assessment method. In particular, assessments should always include some type of semi-structured clinical interview with child and parents/caregivers and at least one self-report instrument. Additional information from relevant teachers, family members, and other persons will also enhance the assessment picture. Relevant multiple sources are superior to only one perspective of the traumatic experience and consequences. Counselors should also assume that additional important assessment data likely will emerge over time as the therapeutic alliance is strengthened with the child and parents. Once the formal assessment is complete, the counselor should provide feedback to both the parent and child. In general, children that are age 7 or 8 and up can be provided assessment feedback with parents present. In the case of younger children or children with significantly below average intelligence, the counselor should consider providing a separate feedback session for the parents in addition to a conjoint session for the parents and child that emphasizes a developmental appropriate level of feedback for the child.

Counseling Interventions

Given the current literature, the following discussion emphasizes the integration of CBT and family interventions for ameliorating trauma-related symptoms and developing a supportive family environment. Play therapy also may be a part of treatment, especially for younger children, in establishing a therapeutic alliance and helping children process their trauma; however, exclusive use may inadvertently support avoidance of trauma issues (Pearce & Pezzot-Pearce, 2007). Children and adolescents must be exposed to painful trauma material in order to extinguish the symptoms and then to reconceptualize their interpretation of the abuse. Furthermore, PCIT can be effective in teaching physically abusive parents

227

appropriate skills to change negative parent–child interactions to more positive and nurturing interactions. Also, the CM clinical literature emphasizes the importance of building and maintaining the therapeutic alliance and addressing trust issues (Briere & Scott, 2006). A safe, trusting relationship with the counselor and family is necessary to effectively implement structured CBT interventions. The therapeutic relationship is a curative factor of itself, by reducing feelings of disconnectedness and increasing the child's sense of trust, safety, security, and control (Siegel, 2003).

The integration of these approaches is only now beginning to surface in the child treatment literature. As such, the particulars of proceeding through the treatment process, including therapy phase progression, have not yet been fully fleshed out in the empirical literature. Consequently, the particulars of the counseling process are informed by a consensus of clinical wisdom and experience. As a result, the following model is informed by existing empirical research, appropriate theory, and widely held clinical wisdom. Much of the material in Chapter 9 of this book for treating female victims of abuse is applicable to treating CM, particularly issues related to treatment stages and the therapeutic environment.

As with adult victims, treatment does not always progress in a continuous linear fashion through the phases. Children and adolescents with different abuse histories will likely progress through treatment at different rates and cycle back through earlier phases at different points in treatment as new material emerges. For example, those who have experienced more severe and frequent abuse episodes over an extended period will tend to need longer-term treatment than those with single-incident, less severe abuse. The former abuse circumstance may require longer treatment periods for each phase, whereas the latter may require a shorter treatment period per phase and may not require the same number of treatment phases as more severe cases. Unlike adults, children's continuation in treatment is greatly influenced by the parents/caregivers. Thus, it is also important to have a strong alliance with the parents/caregivers. Child victims may need an occasional vacation from counseling if the abuse was severe and treatment is intense.

Counseling Phases

Providing treatment in phases is important with traumatized individuals (J. A. Cohen, Mannarino, & Deblinger, 2006; Cook et al., 2003). Attempting to do too much at once or to process the trauma before the child is equipped to do so often overloads the child's ability to process and learn new behaviors, thoughts, and relationship skills. For example, exposure therapy is a critical intervention phase for processing emotionally traumatic material. This intervention provides greater reduction in affect dysregulation (i.e., low-threshold, high-intensity emotional reactions and slow return to nondistressed emotional state)—a major symptom of trauma—than any other intervention. However, by itself, exposure therapy may trigger unmanageable emotional intensity for many clients, hamper a good working relationship with the clinician, and result in high client dropout (Cloitre & Koenen, 2001). Conversely, adding prior treatment phases that enhance safety and the therapeutic relationship and that teach affect and interpersonal regulation skills predicts successful exposure therapy with adults and children (Cloitre et al., 2004). Thus, phases are important as is the order in which each phase is presented.

Four Phases

In general, the empirically supported treatments include three to four phases of treatment (Cloitre et al., 2004; J. A. Cohen, Mannarino, & Deblinger, 2006; Cook et al., 2003). The following discussion enumerates a four-phase model. Phase 1 concentrates on stabilizing the client. This process includes building the working alliance with the child and caregivers, improving affect regulation, providing trauma education, and creating and fortifying a sense of safety and an appropriate level of self- and other-care. Phase 2 focuses on processing the traumatic experience. Phase 3 involves helping children derive new, more hopeful meanings about themselves, the future, and the traumatic experiences, whereas the Phase 4 emphasizes consolidating new learning from the previous stages, enhancing resiliency, and reestablishing secure social networks.

Stabilization

Under most circumstances the counselor will begin the treatment phase with conjoint sessions with parents and child unless one or both parents were the perpetrators of sexual abuse. If the family is lacking in cohesion and has a history of instability, lack of parent support, and/or lack of parenting skills, a series of conjoint family sessions will precede individual and parent–child sessions (Faust & Katchen, 2004). With higher functioning families, a single family session may precede individual sessions, followed by several conjoint family sessions later in the treatment.

Counselors will continue developing the working alliance as they begin clarifying the needs of the child and parents and begin to set both long- and short-term goals. As in any type of treatment, goals may change and/or be reshaped throughout the course of treatment.

Safety

Before using specific interventions, it is critical to address the safety of the child and family. The major task at this juncture is to develop a safe environment for the child and family by accessing necessary resources in the home and community. This process may involve contact with CPS, the legal system, school personnel, law enforcement, and other family and friends who can provide support. This process also may entail a physical move to another location, the removal of a family member from the home, and/or the acquisition of a protective order to prevent contact with the child. In addition, the counselor can help the family develop a safety plan regarding any threatening people outside the home (e.g., "Always stay with a group of other children" and "Do not make eye contact with or talk to strangers").

Trauma Education

The child and parents need to have accurate information on trauma and its effects. This knowledge often begins the healing process simply because the counselor has provided an explanation about unfamiliar symptoms and behaviors (van der Kolk, 1996). This information helps the child and parents begin to derive some meaning from the trauma experience and, as a result, helps them begin to regain a sense of control and hope for improvement. This process also provides an opportunity to begin establishing a collaborative "us" set for treatment tasks. A counselor's credibility and the alliance with the child and parents will be greatly enhanced if the counselor can present this information in a knowledgeable, understandable, and caring manner (see J. A. Cohen, Mannarino, & Deblinger, 2006, Appendix 1, for handouts on abuse).

Emotional Regulation and Stabilization

Emotional regulation is the ability to tolerate and cope effectively with distress (Ford & Courtois, 2009). Some traumatized children have never learned appropriate self-regulation skills because of inappropriate caregiving, whereas some children developed the skills only to have them greatly compromised because of traumatic experiences. The experience of the trauma often results in physiological changes that affect the child's ability to identify, understand, and process the traumatic experience. The intense feelings of fear, confusion, and emotional overstimulation create a sense of turmoil and of being out of control. These reactions may focus only on the traumatic incident, or, most likely, they will generalize to other aspects of the child's life. Both internal and external events may trigger intense fear and flight-or-fight reactions whether or not these triggers are objective threats. These children often are overwhelmed by a myriad of strong emotions that continue long after the child has been removed from the distressing circumstance.

Children must gain some degree of mastery in deescalating trauma-related emotions before they address the trauma thoughts, feelings, and memories. The following skills have been proven to be effective in helping these clients better manage trauma-related emotions.

Stress Management

Children are taught stress management skills such as relaxation through controlled breathing, progressive muscle relaxation, focused breathing, and thought stopping and replacement (J. A. Cohen, Mannarino, & Deblinger, 2000). Relaxation tends to reverse the psychological and physiological effects of stress. Training in stress management skills is followed by training in emotional expression skills. Counselors teach clients to identify and rate the intensity of their emotions and then teach them how to express those feelings in acceptable ways rather than feeling overwhelmed by many emotions that are difficult to identify or connect to a specific experience. Clients are supported in experiencing and communicating their feelings verbally, nonverbally, and physically.

Cognitive Coping

Counselors teach clients cognitive coping skills, such as the relationship between thoughts, feelings, and behavior, as well as how to challenge their inaccurate thinking and replace those thoughts with more accurate thoughts. Other tasks include reducing vulnerability to extreme emotions, increasing the frequency of positive emotions, and developing the ability to experience emotions without judging or reacting to them (J. A. Cohen, Mannarino, & Deblinger, 2006). Children also are taught how to anticipate and prepare to encounter previously distressing situations, how to distract oneself, how to use problem-solving skills, and how physical exercise or activities can increase a sense of control and mastery. J. A. Cohen, Mannarino, & Deblinger (2006) suggested teaching children the following problem-solving steps.

1. Describe the problem.
2. Identify possible solutions.
3. Consider the likely outcome of each solution.
4. Pick a solution most likely to achieve the desired outcome and implement that choice.
5. Evaluate your choice to see how it worked.
6. If it didn't work out as hoped, try to figure out what went wrong.
7. Include what you just learned the next time a problem arises. (p. 95)

Parent Involvement

Parents learn skills similar to those their children learn, because the parents often struggle with strong emotions about the trauma, such as anger, depression, fear, and guilt. In addition, periodic parent–child sessions allow children and their parents to practice the skills together and to promote more effective and supportive communication about the abuse (J. A. Cohen, Mannarino, & Deblinger, 2000). Parenting skills are taught in individual sessions (J. A. Cohen, Mannarino, & Deblinger, 2006). Although skill building is an important aspect of this first phase, counselors work at the client's pace and take time to address issues such as client reluctance, mistrust, vulnerability, and feeling overwhelmed. The importance of the therapeutic alliance cannot be stressed enough, as it provides the substrate and leverage for learning skills. It is critical that counselors be attuned to the strength of the alliance, because it often ebbs and flows during treatment, particularly during more challenging phases such as when processing the trauma or during alliance repair.

Process the Traumatic Experience

If symptoms such as intense fear, intrusive trauma memories, and extensive avoidance behaviors do not resolve on their own, it will be important to help the child or adolescent to integrate the feelings, thoughts, and memories about the trauma into their life history and autobiographical memory—that is, trauma integration, the second phase of treatment. Successful trauma integration results in significant reduction in the ever-present trauma anguish and an increase in the ability to put the traumatic experiences into a historical perspective with a beginning, middle, and end. Specifically, trauma integration helps survivors to do the following:

- control intrusive and upsetting trauma-related imagery;
- reduce avoidance of cues, situations, and feelings associated with trauma exposure;
- identify unhelpful cognitions about traumatic events; and

- recognize, anticipate, and prepare for reminders of the trauma. (J. A. Cohen, Mannarino, & Deblinger, 2006)

Preparation for Direct Trauma Work

The primary focus of this phase of treatment involves exposure to the traumatic experience by either imaginal flooding or gradual exposure to increasingly more intense trauma scenes and related emotions and thoughts over several sessions (J. A. Cohen, Mannarino, & Deblinger, 2006; Cook et al., 2003). The latter approach using gradual exposure and desensitization is arguably becoming the most widely used intervention and is often less distressing for the child and parents.

The prospect of reexposure to the trauma is often difficult for parents, children, and sometimes counselors. They typically want to avoid such a situation because they assume talking about and reexperiencing something traumatic only makes matters worse (J. A. Cohen, Mannarino, & Deblinger, 2006). However, avoidance prevents the processing of the trauma memory, which results in a prolonging of the intense trauma symptoms. Given the tendency to avoid these experiences, the counselor needs to provide a rationale for reexperiencing the trauma as well as the accrued benefits of this intervention. This step may be a sticking point for some children and parents, so it is important to take adequate time and provide appropriate empathy during this process. In addition, the counselor can point out that the skills learned in the earlier treatment phase (e.g., cognitive processing, stress management) can be used to greatly lessen the overwhelming experience of the original trauma. It is often helpful to review these skills with the child and parents and try them out first on a less stressful situation before focusing on the trauma experience.

Trauma Integration Steps

The gradual exposure approach involves encouraging children to begin with a less upsetting aspect of the trauma (e.g., brief, general description) and then increasingly progress toward describing more intense and threatening aspects of the event. This process typically involves eliciting greater details of the trauma as well as emotional reactions to the episode.

J. A. Cohen, Mannarino, and Deblinger (2006) suggested constructing a trauma narrative in the form of a book or other methods of chronicling the trauma, such as a poem, song, pictures, and/or recording. First, select the best format for the child, such as writing, using a computer, drawing pictures, singing songs, or a combination of these. For some children, symbolic play with dolls and puppets may be used to represent the traumatic experience (E. Gil, 2006). Next, counselors can help the child chronicle the abuse events, going into the level of detail that the child can tolerate at the time, describing a beginning, middle, and end. For children, initially using puppets to describe the trauma event may provide manageable distance from intense emotions. New details can be added with each retelling. The narrative may also include related distressing events, such as telling parents, undergoing medical examinations, involving law enforcement, and having a family member removed from the home. The emotionally engaged telling and retelling of the traumatic experience within a safe and therapeutic environment is the active ingredient in the emotional healing process. The number of times necessary to read the trauma narrative depends on the client and the severity of the trauma. Typically, repeating the trauma narrative two or three times is a minimum, with some severe cases necessitating retelling the trauma story six to eight times or more. With multiple types and incidences of abuse, clients may need to create several trauma narratives for different types of trauma.

Reading and Processing the Trauma Narrative

Once the narrative is completed, the child will review the narrative and add more thoughts and feelings with progressively more detail and more distressing feelings and thoughts (J. A. Cohen, Mannarino, & Deblinger, 2006). Children are encouraged to express verbally how they felt about particular events; for some children, this expression may take place through drawings, play, and choreography. With younger children, the counselor may have to help in the reviewing process. The counselor may need to prompt the child, "Can you tell me more about how it felt for you?" "Why don't we add the thoughts you had at the time?" or "Show me with the dolls what he did to you." During the process of reviewing the narrative, the counselor should be attuned to extreme, exaggerated, or inaccurate thoughts the child may have about the traumatic event, for example, "I feel guilty. It's all my fault. I shouldn't have gone over there." The counselor can begin to process those thoughts with the eventual goal of helping the child rethink and replace the inaccurate and problematic thoughts in subsequent sessions. For example, "You're probably right that not going over to his house would have been better, looking at it now. But didn't you tell me you'd never had any reason to think Mr. Jones would touch you like he did? You'd gone over to play with Lucy many times before and nothing like that had ever happened." Child: "Yeah, I guess you're right. I hadn't really thought about it like that before." This will likely be an ongoing process rather than a one-time event in a session. Much of this work will be continued and completed in the next phase of treatment (see section titled *Cognitive Processing*). If the child is highly defensive about his or her perspective, the best strategy would be to pose a second way of thinking about the trauma rather than directly challenging the inaccurate thought. For example, the counselor may say, "I can see how you might think about the abuse that way. I also remember you telling me you were only 8 years old when your mom took you over to their house because she didn't want you to be alone. Maybe you didn't have a lot of control over whether you went to their house or not then." The counselor gently offers a broader context for interpreting the child's traumatic experience.

Dealing With Distress

During the trauma integration process the counselor must be sensitive to the child's anxiety level. Assessing the child's anxiety level can be done periodically on the basis of the child's perceived level of distress. Once distressing emotions and thoughts are identified and expressed, the counselor can ask the child to rate his or her level of discomfort (see earlier section titled *Stress Management*) and if elevated (e.g., a 9 on a 10-point scale with 10 as *most intense* and 0 as *least intense*) use breathing and other relaxation skills learned in the previous phase to lower their distress level. Then, the narrative processing can continue. Throughout this process, children should be praised and encouraged for their courage and willingness to go through a difficult part of treatment.

Cognitive Processing

The third phase of treatment focuses on challenging and replacing inaccurate and distorted thoughts. Older children and adolescents, more so than younger children, tend to foster more complex and distorted thinking about the traumatic event, largely because of a greater capacity for abstract thought and perspective taking. For example, in order to regain some sense of control, they may search for something they did to cause the trauma (J. A. Cohen et al., 2000). Their logic is that if they can identify what they did to cause the trauma, then they will not do the thing that caused it again. Another distortion is viewing their world as unsafe and unfair. Unfortunately, some families contribute to these distortions by attributing most of the blame to the child.

Problematic Beliefs

Counselors should be particularly sensitive to cognitions related to feeling shame, practicing self-blame, having survivor guilt, seeing the world as unsafe, being different, and thinking others do not believe you, as they predict psychological symptoms (e.g., depression, PTSD symptoms; Mannarino & Cohen, 1996). The therapeutic alliance is a crucial for addressing these issues.

Correcting Distorted Beliefs

Counselors first should teach children the relationship between thinking, feelings, and behaving and then should help children process distorted cognitions through a series of steps:

1. Identify inaccurate, troublesome beliefs elicited from processing the trauma narrative.
2. Use thought stopping or focused breathing to interrupt the upsetting thought.
3. Evaluate the child's reasoning and perspective.
4. Replace distorted beliefs with more accurate and logical ones. (J. A. Cohen et al., 2000)

Unlike the previous phase that focused primarily on emotions and, to a lesser degree, on cognitions, this phase emphasizes the child's distorted thoughts, particularly strongly held ones. Socratic questioning, role playing, searching for alternative perspectives, and perspective-taking exercises are used to challenge and then replace distorted thoughts (Briere & Scott, 2006).

Developmental Level

The child's developmental level informs the choice of interventions. Typically, preschool children may have difficulty processing traumatic information cognitively. Some authors suggest that infants and toddlers may benefit more from a focus on parent–child interaction (Lyons Ruth & Jacobvitz, 1999; McNeil & Hembree-Kigin, 2010). As such, PCIT might be the preferred intervention for younger children, focusing on the child-directed interaction phase of treatment, especially in cases of child physical abuse. Furthermore, the parent-directed interaction phase teaches parents nonpunitive discipline. On the other hand, Cohen and colleagues (J. A. Cohen & Mannarino, 1996; J. A. Cohen et al., 2000) have used trauma-focused CBT successfully with children as young as 3 years of age with accommodations to the age of the child. Toys and play media may be used with younger children (E. Gil, 2006).

It is important for the child and parents to experience success in changing their thoughts and, as a result, changing their feelings and behaviors. This ability is most successfully developed and reinforced within a supportive and warm family/community environment. It is primarily within a relational context (especially with parents) that new and healthier beliefs about self, other, and world take root and become interiorized for the child (J. A. Cohen & Mannarino, 1998).

It is important for children and parents to gain confidence that they can have a significant influence on reducing their symptoms and regaining normalcy in their lives. Mastery of emotional dysregulation enhances their sense of control and self-efficacy (J. A. Cohen, Mannarino, & Deblinger, 2006).

Consolidation and Relationship Enhancement

This final phase of treatment helps children integrate all the skills, new beliefs, and new behaviors they have learned. Because of the developmental nature of the phases, consolidation occurs to a degree as treatment moves from one phase to the next. However, more than in previous phases, the child and parents are supported in using their learnings from the previous treatment phases. Up to this point, children and parents have been practicing the skills together in-session as well as at home. They are now helped to find low-threat, real-world settings in which to generalize their skills. Thus, they might go to a store or mall, interact with safe but unfamiliar people, or drive near the location of the trauma with parents. Generalizing their learnings beyond the counseling room is a critical part of treatment. Also, it is critical that children reconnect with peers, as this enhances resiliency and recovery (J. A. Cohen, Mannarino, & Deblinger, 2006).

Family Sessions

As stated earlier, parent and family involvement are critical for the child's recovery. In fact, family and other support is one of the strongest predictors of recovery for trauma victims (Briere & Scott, 2006). As such, the counselor must assess for parent and family support throughout the treatment process. More conjoint family work will likely be necessary throughout the treatment process with less cohesive and less supportive family dynamics. With these families, issues related to believing the child, tolerating and managing the child and parent reactions, establishing a safe environment, and establishing clear, functional generational boundaries are important to address (Faust & Katchen, 2004). Children may fail to make progress until such changes in family or caregiver dynamics have taken place (Lieberman, 2004).

In addition, the parent's level of emotional distress at the completion of treatment is the strongest predictor of a child's symptom resolution (J. A. Cohen & Mannarino, 1996). Furthermore, Deblinger, Steer, and Lippman (1999) found that parental use of guilt and anxiety-provoking parenting methods was correlated with increasing levels of PTSD symptoms and significant misbehavior with sexually abused children. Conjoint family sessions and/or parent–child sessions can allow the counselor to observe parent–child interactions and facilitate interactive support from the parents to children. Prior individual sessions with parents should have addressed the parents' distress level as well as parenting skills, making productive family sessions more likely.

Parents' health and involvement cannot be overemphasized in the success of the child's treatment. Recall that in the treatment phases discussed earlier, parents received similar treatment to the child's treatment. Parents will be less likely to provide healthy and necessary parenting to the traumatized child if they, too, have not taken steps to enhance their own emotional and behavioral functioning. Parents' depression, anxiety, drug abuse, and PTSD can greatly hinder successful recovery from abuse and prevention of future abuse of their child. For example, mothers of children who have been sexually abused are likely to be victims of sexual abuse themselves (22% to 42%; DiLillo & Damashek, 2003), with the risk of intergenerational abuse being approximately 30% (Paredes, Leifer, & Kilbane, 2001). A daughter's risk of being sexually abused is 3.6 times greater if her mother was also sexually abused (DiLillo & Damashek, 2003).

Although abused mothers do not necessarily abuse their children, a mother's abuse history may result in her placing her children in situations in which they would be vulnerable to abuse, such as with a male offending partner (D. W. Smith, Davis, & Fricker-Elhai, 2004). Assessment of parents' mental health is critical to their child's recovery and to prevention of future abuse.

Other Restorative Experiences

The experience of trauma and subsequent symptoms and life disruptions tend to dominate a person's life. Gratifying experiences occur less during this time as a result of the trauma. As such, both children and parents need to engage in activities that provide them with a sense of mastery and enjoyment (van der Kolk, 1996). Such activities may be solitary (e.g., having a hobby, reading, caring for pets) or involve others, such as participating in social activities, sports, hiking, games, and other noncompetitive physical activities. In addition to helping parents and children experience pleasure and mastery, such activities are also meant to provide opportunities for spontaneity, which are often greatly diminished post-trauma. These activities also can be encouraged with peer involvement, school personnel, and people in community organizations such as churches and clubs.

Another element of restorative experiences is supporting the child in becoming more independent and self-efficacious within a relatively safe environment. This process likely will be gradual and will vary greatly based on the child's age and maturity and available resources. Part of self-efficacy is teaching children how to keep themselves safe, as abused children are at an increased risk of revictimization (Boney-McCoy & Finkelhor, 1995). Stauffer and Deblinger (2003, 2004) have written books and workbooks addressing safety issues for children that provide resources for parents, counselors, educators, and law enforcement.

Addressing Loss and Grief

For many children, adolescents, and their parents, grief over loss of a loved one is intertwined with trauma symptoms. The sudden death of a loved one, often by some gruesome means, and exposure to graphic aspects such as blood, severed limbs, or maimed body parts may result in childhood traumatic grief. Traumatic grief is defined as "a condition in which both unresolved grief and PTSD symptoms are present, often accompanied by depression" (J. A. Cohen, Mannarino, & Deblinger, 2006, p. 17). As such, treatment for these children needs to focus on trauma symptoms as well as facilitating the process of grieving. Failure to grieve the loss of the loved one may result in the child being fixated on the conditions surrounding the loved one's death. Cohen et al. (p. 170) suggested several additional components to treatment following the treatment of trauma:

- training in grief psychoeducation,
- grieving the loss and resolving the ambivalent feelings about the deceased,
- preserving positive memories of the deceased, and
- redefining the relationship with the deceased and commitment to present relationships.

Research supports a two-module treatment model that includes sequential treatment of trauma followed by traumatic grief using CBT (J. A. Cohen, Mannarino, & Staron, 2006).

Prevention

The seeds for CM are sown in the earliest years of a child's life (Ryan, 2005; Schore, 2003). For example, prenatal exposure to drugs or alcohol, low birth weight, and prematurity can precipitate chronic distress between caregiver and child, thus increasing the risk of CM at birth (P. M. Sullivan & Knutson, 1998). Close pre- and postnatal care and support can moderate or prevent this risk (Ryan, 2005). Furthermore, when the parent of an infant is a young, single, and isolated mother, the risk for CM is increased (Crittenden, 1998). Home visitation interventions for these mothers and infants have been found to be effective in decreasing CM as well as in decreasing delinquency as adolescents (Bilukha et al., 2005). A primary intervention is teaching parents to be responsive to the child's affective cues and physical needs (Prentky, Harris, Frizzell, & Righthand, 2000).

Thus, the most effective prevention begins before the birth of children with parents and caregivers and continues throughout the child's development. Research has identified a number of protective factors that are correlated with reductions in CM (Ryan, 2002):

- parent resilience,
- caregiver nurturing and attachment,
- social connections,
- knowledge of parenting and child development,
- effective problem-solving and communication skills,
- concrete support in times of need,
- social and emotional competence of children, and
- healthy marriages.

Several authors have suggested additional interventions for parents, counselors, and educators to prevent CM:

- Facilitate friendships and mutual support of parents/caregivers in the neighborhood.
- Strengthen parenting skills through parenting classes, support groups, home visits, and tip sheets from pediatricians and resource libraries.
- Offer extra support to families in crises from neighborhood support, churches, community organizations, and schools.
- Connect families to services and opportunities such as job training, education, health care, and mental health facilities.
- Provide specific programs to facilitate children's prosocial skills.
- Teach children safety skills through instruction and practice. (J. A. Cohen, Mannarino, & Deblinger, 2006; Gomby, Culross, & Behrman, 1999; Krug et al., 2002)

Parenting Programs

Parenting programs are effective in enhancing parents' psychological and emotional adjustment, improving parenting skills, increasing knowledge about child development and age-appropriate parenting strategies, reducing parent–child conflict, improving children's behavior, increasing parents' social support, enhancing self-efficacy, and reducing the risk of CM (J. A. Cohen et al., 2006). PCIT is particularly useful with 3- to 9-year-olds.

Prevention Beyond the Family

Experts suggest that prevention of CM must be directed to multiple levels of society beyond the family (i.e., community, social service, and policy; MacLeod & Nelson, 2000; Zeldin, 2004). Mass media campaigns to increase public education include public service announcements on radio and television, in newspapers and magazines, and on billboards and websites—such educational material is effective in increasing awareness of CM (Hoefnagels & Mudde, 2000).

School-based programs help children avoid and report victimization (Plummer, 2005). These programs reach a wide range of children, with some surveys indicating that 85% of elementary schools offer some type of CSA program (Breen, Daro, & Romano, as cited in Finkelhor, Asdigian, & Dziuba-Leatherman, 1995). M. K. Davis and Gidycz (2000) analyzed 27 school-based sexual abuse prevention programs and concluded that participants scored higher on prevention-related knowledge than nonparticipants, although none of the programs was able to show a relationship between the program and a decline in victimization. Gibson and Leitenberg (2000) determined that university female students who received CSA prevention education in childhood were significantly less likely to be sexually abused later.

Developmentally Sequenced Treatment

The treatment of childhood trauma and traumatic grief must be conceptualized within a developmental framework that is based on the child's age and ability to metabolize treatment material. If a child or adolescent experiences serious maltreatment, counseling may need to occur over a period of years, with months and years between a series of sessions. This extended period of counseling does not mean that treatment was unsuccessful. However, as the child develops emotionally, cognitively, psychologically, and socially, it may be necessary to revisit abuse-related issues as they relate to peer relationships, romantic relationships, or sexual relationships. In a similar manner, treatment interventions must be selected on the basis of the child's developmental abilities. For example, although some form of exposure seems to be a critical intervention for overcoming trauma, the form by which it is presented depends on the child's age and developmental capability. For younger children and those who are less verbal, play therapy and play media may be the vehicle through which children process trauma events. With older, more verbal children and adolescents, a trauma narrative can be used that includes writing out the trauma and reading it aloud.

Case Example

A great-grandmother sought services for two of her great-grandchildren, 3- and 4-year-old females who had been removed from their home because of their parents' extensive abuse of drugs. The girls exhibited symptoms associated with CSA, such as intense masturbation, attempts to touch other children's genitals, and other sexualized behaviors (e.g., talking about genitals, asking adults questions about sexual behavior) that are uncharacteristic for their ages. The girls also had been diagnosed with genital warts, which confirmed the suspicion of CSA. Furthermore, they also exhibited a unique sibling language and became extremely distressed when separated. The girls also exhibited underdeveloped language and interpersonal skills. When distressed, one of the girls would freeze and assume a catatonic posture with a dissociative, nonblinking stare while the other would become inconsolably enraged. These behaviors suggested that the girls had been severely sexually abused and neglected. The girls recently had started preschool, resulting in an increase in their symptoms.

The great-grandparents (GGPs) were in their early 70s but were firmly committed to raising the girls and getting them the psychological help they needed. However, they would often become frustrated and overwhelmed by the girls' problematic behavior. Furthermore, they were having to make difficult adjustments to provide proper care for the girls. Therefore, periodic counseling sessions were held with one or the other GGP to address personal distresses. Because of the girls' ages, underdeveloped language skills, insecure attachments to adults, and problematic externalizing behavior problems, the initial treatment of choice was PCIT. This phase of treatment involved weekly or biweekly sessions with the GGPs and the two girls. The counselor took turns with each GGP and each child, facilitating child-focused play counseling. During this period, each GGP learned how to provide specific praise, reflect specific behavior and/or feelings, imitate the child's behavior, and describe the child's behavior. Conversely, the GGPs were coached to minimize giving commands, asking questions, or criticizing during play sessions. They were asked to practice the child-focused aspect of treatment daily with each child for a minimum of 5–10 minutes. The GGPs' interaction with the girls improved over the next 8 weeks as did the girls' behavior, although at a much slower and more uneven rate than the GGPs' skill improvement. The girls engaged in significantly less sexualized behavior (e.g., talking about their genitals and inappropriate touching of others) at home and school and began attempting to interact more with adults and use less twin language by the end of the 8 weeks. The decrease in masturbation was partly attributed to helping the GGPs to view this behavior as a self-soothing behavior when the girls were anxious rather than being viewed as misbehavior that needed to be punished. This behavior was largely ignored while simultaneously distracting and/or redirecting the girls to other behaviors. Once the girls engaged in other behaviors, the GGPs would assume the child-centered orientation mode for a few minutes and attend to the other acceptable behaviors. The GGPs reported that the girls were beginning to seek them out more often for comfort when distressed rather than engaging in sexualized behavior, dissociation, and rage.

At this point the second component of PCIT was implemented: the parent-directed interaction. This component of treatment emphasizes contingency management skills associated with helping the GGPs learn appropriate limit setting, consistency, and problem solving. For example, they learned to state directly what they wanted the girls to do in a positive, respectful, and specific fashion. They also learned appropriate use of time-outs when necessary. They had been overusing time-outs in an ineffective fashion that actually reinforced the girls' misbehavior. The GGPs practiced the child-centered component of PCIT followed by the parent-directed interaction with each child when a command was given, such as to pick up a toy. As was expected, the girls had a difficult time with the new form of time-out (e.g., GGPs controlled the time-out period in the chair or time-out room). With persistence in sessions as well as at home by the GGPs, the new time-out procedure began to work well after about 2 weeks. The in-session coaching of the GGPs was essential for both phases of treatment to be implemented effectively as they had to unlearn many well-intended though ineffective disciplinary methods.

At the end of 12 weeks, the girls had improved significantly at home and school, although there were periodic relapses. They became more appropriately expressive in a tangible manner (e.g., using toys to express negative feelings) about their anger and fear in play therapy sessions with the counselor. They also began to identify the source of anger and fear and to express this verbally in a rudimentary fashion to their GGPs. Numerous small setbacks (e.g., inappropriate touching of self and others, outbursts of anger at school) occurred over these 12 weeks of treatment; however, the girls and GGPs were able to recover within a much shorter period of time than at the onset of treatment. The girls had improved significantly after the 12 weeks of treatment, although their behavior would be considered in the low-average range of behavior for children of their age. Treatment ended at this time because of driving distance, cost of fuel, and the fact that the great-grandfather had gone back to work to support the girls.

This case represents a degree of success in treating two cases of sexual abuse and neglect. A critical factor in the success of this case was the commitment of the GGPs. They truly cared about their great-granddaughters and were open to trying new parenting procedures (no small task for older family members raising great-grandchildren) and receiving feedback from the counselor. At times they would get discouraged, but they continued in treatment until other factors became prohibitive. Only time will tell whether or not treatment is effective long-term.

Summary

Research on the treatment of children who have been maltreated is in its infancy. Current treatment models have borrowed heavily from models for adult trauma victims. Although a wide range of approaches have been used in treating this population, cognitive–behavioral and family/parent interventions along with focused attention to the therapeutic alliance (psychodynamic/attachment approaches) have shown the most success in treatment. However, counselors also must consider such issues as severity and frequency of the trauma, age of the victim, parent/family support, and dosage of treatment in implementing appropriate treatment for each case.

Most experts hold that phase-based treatment models currently are considered the most effective approaches. A widely used phased-based format includes the following phases: stabilizing the client, processing the traumatic experience, cognitive processing, and consolidating learning and enhancing resiliency. Phase-based models consider developmental treatment needs of a victimized child, such that issues related to the therapeutic relationship, self- and emotional regulation, and parent support are necessary prerequisites to effectively addressing the trauma experience.

Existing research supports the effectiveness of integrated, phase-based models of treatment. However, future research must examine more closely the effects of trauma severity and length of treatment on effectiveness and interventions. In addition, more research is necessary to examine the impact of whole family involvement beyond the parents in treatment protocols.

Suggested Readings

Blaustein, M. E., & Kinniburgh, K. M. (2010). *Treating traumatic stress in children and adolescents.* New York, NY: Guilford Press.

Cohen, J. A., Mannarino, A. P., & Deblinger, E. (2006). *Treating trauma and traumatic grief in children and adolescents.* New York, NY: Guilford Press.

Cook, A., Blaustein, M., Spinazzalo, J., & van der Kolk, B. (2003). *Complex trauma in children and adolescents.* White paper from the National Child Traumatic Network Complex Trauma Task Force. Retrieved March 2006 from http://nctsn.org/nctsn_assets/pdfs/edu_materials/ComplexTrauma_All.pdf

Homebuilders. (2012). http://www.cebc4cw.org/program/homebuilders/detailed

McNeil, C. B., & Hembree-Kigin, T. L. (2010). *Parent–child interaction therapy*. New York, NY: Springer.

Pearce, J. W., & Pezzot-Pearce, T. D. (2007). *Psychotherapy of abused and neglected children* (2nd ed.). New York, NY: Guilford Press.

Saunders, B. E., Berliner, L., & Hanson, R. F. (Eds.). (2004). *Child physical and sexual abuse: Guidelines for treatment* (Revised report dated April 26, 2004). Charleston, SC: National Crime Victims Research and Treatment Center. Retrieved April 2006 from http://www.musc.edu/cvc/

Silverman, W. K., Ortiz, C. D., Chockalinghan, V., Burns, B. J., Koklo, D. J., Putnam, F. W., & Amaya-Jackson, L. (2008). Evidence-based psychosocial treatments for children and adolescents exposed to traumatic events. *Journal of Clinical Child & Adolescent Psychology, 37,* 156–183.

chapter 13

Elder Abuse

Case Examples

Marion

Marion was a 63-year-old woman with developmental disabilities who had lived with her brother Hank since her parents died. She had been physically abused by Hank for several years but thought that if she told anyone she would have no place to live. She was also financially exploited by Hank, who was the payee for her Social Security check and used that money to support his drinking habit.

Harry

Harry, age 72, was hospitalized due to the amputation of his leg. He signed over a power of attorney to his son, John. John did not have a job, nor did his wife. Harry had an estate of $400,000, plenty of money to support all of them. The son and his wife moved in and took over, including remodeling the house and spending significant amounts of money on luxury items. Though they said they remodeled a bathroom for Harry, the bathroom was not wheelchair accessible, and no ramps were built to enable Harry to come and go from the house. Harry was very capable of making his own decisions but was told who he could see and was never included in making decisions about how his money was to be spent. Kept hostage in his own home, he never telephoned anyone because his son and daughter-in-law would listen in on the conversation and then yell at him. Other family members were told that they could not visit Harry unless they made prior arrangements with John, who summarily denied all of them contact. (National Center on Elder Abuse [NCEA], 2002)

The cases above are all too common in today's society. Yet they demonstrate how physical abuse, control, and threat can characterize an elder person's life. These examples represent many cases of elder abuse in which the perpetrator is intimately known by the elder person. In fact, elder abuse by a family member is the most common type of abuse (65.6%), with an adult child being the most common perpetrator (32.6%), followed by other family members (21.5%; Teaster et al., 2006). Of elder abusers, 52.7% are female and 47.3% are male. The abuse can take many forms: physical, sexual, neglect, psychological, and financial exploitation. As with abuse of children and women, elder abuse has a long history but was not formally recognized until the late 1970s and 1980s. The World Health Organization brought attention to elder abuse in 2002 (Nelson, 2002), and yet little scholarly work has been conducted on the issue.

This chapter examines the definition and prevalence of elder abuse along with characteristics of abused elders and those who abuse elders. It also examines the few studies that exist on interventions for elder abuse and provides clinical suggestions based on clinical wisdom and experience.

On the basis of information from the U.S. Census Bureau, in 2010 there were over 40.5 million adults 65 years of age and older. This number is an increase of 5.4 million (15.3%) since 2000 (U.S. Census Bureau, 2011). Adults age 65 and over represent 13.1% of the total U.S. population—approximately one in eight Americans. The number of those who are 85 and older grew faster than any age group of the older population. These numbers are expected to continue to increase. By 2030, estimates suggest that elders age 60 and older will more than double to 85 million while elders over the age of 85 will triple to 8 million. Elders are expected to make up 19% of the population by 2030. Older women outnumber older men 23 million to 17.5 million. Anglo American elders are expected to increase by 97% while elderly African Americans are expected to increase by 265% and elder Hispanic Americans by 530%. With increased numbers of elderly is an increased risk of elder abuse.

Extent of Elder Abuse

What Is Elder Abuse?

One of the difficulties in defining elder abuse is related to such issues as independence, self-sufficiency, and self-neglect. For example, what if an elderly father who is diabetic eats too much of the wrong foods, drinks alcohol excessively, and consistently fails to keep doctor appointments. If his adult children see this behavior and do nothing, are they being abusive? If not, where is the line distinguishing abuse from nonabuse? The concept of self-neglect must be weighed in the balance of independence and self-determination on one hand and the ability to engage in self-care on the other. Finding the appropriate balance on these issues must be considered on a case-by-case basis and sometimes through legal means. These circumstances make categorical definitions of elder abuse difficult.

Regarding age designation, *elder* is most consistently defined as someone who is 60 years of age and older (Joint Commission on Accreditation of Healthcare Organizations, 2002). The U.S. Congress also accepts this age designation (Stiegel, 2003).

A widely accepted definition of elder abuse is any knowing, intentional, or negligent act by a caregiver or other person that causes harm or serious risk of harm to an elderly person or failure to meet an elder's basic needs (National Research Council, 2003).

The specificity of laws varies from state to state, but broadly defined, abuse may be any of the following:

- *Physical abuse:* Inflicting, or threatening to inflict, physical pain or injury on a vulnerable elder. Physical abuse may include, but is not limited to, such acts of violence as striking, hitting, beating, pushing, shoving, shaking, slapping, kicking, pinching, and burning. Other examples include unacceptable use of drugs, physical restraints, force-feeding, and physical punishment of any kind.
- *Emotional/psychological abuse:* Inflicting mental pain, anguish, or distress on an elder person through verbal or nonverbal acts. Examples include verbal assaults, insults, threats, intimidation, humiliation, and harassment. Further examples include treating an older person like an infant; isolating an elderly person from family, friends, or regular activities; giving an older person the "silent treatment"; and enforced social isolation.
- *Sexual abuse:* Nonconsensual sexual contact of any kind. Sexual contact with any person incapable of giving consent is also considered sexual abuse. It includes, but is not limited to, unwanted touching and all types of sexual assault or battery, such as rape, sodomy, coerced nudity, and sexually explicit photographing.
- *Neglect:* Refusal or failure by those responsible to provide food, shelter, health care, or protection for a vulnerable elder. Neglect also includes failure of a person who has fiduciary responsibilities to provide care for an elder (e.g., pay for home-care services) or the failure on the part of an in-home service provider to provide necessary care. Other examples consist of refusal or failure to provide an elder with such life necessities as food, water, clothing, shelter, personal hygiene, medicine, comfort, personal safety, and other essentials included in an implied or agreed-upon responsibility to an elder.
- *Self-neglect:* Self-neglect is characterized as the behavior of an elderly person that threatens his or her own health or safety. Self-neglect generally manifests itself in older persons as a refusal or failure to provide themselves with adequate food, water, clothing, shelter, personal hygiene, medication, and safety precautions. Self-neglect does not include a situation in which a mentally competent older person, who understands the consequences of his or her decisions, makes a conscious and voluntary decision to engage in acts that threaten his or her health or safety as a matter of personal choice.
- *Abandonment:* The desertion of a vulnerable elder by anyone who has assumed the responsibility for care or custody of that person. Examples include the desertion of an elder at a hospital, a nursing facility, or similar institutions; the desertion of an elder at a shopping center or other public location; and an elder's own report of being abandoned.

- *Financial or material exploitation:* Illegal or improper use of an elder's funds, property, or assets. Examples include, but are not limited to, cashing an elderly person's checks without authorization or permission; forging an older person's signature; misusing or stealing an older person's money or possessions; coercing or deceiving an older person into signing any document (e.g., contracts or will); and the improper use of conservatorship, guardianship, or power of attorney. (NCEA, 2012)

Elder abuse can affect people of all ethnic backgrounds, social status, and both men and women, although research indicates that certain groups of people are at higher risks than others.

Prevalence of Elder Abuse

Approximately 11% of cognitively intact elders experience mistreatment (Acierno, Hernandez-Tejada, Muzzy, & Steve, 2009), and 47.3% of cognitively impaired elders experience mistreatment (Wiglesworth et al., 2010). The State Adult Protective Services survey (APS survey; Teaster et al., 2006) includes data about elder abuse from state APS agencies in 2004. APS received 565,747 reports of suspected elder abuse and investigated 461,135 of these cases. Of these cases, 191,908 (41.6%) cases were substantiated, an increase of 15.6% from the 2000 survey (166,019 substantiated cases).

Two groups of researchers conducted national random sample surveys and found much lower incidence rates of elder abuse (see Table 13.1). Lower rates of abuse would be expected with a community random sample as opposed to suspected abuse cases reported to APS. Amstadter et al. (2011) surveyed 5,777 elders, 60 years of age and older, using a computer-assisted telephone interview procedure. One in ten reported some type of maltreatment. Of those who reported abuse, 4.6% reported emotional mistreatment, 1.6% reported physical mistreatment, and 0.6% reported sexual mistreatment in the past year. Laumann et al. (2008) surveyed 3,005 individuals between the ages of 57 and 85 about mistreatment by *family members* and found that 9.0% reported emotional mistreatment, 0.2% reported physical mistreatment, and 3.5% reported financial mistreatment.

Table 13.1
Elder Abuse as Reported in Two National Random Sample Self-Reported Surveys

Type of Abuse	Percentage Abused by Others[a]	Percentage Abused by Family Members[b]
Physical	1.6	0.2
Sexual	0.6	—
Emotional	4.6	9.0
Neglect	5.1	—
Financial	5.2	3.5

[a]$N = 5,777$ and elders were age 60 and up. Information from Amstadter et al. (2011).
[b]$N = 3,005$ and elders were age 57—85. Information from Laumann et al. (2008).

Sources of elder abuse reports include family members (17%), social service staff (10.6%), friends and neighbors (8%), self (6.3%), long-term care facility staff (5.5%), law enforcement personnel (5.3%), nurses and nurses aids (4.7%), home health workers (2.9), physicians (1.4%), and others (26.6%). The greatest number of reports came from the abusers themselves, municipal agents, postal service workers, utility workers, and hospital discharge planners.

On the APS survey, the following were the substantiated types of elder abuse:

- self-neglect (37.2%),
- caregiver neglect (20.4%),
- financial exploitation (14.7%),
- emotional/psychological/verbal abuse (14.8%),
- physical abuse (10.7%),
- sexual abuse (1.0%), and
- other (1.2%).

The vast majority of the victims were Euro Americans (77.1%), followed by African Americans (21.2%). American Indians, Asian Americans, and Pacific Is-landers comprised less than 1% each of the remaining substantiated cases. The majority of abuse cases (89.3%) took place in a domestic context. The extremely low rates of substantiated cases of elder abuse for some groups (e.g., American In-dians, Asians) likely reflect cultural differences in defining elder abuse as well as in choosing not to report elder abuse (Moon & Benton, 2000). There is evidence that as Asians become more acculturated into Western culture, their attitudes and practices toward the elderly change. For example, many young Americanized Asians are beginning to put their elder parents in assisted living centers rather than keeping them at home (Kershaw, 2003).

Self-Neglect

Elders who self-neglect make up the largest group of abused elders. Self-neglect occurs when elders engage in behavior or fail to engage in behavior that threatens their health and safety. Females comprise the approximately two thirds (65.3%) of substantiated self-neglecting elders, and approximately two thirds (65.1%) of self-neglect cases were with people age 75 or older. The majority of self-neglecting elders are Caucasian (77.4%). Understandably, 93.3% have great difficulty caring for themselves, and 75.3% suffer from varying degrees of confusion: 30% are very confused or disoriented. Depression and cognitive impairment predict self-neglect (Abrams, Lachs, McAvay, Keohane, & Bruce, 2002).

Reluctance to Disclose

A number of researchers believe that elder abuse is significantly underreported (Bulman, 2010), with some suggesting that as much as 5 times more goes un-reported as reported (Tatara et al., 1998). Some suggest abuse goes unreported because elders often do not believe they are being abused. Other reasons include fear of loss of independence, fear of being institutionalized, fear of losing the rela-tionship and care from a family member, and abuse is considered a private family matter not to be shared outside the family.

Injury Estimates

The National Electronic Injury Surveillance System (CDC, 2003) keeps information on people seeking treatment for injuries in hospital emergency rooms. In 2001, approximately 33,000 elders sought treatment in emergency rooms. Of these, 55.4% were men. Most of the injuries fell in the following categories: (a) contusions/abrasions (31.9%), (b) lacerations (21.1%), and fractures (12.7%). Injury rates may be as high as 6% for physically abused elderly husbands and 57% for physically abused elderly wives (Pillemer & Finkelhor, 1988).

Characteristics of Abused Elders

Few differences exist between victims and nonvictims of elder abuse (Brandl & Cook-Daniels, 2002). When compared with other elders across age groups and ethnic groups, older Caucasian females were the least likely group of elders to be victimized (Klaus, 2000), whereas the majority of victims were Caucasian (Teaster et al., 2006).

Several factors have been identified to be associated with a greater risk for elder mistreatment: cognitive impairment (Wiglesworth et al., 2010), social isolation (Lachs, Berkman, Fulmer, & Horwitz, 1994), lower household income (Acierno et al., 2009), and previous traumatic event (Acierno et al., 2009). A shared living arrangement (usually family members) is a major risk factor for elder mistreatment (Lachs, Williams, O'Brien, Hurst, & Horwitz, 1997). The inability to care for themselves often results in elders living with their caregivers and thus having more consistent and intense interaction with them and an increased possibility for conflict and maltreatment. Viable options for dealing with interpersonal tensions that would normally be addressed by simply leaving the situation are often not available for the elderly or the caregiver. Wolf and Pillemer (1989) found that a change in living arrangements for abused elderly was viewed as the most effective intervention, whereas focus on changing the abusers was seen as least effective by case workers involved in 266 elder abuse cases. However, victim's willingness to consider change was critical to successful intervention.

Age and Gender

Although elder abuse is typically defined as occurring to individuals age 60 and up, abuse does not occur equally in all age groups. On the basis of data from the 2004 APS survey, ages of abuse victims were totaled in increments of 10 years as follows:

- 20.8% of elder victims were between the ages 60 and 69,
- 36.5% were between ages 70 and 79, and
- 42.8% were age 80 or over.

The fact that the oldest elders (age 80 and up) make up 19% of the U.S. elderly population speaks to the increased vulnerability to abuse with increasing age. As the age-80-and-up group is the fastest growing group of elderly persons, more attention needs to be given to prevention of abuse with this group. This age group likely is more vulnerable to abuse because of their increasing dependency on others for care (Bonnie & Wallace, 2003). Furthermore, the vast majority of abused elders (65.7%) are older women (Teaster et al., 2006). This finding was true for all categories of abuse except abandonment, in which elderly males were the most likely victims.

Ethnicity

The majority of surveys indicate that Euro Americans are overly represented in every category of elder abuse except abandonment, in which African Americans were the majority of victims (57.3%; NCEA, 2002). One explanation for this phenomenon is that the various ethnic groups likely differ more in what behaviors they view as abusive than in the frequency of abusive behavior (Bonnie & Wallace, 2003; Moon & Williams, 1993).

Characteristics of Elder Abusers

Perpetrator risk factors include family relation (Lachs et al, 1994), substance abuse (Anetzberger, Korbin, & Austin, 1994), mental illness (Williamson & Shaffer, 2001), dependency (Pillemer & Finkelhor, 1989), and unemployment (Acierno et al., 2009). The most common perpetrators of elder violence are as follows: adult children (32.6%), other family members (21.5%), unknown (16.3%), and spouses and other intimate partners of the perpetrators (11.3%; Teaster et al., 2006). Identifying a consistent profile of an elder abuser is probably more difficult than compiling a profile of an abused elder, as existing studies often contradict each other.

Age and Gender

Results of the APS 2004 survey indicated that most perpetrators are under the age of 60, with the following age break-down:

- 4.3% were under age 18,
- 10.6% were between 18 and 29,
- 16.1% were between 30 and 39,
- 25.6% were between 40 and 49,
- 18.5% were between 50 and 59,
- 11.2% were between 60 and 69,
- 7.9% were between 70 and 79, and
- 5.8% were over 80 years of age.

These figures are roughly consistent with both the APS 2000 survey (Teaster, Nerenberg, & Stansbury, 2003) and the Boston survey (Pillemer & Finkelhor, 1988) indicating that elder abusers tend to be middle-age individuals between 36 and 55. In more than half (52.7%) of the cases, the alleged perpetrators were female, and the majority of these (75.1%) were under the age of 60 (Teaster et al., 2003). The Boston survey found that spouses were most often the perpetrators, with victims split almost equally for men and women, although women suffered more serious injuries.

Explanations for Elder Abuse

Intraindividual Theories

The intraindividual theory assumes that some type of mental impairment causes a person to abuse another person. This impairment could include mental illness, personality problems, or alcohol and/or drug abuse. In three samples of caregivers, Wolf and Pillemer (1989) found that 38% had some history of mental illness. Similarly, Reis and Nahmiash (1998) interviewed 341 caregivers and found that the caregivers' mental health and behavior problems were strong predictors of abuse. The most common intraindividual characteristics associated with caregiver abuse include mental illness (Williamson & Shaffer, 2001), hostility (Quayhagen et al., 1997), and alcohol or drug abuse (Anetzberger et al., 1994). These characteristics are significantly higher in caregivers who abuse elders than those caregivers who do not. Abuser characteristics are the strongest explanation for elder abuse (Pillemer, 2005).

Social Exchange Theory

Social exchange theory explains interpersonal behavior as based on the process of negotiated exchange. This theory also acknowledges potential dependency that is based on who is contributing the most to the relationship. In the case of elder abuse, it is assumed that abusers tend to be dependent on the person they are mistreating. One view holds that increasing dependency increases the risk of abuse (Wolf, Strugnell, & Godkin, 1982). Financial dependency on the elder by the abuser is a consistent issue in many cases. Related to the previous intraindividual factors, Pillemer (2005) asserted that as opposed to stable or well-intentioned caregivers, "elder abusers tend to suffer from a variety of mental health, substance abuse, and stress-related problems" (p. 215) that contribute to the caregiver's dependency on the elder, rather than the elder being dependent on the abuser. Pillemer (1985, 1986) found abusers to be more dependent on elders in four major areas: housing, household repair, financial assistance, and transportation. Abusing the elder is one way to regain some sense of control in the relationship.

Caregiver Stress Theory

Although some research offers evidence that elder abusers are disturbed people and dependent on the elders they abuse (Pillemer, 2005), another group holds that caregiver stress is the major cause of elder abuse. Mace (1981) referred to the "36 hour day" to highlight the heightened stress and demands that caregivers often experience. This view holds that caring for the elder brings on economic hardship, loss of sleep, disruptions in normal family life, and loss of privacy; this stress creates resentment and ultimately can result in a loss of control and the occurrence of abuse (Steinmetz, 2005). In particular, Steinmetz (1983, 1988) found that there was a moderate relationship between elder abuse and objective levels of elder impairment and demands on the caregiver. An even stronger relationship existed between abuse and caregivers' subjective feelings of burden and stress related to the need to help the elder. This research suggests that it is the elder's dependency on the caregiver that is related to elder abuse (Fulmer & Ashley, 1989; Fulmer & O'Malley, 1987). Elders with Alzheimer's present a particular challenge for caregivers, and those elders who have this disease are at a higher risk for abuse than those elders who do not have Alzheimer's (Paveza et al., 1992).

The issue of whether it is caregivers who endure stress or caregivers who are dependent and troubled that cause elder abuse is a hotly debated issue (see Steinmetz, 2005; Pillemer, 2005). With both sides marshalling research to support their particular points of view, it is likely that both positions are valid with certain samples of abused elders. As well, there is probably a mid-point between the two positions that includes an interactional contribution of the abusers and the elderly (Phillips, Torres de Ardon, & Briones, 2000). However, care must be exercised not to blame the victim. Interventions derived from this framework emphasize support to the caregiver.

Social Cognitive Theory

Social cognitive theory (Bandura, 1979) is a major explanation for most forms of family violence. Briefly, the theory assumes that people learn from observing others. Thus, if a child observes his or her caregiver abuse another family member, including an elderly person, then an increased risk exists for a continuation of such behavior in the next generation. Interventions focus on identifying maladaptive learning and teaching new, more adaptive behaviors.

Sociocultural Theories

Sociocultural theories emphasize power and control and have been the mainstay of feminist theory. From this perspective, elder abusers believe they have rights entitling them to abuse and/or neglect older adults. Treatments focuses not on the needs and demands of the elder but on the deviance and sense of entitlement of the abusers (Pillemer & Finkelhor, 1989). Interventions focus on safety for the elder and holding abusers accountable for their behavior.

As with most explanations for abuse of any kind, individual explanations and theories account for only a piece of the pie. In all likelihood, several of these explanations provide the best explanation for any given elder-abuse situation. Thus, clinicians must consider the unique circumstances for any given abuse case and determine if one or several of these explanations fit the case and then consider interventions accordingly. However, having said this, some experts believe that caregiver stress theory and mental impairment of the abuser (intrapersonal theories) best account for a large portion of elder abuse (O. Barnett et al., 2011).

Elder Abuse in Long-Term Care Facilities

Little research has been conducted with the elderly who live in residential settings (Hawes, 2003). However, existing research suggests that elderly people who live in long-term care facilities are at high risk for abuse or neglect because most suffer with chronic illnesses that greatly compromise their physical and cognitive functioning (Hawes, Blevins, & Shanley, 2001; Schiamberg et al., 2012). These elderly people are highly dependent on others and often are unable or unwilling to report abuse or neglect because of a fear of retaliation or compromised services. Burgess, Dowdell, and Prentky (2000) argued, "The risk for abuse increases simply as a function of their dependence on staff for safety, protection, and care" (p. 12). Elderly with Alzheimer's or other types of dementia and behavior problems are at an increased risk for abuse in domestic settings. These same factors are strong risk factors for abuse in residential settings (Hawes et al., 2001).

Although the quality of care varies widely across residential facilities, abuse rates of elderly are significant. Estimated prevalence of physical abuse in residential settings has been reported to be 24.3% in a random community sample in Michigan that was based on 453 noninstitutionalized adults with a relative in a residential setting (Schiamberg et al., 2012). The Atlanta Long-Term Care Ombudsman Program (2000) interviewed 80 residents in 23 nursing homes in Georgia and found that 44% reported being abused in some fashion. As well, 38% stated they had seen other residents abused. Ninety-five percent of these residents reported that they had experienced neglect and/or had seen other residents being neglected. Examples of neglect included being left wet or soiled with feces; not being turned, which can result in pressure ulcers; having staff members shut off call lights without giving help; and not receiving adequate help at mealtime. In a survey of 577 nursing home staff from 31 facilities, 36% reported witnessing at least one incident of physical abuse, while 10% of the staff acknowledged they had committed abusive acts as well (Pillemer & Moore, 1989). Incidents of abuse against residents included using excessive physical restraint (21%); pushing, shoving, grabbing, or pinching (17%); and slapping or hitting (13%). Of the 3,443 statewide complaints of nursing home residents in Connecticut, 47% were reports of abuse (Hawes, 2003). Clearly, nursing homes can be a high-risk factor for elder abuse.

Predictors of Abuse

Using surveys from 577 nursing staff within 31 long-term care facilities, Pillemer and Bachman-Prehn (1991) examined predictors of physical and psychological abuse related to institutional characteristics, staff characteristics, and situational characteristics. Predictors of psychological abuse were staff burnout, physical aggression from patients, negative attitudes toward patients, and age of staff worker. Younger staff members were most likely to become involved in psychological abuse. Physical abuse was predicted by staff burnout, patient aggression, and degree of conflict with patients. Other studies have identified similar risk factors, including (a) stressful working conditions related to staff shortages, (b) staff burnout, (c) resident aggression, (d) poor training in managing problem behavior, (e) poor hiring, (f) chronic staff problems, and (g) lack of supervisory oversight (Hawes, 2003; Pillemer, 1986).

Researchers contend that elder abuse in nursing facilities is vastly underreported by all concerned parties, including the elderly residents and their families, facility staff, and outside health care professionals such as physicians and nurses

(Hawes, 2003). Advocates, researchers, practitioners, and government must work together to improved detection. More active ombudsman programs and better training with nursing and other staff members could improve reporting as well as prevention strategies. Training for staff should include both training to enhance reporting as well as training to deal with stress, anger management, and conflict resolution (Menio & Keller, 2000). Facility administrators must also do a more thorough screening of applicants for criminal backgrounds and appropriate credentials along with reporting all cases of abuse to law enforcement and abuse registries (O. Barnett et al., 2011).

Consequences of Elder Maltreatment

There is a lack of research or scholarly activity on the consequences of elder abuse beyond increased risk for injuries and neglect-related medical issues such as bruises, dehydration, burns, malnutrition, bedsores, and fractures (Dyer, Connolly, & McFeeley, 2003). However, in many ways, elders who experience abuse are subject to the same psychological and emotional symptoms as people who experience other types of interpersonal maltreatment: depression, learned helplessness, PTSD, guilt, shame, and denial (O. Barnett et al., 2011). Well-conducted studies are rare, though, and those that exist are small and methodologically questionable. Depression seems to be a consistent factor for the elderly who experience abuse. However, it is often difficult to determine if the depression is solely a result of the abuse or if depressed elders are more susceptible to abuse (Brandl & Cook-Daniels, 2002).

Research indicates that a percentage of elders live in abusive relationships with their spouses. The APS 2004 survey indicated that spouses were the perpetrators of elder abuse in 11.3% of the cases (Teaster et al., 2006). Two studies used data from domestic violence programs and found that 58% to 95% of elderly women clients were abused by partners (Seaver, 1996; Vinton, 1992). On the basis of IPV research, it is likely that at least a portion of these cases would experience some degree of depression, anxiety, PTSD, and CPTSD as result of abuse. Research is needed in the area of elder partner/spouse IPV, particularly as it pertains to distinctions between CCV and terroristic violence.

Fatalities

Both elder abuse and self-neglect are related to mortality rate. A recent study with a community sample of elders found a significant relationship between elder abuse, self-neglect, and mortality 1 year after a report to social services as compared with nonabused elders (Dong et al., 2009). Lachs, Williams, O'Brien, Pillemer, and Charlson (1998) tracked elderly residents in Connecticut for 13 years. Elderly adults who experienced abuse at any time during this period had a poorer survival rate (9%) than either those who were self-neglecting (17%) or who were never abused (40%). None of the deaths were attributed to injuries from the abuse. The authors concluded that abuse and self-neglect are associated with shorter survival.

Abuse of Caregivers

Some research indicates that 29% to 33% of elderly adults are physically abusive to their caregivers (Coyne, Reichman, & Berbig, 1993; Phillips et al., 2000), with 16% being severely physically abusive (Paveza et al., 1992). Yet elders who are abusive with caregivers are at a greater risk for retaliatory violence from caregivers (Coyne et al., 1993). Phillips et al. (2000) identified four factors that predicted an elderly person's abuse of his or her caregiver: (a) younger age of the elder, (b) greater difference between the caregiver's past versus present image of the elder, (c) a perception of power imbalance toward the elder, and (d) greater interpersonal conflict.

Interventions

Successfully addressing elder abuse is multifaceted and involves legal, mental health, community, and educational components. However, many elder-care providers are ill-prepared to address elder abuse even at the most basic level. Of the three most critical groups needing education on elder abuse—professionals, community leaders, and the elderly (O. Barnett et al., 2011)—only professionals working with the elderly receive any type of training. Even then, 40% receive no training (Pagano, Mihaly, Dauenhauer, & Mason, 2007). This lack of education is often borne out in daily practice. Lachs and Pillemer (1995) surveyed health care providers regarding elder abuse and found the following problems reported: lack of knowledge of reporting requirements, confusion on what constitutes elder abuse, hesitancy to report cases because of victim's denial of abuse, and low suspicion level for elder abuse. In addition, state laws on elder abuse vary greatly. Although all states have laws related to elder abuse, only 44 states and the District of Columbia have mandatory reporting laws. States not regulating mandatory reporting are Colorado, New Jersey, New York, North Dakota, South Dakota, and Wisconsin.

In recent years, there has been a growing focus on elder abuse both by government-sponsored and advocacy-group-sponsored programs and by organizations to enhance awareness, to provide training and skills for intervention, and to change policy. The U.S. DHHS Administration on Aging (http://www.aoa.gov/about/about.asp), the NCEA (http://www.elderabusecenter.org/default.cfm), and the National Committee for the Prevention of Elder Abuse (http://www.preventelderabuse.org/index.html) are a few of the organizations that strongly advocate for elders and the prevention of elder abuse. These organizations often include professionals from a variety of professions, such as medicine, public health, psychology, social work, sociology, nursing, and law to name a few.

Most intervention programs include a number of change strategy components, such as legal, therapeutic, educational, and advocacy (Reis & Nahmiash, 1995). Anetzberger (2000) noted that existing approaches to elder abuse focus on three overlapping goals and strategies: (a) legislative interventions, particularly adult protection services; (b) community services that use integrative models that include legal, medical, and psychosocial needs of at-risk elderly people; and (c) education and prevention services, such as advocacy and empowerment.

Recently, an extensive review of interventions for elder abuse found only eight well-designed studies (e.g., included a comparison group), with results indicating little effect for interventions (e.g., psychoeducational support group, legal interventions, social services, home visits, and advocacy interventions) targeting victims, perpetrators, and caregivers. In some cases, interventions actually increased the risk of recurrence (e.g., assistance in using the legal system, home visits plus education) when compared with a no-intervention control group (Ploeg, Fear, Hutchison, MacMillan, & Bolan, 2009). Three studies examined psychosocial interventions and found no difference between interventions and control groups on measures of depression, guilt, self-esteem, family relations, and sense of well-being. The authors concluded that there is insufficient evidence to support any particular intervention for elder abuse. However, they suggest that professionals continue to use interventions that provide support to victims and caregivers, training for caregivers and professionals, and legal advocacy.

Reporting Maltreatment

In most instances of abuse, reports are made to APS. However, there is a lack of consistency across state laws with regard to defining elder abuse and who is required to report. For example, 15 of the 44 states require reporting not only by professionals but also by anyone who might suspect elder abuse (Bonnie & Wallace, 2003). Sadly, many elderly victims do not report abuse or seek services for the following reasons: (a) They do not see themselves as abused, (b) they would prefer services for their abusers rather than themselves, and (c) embarrassment or fear of losing the abusing family member's support (Brandl & Cook-Daniels, 2002). Underreporting by elderly is a major hurdle to appropriate action. The National Elder Abuse Incidence Study (NCEA, 1998) found that there are 5 times as many unreported cases of elder abuse as reported. This underreporting is a critical issue that needs to be addressed.

Elders tend to see medical professionals on a regular basis, and yet many physicians and nurses knowingly fail to report suspected elder abuse (Blakely & Dolon, 1991). Medical personnel are reluctant to report elder abuse for a number of reasons. For example, some physicians believe that reporting elder abuse undermines rapport; reporting often involves APS or law enforcement, which in turn disrupts the victim's quality of life; and reporting may result in the physician losing decision-making power regarding the best interests of the elderly patient (M. A. Rodriguez, Wallace, Woolf, & Mangione, 2006). Obviously, medical professionals must take the issue of elder abuse much more seriously. As well, counselors are required to report suspected elder abuse.

APS agencies are the primary responders to elder mistreatment once a report has been made. Following the report, APS will (a) determine whether there is sufficient information to warrant an investigation, (b) determine whether or not maltreatment actually occurred, (c) assess the elderly person's ability to make informed decisions about his or her own care, and (d) determine the appropriate services (McClennen, 2010). Several screening devices are available for identifying elder abuse in the community and in nursing homes (McGarry & Simpson, 2009).

Assessment and Services

Once elder abuse is identified, an assessment should be conducted to understand the dynamics surrounding the abuse; this assessment should be done before implementing a plan to address the abuse. A *capacity assessment* involves gathering and integrating information pertaining to neuropsychiatric illness, cognitive and behavioral capacity to make competent decisions, living conditions, financial circumstances, treatment consent, caregiver functioning, and vulnerability to others' influence that primarily benefits a coercer (McClennen, 2010). Capacity assessments are especially useful when dealing with elders who self-neglect because of some physical or cognitive limitation.

Once a capacity assessment has been concluded, services can be offered to the elderly person based on need, such as police intervention, case management, protective orders, health care services, homemaker services, individual counseling, peer support groups, and 24-hour help line (Brownell, Berman, & Salamone, 1999). There is some support for the effectiveness of these interventions. Nahmiash and Reis (2000) used a qualitative content analysis to evaluate the effects of 473 strategies with 83 elder abuse cases. The most successful strategies noted were as follows: nursing and other medical care and homemaking assistance; followed by empowerment strategies, such as support groups; and information about rights and resources and volunteer buddies/advocates. The least successful strategies were referrals to general community activities and programs. The most successful psychological interventions included education and individual counseling to reduce anxiety, stress, and depression. A combination of CBT and person-centered therapy has been used with abused elders, with anecdotal reports supporting its effectiveness (Fraser, 2006).

Another study examined the effectiveness of education and anger management with individuals who abused or neglected elderly people and found that participants reported significant reductions in strain, depression, and anxiety following the interventions (Reay & Browne, 2002). Subjects also reported fewer conflicts with regard to elders. Although neither study involved a control group, it would seem that the interventions cited might be promising interventions for further research. Several other studies have found a reduction or elimination of abuse by using similar interventions (Lithwick, Beaulieu, Gravel, & Straka, 1999; Vladescu, Eveleigh, & Patterson, 1999).

Multidisciplinary teams (MDTs) composed of law enforcement personnel, attorneys, medical personnel, clergy, and forensic pathologists are being used more widely with elder abuse cases (Anetzberger, Dayton, Miller, McGreevey, & Schimer, 2005). These teams have been successful in dealing with child abuse and partner abuse (Wolfe, 2003). MDTs receive training to identify and prevent elder abuse and, once trained, provide consultation on abuse cases and help coordinate and assist agencies in providing services.

Prevention

Elder abuse prevention typically targets providers, community leaders, elderly people, and their families (O. Barnett et al., 2011). Many professionals such as nurses, psychologists, counselors, social workers, and physicians are required to accrue a number of continuing education (CE) hours yearly to maintain their licenses/certifications. In fact, many agencies require their providers to attend seminars or conferences on abuse. In addition, states could take a proactive step by requiring professionals to complete a certain number of CE hours each year on abuse, including elder abuse. Just as many professions have made cultural awareness and sensitivity an integral part of training and CE, abuse and elder abuse in particular should achieve a similar status in the helping professions, particularly for those working with the elderly.

Educating elderly people is another critical step in prevention of elder abuse. Providing them with accurate information about their rights, self-protection measures, and solution-oriented behaviors greatly contributes to their sense of self-efficacy. One group of researchers compared three prevention strategies (i.e., public awareness campaigns, home visits, or both) with a group of 403 abused elders with a goal of preventing revictimization. Results indicated that none of the interventions significantly increased elder's knowledge about abuse or social services, nor did any intervention improve their psychological well-being. However, those elders who were exposed to both interventions were more likely to report abuse to the researchers and contact the police (R. C. Davis, Medina, & Avitabile, 2001).

A promising prevention tool is the use of support activities that use individual and group formats to create a supportive culture to further empower elderly people. For example, Project Care in Montreal matches up abused elders with volunteer "buddies" who meet regularly to encourage, to reduce social isolation, and to monitor elder treatment. Weekly group meetings allow participants to share their experiences and suggestions in dealing with various problems (Reis & Nahmiash, 1995). Regular group meetings also provide the abused elders with a sense of hope, a chance to identify with other elders who have similar problems, and an opportunity to learn new problem-solving skills.

Public education raises the awareness level of the general public and helps create and maintain a social attitude that disapproves of elder abuse. Activities include pamphlets on advocacy, newspaper ads, billboard advertisements, lobbying, public media, and conferences.

Finally, respite care—having someone else care for the elder, even for a few hours each week—is critical in reducing caregiver stress, a major contributing factor in elder abuse. Most caregivers benefit from time away from caring for someone else. Time away is especially important for caregivers of people suffering from Alzheimer's or other forms of significant dementia or of elders who are severely disabled (American Psychological Association, 2006).

Summary

Elder abuse is probably the least researched and the least developed sub-area of family violence. A lack of uniformity in its definition and in reporting requirements across states—and even between professional groups—creates considerable difficulty for reporting and for developing prevention and intervention plans. As well, research is sorely lacking that provides clear direction for effective interventions and a clear understanding of the phenomenon. Recent years have seen an increase in awareness by government and private organizations. However, much remains to be accomplished to bring the field of elder abuse to a level of awareness, advocacy, interventions, and research similar to that in other sub-areas of intimacy violence.

Current efforts have begun to identify promising prevention and intervention strategies, such as education for professionals, elders, and their families; MDTs; support groups; and anger management groups. However, few studies have been conducted to test their effectiveness. Such research efforts must be a major thrust of future activities in addressing elder abuse. Furthermore, state and federal government must take a more active role in helping clarify and define elder abuse to make reporting laws more viable and effective.

Suggested Readings

American Law Sources On-line. *www.lawsource.com/also/* [an on-line link to state laws].

Bonnie, R. J., & Wallace, R. B. (Eds.). (2003). *Elder maltreatment: Abuse, neglect, and exploitation in an aging America.* Washington, DC: The National Academies Press (www.nap.edu).

Brandl, B., & Cook-Daniels, L. (2002). *Domestic abuse in later life.* Washington, DC: National Resource Center on Domestic Violence. http://www.vawnet.org/DomesticViolence/Research/VAWnetDocs/AR_later-life.php

Fraser, A. (2006). Psychological therapies in the treatment of abused adults. *Journal of Adult Protection, 8,* 31–38.

Harris, D. K., & Benson, M. L. (2006). *Maltreatment of patients in nursing homes: There is no safe place.* Binghamton, NY: Haworth Pastoral Press.

Hederson, D., Varble, D., & Buchanan, J. A. (2004). Elder abuse: Guidelines for treatment. In W. T. O'Donohue & E. R. Levensky (Eds.), *Handbook of forensic psychology: Resource for mental health and legal professionals* (pp. 743–766). Atlanta, GA: Elsevier Science.

Kaye, L. W., Kay, D., & Crittenden, J. A. (2007). Intervention with abused older males: Conceptual and clinical perspectives. *Journal of Elder Abuse & Neglect, 19,* 153–172.

Nerenberg, L. (2008). *Elder abuse prevention: Emerging trends and promising strategies.* New York, NY: Springer.

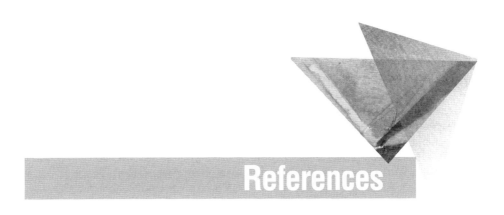

References

Abbey, A. (2002). Alcohol-related sexual assault: A common problem among college students. *Journal of Studies on Alcohol, Supplement No. 14,* 118–128.

Abbey, A., McAuslan, P., Zawacki, T., Clinton, A. M., & Buck, P. O. (2001). Attitudinal, experiential, and situational predictors of sexual assault perpetration. *Journal of Interpersonal Violence, 16,* 784–807.

Abrams, R., Lachs, M., McAvay, G., Keohane, D., & Bruce, M. (2002). Predictors of self-neglect in community dwelling elders. *American Journal of Psychiatry, 159,* 1724–1730.

Achenbach, T. M. (1991). *Manual for the Child Behavior Checklist/4-18 and 1991 profile.* Burlington: Department of Psychiatry, University of Vermont.

Achenbach, T. M. (2002). *Achenbach System of Empirically Based Assessment* (ASEBA). Burlington, VT: Research Center for Children, Youth, and Families.

Acierno, R., Hernandez-Tejada, M., Muzzy, W., & Steve, K. (2009). *Prevalence and correlates of emotional, physical, sexual, and financial abuse and potential neglect in the United States: The National Elder Mistreatment Study* (NCJ Publication No. 226456). Washington, DC: U.S. Department of Justice.

Agbayani-Siewert, P., & Flanagan, A. (2001). Filipino American dating violence: Definitions, contextual justifications, and experiences of dating violence. *Journal of Human Behavior in the Social Environment, 3,* 115–133.

Aguilar, R. J., & Nightingale, N. N. (1994). The impact of specific battering experiences on the self-esteem of abused women. *Journal of Family Violence, 9,* 35–45.

Ahrens, C. E., Campbell, R., Wasco, S. M., Aponte, G., Grubstein, L., & Davidson, W. S., II. (2000). Sexual Assault Nurse Examiner (SANE) programs. *Journal of Interpersonal Violence, 15,* 921–943.

Ahrens, C. E., Rios-Mandel, L. C., Isas, L., & del Carment Lopez, M. (2010). Talking about interpersonal violence: Cultural influences on Latinas' identification and disclosure of sexual assault and intimate partner violence. *Psychological Trauma, Theory, Research, Practice, and Policy, 2,* 284–295.

Aldarondo, E. (2002). Evaluating the efficacy of interventions with men who batter. In E. Aldarondo & F. Mederos (Eds.), *Programs for men who batter: Intervention and prevention strategies in a diverse society* (pp. 3–20). Kingston, NJ: Civic Research Institute.

Aldarondo, E., & Castro-Fernandez, M. (2011). Risk and protective factors for domestic violence. In J. W. White, M. P. Koss, & Kazdin, A. E. (2011). *Violence against women and children: Mapping the terrain* (Vol. 1, pp. 221–242). Washington, DC: American Psychological Association.

Aldarondo, E., & Kaufman Kantor, G. (1997). Social predictors of wife assault cessation. In G. Kaufman Kantor & J. L. Jasinski (Eds.), *Out of darkness: Contemporary perspectives on family violence* (pp. 183–193). Thousand Oaks, CA: Sage.

Aldarondo, E., Kaufman Kantor, G., & Jasinski, J. L. (2002). Risk marker analysis for wife assault in Latino families. *Violence Against Women: An International and Interdisciplinary Journal, 8,* 429–454.

Aldarondo, E., & Mederos, F. (2002). *Programs for men who batter: Intervention and prevention strategies in a diverse society.* Kingston, NJ: Civic Research Institute.

Aldarondo, E., & Sugarman, D. B. (1996). Risk marker analysis of the cessation and persistence of wife assault. *Journal of Consulting and Clinical Psychology, 64,* 1010–1019.

Alink, L. R. A., Cicchetti, D., Kim, J., & Rogosch, F. A. (2009). Mediating and moderating processes in the relation between maltreatment and psychopathology: Mother–child relationship quality and emotion regulation. *Journal of Abnormal Child Psychology, 37,* 831–843.

American Academy of Family Physicians. (2000). *Violence position paper.* Retrieved March 10, 2008, from http://www.aafp.org/online/en/home/policy/policies/v/violencepositionpaper.preinterview.ht

American Professional Society on the Abuse of Children. (1995). *Guidelines for the psychological evaluation of suspected psychological maltreatment in children and adolescents.* Chicago, IL: Author.

American Psychiatric Association. (1994). *Diagnostic and statistical manual of mental disorders* (4th ed.). Washington, DC: Author.

American Psychiatric Association. (2000). *Diagnostic and statistical manual of mental disorders* (4th ed., text rev.). Washington, DC: Author.

American Psychological Association. (1996a). *Issues and dilemmas in family violence.* Washington, DC: Author.

American Psychological Association. (1996b). *Violence and the family.* Washington, DC: Author.

American Psychological Association. (2006). *Elder abuse and neglect: In search of solutions.* Retrieved from www.apa.org/pi/aging/eldabuse.html

Amstadter, A. B., Cisler, J. M., McCauley, J. L., Hernandez, M. A., Muzzy, W., & Acierno, R. (2011). Do incident and perpetrator characteristics of elder mistreatment differ by gender of the victim? Results from the National Elder Mistreatment Study. *Journal of Elder Abuse & Neglect, 23,* 43–57

Anderson, D. K., & Saunders, D. G. (2003). Leaving an abusive partner: An empirical review of predictors, the process of leaving, and psychological well-being. *Trauma, Violence, & Abuse, 4,* 163–191.

Anderson, L. A., & Whiston, S. C. (2005). Sexual assault education programs: An meta-analytic examination of their effectiveness. *Psychology of Women Quarterly, 29,* 374–388.

Andrews, B., Brewin, C. R., Rose, S., & Kirk, M. (2000). Predicting PTSD symptoms in victims of violent crime: The role of shame, fear, anger, and childhood abuse. *Journal of Abnormal Behavior, 109,* 69–73.

Anetzberger, G. J. (2000). Caregiving: Primary cause of elder abuse? *Journal of the American Society on Aging, 2,* 46–51.

Anetzberger, G. J., Dayton, C. Miller, C. A., McGreevey, J. F., & Schimer, M. (2005). Multidisciplinary teams in the clinical management of elder abuse. *Clinical Gerontologist, 28,* 157–171.

Anetzberger, G. J., Korbin, J. E., & Austin, C. (1994). Alcoholism and elder abuse. *Journal of Interpersonal Violence, 9,* 184–193.

Antoun, R. T. (1968). On the modesty of women in Arab Muslim villages: A study in the accommodation of traditions. *American Anthropologist, 70,* 671–697.

Aponte, J., & Johnson, L. (2000). The impact of culture on the intervention and treatment of ethnic populations. In J. Aponte & J. Wohl (Eds.), *Psychological intervention and cultural diversity* (pp. 18–39). Boston, MA: Allyn & Bacon.

Appleby, G. A. (2001). Ethnographic study of gay and bisexual working-class men in the United States. *Journal of Gay & Lesbian Social Services: Issues in Practice, Policy & Research, 12,* 51–62.

Arata, C. M. (2002). Child sexual abuse and sexual revictimization. *Clinical Psychology: Science and Practice, 9,* 135–164.

Archambeau, O. G., Frueh, B. C., Deliramich, A. N., Herman, S., Kim, B. S. K., Ilhai, J. D., & Grubaugh, A. L. (2010). Interpersonal violence and mental health outcomes among Asian American and Native Hawaiian/other Pacific Islander college students. *Psychological Trauma: Theory, Research, Practice, and Policy, 2,* 273–283.

Archer, J. (2000). Sex differences in aggression between heterosexual partners: A meta-analytic review. *Psychological Bulletin, 126,* 651–680.

Arias, I., & Pape, K. T. (1999). Psychological abuse: Implications for adjustment and commitment to leave violent partners. *Violence and Victims, 14,* 55–67.

Armstrong, T. G., Wernke, J. Y., Medina, K. L., & Schafer, J. (2002). Do partners agree about the occurrence of intimate partner violence? *Trauma, Violence, & Abuse, 3,* 181–193.

Ashcraft, C. (2000). Naming knowledge: A language for reconstructing domestic violence and gender inequity. *Women and Language, 23,* 3–10.

Atlanta Long-Term Care Ombudsman Program. (2000). *The silenced voice speaks out: A study of abuse and neglect of nursing home residents.* Atlanta, GA: Atlanta Legal Aid Society; and Washington, DC: National Citizens Coalition for Nursing Home Reform.

Azar, S. T., & Wolfe, D. A. (2006). Child physical abuse and neglect. In E. J. Mash & R. A. Barkley (Eds.), *Treatment of childhood disorders* (3rd ed., pp. 595–646). New York, NY: Guilford Press.

Babcock, J. C., Green, C. E., & Robie, C. (2004). Does batterers' treatment work? A meta-analytic review of domestic violence treatment. *Clinical Psychology Review, 23,* 1023–1053.

Babcock, J. C., & La Taillade, J. L. (2000). Evaluating interventions for men who batter. In J. P. Vincent & E. N. Jouriles (Eds.), *Domestic violence: Guidelines for research-informed practice* (pp. 37–77). London, England: Jessica Kingsley.

Babcock, J. C., & Steiner, R. (1999). The relationship between treatment, incarceration, and recidivism of battering: A program evaluation of Seattle's coordinated community response to domestic violence. *Journal of Family Psychology, 13,* 46–59.

Babcock, J. C., Waltz, J., Jacobson, N. S., & Gottman, J. M. (1993). Power and violence: The relation between communication patterns, power discrepancies, and domestic violence. *Journal of Consulting and Clinical Psychology, 61,* 40–50.

Bachman, R., & Saltzman, L. E. (1995). *Violence against women: Estimates from the redesigned survey* (NCJ Publication No. 154348). Rockville, MD: U.S. Department of Justice.

Bala, N. (2008). An historical perspective on family violence and child abuse: Comment on Moloney et al., Allegations of family violence, June 12, 2007. *Journal of Family Studies, 14,* 271–278.

Balsam, K. F., Martell, C. R., & Safren, S. A. (2006). Affirmative cognitive–behavioral therapy with lesbian, gay, and bisexual people. In P. A. Hays & G. Y. Iwamasa (Eds.), *Culturally responsive cognitive–behavioral therapy: Assessment, practice, and supervision* (pp. 223–243). Washington, DC: American Psychological Association.

Balsam, K. F., & Szymanski, D. M. (2005). Relationship quality and domestic violence in women's same-sex relationships: The role of minority stress. *Psychology of Women Quarterly, 29,* 258–269.

Bandura, A. (1979). The social leaning perspective: Mechanisms of aggression. In A. Toch (Ed.), *Psychology of crime and criminal justice* (pp. 298–336). New York, NY: Holt, Rinehart & Winston.

Banyard, V. L., Ward, S., Cohn, E. S., Plante, E. G., Moorhead, C., & Walsh, W. (2007). Unwanted sexual contact on campus: A comparison of women's and men's experiences. *Violence and Victims, 22,* 52–70.

Barbaree, H. E., Marshall, W. L., & McCormick (1998). The development of deviant sexual behaviour among adolescents and its implications for prevention and treatment. *Irish Journal of Psychology, 19,* 1–31.

Barelds, D. P. H., & Barelds-Dijkstra, P. (2007). Relations between different types of jealousy and self and partner perceptions of relationship quality. *Clinical Psychology & Psychotherapy, 14,* 176–188.

Barelds, D. P. H., & Dijkstra, P. (2006). Reactive, anxious and possessive forms of jealousy and their relation to relationship quality among heterosexuals and homosexuals. *Journal of Homosexuality, 51,* 183–198.

Barnett, D., Ganiban, J., & Cicchetti, D. (1999). Maltreatment, negative expressivity, and the development of Type D attachments from 12 to 24 months of age. *Monographs of the Society for Research in Child Development, 64,* 97–118.

Barnett, O. W. (2000). Why battered women do not leave, part 1: External inhibiting factors within society. *Trauma, Violence, & Abuse, 1,* 343–372.

Barnett, O., Miller-Perrin, C. L., & Perrin, R. D. (2005). *Family violence across the lifespan: An introduction* (2nd ed.). Thousand Oaks, CA: Sage.

Barnett, O., Miller-Perrin, C. L., & Perrin, R. D. (2011). *Family violence across the lifespan: An introduction* (3rd ed.). Thousand Oaks, CA: Sage.

Bartkowski, J. (1996). Beyond Biblical literalism and inerrancy: Conservative Protestants and the hermeneutic interpretation of Scripture. *Sociology of Religion, 57,* 259–272.

Basile, K. C. (2002). Prevalence of wife rape and other intimate partner sexual coercion in a nationally representative sample of women. *Violence and Victims, 17,* 511–524.

Bassuk, E., Dawson, R., & Huntington, N. (2006). Intimate partner violence in extremely poor women: Longitudinal patterns and risk markers. *Journal of Family Violence, 21,* 387–399.

Bauer, H., Rodriquez, M., Quiroga, S., & Flores-Ortiz, Y. (2000). Barriers to health care for abused Latina and Asian immigrant women. *Journal of Health Care for the Poor and Underserved, 11,* 33–44.

Baum, K., Catalano, S., Rand, M., & Rose, K. (2009). *Stalking victimization in the United States* (NCJ Publication No. 224527). U.S. Department of Justice, NCVS. Available at http://www.ojp.usdoj.gov/bjs/abstract/svus.htm

Baumeister, R. F., & Sommer, K. L. (1997). What do men want? Gender differences and two spheres of belongingness: Comment on Cross and Madison (1997). *Psychological Bulletin, 122,* 38–44.

Baumrind, D. (1996). A blanket injunction against disciplinary use of spanking is not warranted by the data. *Pediatrics, 98,* 828–831.

Baumrind, D., Larzelere, R. E., & Cowan, P. A. (2002). Ordinary physical punishment: Is it harmful? Comment on Gershoff (2002). *Psychological Bulletin, 128,* 580–589.

Becerra, R. (1988). The Mexican American family. In C. H. Mindel, R. W. Habenstein, & R. Wright, Jr. (Eds.), *Ethnic families in American: Patterns and variations* (pp. 141–159). New York, NY: Elsevier.

Beck, A. T., Steer, R. A., & Brown, G. K. (1996). *BDI-II: Beck Depression Inventory manual* (2nd ed.). San Antonio, TX: Psychological Corporation.

Beck, J. S., Beck, A. T., & Jolly, J. B. (2001). *Beck Youth Depression Inventory.* San Antonio, TX: Psychological Corporation.

Belknap, J. (1992). Perceptions of woman battering. In I. L. Moyer (Ed.), *The changing roles of women in the criminal justice system* (2nd ed., pp. 181–201). Prospect Heights, IL: Waveland Press.

Bell, M. D., Goodman, L. A., & Dutton, M. A. (2007). The dynamics of staying and leaving: Implications for battered women's emotional well-being and experiences of violence at the end of a year. *Journal of Family Violence, 23,* 69–80.

Belle, D., & Doucet, J. (2003). Poverty, inequality, and discrimination as sources of depression among U.S. women. *Psychology of Women Quarterly, 27,* 101–113.

Belsky, J. (1980). Child maltreatment: An ecological integration. *American Psychologist, 35,* 320–335.

Belsky, J. (1993). Etiology of child maltreatment: A developmental–ecological approach. *Psychological Bulletin, 114,* 413–434.

Ben-David, S. (1993). The two facets of female violence: The public and the domestic domains. *Journal of Family Violence, 8,* 345–359.

Berns, S. B., Jacobson, N. S., & Gottman, J. M. (1999). Demand–withdraw interaction in couples with a violent husband. *Journal of Consulting and Clinical Psychology, 67,* 666–674.

Bernstein, E. M., & Putnam, F. W. (1986). Development, reliability, and validity of a dissociation scale. *Journal of Nervous and Mental Disease, 174,* 727–735.

Beyer, L. (1999, January 18). The price of honor. *Time,* p. 55.

Bilukha, O., Hahn, R. A., Crosby, A., Fullilove, M. T., Liberman, A., Moscicki, E., . . . Briss, P. A. (2005). The effectiveness of early childhood home visitation in preventing violence: A systematic review. *American Journal of Preventative Medicine, 28* (suppl. 1), Feb, 11–39.

Binggeli, N. J., Hart, S. N., & Brassard, M. R. (2001). *Psychological maltreatment of children.* Thousand Oaks, CA: Sage.

Blaauw, E., Winkel, F. W., Arensman, E., Sheridan, L. P., & Freeve, A. (2002). The toll of stalking: The relationship between features of stalking and psychopathology of victims. *Journal of Interpersonal Violence, 17,* 50–63.

Black, D. A., Heyman, R. E., & Slep, A, M. S. (2001a). Risk factors for child physical abuse. *Aggression and Violent Behavior, 6,* 121–188.

Black, D. A., Heyman, R. E., & Slep, A, M. S. (2001b). Risk factors for child sexual abuse. *Aggression and Violent Behavior, 6,* 203–229.

Black, M. C., Basile, K. C., Breiding, M. J., Smith, S. G., Walters, M. L., Merrick, M. T., . . . Stevens, M. R. (2011). *The National Intimate Partner and Sexual Violence Survey (NISVS): 2010 summary report.* Atlanta, GA: National Center for Injury Prevention and Control, Centers for Disease Control and Prevention.

Blake, D. D., Wethers, F. W., Nagy, L. M., Kaloupek, D. G., Charney, D. S., & Keane, T. M. (1996). *The Clinician-Administered PTSD Scale (CAPS).* Boston, MA: National Center for PTSD, Boston VA Medical Center.

Blakely, B. E., & Dolon, R. (1991). Area agencies on aging and the prevention of elder abuse: The results of a national study. *Journal of Elder Abuse & Neglect, 3,* 21–40.

Bletzer, K., & Koss, M. (2006). After-rape among three populations in the Southwest: A time of mourning, a time for recovery. *Violence Against Women, 12,* 5–29.

Bodnarchuk, M., Kropp, P., Ogloff, J., Hart, S., & Dutton, D. (1995). *Predicting cessation of intimate assaultiveness after group treatment.* Vancouver, British Columbia, Canada: British Columbia Institute of Family Violence; Beachwood, OH: Center for the Prevention of Domestic Violence.

Bograd, M. J. (1988). Feminist perspectives on wife abuse: An introduction. In M. Bograd & K. Yllo (Eds.), *Feminist perspectives on wife abuse* (pp. 11–26). Beverly Hills, CA: Sage.

Bolen, R. M., & Scannapieco, M. (1999). Prevalence and child sexual abuse: A corrective meta-analysis. *Social Service Review, 73,* 281–313.

Bondurant, B. (2001). University women's acknowledgment of rape. *Violence Against Women, 7,* 294–314.

Boney-McCoy, S., & Finkelhor, D. (1995). Prior victimization: A risk factor for child sexual abuse and for PTSD related symptomatology among sexually abused youth. *Child Abuse and Neglect, 19,* 1401–1421.

Bonnie, R. J., & Wallace, R. B. (Eds.). (2003). *Elder maltreatment: Abuse, neglect, and exploitation in an aging America.* Washington, DC: The National Academies Press (www.nap.edu).

Bordin, E. S. (1979). The generalizability of the psychoanalytic concept of the working alliance. *Psychotherapy: Theory, Research, Practice, Training, 16,* 252–260.

Boroughs, D. S. (2004). Female sexual abusers of children. *Children and Youth Services Review, 26,* 481–487.

Bottoms, B. L., Shaver, P. R., Goodman, G. S., & Qin, J. (1995). In the name of God: A profile of religion-related child abuse. *The Society for the Psychological Study of Social Issues, 51,* 85–111.

Bourg, S., & Stock, H. V. (1994). A review of domestic violence arrest statistics in police department using a pro-arrest policy: Are pro-arrest policies enough? *Journal of Family Violence, 9,* 177–192.

Bowen, M. (1978). *Family therapy in clinical practice.* New York, NY: Aronson.

Bowker, L. H., Arbitell, M., & McFerron, J. R. (1988). On the relationship between wife beating and child abuse. In K. Yllo & M. Bograd (Eds.), *Feminist perspectives on wife abuse* (pp. 158–174). Newbury Park, CA: Sage.

Bowlby, J. (1973). *Attachment and loss: Vol. 2. Separation.* New York, NY: Penguin Books.

Bowlby, J. (1988). *A secure base: Parent–child attachment and healthy human development.* New York, NY: Basic Books.

Brady, K. T., Killeen, T., Brewerton, T. D., & Lucerini, S. (2000). Comorbity of psychiatric disorders and posttraumatic stress disorder. *Journal of Clinical Psychiatry, 61*(Suppl. 7), 22–32.

Brandl, B., & Cook-Daniels, L. (2002). *Domestic abuse in later life.* Washington, DC: National Resource Center on Domestic Violence. Retrieved from http://www.ncea.aoa.gov/ncearoot/main_site/pdf/research/culture.pdf

Brannen, S. J., & Rubin, A. (1996). Comparing the effectiveness of gender-specific and couples groups in a court-mandated spouse abuse treatment program. *Research on Social Work Practice, 6,* 405–424.

Brassard, M. R., & Donovan, K. L. (2006). Defining psychological maltreatment. In M. M. Feerick, J. F. Knutson, P. K. Trickett, & S. M. Flanzer (Eds.), *Child abuse and neglect: Definitions, classifications, and a framework for research* (pp. 151–197). Baltimore, MD: Paul H. Brookes.

Breslau, N., Chilcoat, H. D., Kessler, R. C., & Davis, G. C. (1999). Previous exposure to trauma and PTSD effects of subsequent trauma: Results from the Detroit Area Survey of Trauma. *American Journal of Psychiatry, 156,* 902–907.

Breslau, N., Wilcox, H. C., Storr, C. L., Lucia, V., & Anthony, J. C. (2004). Trauma exposure and PTSD: A non-concurrent prospective study of youth in urban America. *Journal of Urban Health, 81,* 530–544.

Bretherton, I., & Munholland, K. A. (2008). Internal working models in attachment relationships: Elaborating a central construct in attachment theory. In J. Cassidy & P. R. Shaver (Eds.), *Handbook of attachment* (2nd ed., pp. 102–130). New York, NY: Guilford Press.

Brewin, C. R., Andrews, B., & Rose, S. (2000). Fear, helplessness, and horror in posttraumatic stress disorder: Investigating *DSM-IV* Criterion A2 in victims of violent crime. *Journal of Traumatic Stress, 13,* 499–509.

Briere, J. (1995). *Trauma Symptom Inventory (TSI) professional manual.* Odessa, FL: Psychological Assessment Resources.

Briere, J. (1996). *Trauma Symptom Checklist for Children (TSCC) professional manual.* Odessa, FL: Psychological Assessment Resources.

Briere, J. (2000). *Inventory of Altered Self Capacities (IASC).* Odessa, FL: Psychological Assessment Resources.

Briere, J. (2001). *Detailed Assessment of Posttraumatic Stress (DAPS).* Odessa, FL: Psychological Assessment Resources.

Briere, J. (2004). *Psychological assessment of adult posttraumatic stress: Phenomenology, diagnosis, and measurement.* Washington, DC: American Psychological Association.

Briere, J. (2005). *Trauma Symptom Checklist for Young Children (TSCYC).* Odessa, FL: Psychological Assessment Resources.

Briere, J., & Elliott, D. M. (2000). Prevalence, characteristics, and long-term sequelae of natural disaster exposure in the general population. *Journal of Traumatic Stress, 13,* 661–679.

Briere, J., & Elliott, D. M. (2003). Prevalence and symptomatic sequelae of self-reported childhood physical and sexual abuse in a general population sample of men and women. *Child Abuse and Neglect, 27,* 1205–1222.

Briere, J., & Jordon, C. E. (2004). Violence against women: Outcome complexity and implications for assessment and treatment. *Journal of Interpersonal Violence, 19,* 1252–1276.

Briere, J., & Scott, C. (2006). *Principles of trauma therapy: A guide to symptoms, evaluations, and treatment.* Thousand Oaks, CA: Sage.

Briere, J., Woo, R., McRae, B., Foltz, J., & Sitzman, R. (1997). Lifetime victimization history, demographics, and clinical status in female psychiatric emergency room patients. *Journal of Nervous and Mental Disease, 185,* 95–101.

Briere, J., & Zaidi, L. Y. (1989). Sexual abuse histories and sequelae in female psychiatric emergency room patients. *American Journal of Psychiatry, 146,* 1602–1606.

Brinkerhoff, M. B., & Lupri, E. (1988). Interpersonal violence. *Canadian Journal of Sociology, 13,* 407–434.

Bronfenbrenner, U. (1979). *The ecology of human development: Experiments by nature and design.* Cambridge, MA: Harvard University Press.

Brown, C. (2008). Gender-role implications on same-sex intimate partner abuse. *Journal of Family Violence, 23,* 457–462.

Brown, E. J., Albrecht, A., McQuaid, J., Munoz-Silva, D. M., & Silva, R. R. (2004). Treatment of children exposed to trauma. In R. R. Silva (Ed.), *Posttraumatic stress disorder in children and adolescents* (pp. 257–286). New York, NY: Norton.

Brown, G. (2004). Gender as a factor in the response of the law-enforcement system to violence against partners. *Sexuality and Culture, 8,* 1–87.

Brown, J., Cohen, P., Johnson, J. G., & Salzinger, S. (1998). A longitudinal analysis of risk factors for child maltreatment: Findings of a 17-year prospective study of officially recorded and self-reported child abuse and neglect. *Child Abuse & Neglect, 22,* 1065–1078.

Browne, A. (1987). *When battered women kill.* New York, NY: Free Press.

Browne, A., & Finkelhor, D. (1986). Impact of child sexual abuse: A review of the research. *Psychological Bulletin, 99,* 66–77.

Browne, A., Salomon, A., & Bassuk, S. S. (1999). The impact of recent partner violence on poor women's capacity to maintain work. *Violence Against Women, 5,* 393–426.

Brownell, P., Berman, J., & Salamone, A. (1999). Mental health and criminal justice issues among perpetrators of elder abuse. *Journal of Elder Abuse & Neglect, 11,* 81–94.

Brutz, J. L., & Ingoldsby, B. B. (1984). Conflict resolution in Quaker families. *Journal of Marriage and the Family, 46,* 21–26.

Bulman, P. (2010, April). Elder abuse emerges from the shadows of public consciousness. *NIJ Journal, 265,* 4–7.

Bunting, L. (2007). Dealing with the problem that doesn't exist? Professional responses to female perpetrated child sexual abuse. *Child Abuse Review, 16,* 252–267.

Burack, J. A., Flanagan, T., Peled, T., Sutton, H. M., Zygmuntowicz, C., & Manly, J. T. (2006). Social perspective-taking skills in maltreated children and adolescents. *Developmental Psychology, 42,* 207–217.

Bureau of Justice Statistics. (2002). *Rape and sexual assault: Reporting to police and medical attention 1992–2000.* Washington, DC: U.S. Department of Justice, Bureau of Justice Statistics.

Burgess, A. W., Dowdell, E., and Prentky, R. (2000). Sexual abuse of nursing home residents. *Journal of Psychosocial Nursing, 38,* 11–18.

Bushman, B. J., & Anderson, C. A. (2009). Comfortably numb: Desensitizing effects of violent media on helping others. *Psychological Science, 20,* 273–277.

Buss, D. M., Larsen, R. J., Westen, D., & Semmelroth, J. (1992). Sex differences in jealousy: Evolution, physiology, and psychology. *Psychological Science, 3,* 251–255.

Butcher, J. N., Dahlstrom, W. G., Graham, J. R., Tellegen, A., & Kaemmer, B. (1989). *MMPI-2: Manual for administration and scoring.* Minneapolis, MN: University of Minnesota Press.

Butcher, J. N., & Williams, C. L. (2000). *Essentials of MMPI-2 and MMPI-A* (2nd ed.). Minneapolis, MN: University of Minnesota Press.

Button, D. M., & Gealt, R. (2010). High risk behaviors among victims of sibling violence. *Journal of Family Violence, 25,* 131–140.

Buzawa, E. S., & Buzawa, C. G. (1996). *Domestic violence: The criminal justice response* (2nd ed.). Thousand Oaks, CA: Sage.

Buzawa, E. S., & Buzawa, C. G. (2003). *Domestic violence: The criminal justice response* (3rd ed.). Thousand Oaks, CA: Sage.

Caetano, R., Field, C. A., Ramisetty-Mikler, S., & McGrath, C. (2005). The 5-year course of intimate partner violence among White, Black, and Hispanic couples in the United States. *Journal of Interpersonal Violence, 20,* 1039–1057.

Campbell, J. C. (1995). Prediction of homicide of and by battered women. In J. C. Campbell (Ed.), *Assessing dangerousness: Violence by sexual offenders, batterers, and child abusers* (pp. 96–113). Thousand Oaks, CA: Sage.

Campbell, J. C., & Alford, P. (1989). The dark consequences of marital rape. *American Journal of Nursing, 89,* 946–949.

Campbell, J. C., Glass, N., Sharps, P., Laughon, K., & Bloom, T. (2007). Intimate partner homicide: Review and implications of research and policy. *Trauma, Violence, & Abuse, 8,* 246–269.

Campbell, J. C., & Soeken, K. L. (1999). Women's responses to battering over time. *Journal of Interpersonal Violence, 14,* 21–40.

Campbell, J. C., Sullivan, C. M., & Davidson, W. S. (1995). Depression in women who use domestic violence shelters: A longitudinal analysis. *Psychology of Women Quarterly, 19,* 237–255.

Campbell, J. C., Webster, D., Korziol-McLain, J., Bolck, C., Campbell, D., Curry, M., & Laughon, K. (2003). Risk factors for femicide in abusive relationships: Results from a multisite case control study. *American Journal of Public Health, 93,* 1089–1097.

Campbell, R. (1989). *How to really love your child.* Wheaton, IL: Victor Books.

Campbell, R. Wasco, S., Ahrens, C., Sefl, T., & Barnes, H. (2001). Preventing the "second rape": Rape survivors' experiences with community service providers. *Journal of Interpersonal Violence, 16,* 1239–1259.

Candib, L. M. (1999). Incest and other harms to daughters across cultures: Maternal complicity and patriarchal power. *Women's Studies International Forum, 22,* 185–201.

Cano, A., & Vivian, D. (2001). Life stressors and husband-to-wife violence. *Aggression and Violent Behavior, 6,* 459–480

Cantos, A. L., Neidig, P. H., & O'Leary, K. D. (1994). Injuries of men and women in a treatment program for domestic violence. *Journal of Family Violence, 9,* 113–124.

Capaldi, D. M., & Clark, S. (1998). Prospective family predictions of aggression toward female partners for at-risk young men. *Developmental Psychology, 34,* 1175–1188.

Capaldi, D. M., Kim, H. K., & Shortt, J. W. (2007). Observed initiation and reciprocity of physical aggression in young, at-risk couples. *Journal of Family Violence, 22,* 101–111.

Cappell, C., & Heiner, R. B. (1990). The intergenerational transmission of family aggression. *Journal of Family Violence, 5,* 135–152.

Carden, A. D. (1994). Wife abuse and the wife abuser: Review and recommendations. *Counseling Psychologist, 22,* 539–582.

Carlson, E. B., & Dalenberg, C. J. (2000). A conceptual framework for the impact of traumatic experiences. *Trauma, Violence, & Abuse, 1,* 4–28.

Carney, M. M., & Buttell, F. P. (2004). A multidimensional evaluation of a treatment program for female batterers: A pilot study. *Research on Social Work Practice, 14,* 249–258.

Carney, M. M., & Buttell, F. P. (2006). An evaluation of a court-mandated batterer intervention program: Investigating differential program effect for African American and White women. *Research in Social Work, 16,* 571–581.

Carr, J. L., & VanDeusen, K. M. (2002). The relationship between family of origin violence and dating violence in college men. *Journal of Interpersonal Violence, 17,* 630–646.

Carson, D. K. (1995). American Indian elder abuse: Risk and protective factors among the oldest Americans. *Journal of Elder Abuse and Neglect, 7,* 17–39.

Cascardi, M., Langhinrichsen, J., & Vivian, D. (1992). Marital aggression: Impact, injury, and health correlates for husbands and wives. *Archives of Internal Medicine, 152,* 1178–1184.

Cascardi, M., & O'Leary, K. D. (1992). Depressive symptomatology, self-esteem, and self-blame in battered women. *Journal of Family Violence, 7,* 249–259.

Cascardi, M., O'Leary, K. D., & Schlee, K. A. (1999). Co-occurrence and correlates of post traumatic stress disorder and major depression in physically abused women. *Journal of Family Violence, 14,* 227–249.

Cascardi, M., & Vivian, C. (1995). Context for specific episodes of marital violence: Gender and severity of violence differences. *Journal of Family Violence, 10,* 265–293.

Caselles, C. E., & Milner, J. S. (2000). Evaluation of child transgressions, disciplinary choices, abusive and comparison mothers. *Child Abuse & Neglect, 24,* 477–491.

Castonguay, L. G., Constantino, M. J., & Holtforth, M. G. (2006). The working alliance: Where are we and where should we go? *Psychotherapy, 43,* 271–279.

Catalano, S. (2006). *Intimate partner violence in the United States* [electronic version]. Washington, DC: U.S. Department of Justice, Bureau of Justice Statistics. Retrieved from http://www.ojp.usdoj.gov/bjs/intimate/ipv.htm

Catalona, S. (2007). *Intimate partner violence in the United States* (NCJ Publication No. 210675). Retrieved from U.S. Department of Justice Statistics, http://www.ojp.usdoj.gov

Cazenave, N. A., & Zahn, M. A. (1992). Women, murder, and male domination: Police reports of domestic homicide in Chicago and Philadelphia. In E. C. Viano (Ed.), *Intimate violence: Interdisciplinary perspectives* (pp. 83–96). Washington, DC: Hemisphere.

Centers for Disease Control and Prevention. (2003). Public health and aging: Nonfatal physical assault—Related injuries among persons aged > 60 years treated at hospital emergency departments—United States, 2001. *Morbidity and Mortality Weekly Report, 52,* 812–816.

Centers for Disease Control and Prevention. (2011). Youth risk behavior surveillance—United States, 2001–2009. *Morbidity and Mortality Weekly Report, Early Release, 60,* 1–35.

Chaffin, M., Silovsky, J. F., Funderburk, B., Valle, L. A., Brestan, E. V., Balachova, T., . . . Bonner, B. L. (2004). Parent–child interaction therapy with physically abusive parents: Efficacy for reducing future abuse reports. *Journal of Consulting and Clinical Psychology, 72,* 500–510.

Chalk, R., Gibbons, A., & Scarupa, H. J. (2002). *The multiple dimensions of child abuse and neglect: New insights into an old problem.* Washington, DC: Child Trends. Retrieved from www.childtrends.org/Files/ChildAbuseRB.pdf

Champion, K. M., Shipman, K., Bonner, B. L., Hensley, L., & Howe, A. C. (2003). Child maltreatment training in doctoral programs in clinical, counseling, and school psychology: Where do we go from here? *Child Maltreatment, 8*, 211–217.

Chapple, C. L. (2003). Examining intergenerational violence: Violent role modeling or weak parental controls? *Violence and Victims, 18,* 142–162.

Chard, K. M. (2005). An evaluation of cognitive processing therapy for the treatment of posttraumatic stress disorder related to childhood sexual abuse. *Journal of Consulting and Clinical Psychology, 73,* 965–971.

Chase, K. A., O'Leary, K. D., & Heyman, R. E. (2001). Categorizing partner-violent men within the reactive–proactive typology model. *Journal of Consulting and Clinical Psychology, 69,* 567–572.

Chester, B., Robin, R. W., Koss, M. P., Lopez, J., & Goldman, D. (1994). Grandmother dishonored: Violence against women by male partners in American Indian communities. *Violence and Victims, 9,* 249–258.

Child Abuse Prevention and Treatment Act (CAPTA), the Keeping Children and Families Safe Act of 2003, Pub. L. No. 108-36.

Child Welfare Information Gateway. (2007). *Abuse-focused cognitive behavioral therapy*. Retrieved from http://www.childwelfare.gov/pubs/cognitive/

Child Welfare Information Gateway. (2008). *National Child Abuse and Neglect Data System (NCANDS; 2008). Child abuse and neglect fatalities: Statistics and interventions*. Washington, DC: Author.

Christensen, A., & Heavey, C. L. (1990). Gender and social structure in the demand/withdrawal pattern of marital conflict. *Journal of Personality and Social Psychology, 59,* 73–82.

Cicchetti, D., & Barnett, D. (1991). Toward the development of a scientific nosology of child maltreatment. In D. Cicchetti & W. Grove (Eds.), *Thinking clearly about psychology: Essays in honor of Paul E. Meehl* (pp. 346–377). Minneapolis: University of Minnesota Press.

Cicchetti, D., & Toth, S. L. (2005). Child maltreatment. *Annual Review of Clinical Psychology, 1,* 409–438.

Classen, C. C., Palesh, O. G., & Aggarwal, R. (2005). Sexual revictimization: A review of the empirical literature. *Trauma, Violence, & Abuse, 6,* 103–129.

Clements, K., Holtzworth-Munroe, A., Gondolf, E., & Meehan, J. (2002, November). *Testing the Holtzworth-Munroe et al. (2000) batterer typology among court-referred maritally violent men.* Poster presented at the annual meeting of the Association for the Advancement of Behavior Therapy, Reno, NV.

Cloitre, M., Cohen, L. R., & Koenen, K. C. (2006). *Treating survivors of childhood abuse: Psychotherapy for the interrupted life*. New York, NY: Guilford Press.

Cloitre, M., & Koenen, K. (2001). Interpersonal group process treatment for CSA-related PTSD: A comparison study of the impact of borderline personality disorder on outcome. *International Journal of Group Psychotherapy, 51,* 379–398.

Cloitre, M., Koenen, K. C., Cohen, L. R., & Han, H. (2002). Skills training in affective and interpersonal regulation followed by exposure: A phase-based treatment for PTSD related to childhood abuse. *Journal of Consulting and Clinical Psychology, 70,* 1067–1074.

Cloitre, M., Stovall-McClough, K. C., Miranda, R., & Chemtob, C. M. (2004). Therapeutic alliance, negative mood regulation, and treatment outcome in child abuse-related posttraumatic stress disorder. *Journal of Consulting and Clinical Psychology, 72,* 411–416.

Close, S. M. (2005). Dating violence prevention in middle school and high school youth. *Journal of Child and Adolescent Psychiatric Nursing, 18,* 2–9.

Cloud, K. (1998, May 4). A matter of hearts. *Seattle Times*, pp. 60–64.

Cochran, S. D., Keenan, C., Schober, C., & Mays, V. M. (2000). Estimates of alcohol use and clinical treatment needs among homosexually active men and women in the U.S. population. *Journal of Consulting and Clinical Psychology, 68,* 1062–1071.

Cohen, D. (1998). Culture, social organization, and patterns of violence. *Journal of Personality and Social Psychology, 75,* 408–419.

Cohen, D. (2001). Cultural variation: Considerations and implications. *Psychological Bulletin, 127,* 451–471.

Cohen, J. A., & Mannarino, A. P. (1996). A treatment outcome study for sexually abused preschool children: Initial findings. *Journal of the American Academy of Child and Adolescent Psychiatry, 35,* 42–50.

Cohen, J. A., & Mannarino, A. P. (1998). Interventions for sexually abused children: Initial treatment findings. *Child Maltreatment, 3,* 17–26.

Cohen, J. A., Mannarino, A. P., Berliner, L. & Deblinger, E. (2000). Trauma-focused cognitive behavioral therapy for children and adolescents. *Journal of Interpersonal Violence, 15,* 1202–1223.

Cohen, J. A., Mannarino, A. P., & Deblinger, E. (2006). *Treating trauma and traumatic grief in children and adolescents.* New York, NY: Guilford Press.

Cohen, J. A., Mannarino, A. P., & Knudsen, K. (2005). Treating sexually abused children: 1 year follow-up of a randomized controlled trial. *Child Abuse & Neglect, 29,* 135–145.

Cohen, J. A., Mannarino, A. P., & Murray, L. K. (2011). Trauma-focused CBT for youth who experience ongoing traumas. *Child Abuse & Neglect, 35,* 637–646.

Cohen, J. A., Mannarino, A. P., & Staron, V. R. (2006). A pilot study of modified cognitive–behavioral therapy for childhood traumatic grief (CBT-CTG). *Journal of the American Academy of Child & Adolescent Psychiatry, 45,* 1465–1473

Cohen, L. J., Gans, S. W., McGeoch, P. G., Poznnsky, O., Itskovich, Y., Murphy, S., . . . Galynker, I. I. (2002). Impulsive personality traits in male pedophiles versus healthy controls: Is pedophilia an impulsive–aggressive disorder? *Comprehensive Psychiatry, 43,* 127–134.

Coid, J., Petruckevitch, A., Feder, G., Chung, W., Richardson, J., & Moorey, S. (2001). Relation between childhood sexual abuse and physical abuse and risk of revictimization in women. A cross-sectional survey. *The Lancet, 358,* 450–454.

Coker, A. L., Davis, K. E., Arias, I., Desai, S., Sanderson, M., Brandt, H. M., & Smith, P. H. (2002). Physical and mental health effects of intimate partner violence for men and women. *American Journal of Preventative Medicine, 23,* 260–268.

Coker, A. L., Derrick, C., Lumpkin, J. L., Aldrich, T. E., & Oldendick, R. (2000). Help-seeking for intimate partner violence and forced sex in South Carolina. *American Journal of Preventive Medicine, 19,* 316–320.

Collins, P. G., & O'Connor, A. (2000). Rape and sexual assault of the elderly: An exploratory study of 10 cases referred to the Irish Forensic Psychiatry Service. *Irish Journal of Psychological Medicine, 17,* 128–131.

Comas-Diaz, L. (1995). Puerto Ricans and sexual child abuse. In L. A. Fontes (Ed.), *Sexual abuse in nine North American cultures: Treatment and prevention* (pp. 31–66). Thousand Oaks, CA: Sage.

Conner, K. R., & Ackerly, G. D. (1994). Alcohol-related battering: Developing treatment strategies. *Journal of Family Violence, 9,* 143–155.

Connolly, J., & Friedlander, L. (2009). Peer group influences on adolescent dating aggression. *The Prevention Researcher, 16,* 8–11.

Conron, K. J., Beardslee, W., Koenen, K. C., Buka, S. L., & Gortmaker, S. L. (2009). A longitudinal study of maternal depression and child maltreatment in a national sample of families investigated by Child Protective Services. *Archives of Pediatrics & Adolescent Medicine, 163,* 922–930.

Conway, E. E. (1998). Nonaccidental head injury in infants: The shaken baby syndrome revisited. *Pediatric Annals, 27,* 677–690.

Coohey, C. (1995). Neglectful mothers, their mothers, and partners: The significance of mutual aid. *Child Abuse and Neglect, 19,* 885–895.

Coohey, C. (2000). The role of friends, in-laws, and other kin in father-perpetrated child physical abuse. *Child Welfare, 79,* 372–402.

Cook, A., Blaustein, M., Spinazzalo, J., & van der Kolk, B. (2003). *Complex trauma in children and adolescents.* White paper from the National Child Traumatic Network Complex Trauma Task Force. Retrieved from http://nctsn. org/nctsn_assets/pdfs/edu_materials/ComplexTrauma_All.pdf

Cook, A., Spinazzola, J., Ford, J., Lanktree, C., Blaustein, M., Cloitre, M., . . . van der Kolk, B. (2005). Complex trauma in children and adolescents. *Psychiatric Annals, 35,* 390–398.

Corliss, H. L., Cochran, S. D., & Mays, V. M. (2002). Reports of parental maltreatment during childhood in a United States population based survey of homosexual, bisexual and heterosexual adults. *Child Abuse and Neglect, 26,* 1165–1178.

Corvo, K., & Carpenter, E. (2000). Effects of parental substance abuse on current levels of domestic violence: A possible elaboration of intergenerational transmission process. *Journal of Family Violence, 15,* 123–137.

Coulton, C. J., Crampton, D. S., Irwin, M., Spilsbury, J. C., & Korbin, J. E. (2007). How neighborhoods influence child maltreatment: A review of the literature and alternative pathways. *Child Abuse & Neglect, 25,* 1117–1142.

Courtois, C. A. (1999). *Recollections of sexual abuse: Treatment principles and guidelines.* New York, NY: Norton.

Courtois, C. A. (2002). Traumatic stress studies: The need for curricula inclusion. *Journal of Trauma Practice, 1,* 33–57.

Courtois, C. A. (2008). Complex trauma, complex reactions: Assessment and treatment. *Psychological Trauma: Theory, Research, Practice, and Policy, 5,* 86–100.

Courtois, C. A., & Ford, J. D. (Eds.). (2009). *Treating complex traumatic stress disorders: An evidence-based guide.* New York, NY: Guilford Press.

Courtois, C. A., & Gold, S. N. (2009). The need for inclusion of psychological trauma in the professional curriculum: A call to action. *Psychological Trauma: Theory, Research, Practice, and Policy, 1,* 3–23

Covell, C. M., & Scalora, M. J. (2002). Empathic deficits in sexual offenders: An integration of affective, social, and cognitive constructs. *Aggression and Violent Behavior, 7,* 251–270.

Cox, L., & Speziale, B. (2009). Survivors of stalking. *Affilia, 24,* 5–18.

Coyne, A. C., Reichman, W. E., & Berbig, L. J. (1993). The relationship between dementia and elder abuse. *American Journal of Psychiatry, 150,* 643–663.

Craft, S. M., & Serovich, J. M. (2005). Family of origin factors and partner violence in the intimate relationships of gay men who are HIV positive. *Journal of Interpersonal Violence, 20,* 777–791.

Craft, S. M., Serovich, J. M., McKenry, P. C., & Lim, J.-Y. (2008). Stress, attachment style, and partner violence among same-sex couples. *Journal of GLBT Family Studies, 4,* 57–73.

Crittenden, P. M. (1998). Dangerous behavior and dangerous contexts: A 35-year perspective on research on the developmental effects of child physical abuse. In P. K. Trickett & C. J. Schellenbach (Eds.), *Violence against children in family and the community* (pp. 11–38). Washington, DC: American Psychological Association.

Crittenden, P. M., Claussen, A. H., & Sugarman, D. B. (1994). Physical and psychological maltreatment in middle childhood and adolescence. *Development and Psychopathology, 6,* 145–164.

Cross, T. (1986). Drawing on cultural traditions in Indian child welfare practices. *Social Casework, 67,* 283–289.

Cross, T., Earle, K. A., & Simmons, D. (2000). Child abuse and neglect in Indian country: Policy issues. *Families in Society: The Journal of Contemporary Human Services, 81,* 49–58.

Cruz, J. M. (2003). "Why doesn't he just leave?": Gay male domestic violence and the reasons victims stay. *Journal of Men's Studies, 11,* 309–324.

Cryder, C. H., Kilmer, R. P., Tedeschi, R. G., & Calhoun, L. G. (2006). An exploratory study of posttraumatic growth in children following a natural disaster. *American Journal of Orthopsychiatry, 76,* 65–69.

Culbertson, K. A., & Dehle, C. (2001). Impact of sexual assault as a function of perpetrator type. *Journal of Interpersonal Violence, 16,* 992–1007.

Cunradi, C. B., Caetano, R., Clark, C., & Schafer, J. (2000). Neighborhood poverty as a predictor of intimate partner violence among White, Black, and Hispanic couples in the United States. *Annals of Epidemiology, 10,* 297–308.

Cupach, W. R., & Spitzberg, B. H. (2000). Obsessive relational intrusion: Incidence, perceived severity, and coping. *Violence and Victims, 15,* 357–372.

Dahlberg, L. L., & Krug, E. G. (2002). Violence: A global public health problem. In E. G. Krug, L. L. Dahlberg, J. A. Mercy, A. B. Zwi, & R. Lozano (Eds.), *World report on violence and health* (pp. 1–21). Geneva, Switzerland: World Health Organization.

Dalenberg, C. J. (2004). Maintaining the safe and effective therapeutic relationship in the context of distrust and anger: Countertransference and complex trauma. *Psychotherapy: Theory, Research, Practice, Training, 41,* 438–447.

Daly, M., Wilson, M., & Weghorst, S. J. (1982). Male sexual jealousy. *Ethology and Sociobiology, 3,* 11–27.

Damant, D., Lapierre, S., Kouraga, A., Fortin, A., Hamelin-Brabant, L., Lavergne, C., . . . Lessard, G. (2008). Taking child abuse and mothering into account: Intersectional feminism as an alternative for the study of domestic violence. *Affilia: Journal of Women and Social Work, 23,* 123–133.

Daniels, J. W., & Murphy C. M. (1997). Stages and processes of change in batterers' treatment. *Cognitive and Behavioral Practice, 4,* 123–145.

Dasgupta, S. D. (1999). Just like men? A critical view of violence by women. In M. F. Shepard & E. L. Pence (Eds.), *Coordinating community responses to domestic violence: Lessons from Duluth and beyond* (pp. 195–222). Thousand Oaks, CA: Sage.

Dasgupta, S. D. (2002). A framework for understanding women's use of nonlethal violence in intimate heterosexual relationships. *Violence Against Women, 8,* 1364–1389.

Dasgupta, S. D., & Warrier, S. (1996). In the footsteps of "Arundhati": Asian Indian women's experience of domestic violence in the United States. *Violence Against Women, 2,* 238–259.

Davey, G. C. I. (1992). Classical conditioning and the acquisition of human fears and phobias: A review and synthesis of the literature. *Advances in Behaviour Research and Therapy, 14,* 29–66.

Davidson, J. R. T., & van der Kolk, B. A. (1996). The psychopharmacological treatment of posttraumatic stress disorder. In B. A. van der Kolk, A. C. McFarlan, & L. Weisaeth (Eds.), *Traumatic stress: The effects of overwhelming experience on mind, body, and society* (pp. 510–524).New York, NY: Guilford Press.

Davidson, T. (1977). Wifebeating: A recurring phenomenon throughout history. In M. Roy (Ed.), *Battered women: A psychosociological study of domestic violence* (pp. 19–57). New York, NY: Van Nostrand Reinhold.

Davidson, T. (1978). *Conjugal crime: Understanding and changing the wife-beating pattern.* New York, NY: Hawthorn.

Davin, P. A. (1999). Secrets revealed: A study of female sex offenders. In P. A. Davin, J. C. R. Hislop, & T. Dunbar (Eds.), *The female sexual abuser: Three views* (pp. 1–134). Brandon, VT: Safer Society Press.

Davis, K. E., Ace, A., & Anda, M. (2000). Stalking perpetrators and psychological maltreatment of partners: Anger–jealously, attachment insecurity, and break-up context. *Violence and Victims, 15,* 407–425.

Davis, M. K., & Gidycz, C. A. (2000). Child sexual abuse prevention programs: A meta-analysis. *Journal of Clinical Child Psychology, 29,* 257–265.

Davis, R. C., Medina, J., & Avitabile, N. (2001). *Reducing repeat incidents of elder abuse: Results of a randomized experiment, final report* (NCJRS Publication No. 189086). Washington, DC: U.S. Department of Justice.

De Bellis, M. D. (2001). Developmental traumatology: The psychobiological development of maltreated children and its implications for research, treatment, and policy. *Development and Psychopathology, 13,* 539–564.

Deblinger, E., Steer, R., & Lippman, J. (1999). Two-year follow-up study of cognitive–behavioral therapy for sexually abused children suffering posttraumatic stress symptoms. *Child Abuse & Neglect, 23,* 1371–1378.

DeKeseredy, W. S. (2011). Feminist contributions to understanding women abuse: Myths, controversies, and realities. *Aggression and Violent Behavior, 16,* 297–302.

DeKeseredy, W. S., & Schwartz, M. D. (1998). *Woman abuse on campus: Results from the Canadian National Survey.* Thousand Oaks, CA: Sage.

DeKeseredy, W. S., & Schwartz, M. D. (2001). Definitional issues. In C. M. Renzetti, J. L. Edleson, & R. K. Bergen (Eds.), *Sourcebook on violence against women* (2nd ed., pp. 23–34). Thousand Oaks, CA: Sage.

Delsol, C., & Margolin, G. (2004). The role of family-of-origin violence in men's marital violence perpetration. *Clinical Psychology Review, 24,* 99–123.

Denov, M. S. (2001). A culture of denial: Exploring professional perspectives on female sex offending. *Canadian Journal of Criminology, 43,* 303–329.

Denov, M. S. (2003). The myth of innocence: Sexual scripts and the recognition of child sexual abuse by female perpetrators. *Journal of Sex Research, 40,* 303–314.

de Paul, J., & Arruabarrena, M. I. (1995). Behavior problems in school-aged physically abused and neglected children in Spain. *Child Abuse & Neglect, 19,* 409–418.

DePrince, A. P., & Freyd, J. J. (2007). Trauma-induced dissociation. In M. J. Friedman, T. M. Keane, & P. A. Resick (Eds.), *Handbook of PTSD: Science and practice* (pp. 135–150). New York, NY: Guilford Press.

Derogatis, L. R. (1993). *Brief Symptom Inventory: Administration, scoring, and procedures manual–II.* Minneapolis, MN: National Computer Systems.

DiLillo, D., & Damashek, A. (2003). Parenting characteristics of women reporting a history of childhood sexual abuse. *Child Maltreatment, 8,* 319–333.

Dimidjian, S., Martell, C. R., & Christensen, A. (2002). Integrative behavioral couple therapy. In A. S. Gurman & N. S. Jacobson (Eds.), *Clinical handbook of couple therapy* (3rd ed., pp. 251–277). New York, NY: Guilford Press.

Dixon, L., & Browne, K. (2003). The heterogeneity of spouse abuse: A review. *Aggression and Violent Behavior, 8,* 107–130.

Dobash, R. E., & Dobash, R. P. (1978). Wives: The appropriate victims of marital violence. *Victimology, 2,* 426–439.

Dobash, R. E., & Dobash, R. P. (1979). *Violence against wives: A case against patriarchy.* New York, NY: Free Press.

Dobson, J. C. (1987). *Parenting isn't for cowards.* Waco, TX: Word.

Dodge, K. A., Pettit, G. S., & Bates, J. E. (1994). Socialization mediators of the relation between socioeconomic status and child conduct problems. *Child Development, 65,* 649–665.

Dong, X. Q., Simon, M., de Leon, C. M., Fulmer, T., Beck, T., Hebert, L., . . . Evans, D. (2009). Elder self-neglect and abuse and mortality risk in a community-dwelling population. *JAMA: Journal of the American Medical Association, 302,* 517–526.

Donnelly, C. L., & Amaya-Jackson, L. (2002). Post-traumatic stress disorder in children and adolescents: Epidemiology, diagnosis and treatment options. *Paediatric Drugs, 4,* 159–170.

Donnelly, D. A., Smith, L. G., & Williams, O. J. (2002). The batterer education program for incarcerated African-American men, 1997–2000. In E. Aldarondo & F. Mederos (Eds.), *Programs for men who batter: Intervention and prevention strategies in a diverse society* (pp. 11–19). Kingston, NJ: Civic Research Institute.

Douglas, E. M., & Straus, M. A. (2006). Assault and injury of dating partners by university students in 19 countries and its relation to corporal punishment experienced as a child. *European Journal of Criminology, 3,* 293–318.

Doumas, D. M., Pearson, C. L., Elgin, J. E., & McKinley, L. L. (2008). Adult attachment as a risk factor for intimate partner violence. *Journal of Interpersonal Violence, 23,* 616–634.

Dowd, L. (2001). Female perpetrators of partner aggression: Relevant issues and treatment. *Journal of Aggression, Maltreatment & Trauma, 5,* 73–104.

Dowd, L., & Leisring, P. A. (2008). A framework for treating partner aggressive women. *Violence and Victims, 23,* 249–263.

Dowd, L., Leisring, P. A., & Rosenbaum, A. (2005). Partner aggressive women: Characteristics and treatment attrition. *Violence and Victims, 20,* 219–233.

Dubble, C. (2006). A policy perspective on elder justice through APS and law enforcement collaboration. *Journal of Gerontological Social Work, 45,* 33–55.

Dubowitz, H. (1994). Neglecting the neglect of neglect. *Journal of Interpersonal Violence, 9,* 556–560.

Dubowitz, H., Black, M., Harrington, D., & Verschoore, A. (1993). A follow-up study of behavior problems associated with child sexual abuse. *Child Abuse & Neglect, 17,* 734–754.

Duminy, F. J., & Hudson, D. A. (1993). Assault inflicted by hot water. *Burns, 19,* 426–428.

Duran, E., Duran, B., Woodis, W., & Woodis, P. (2008). A postcolonial perspective on domestic violence in Indian country. In R. Carrillo & J. Tello (Eds.), *Family violence and men of color: Healing the wounded male spirit* (2nd ed., pp. 143–162)

Durose, M., Harlow, C. W., Langan, P. A., Motivans, M., Rantala, R. R., & Smith, E. L. (2005). *Family violence statistics: Including statistics on strangers and acquaintances* (NCJ Publication No. 207846). Washington, DC: Bureau of Justice Statistics.

Dutcher-Walls, P. (1999). Sociological directions in feminist biblical studies. *Social Compass, 46,* 441–453.

Duterte, E. E., Bonomi, A. E., Kernic, M. A., Schiff, M. A., Thompson, R. S., & Rivara, F. P. (2008). Correlates of medical and legal help seeking among women reporting intimate partner violence. *Journal of Women's Health, 17,* 85–95.

Dutton, D. G. (1985). An ecologically nested theory of male violence toward intimates. *International Journal of Women's Studies, 8,* 404–413.

Dutton, D. G. (1988). *Domestic assault of women: Psychological and criminal justice perspectives.* Boston, MA: Allyn & Bacon.

Dutton, D. G. (1994). Behavioral and affective correlates of borderline personality organization in wife assaulters. *International Journal of Law and Psychiatry, 17,* 265–277.

Dutton, D. G. (1995). *The domestic assault of women.* Vancouver, BC, Canada: UBC Press.

Dutton, D. G. (1996). Patriarchy and wife assault. In L. K. Hamberger & C. Renzetti (Eds.), *Domestic partner abuse* (pp. 125–151). New York, NY: Springer.

Dutton, D. G. (1998). *The abusive personality*. New York, NY: Guilford Press.

Dutton, D. G. (2000). Witnessing parental violence as a traumatic experience shaping the abusive personality. *Journal of Aggression, Maltreatment & Trauma, 3,* 59–67.

Dutton, D. G. (2006). *Rethinking domestic violence*. Vancouver, British Columbia, Canada: UBC Press.

Dutton, D. G. (2007). *The abusive personality* (2nd ed.). New York, NY: Guilford Press.

Dutton, D. G., Bodnarchuk, M., Kropp, R., Hart, S. K., & Ogloff, J. R. P. (1997). Wife assault treatment and criminal recidivism: An 11-year follow-up. *International Journal of Offender Therapy and Comparative Criminology, 41,* 9–23.

Dutton, D. G., & Corvo, K. (2006). Transforming a flawed policy: A call to revive psychology and science in domestic violence research and practice. *Aggression and Violent Behavior, 11,* 457–483.

Dutton, D. G., & Golant, S. K. (1995). *The batterer: A psychological profile*. New York, NY: Basic Books.

Dutton, D. G., & Nichols, T. (2005). The gender paradigm in domestic violence research and theory: The conflict of theory and data. *Aggression and Violent Behavior, 10,* 680–714.

Dutton, D. G., & Painter, S. (1981). Traumatic bonding: The development of emotional attachments in battered women and other relations of intermittent abuse. *Victimology: An International Journal, 6,* 139–155.

Dutton, D. G., & Painter, S. (1993). Emotional attachments in abusive relationships: A test of traumatic bonding theory. *Violence and Victims, 8,* 105–120.

Dutton, D. G., Saunders, K., Starzomski, A., & Bartholomew, K. (1994). Intimacy, anger and insecure attachment as precursors of abuse in intimate relationships. *Journal of Applied Social Psychology, 24,* 1367–1386.

Dutton, D. G., & Starzomski, A. J. (1993). Borderline personality in perpetrators of psychological and physical abuse. *Violence and Victims, 8,* 327–337.

Dutton, M. A., & Dionne, D. (1991). Counseling and shelter for battered women. In M. Steinman (Ed.). *Women battering: Policy responses* (pp. 113–130). Cincinnati, OH: Anderson.

Dyer, C. B., Connolly, M., & McFeeley, P. (2003). The clinical and medical forensics of elder abuse and neglect. In R. J. Bonnie & R. B. Wallace (Eds.), *Elder maltreatment: Abuse, neglect, and exploitation in an aging America* (pp. 303–338). Washington, DC: National Academy Press.

Eckhardt, C. E., Babcock, J., & Homack, S. (2004). Partner assaultive men and the stages and processes of change. *Journal of Family Violence, 19,* 81–93.

Eckhardt, C. E., & Dye, M. L. (2000). The cognitive characteristics of maritally violent men: Theory and evidence. *Cognitive Therapy and Research, 24,* 139–158.

Eckhardt, C. E., Holtzworth-Munroe, A., Norlander, B., Sibley, A., Togun, I., & Cahill, M. (2003, July). *Readiness to change, partner violence subtypes, and treatment outcomes among men in treatment for partner assault.* Paper presented at the International Family Violence Conference, Portsmouth, NH.

Edleson, J. (1999). Children's witnessing of adult domestic violence. *Journal of Interpersonal Violence, 14,* 839–870.

Edleson, J. L., Mbilinyi, L. F., Beeman, S. K., & Hagemeister, A. K. (2003). How children are involved in adult domestic violence: Results from a four-city telephone survey. *Journal of Interpersonal Violence, 18,* 18–32.

Ehrensaft, M. K., Cohen, P., Brown, J., Smailes, E. M., Chen, H., & Johnson, J. G. (2003). Intergenerational transmission of partner violence: A 20-year prospective study. *Journal of Consulting and Clinical Psychology, 71,* 741–753.

Ehrensaft, M. K., Cohen, P., & Johnson, J. G. (2006). Development of personality disorder symptoms and the risk for partner violence. *Journal of Abnormal Psychology, 115,* 474–483.

Ehrensaft, M. K., Moffitt, T. E., & Caspi, A. (2004). Clinically abusive relationships in an unselected birth cohort: Men's and women's participation and developmental antecedents. *Journal of Abnormal Psychology, 113,* 258–271.

Ehrensaft, M. K., & Vivian, D. (1996). Spouses' reasons for not reporting existing physical aggression as a marital problem. *Journal of Family Psychology, 10,* 443–453.

Eitle, D. (2005, October). The influence of mandatory arrest policies, police organizational characteristics, and situational variables on the probability of arrest in domestic violence cases. *Crime & Delinquency, 51,* 573–597.

Elliott, D. M. (1994). Impaired object relations in professional women molested as children. *Psychotherapy: Theory, Research, Practice, & Training, 21,* 79–86.

Elliott, D. M., & Briere, J. (1992). Sexual abuse trauma among professional women: Validating the Trauma Symptom Checklist–40 (TSC-40). *Child Abuse and Neglect, 16,* 391–398.

Elliott, D. M., & Briere, J. (1994). Forensic sexual abuse evaluations of older children: Disclosures and symptomatology. *Behavioral Sciences and the Law, 12,* 261–277.

Elliott, K., & Urquiza, A. (2006). Ethnicity, culture, and child maltreatment. *Journal of Social Issues, 62,* 787–809.

Elliott, M. (1993). *Female sexual abuse of children: The ultimate taboo.* New York, NY: Guilford Press.

Ellison, C. G., & Bradshaw, M. (2009). Religious beliefs, sociopolitical ideology, and attitudes toward corporal punishment. *Journal of Family Issues, 30,* 320–340.

Ellison, C. G., & Sherkat, D. E. (1993). Conservative Protestantism and support for corporal punishment. *American Sociological Review, 58,* 131–144.

Emerson, R. M., Ferris, K. O., & Gardner, C. B. (1998). On being stalked. *Social Problems, 45,* 289–314.

Emery, R. E., & Laumann-Billings, L. (1998). An overview of the nature, causes, and consequences of abusive family relationship: Toward differentiating maltreatment and violence. *American Psychologist, 53,* 121–135.

Empey, L. T., Stafford, M. C., & Hay, H. H. (1999). *American delinquency: Its meaning and construction.* Belmont, CA: Wadsworth.

Enns, C. Z., Campbell, J., & Courtois (1997). Recommendations for working with domestic violence survivors, with special attention to memory issues and posttraumatic process. *Psychotherapy: Theory, Research, Practice, Training, 34,* 459–477.

Erchak, G. M., & Rosenfeld, R. (1994). Societal isolation, violent norms, and gender relations: A reexamination and extension of Levinson's model of wife beating. *Cross-Cultural Research: The Journal of Comparative Social Science, 28,* 111–133.

Erickson, M. F., & Egeland, B. (2010). Child neglect. In J. E. B. Myers (Ed.), *The APSAC handbook on child maltreatment* (3rd ed., pp. 103–124). Thousand Oaks, CA: Sage.

Eriksen, S., & Jensen, V. (2009). A push or a punch: Distinguishing the severity of sibling violence. *Journal of Interpersonal Violence, 24,* 183–208.

Ezzell, C. E., Swenson, C. C., & Brondino, M. J. (2000). The relationship of social support to physically abused children's adjustment. *Child Abuse and Neglect, 24,* 641–651.

Faller, K. C. (2011). Victim services for child abuse. In M. P. Koss, J. W. White, & A. E. Kazdin (Eds.), *Violence against women and children: Vol. 2. Navigating solutions* (pp. 11–26). Washington, DC: American Psychological Association.

Fals-Stewart, W., Kashdan, T. B., O'Farrell, T. J., & Birchler, G. R. (2002). Behavioral couples therapy for drug-abusing patients: Effects on partner violence. *Journal of Substance Abuse Treatment, 22,* 87–96.

Fang, X., Brown, D. S., Florence, C. S., & Mercy, J. A. (2012). The economic burden of child maltreatment in the United States and implications for prevention. *Child Abuse & Neglect, 36,* 156–165.

Fantuzzo, J. W. (1990). Behavioral treatment of the victims of child abuse and neglect. *Behavior Modification, 14,* 316–339.

Fantuzzo, J. W., & Lindquist, C. U. (1989). The effects of observing conjugal violence on children: A review and analysis of research methodology. *Journal of Family Violence, 4,* 77–94.

Fauerbach, J. A., Richter, L., & Lawrence, J. W. (2002). Regulating acute posttrauma distress. *Journal of Burn Care and Rehabilitation, 23,* 249–257.

Faust, J., & Katchen, L. B. (2004). Treatment of children with complicated posttraumatic stress reactions. *Psychotherapy: Theory, Research, Practice, Training, 41,* 426–437.

Feazell, C. S., Mayers, R. S., & Deschner, J. (1984). Services for men who batter: Implications for programs and policies. *Family Relations, 33,* 217–233.

Feder, L., & Wilson, D. B. (2005). A meta-analytic review of court-mandated batterer intervention programs: Can courts affect abusers' behavior? *Journal of Experimental Criminology, 1,* 239–262.

Feeney, J. A. (1999). Adult romantic attachment and couple relationships. In J. Cassidy & P. R. Shaver (Eds.), *Handbook of attachment: Theory, research, and clinical applications* (pp. 355–377). New York, NY: Guilford Press.

Feeny, N. C., Zoellner, L. A., & Foa, E. B. (2000). Anger, dissociation, and posttraumatic stress disorder among female assault victims. *Journal of Traumatic Stress, 13,* 89–100.

Feindler, E. L., Rathus, J. H., & Silver, L. B. (2002). *Assessment of family violence: A handbook for researchers and practitioners*. Washington, DC: American Psychological Association.

Feiring, C., Taska, L., & Lewis, M. (2002). Adjustment following sexual abuse discovery: The role of shame and attributional style. *Developmental Psychology, 38,* 79–92.

Feld, S. L., & Straus, M. A. (1989). Escalation and desistance of wife assault in marriage. *Criminology, 27,* 141–161.

Feldman, C. M., & Ridley, C. A. (1995). The etiology and treatment of domestic violence between adult partners. *Clinical Psychology: Science and Practice, 2,* 317–348.

Felson, R. B., & Outlaw, M. C. (2007). The control motive and marital violence. *Violence and Victims, 22,* 387–407.

Ferrara, F. F. (2002). *Childhood sexual abuse*. Pacific Grove, CA: Brooks/Cole.

Fiebert, M. S. (2004). References examining assaults by women on their spouses or male partners: An annotated bibliography. *Sexuality and Culture, 8,* 140–177.

Finkelhor, D. (1980). Sex among siblings: A survey of prevalence, variety, and effects. *Archives of Sexual Behavior, 9,* 171–193.

Finkelhor, D. (1984). *Child sexual abuse: New theory and research*. New York, NY: Free Press.

Finkelhor, D. (1994). The international epidemiology of child sexual abuse. *Child Abuse & Neglect, 18,* 409–417.

Finkelhor, D. (1996). *Introduction*. In J. Briere, L. Berlinger, J. A. Bulkley, C. Jenny, & T. A. Reid (Eds.), *The APSAC handbook on child maltreatment* (pp. ix–xiii). Thousand Oaks, CA: Sage.

Finkelhor, D., Asdigian, N., & Dziuba-Leatherman, J. (1995). The effectiveness of victimization prevention instruction: An evaluation of children's responses to actual threats and assaults. *Child Abuse & Neglect, 19,* 141–153.

Finkelhor, D., Hotaling, C. T., Lewis, I. A., & Smith, C. (1990). Sexual abuse in a national survey of adult men and women: Prevalence, characteristic and risk factors. *Child Abuse and Neglect, 14,* 19–28.

Finkelhor, D., & Jones, L. M. (2006). Why have child maltreatment and child victimization declined? *Journal of Social Forces, 62,* 685–716.

Finkelhor, D., Mitchell, K., & Wolak, J. (2000). *Online victimization: A report on the nation's youth*. Retrieved from www.unh.edu/ccrc/Youth_Internet_for_page.html

Finkelhor, D., Moore, D., Hamby, S. L., & Straus, M. A. (1997). Sexually abused children in a national survey of parents: Methodological issues. *Child Abuse and Neglect, 21,* 1–9.

Finkelhor, D., Ormrod, R., Turner, H., & Hamby, S. L. (2005). The victimization of children and youth: A comprehensive national survey. *Child Maltreatment: Journal of the American Professional Society on the Abuse of Children, 10,* 2–5.

Finkelhor, D., & Yllo, K. A. (1987). *License to rape: Sexual abuse of wives*. New York, NY: Free Press.

Fischer, D. H. (1989). *Albion's seed*. New York, NY: Oxford University Press.

Fisher, B. S., Cullen, F. T., & Turner, M. G. (2000). *The sexual victimization of college women* (NCJ Publication No. 182369). Washington, DC: U.S. Department of Justice.

Fletcher, K. E. (1996). Childhood posttraumatic stress disorder. In E. J. Mash & R. A. Barkley (Eds.), *Child psychopathology* (pp. 242–276). New York, NY: Guilford Press.

Flowers, R. B. (1984). Withholding medical care for religious reasons. *Journal of Religion and Health, 23,* 268–282.

Foa, E. B., Keane, T. M., & Friedman, M. J. (Eds.). (2000). *Effective treatments of PTSD: Practice guidelines from the International Society of Traumatic Stress Studies.* New York, NY: Guilford Press.

Follette, V. M., Polusny, M. A., Bechtle, A. E., & Naugle, A. E. (1996). Cumulative trauma: The impact of child sexual abuse, adult sexual assault, and spouse abuse. *Journal of Traumatic Stress, 9,* 25–35.

Follingstad, D. R. (2009). The impact of psychological aggression on women's mental health and behavior. *Trauma, Violence, & Abuse, 10,* 271–289.

Follingstad, D. R., Wright, S., Lloyd, S., & Sebastian, J. A. (1991). Sex differences in motivations and effects in dating violence. *Family Relations, 40,* 51–57.

Foran, H., & O'Leary, K. D. (2008). Alcohol and intimate partner violence: A meta-analytic review. *Clinical Psychology Review, 28,* 1222–1234.

Ford, J. D. (2009). Neurobiological and developmental research. In C. A. Courtois & J. D. Ford (Eds.), *Treating complex traumatic stress disorders* (pp. 31–58). New York, NY: Guilford Press.

Ford, J. D., & Courtois, C. A. (2009). Defining and understanding complex trauma and complex traumatic stress disorders. In C. A. Courtois & J. D. Ford (Eds.), *Treating complex traumatic stress disorders* (pp. 13–30). New York, NY: Guilford Press.

Ford, J. D., Courtois, C. A., Steele, K., van der Hart, O., & Nijenhuis, E. R. S. (2005). Treatment of complex posttraumatic self-regulation. *Journal of Traumatic Stress, 18,* 437–447.

Fortunata, B., & Kohn, C. S. (2003). Demographic, psychosocial, and personality characteristics of lesbian batterers. *Violence and Victims, 18,* 557–568.

Foshee, V. A., Bauman, K. E., Arriaga, X. B., Helms, R. W., Koch, G. G., & Linder, G. F. (1998). An evaluation of Safe Dates: A adolescent dating violence prevention program. *American Journal of Public Health, 88,* 45–50.

Foshee, V. A., Bauman, K. E., Greene, W. F., Koch, G. G., Linder, G. F., & MacDougall, J. E. (2000). The Safe Dates Program: 1-year follow-up results. *American Journal of Public Health, 90,* 1619–1622.

Foshee, V. A., Benefield, T. S., Ennett, S. T., Bauman, K. E., & Suchindran, C. (2004). Longitudinal predictors of serious physical and sexual dating violence victimization during adolescence. *Preventive Medicine: An International Journal Devoted to Practice and Theory, 39,* 1007–1016.

Foshee, V. A , & Langwick, S. (2004). *Safe Dates: An adolescent dating abuse prevention curriculum* [program manual]. Center City, MN: Hazelden Publishing and Educational Services.

Foshee, V. A., & Langwick, S. (2010). *Safe Dates: An adolescent dating abuse prevention curriculum* (2nd ed.) [program manual]. Center City, MN: Hazelden Publishing and Educational Services.

Foshee, V. A., Linder, G. F. & Bauman, K. E., Langwick, S. A., Arriaga, X. B., Heath, J. L., . . . Bangdiwala, S. (1996). The Safe Dates Program: Theoretical basis, evaluation design, and selected baseline findings. *American Journal of Preventative Medicine, 12*, 39-47.

Foshee, V. A., Linder, G. F., MacDougall, J. E., & Bangdiwala, S. (2001). Gender differences in the longitudinal predictors of adolescent dating violence. *Prevention Medicine: An International Journal Devoted to Practice and Theory, 32*, 128–141.

Foshee, V. A., & Reyes (2009). Primary prevention of adolescent dating abuse perpetration: When to begin, whom to target, and how to do it. In D. J. Whitaker & J. R. Lutzker (Eds.), *Preventing partner violence: Research and evidence-based intervention strategies* (pp. 141–168). Washington, DC: American Psychological Association.

Foshee, V. A., Reyes, H. L. M., & Wyckoff, S. C. (2009). Approaches to preventing psychological, physical and sexual abuse. In K. D. O'Leary & E. M. Woodin (Eds.), *Psychological and physical aggression in couples: Causes and interventions* (pp. 165–181). Washington, DC: American Psychological Association.

Foster, H. J. (1983). African patterns in the Afro-American family. *Journal of Black Studies, 14*, 201–232.

Foubert, J. D., & Marriott, D. A. (1997). Effects of a sexual assault peer education program on men's belief in rape myths. *Sex Roles, 36*, 257–266.

Fox, J. (2005). *Uniform crime reports, United States: Supplementary homicide reports, 1976–2002* [computer file]. Ann Arbor, MI: Inter-University Consortium for Political and Social Research.

Francis, K. J., & Wolfe, D. A. (2008). Cognitive and emotional differences between abusive and non-abusive fathers. *Child Abuse & Neglect, 32*, 1127–1137.

Fraser, A. (2006). Psychological therapies in the treatment of abused adults. *Journal of Adult Protection, 8*, 31–38.

Freedner, N., Freed, L. H., Yang, Y. W., & Austin, S. B. (2002). Dating violence among gay, lesbian, and bisexual adolescents: Results from a community survey. *Journal of Adolescent Health, 31*, 469–474.

Frias-Armenta, M. (2002). Long-term effects of child punishment on Mexican women: A structural model. *Child Abuse & Neglect, 26*, 371–386.

Friedman, M. J., Davidson, J. R. T., Mellman, T. A., & Southwick, S. M. (2000). *Pharmacotherapy*. In E. B. Foa, T. M. Keane, & M. J. Friedman (Eds.), *Effective treatments of PTSD: Practice guidelines from the International Society of Traumatic Stress Studies* (pp. 84–105, 326–329). New York, NY: Guilford Press.

Friedman, M. J., Resick, P. A., & Keane, T. M. (2007). PTSD: Twenty-five years of progress and challenges. In M. J. Friedman, T. M. Keane, & Resick, P. A. (Eds.), *Handbook of PTSD: Science and practice* (pp. 3–18). New York, NY: Guilford Press.

Friedrich, W. N. (1998). *The Child Sexual Behavior Inventory professional manual*. Odessa, FL: Psychological Assessment Resources

Friess, S. (1997). Behind closed doors: Domestic violence. *The Advocate, 748*, 48–52.

Fromuth, M. E., & Conn, V. E. (1997). Hidden perpetrators: Sexual molestation in a nonclinical sample of college women. *Journal of Interpersonal Violence, 12*, 456–465.

Fulmer, T., & Ashley, J. (1989). Clinical indicators which signal elder neglect. *Applied Nursing Research Journal, 2,* 161–167.

Fulmer, T., & O'Malley, T. (1987). *Inadequate care of the elderly: A health care perspective on abuse and neglect.* New York, NY: Springer.

Garbarino, J., & Collins, C. C. (1999). Child neglect: The family with a hole in the middle. In H. Dubowitz (Ed.), *Neglected children: Research, practice, and policy* (pp. 1–23). Thousand Oaks, CA: Sage.

Garrido, V., Esteban, C., & Molero, C. (1996). The effectiveness in the treatment of psychopathy: A meta-analysis. In D. J. Cook, A. E. Forth, J. P. Newman, & R. D. Hare (Eds.), *Issues in criminological and legal psychology: No. 24* (pp. 57–59). Liecester, UK: British Psychological Society.

Gelles, R. J. (1983). An exchange/social control theory. In D. Finkelhor, R. J. Gelles, G. T. Hotaling, & M. A. Straus (Eds.), *The dark side of families: Current family violence research* (pp. 151–165). Beverly Hills, CA: Sage.

Gelles, R. J. (1985). Family violence. *Annual Review of Sociology, 11,* 347–367.

Gelles, R. J. (1995). *Violence toward men: Fact or fiction?* (Report prepared for the American Medical Association, Council on Scientific Affairs). Kingston, RI: Family Violence Research Program, University of Rhode Island.

Gelles, R. J., & Cornell, C. P. (1990). *Intimate violence in families* (2nd ed.). Newbury Park, CA: Sage.

Gelles, R. J., & Loseke, D. R. (1993). Conclusions: Social problems, social policy, and controversies on family violence. In R. J. Geles & D. R. Loseke (Eds.), *Current controversies on family violence* (pp. 357–366). Newbury Park, CA: Sage.

George, C. (1996). A representational perspective of child abuse and prevention: Internal working models of attachment and caregiving. *Child Abuse Neglect, 20,* 411–424.

George, C., & Main, M. (1979). Social interaction of young abused children: Approach, avoidance, and aggression. *Child Development, 50,* 306–318.

Gershoff, E. T. (2002). Corporal punishment by parents and associated child behaviors and experiences: A meta-analytic and theoretical review. *Psychological Bulletin, 128,* 539–579.

Gershoff, E. T., Miller, P. C., & Holden, G. W. (1999). Parenting influences from the pulpit: Religious affiliation as a determinant of parental corporal punishment. *Journal of Family Psychology, 13,* 307–329

Gibb, B. E., Chelminski, L., & Zimmerman, M. (2007). Childhood emotional, physical, and sexual abuse, and diagnoses of depression and anxiety disorders in adult psychiatric patients. *Depression and Anxiety, 24,* 256–263.

Gibson, L. E., & Leitenberg, H. (2000). Child sexual abuse prevention programs: Do they decrease the occurrence of child sexual abuse? *Child Abuse and Neglect, 24,* 1115–1125.

Gidycz, C. A., Layman, M. J., Rich, C. L., Crothers, M., Cyls, J., Matorin, A., . . . Dine, C. (2001). An evaluation of acquaintance rape prevention program. *Journal of Interpersonal Violence, 16,* 1120–1138.

Gil, E. (2006). *Helping abused and traumatized children: Integrating directive and nondirective approaches.* New York, NY: Guilford Press.

Gil, V. E. (1988). In thy father's house: Self-report findings of sexually abused daughters from conservative Christian homes. *Journal of Psychology and Theology, 16,* 144–152.

Gilbert, N. (2005). Advocacy research overstates the incidence of date and acquaintance rape. In D. R. Loseke, R. J. Gelles, & M. M. Cavanaugh (Eds.), *Current controversies on family violence* (2nd ed., pp. 117–130). Thousand Oaks, CA: Sage.

Gilbert, R., Widom, C. S., Browne, K., Fergusson, D., Webb, E., & Janson, S. (2008). Burden and consequences of child maltreatment in high-income countries. *The Lancet, 373,* 68–81.

Giles-Sims, J. (1998). The aftermath of partner violence. In J. L. Jasinski & L. M. Williams (Eds.), *Partner violence: A comprehensive review of 20 years of research* (pp. 44–72). Thousand Oaks, CA: Sage.

Giles-Sims, J., Straus, M. A., & Sugarman, D. B. (1995). Child, maternal and family characteristics associated with spanking. *Family Relations, 44,* 170–176.

Gilligan, C. (1993). *In a different voice: Psychological theory and women's development.* Cambridge, MA: Harvard University Press.

Gilmore, D. (1990). *Manhood in the making.* New Haven, CT: Yale University Press.

Giordano, P. C., Millhollin, T. J., Cernkovich, S. A., Pugh, M. D., & Rudolph, J. L. (1999). Delinquency, identity, and women's involvement in relationship violence. *Criminology, 37,* 17–40.

Glazer, I. M., & Abu Ras, W. (1994). On aggression, human rights, and hegemonic discourse: The case of a murder for family honor in Israel. *Sex Roles, 30,* 269–288.

Golding, J. M. (1999). Intimate partner violence as a risk factor for mental disorders. A meta-analysis. *Journal of Family Violence, 14,* 99–132.

Gomby, D., Culross, P., & Behrman, R. (1999). Home visiting: Recent program evaluations—Analysis and recommendations. *Future of Children, 9,* 2–26.

Gondolf, E. W. (1988). The effect of batterer counseling on shelter outcome. *Journal of Interpersonal Violence, 3,* 275–289.

Gondolf, E. W. (1997). Batterer program: What we know and need to know. *Journal of Interpersonal Violence, 12,* 83–98.

Gondolf, E. W. (2002). *Batterer intervention systems: Issues, outcomes, and recommendations.* Thousand Oaks, CA: Sage.

Gondolf, E. W., & Fisher, E. R. (1988). *Battered women as survivors: An alternative to treating learned helplessness.* Lexington, MA: Lexington Books.

Gondolf, E. W., & Russell, D. (1986). The case against anger control treatment programs for batterers. *Response, 9,* 2–5.

Gondolf, E. W., & White, R. J. (2001). Batterer program participants who repeatedly reassault: Psychopathic tendencies and other disorders. *Journal of Interpersonal Violence, 16,* 361–380.

Gondolf, E. W., & Williams, O. (2001). Culturally focused batterer counseling for African American men. *Trauma, Violence, & Abuse, 4,* 283–295.

Goode, W. J. (1971). Force and violence in the family. *Journal of Marriage and the Family, 33,* 624–636.

Goodman, L., Dutton, M. A., Vankos, N., & Weinfurt, K. (2005). Women's resources and use of strategies as risk and protective factors for reabuse over time. *Violence Against Women, 11,* 311–336.

Gordon, L. (1989). *Heroes of their own lives: The politics and history of family violence.* New York, NY: Penguin Books.

Gortner, E., Berns, S. B., Jacbson, N. S., & Gottman, J. M. (1997). When women leave violent relationships: Dispelling clinical myths. *Psychotherapy: Theory, Research, Practice, Training, 34,* 343–352.

Gosselin, D. K. (2003). *Heavy hands: An introduction to the crimes of family violence.* Upper Saddle River, NJ: Prentice Hall.

Gottman, J. M. (1999). *The marriage clinic: A scientifically based marital therapy.* New York, NY: Norton.

Gottman, J. M., Driver, J., & Tabares, A. (2002). Building the sound marital house: An empirically derived couple therapy. In N. S. Jacobson & A. S. Gurman (Eds.), *Clinical handbook of couple therapy* (pp. 373–399). New York, NY: Guilford Press.

Gottman, J. M., Jacobson, N. S., Rushe, R. H., Shortt, J. W., Babcock, J., La Tallade, J. J.,& Waltz, J. (1995). The relationship between heart rate reactivity, emotionally aggressive behavior, and general violence in batterers. *Journal of Family Psychology, 9,* 227–248.

Graham-Kevan, N., & Archer, J. (2008). Does controlling behavior predict physical aggression and violence to partners? *Journal of Family Violence, 23,* 539–548.

Greenwood, G. L., Relf, M. V., Huang, B., Pollack, L. M., Canchola, J. A., & Catania, J. A. (2002). Battering victimization among a probability-based sample of men who have sex with men. *American Journal of Public Health, 92,* 1964–1969.

Greven, P. (1990). *Spare the child: The religious roots of punishment and the psychological impact of physical abuse.* New York, NY: Alfred A. Knopf.

Griffing, S., Ragin, D. F., Morrison, S. M., Sage, R. E., Madry, L., & Primm, B. J. (2005). Reasons for returning to abusive relationships: Effects of prior victimization. *Journal of Family Violence, 20,* 341–348.

Grigsby, N., & Hartman, B. R. (1997). The barriers model: An integrated strategy for intervention with battered women. *Psychotherapy, 34,* 484–497.

Gunther, J., & Jennings, M. A. (1999). Sociocultural and institutional violence and their impact on same-gender partner abuse. In J. C. McClennen & J. Gunther (Eds.), *A professional guide to understanding gay and lesbian domestic violence: Understanding practice interventions* (pp. 29–34). Lewiston, NY: Edwin Mellen Press.

Halpern, C. T., Young, M. L., Waller, M. W., Martin, S. L., & Kupper, L. L. (2004). Prevalence of partner violence among same-sex romantic and sexual relationships in a national sample of adolescents. *Journal of Adolescent Health, 35,* 131–135.

Hamberger, L. K. (1997). Cognitive behavioral treatment of men who batter their partners. *Cognitive and Behavioral Practice, 4,* 147–170.

Hamberger, L. K., & Guse, C. E. (2002). Men's and women's use of intimate partner violence in clinical samples. *Violence Against Women, 8,* 1301–1331.

Hamberger, L. K., & Hastings, J. E. (1986). Personality correlates of men who abuse their partners: A cross-validation study. *Journal of Family Violence, 1,* 323–341.

Hamberger, L. K., & Hastings, J. E. (1993). Court-mandated treatment of men who batter their partners: Issues, controversies, and outcomes. In Z. Hilton (Ed.), *Legal responses to wife assault* (pp. 188–229). New York, NY: Springer.

Hamberger, L. K., Lohr, J. M., Bonge, D., & Tolin, D. F. (1996). A large sample empirical typology of male spouse abusers and its relationship to dimensions of abuse. *Violence and Victims, 11,* 277–292.

Hamberger, L. K., & Potente, T. (1994). Counseling heterosexual women arrested for domestic violence: Implications for theory and practice. *Violence and Victims, 2,* 125–137.

Hamby, S. L. (2000). The importance of community in a feminist analysis of domestic violence among American Indians. *American Journal of Community Psychology, 28,* 649–669.

Hamby, S. L., & Skupien, M. B. (1998). Domestic violence on the San Carlos Apache Reservation: Rates, associated psychological symptoms, and current beliefs. *The HIS Provider, 23,* 103–106.

Hamel, J. (2005). *Gender inclusive treatment of intimate partner abuse: A comprehensive approach.* New York, NY: Springer.

Hammer, R. (2003). Militarism and family terrorism. A critical feminist perspective. *The Review of Education, Pedagogy, and Cultural Studies, 25,* 231–236.

Hampton, R. L., Carrillo, R., & Kim, J. (2005). Domestic violence in African American communities. In B. E. Richie, N. J. Sokoloff, & C. Pratt (Eds.), *Domestic violence at the margins: Readings on race, class, gender, and culture* (pp. 127–141). New Brunswick, NJ: Rutgers University Press.

Hansen, K. K. (1997). Folk remedies and child abuse: A review with emphasis on *caida de mollera* and its relationship to shaken baby syndrome. *Child Abuse and Neglect, 22,* 117–127.

Hansen, M., Harway, M., & Cervantes, N. (1991). Therapists' perceptions of severity in cases of family violence. *Violence and Victims, 6,* 225–234.

Hanson, R. K., & Morton-Bourgon, K. E. (2005). The characteristics of persistent sexual offenders: A meta-analysis of recidivism studies. *Journal of Consulting and Clinical Psychology, 73,* 1154–1163.

Hardesty, J. L., Oswald, R. F., Khaw, L., & Fonseca, C. (2011). Lesbian/bisexual mothers and intimate partner violence: Help seeking in the context of social and legal vulnerability. *Violence Against Women, 17,* 28–46.

Hardesty, J. L., Oswald, R. F., Khaw, L., Fonseca, C., & Chung, G. H. (2008). Lesbian mothering in the context of intimate partner violence. *Journal of Lesbian Studies, 12,* 191–210.

Hare, R. D. (1993). *Without conscience: The disturbing world of the psychopaths among us.* New York, NY: Pocket Books.

Harrington, D., & Dubowitz, H. (1999). Preventing child maltreatment. In R. L. Hampton (Ed.), *Family violence: Prevention and treatment* (2nd ed., 122–147). Thousand Oaks, CA: Sage.

Harris, M. B., & Valentiner, D. P. (2002). World assumptions, sexual assault, depression, and fearful attitudes toward relationships. *Journal of Interpersonal Violence, 17,* 286–305.

Hart, S. N., Brassard, M. R., & Karlson, H. C. (1996). Psychological maltreatment. In J. Briere, L. Berliner, J. A. Bulkley, C. Jenny, & T. Reid (Eds.), *The APSAC handbook on child maltreatment* (pp. 125–146). Thousand Oaks, CA: Sage.

Hart, S. D., Hare, R. D., & Harpur, T. J. (1992). The Psychopathy Checklist–Revised (PCL-R): An overview for researchers and clinicians. In J. C. Rosen, & P. McReynolds (Eds.), *Advances in psychological assessment* (Vol. 8, pp. 103–130). New York, NY: Plenum Press.

Harway, M., & Evans, K. (1996). Working in groups with men who batter. In M. P. Andronicus (Ed.), *Men in groups: Insights, interventions, and psychoeducational work*. Washington DC: American Psychological Association.

Harway, M., & Hansen, M. (1994). *Spouse abuse: Assessing & treating battered women, batterers, & their children*. Sarasota, FL: Professional Resource Press/ Professional Resource Exchange.

Hassouneh-Phillips, D. (2001). Polygamy and wife abuse: A qualitative study of Muslim women in America. *Heath Care for Women International, 22,* 735–748.

Hastings, B. M. (2000). Social information processing and the verbal and physical abuse of women. *Journal of Interpersonal Violence, 15,* 651–664.

Hattery, A. J. (2009). *Intimate partner violence*. New York, NY: Rowman & Littlefield.

Hawes, C. (2003). Elder abuse in residential long-term care settings: What is known and what information is needed? In R. J. Bonnie & R. B. Wallace (Eds.), *Elder maltreatment: Abuse, neglect, and exploitation in an aging America* (pp. 446–500). Washington, DC: National Academy Press.

Hawes, C., Blevins, D., & Shanley, L. (2001). *Preventing abuse and neglect in nursing homes: The role of the nurse aide registries* (Report to the Centers for Medicare and Medicaid Services [formerly HCFA]). College Station, TX: School of Rural Public Health, Texas A&M University System Health Science Center.

Healey, K. M., Smith, C., & O'Sullivan, C. (1998). *Batterer intervention: Program approaches and criminal justice strategies. Report*. Washington, DC: National Institute of Justice.

Hechler, D. (1988). *The battle and the backlash: The child sexual abuse war*. Lexington, MA: Lexington Books.

Heckert, D. A, & Gondolf, E. W. (2000). Predictor of underreporting of male violence by batterer program participants and their partners. *Journal of Family Violence, 15,* 423–443.

Heffer, R. W., & Kelly, M. L. (1987). Mothers' acceptance of behavioral interventions for children: The influence of parental race and income. *Behavior Therapy, 2,* 153–163.

Heise, L. L., Pitanguy, A., & Germain, A. (1994). *Violence against women: The hidden health burden*. Washington, DC: World Bank.

Hemenway, D., Shinoda-Tagawa, T., & Miller, M. (2002). Firearm availability and female homicide victimization rates among 25 populous high-income countries. *Journal of the American Medical Women's Association, 57,* 100–104.

Hendricks, S. S. (1998, August). *Authority and the abuse of power in Muslim marriages.* Paper presented at the Women's Conference of the 2nd International Islamic Unity Conference, Washington, DC. Retrieved April 2005 from www. themodernreligion.com/women/abuse-marriage.html

Henman, M. (1996). Domestic violence: Do men under report? *Forensic Update, 47,* 3–8.

Herman, J. L. (1992). Complex PTSD: A syndrome in survivors of prolonged and repeated trauma. *Journal of Traumatic Stress, 5,* 377–391.

Herman, B. (2007). CAPTA and early childhood intervention: Policy and the role of parents. *Children & Schools, 29,* 17–24.

Hershsberger, S. L., & D'Augelli, A. R. (2000). Issues in counseling lesbian, gay, and bisexual adolescents. In R. M. Perez, K. A. DeBord, & K. J. Bieschke (Eds.), *Handbook of counseling and psychotherapy with lesbian, gay, and bisexual clients* (pp. 225–247). Washington, DC: American Psychological Association.

Hesse, E., & Main, M. (2000). Disorganized infant, child and adult attachment: Collapse in behavioral and attentional strategies. *Journal of the American Psychoanalytic Association, 48,* 1097–1127.

Hesse, E., & Main, M. (2006). Frightened, threatening, and dissociative parental behavior in low-risk samples: Description, discussion and interpretations. *Development and Psychopathology, 18,* 309–343.

Hettrich, E. L., & O'Leary, K. D. (2007). Females' reasons for their physical aggression in dating relationships. *Journal of Interpersonal Violence, 22,* 1131–1143.

Heyman, R. E., & Schlee, K. A. (1997). Toward a better estimate of the prevalence of partner abuse: Adjusting rates based on the sensitivity of the Conflict Tactics Scale. *Journal of Family Psychology, 11,* 332–338.

Hickman, L. J., Jaycox, L. H., & Aronoff, J. (2004). Dating violence among adolescents: Prevalence, gender distribution, and prevention program effectiveness. *Trauma, Violence, & Abuse, 5,* 123–142.

Hildyard, K. L., & Wolfe, D. A. (2002). Child neglect: Developmental issues and outcomes. *Child Abuse & Neglect, 26,* 679–695.

Hill, M. S., & Fischer, A. R. (2001). Does entitlement mediate the link between masculinity and rape-related variables? *Journal of Counseling Psychology, 48,* 39–50.

Hillis, S. D., Anda, R. F., Felitti, V. J., Nordenberg, D., & Marchbanks, P. A. (2000). Adverse childhood experiences and sexually transmitted diseases in men and women: A retrospective study. *Pediatrics, 106,* 257–267.

Hines, D. A., & Douglas, E. M. (2009). Women's use of intimate partner violence against men: Prevalence, implications, and consequences. *Journal of Aggression, Maltreatment & Trauma, 18,* 572–586. doi: 10.1080/10926770903103099

Hines, D. A., & Malley-Morrison, K. (2001). Psychological effects of partner abuse against men: A neglected research area. *Psychology of Men and Masculinity, 2,* 75–85.

Hines, D. A., & Malley-Morrison, K. (2005). *Family violence in the United States: Defining, understanding, and combating abuse.* Thousand Oaks, CA: Sage.

Hines, D. A., & Saudino, K. J. (2003). Gender differences in psychological, physical, and sexual aggression among college students using the Revised Conflict Tactics Scales. *Violence and Victims, 18,* 197–218.

Hines, D. A., & Saudino, K. J. (2004). Genetic and environmental influences on intimate partner aggression. *Violence and Victims, 19,* 701–718.

Hines, D. A., & Saudino, K. J. (2009). How much variance in psychological and physical aggression is predicted by genetics? Psychological and physical aggression in couples: Causes and interventions. In K. D. O'Leary & E. M. Woodin (Eds.), *Psychological and physical aggression in couples: Causes and interventions* (pp. 141–162). Washington, DC: American Psychological Association.

Ho, C. K. (1990). An analysis of domestic violence in Asian American communities: A multicultural approach to counseling. *Women & Therapy, 9,* 129–150.

Hobfoll, S. E., Bansal, A., Schurg, R., Young, S., Peirce, C. A., Hobfoll, I., . . . Johnson, R. (2002). The impact of perceived child physical and sexual abuse history on Native American women's psychological well-being and AIDS risk. *Journal of Consulting and Clinical Psychology, 70,* 252–257.

Hoefnagels, C., & Mudde, A. (2000). Mass media and disclosures of child abuse in the perspective of secondary prevention: Putting ideas into practice. *Child Abuse & Neglect, 24,* 1091–1101.

Holtzworth-Munroe, A. (2000). Social information processing skills deficits in maritally violent men: Summary of a research program. In J. P. Vincent & E. N. Jouriles (Eds.), *Domestic violence: Guidelines for research-informed practice* (pp. 13–36). London, England: Jessica Kingsley.

Holtzworth-Munroe, A., Beatty, S. B., & Anglin, K. (1995). The assessment and treatment of marital violence: An introduction for the marital therapist. In N. S. Jacobson & A. S. Gurman (Eds.), *Clinical handbook of couple therapy* (pp. 317–339). New York, NY: Guilford Press.

Holtzworth-Munroe, A., & Meehan, J. C. (2004). Typologies of men who are maritally violent: Scientific and clinical implications. *Journal of Interpersonal Violence, 19,* 1369–1389.

Holtzworth-Munroe, A., Meehan, J. C., Herron, K., Rehman, U., & Stuart, G. L. (2000) Testing the Holtzworth-Munroe and Stuart (1994) batterer typology. *Journal of Consulting and Clinical Psychology, 68,* 1000–1019.

Holtzworth-Munroe, A., Meehan, J. C., Herron, K., Rehman, U., & Stuart, G. L. (2003). Do subtypes of maritally violent men continue over time? *Journal of Consulting and Clinical Psychology, 71,* 728–740.

Holtzworth-Munroe, A., Meehan, J. C., Rehman, U., & Marshall, A. D. (2002). Intimate partner violence: An introduction for couple therapists. In A. S. Gurman & N. S. Jacobson (Eds.), *Clinical handbook of couple therapy* (3rd ed., pp. 441–465). New York, NY: Guilford Press.

Holtzworth-Munroe, A., & Stuart, G. L. (1994). Typologies of male batterers: Three subtypes and the differences among them. *Psychological Bulletin, 116,* 476–497.

Holtzworth-Munroe, A., Stuart, G. L., & Hutchinson, G. (1997). Violent versus nonviolent husbands: Differences in attachment patterns, dependency, and jealousy. *Journal of Family Psychology, 11,* 314–331.

Hong, G. K., & Hong, L. K. (1991). Comparative perspective in child abuse and neglect: Chinese versus Hispanics and Whites. *Child Welfare, 70,* 463–475.

Horton, A. L., Wilkins, M. M., & Wright, W. (1988). Women who ended abuse: What religious leaders and religion did for these victims. In A. L. Horton & J. A. Williamson (Eds.), *Abuse and religion: When praying isn't enough* (pp. 235–246). Lexington, MA: Lexington Books.

Hotaling, G. T., & Sugarman, D. B. (1986). An analysis of risk markers in husband to wife violence: The current state of knowledge. *Violence and Victims, 1,* 101–124.

House, E. (2001). When women use force. *Wisconsin Coalition Against Domestic Violence Newsletter, 20,* 18–19.

Howard, D. E., Wang, M. Q., & Yan, F. (2007a). Prevalence and psychosocial correlates of forced sexual intercourse among U.S. high school adolescents. *Adolescence, 42,* 629–643.

Howard, D. E., Wang, M. Q., & Yan, F. (2007b). Psychosocial factors associated with reports of physical dating violence among U.S. adolescent females. *Adolescence, 42,* 311–324.

Howell, K. H., Graham-Bermann, S. A., Czyz, E., & Lilly, M. (2010). Assessing resilience in preschool children exposed to intimate partner violence. *Violence and Victims, 25,* 150–164.

Hucker, S., Langevin, R., Wortzman, G., Dickey, R., Bain, J., Handy, L., . . . Wright, S. (1988). Cerebral damage and dysfunction in sexually aggressive men. *Annals of Sex Research, 1,* 33–47.

Huesmann, L. R., Moise-Titus, J., & Podolski, C. (2003). Longitudinal relations between children's exposure to TV violence and their aggressive and violent behavior in young adulthood: 1977–1992. *Developmental Psychology, 39,* 201–221.

Hughes, T. L. (2003). Lesbians' drinking patterns: Beyond the data. *Substance Use & Misuse, 38,* 1739–1758.

Huss, M. T., & Langhinrichsen-Rohling, J. (2000). Identification of the psychopathic batterer: The clinical, legal and policy implications. *Aggression and Violent Behavior, 5,* 403–422.

Island, D., & Letellier, P. (1991). *Men who beat the men who love them.* New York, NY: Harrington Park Press.

Iverson, T. J., & Segal, M. (1990). *Child abuse and neglect: An information and reference guide.* New York, NY: Garland Press.

Iwasaki, Y., & Ristock, J. L. (2007). The nature of stress experienced by lesbians and gay men. *Anxiety, Stress, & Coping: An International Journal, 20,* 299–319.

Jacobson, N. S., & Christensen, A. (1996). *Integrative couple therapy: Promoting acceptance and change.* New York, NY: Norton.

Jacobson, N. S., Gottman, J. M., Gortner, E., Berns, S, & Shortt, J. W. (1996). Psychological factors in the longitudinal course of battering: When do the couples split up? When does the abuse decrease? *Violence and Victims, 11,* 371–392.

Jasinski, J. L. (2001). Physical violence among Anglo, African Americans, Hispanic couples: Ethnic differences in persistence and cessation. *Violence and Victims, 16,* 479–490.

Jennings, J. L., & Murphy, C. M. (2000). Male–male dimensions of male–female battering: A new look at domestic violence. *Psychology of Men & Masculinity, 1,* 21–29.

Johnson, D. M., Zlotnick, C., & Perez, S. (2011). Cognitive behavioral treatment of PTSD in residents of battered women's shelters: Results of a randomized clinical trial. *Journal of Consulting and Clinical Psychology, 79,* 542–551.

Johnson, H., & Bunge, V. P. (2001). Prevalence and consequences of spousal assault in Canada. *Canadian Journal of Criminology, 43,* 27–45.

Johnson, L. L., & Lipsett-Rivera, S. (Eds.). (1998). *The faces of honor: Sex, shame, and violence in colonial Latin America.* Albuquerque: University of New Mexico Press.

Johnson, M. P. (2001). Conflict and control: Images of symmetry and asymmetry in domestic violence. In A. Booth, A. C. Crouter, & M. Clement (Eds.), *Couples in conflict* (pp. 95–104). Mahwah, NJ: Erlbaum.

Johnson, M. P. (2006). Conflict and control: Gender symmetry and asymmetry in domestic violence. *Violence Against Women, 12,* 1003–1018.

Johnson, M. P., & Ferraro, K. J. (2000). Research on domestic violence in the 1990s: Making distinctions. *Journal of Marriage & the Family, 62,* 948–963.

Johnson, M. P., & Leone, J. M. (2005). The differential effects of intimate terrorism and situational couple violence: Findings from the National Violence Against Women Survey. *Journal of Family Issues, 26,* 322–349.

Johnson, S. M. (2002). *Emotionally focused couple therapy with trauma survivors.* New York, NY: Guilford Press.

Johnson, S. M. (2004). *The practice of emotionally focused couple therapy* (2nd ed.). New York, NY: Brunner-Routledge.

Joint Commission on Accreditation of Healthcare Organizations. (2002). *How to recognize abuse and neglect.* Oakbook Terrace, IL: Author.

Jones, A. S., D'Agostino, R. B., Jr., Gondolf, E. W., & Heckert, A. (2004). Assessing the effect of batterer program completion on reassault using propensity scores. *Journal of Interpersonal Violence, 19,* 1002–1020.

Jordon, C. E., Logan, T., Walker, R., & Nigoff, A. (2003). Stalking: An examination of the criminal justice response. *Journal of Interpersonal Violence, 18,* 148–165.

Jouriles, E. N., Platt, C., & McDonald, R. (2009). Violence in adolescent dating relationships. *The Prevention Researcher, 16,* 3–7.

Kairys, S. W., Johnson, C. F., & Committee on Child Abuse and Neglect. (2002). The psychological maltreatment of children—Technical report. *Pediatrics, 109,* 68–73.

Kalmuss, D. S. (1984, February). The intergenerational transmission of marital aggression. *Journal of Marriage and the Family, 46,* 11–19.

Kamphuis, J., & Emmelkamp, P. (2005). 20 years of research into violence and trauma. *Journal of Interpersonal Violence, 20,* 167–174.

Kamphuis, J., Emmelkamp, P., & Bartak, A. (2003). Individual differences in post-traumatic stress following post-intimate stalking: Stalking severity and psychosocial variables. *British Journal of Clinical Psychology, 42,* 145–156.

Kantor, G. K., & Straus, M.A. (1989). Substance abuse as a precipitant of wife abuse victimization. *Journal of Drug and Alcohol Abuse, 15,* 173–189.

Kanuga, M,, & Rosenfeld, W. D. (2004). Adolescent sexuality and the Internet: The good, the bad, and the URL. *Journal of Pediatric and Adolescent Gynecology, 17,* 117–124.

Kapitanoff, S. H., Lutzker, J. R., & Bigelow, K. M. (2000). Cultural issues in the relation between child disabilities and child abuse. *Aggression and Violent Behavior, 5,* 227–244.

Kasturirangan, A., Krishnan, S., & Riger, S. (2004). The impact of culture and minority status on women's experience of domestic violence. *Trauma, Violence, & Abuse, 5,* 318–332.

Kaufman, G. (1992). The mysterious disappearance of battered women in family therapists' offices: Male privilege colluding with male violence. *Journal of Marital and Family Therapy, 18,* 233–243.

Kaufman, J. G., & Widom, C. S. (1999). Childhood victimization, running away, and delinquency. *Journal of Research in Crime and Delinquency, 36,* 347–370.

Kaufman, J. G., & Zigler, E. (1987). Do abused children become abusive parents? *American Journal of Orthopsychiatry, 57,* 516–524.

Kaura, S. A., & Allen, C. M. (2004). Dissatisfaction with relationship power and dating violence perpetration by men and women. *Journal of Interpersonal Violence, 19,* 576–588.

Kazdin, A. E., Siegel, T. C., & Bass, D. (1990). Drawing on clinical practice to inform research on child and adolescent psychotherapy: Survey of practitioners. *Professional Psychology: Research and Practice, 21,* 189–198.

Keiley, M. K., Howe, T. R., Dodge, K. A., Bates, J. E. M., & Pettit, G. E. (2001). The timing of child physical maltreatment: A cross-domain growth analysis of impact on adolescent externalizing and internalizing problems. *Developmental and Psychopathology, 13,* 891–912.

Kelley, B. T., Thornberry, T. P., & Smith, C. A. (1997). *In the wake of childhood maltreatment.* Washington, DC: National Institute of Justice. Retrieved May 2009 from http://www.ncjrs.gov/pdffiles1/165257.pdf

Kelly, J. B., & Johnson, M. P. (2008). Differentiation among types of intimate partner violence: Research update and implications for interventions. *Family Court Review, 46,* 476–499.

Kelly, R. J., Wood, J. J., Gonzalez, L. S., MacDonald, V., & Waterman, J. (2002). Effects of mother–son incest and positive perceptions of sexual abuse experience on the psychosocial adjustment of clinic-referred men. *Child Abuse and Neglect, 26,* 425–441.

Kemp, A., Rawlings, E. I., & Green, B. L. (1991). Posttraumatic stress disorder (PTSD) in battered women: A shelter example. *Journal of Traumatic Stress Studies, 4,* 137–148.

Kendall-Tackett, K. A., & Eckenrode, J. (1996). The effects of neglect on academic achievement and disciplinary problems: A developmental perspective. *Child Abuse &Neglect, 20,* 161–169.

Kershaw, S. (2003, October 20). Elder care Americanized. *Los Angeles Daily News,* p. 12.

Kessler, R. C., Molnar, B. E., Feurer, J. D., & Appelbaum, M. (2001). Patterns and mental health predictors of domestic violence in the United States: Results from the National Comorbidity Survey. *International Journal of Law and Psychology, 24,* 487–508.

Kessler, R. C., Sonnega, A., Bromet, E., Hughes, M., & Nelson, C. B. (1995). Post-traumatic stress disorder in the National Comorbidity Survey. *Archives of General Psychiatry, 52,* 1048–1060.

Kim, J. Y., & Sung, K. (2000). Conjugal violence in Korean American families: A residue of the cultural tradition. *Journal of Family Violence, 15,* 331–345.

Kinsfogel, K. M., & Grych, J. H. (2004). Interparental conflict and adolescent dating relationships: Integrating cognitive, emotional, and peer influences. *Journal of Family Psychology, 18,* 505–515.

Kinsler, P. J., Courtois, C. A., & Frankel, A. S. (2009). Therapeutic alliance and risk management. In C. A. Courtois & J. D. Ford (Eds.), *Treating complex traumatic stress disorders* (pp. 183–201). New York, NY: Guilford Press.

Kistenmacher, B. R., & Weiss, R. L. (2008). Motivational interviewing as a mechanism for change in men who batter: A randomized controlled trial. *Violence and Victims, 23,* 558–570.

Kitzmann, K. M., Gaylord, N. K., Holt, A. R., & Kenny, E. D. (2003). Child witnesses to domestic violence: A meta-analytic review. *Journal of Consulting and Clinical Psychology, 71,* 339–352.

Klaus, P. A. (2000). Crimes against persons age 65 or older, 1992–1997. Washington, DC: U. S. Department of Justice. Retrieved from http://www.ojp.usdoj.gov/bjs/pub/pdf/cpa6597.pdf

Klohnen, E., & John, O. (1998). Working models of attachment: A theory-based approach. In J. Simpson & W. Rholes (Eds.), *Attachment theory and close relationships* (pp. 115–140). New York, NY: Guilford Press.

Knox, M. (2010). On hitting children: A review of corporal punishment in the United States. *Journal of Pediatric Health Care, 24,* 103–107.

Kobak, R., Cassidy, J., & Ziv, Y. (2004). Attachment-related trauma and posttraumatic stress disorder: Implications for adult adaptation. In W. S. Rholes & J. A. Simpson (Eds.), *Adult attachment: Theory, research, and clinical implications* (pp. 388–407). New York, NY: Guilford Press.

Kocher, M. S., & Kasser, J. R. (2000). Orthopaedic aspects of child abuse. *Journal of the American Academy of Orthopedic Surgeons, 8,* 10–20.

Koenen, K. C., Harley, R. M., Lyons, M. J., Wolfe, J., Simpson, J. C., Goldberg, J., . . . Tsuang, M. T. (2002). A twin registry study of familial and individual risk factors for trauma exposure and posttraumatic stress disorder. *Journal of Nervous and Mental Disease, 190,* 209–218.

Koepsell, J. K., Kernic, M. A., & Holt, V. L. (2006). Factors that influence battered women to leave their abusive relationships. *Violence and Victims, 21,* 131–147.

Kolko, D. J., & Swenson, C. C. (2002). *Assessing and treating physically abused children and their families: A cognitive behavioral approach.* Thousand Oaks, CA: Sage.

Korbin, J. E. (2002). Culture and child maltreatment: Cultural competence and beyond. *Child Abuse & Neglect, 26,* 637–644.

Korbin, J. E., Coulton, C. J., Lindstrom-Ufuti, H., & Spilsbury, J. (2000). Neighborhood views on the definition and etiology of child maltreatment. *Child Abuse and Neglect, 24,* 1509–1527.

Kovacs, M. (1985). The Children's Depression Inventory (CDI). *Psychopharmacology Bulletin, 113,* 164–180.

Krienert, J. L., & Walsh, J. A. (2011): Sibling sexual abuse: An empirical analysis of offender, victim, and event characteristics in National Incident-Based Reporting System (NIBRS) data, 2000–2007. *Journal of Child Sexual Abuse, 20,* 353–372.

Kropp, P. R., Hart, S. D., Webster, C. W., & Eaves, D. (1995). *Manual for the Spousal Assault Risk Assessment Guide* (2nd ed.). Vancouver, British Columbia, Canada: B. C. Institute on Family Violence.

Krug, E. G., Dahlberg, L. L., Mercy, J. A., Zwi, A. B., & Lozano, R. (Eds.). (2002). *World report on violence and health.* Geneva, Switzerland: World Health Organization.

Kubany, E. S., Owens, J. A., McCaig, M. A., Williams, P., Hill, E. E., Iannce-Spencer, C., & Tremayne, K. J. (2004). Cognitive trauma therapy for battered women with PTSD (CTT-BW). *Journal of Consulting and Clinical Psychology, 72,* 3–18.

Kurz, D. (1993). Physical assaults by husbands: A major social problem. In R. J. Gelles & D. R. Loseke (Eds.), *Current controversies in family violence* (1st ed., pp. 257–272). Thousand Oaks, CA: Sage.

Lachs, M. S., Berkman, I., Fulmer, T., & Horwitz, R. (1994). Prospective community-based pilot study of risk factors for the investigation of elder mistreatment. *Journal of the American Geriatrics Society, 42,* 169–173.

Lachs, M. S., & Pillemer, K. (1995). Current concepts: Abuse and neglect of elderly persons. *New England Journal of Medicine, 332,* 437–443.

Lachs, M. S., Williams, C., O'Brien, S., Hurst, L., & Horwitz, R. (1997). Risk factors for reported elder abuse and neglect: A nine-year observational cohort study. *Gerontologist, 37,* 469–474.

Lachs, M. S., Williams, C., O'Brien, S., Pillemer, K., & Charlson, M. (1998). The mortality of elder mistreatment. *Journal of the American Medical Association, 280,* 428–432.

Lakes, K., Lopez, S. R., & Garro, L. C. (2006). Cultural competence and psychotherapy: Applying anthropologically informed conceptions of culture. *Psychotherapy, 43,* 380–396.

Lambert, L. C., & Firestone, J. M. (2000). Economic context and multiple abuse techniques. *Violence Against Women, 6,* 49–67.

Lambert, L. C., & Ogles, B. M. (2004). The efficacy and effectiveness of psychotherapy. In M. J. Lambert (Ed.), *Bergin and Garfield's handbook of psychotherapy and behavior change* (5th ed., pp. 139–193). New York, NY: Wiley.

Landes, A., Siegel, M. A., & Foster, C. D. (1993). *Domestic violence: No longer behind the curtains.* Wylie, TX: Information Plus.

Landholt, M. A., & Dutton, D. G. (1997). Power and personality: An analysis of gay male intimate abuse. *Sex Roles, 37,* 335–359.

Langhinrichsen-Rohling, J. (2005). Top 10 greatest "hits": Important findings and future directions for intimate partner violence research. *Journal of Interpersonal Violence, 20,* 108–118.

Langhinrichsen-Rohling, J. (2010). Controversies involving gender and intimate partner violence in the United States. *Sex Roles, 62,* 179–193.

Langhinrichsen-Rohling, J., Huss, M. T., & Ramsey, S. (2000). The clinical utility of batterer typologies. *Journal of Family Violence, 15,* 37–53.

Langhinrichsen-Rohling, J., Huss, M. T., & Rohling, M. L. (2006). Aggressive behavior. In M. Hersen (Ed.), *Clinicians handbook of adult behavioral assessment* (pp. 371–395). San Diego, CA: Elsevier.

Langley, R., & Levy, R.C. (1977). *Wife-beating: The silent crisis.* New York, NY: Dutton.

Larimer, M. E., & Cronce, J. M. (2007). Identification, prevention, and treatment revisited: Individual-focused college drinking prevention strategies 1999–2006. *Addictive Behaviors, 32,* 2439–2468.

Lanier, C., & Maume, M. O. (2009). Intimate partner violence and social isolation across the rural/urban divide. *Violence Against Women, 15,* 1311–1330.

Laroche, D. (2005). *Aspects of the context and consequences of domestic violence, situational couple violence, and intimate terrorism in Canada in 1999*. Quebec City, Canada: Government of Quebec.

Larzelere, R. E. (2000). Weak evidence for a smacking ban. *British Medical Journal, 320*, 1538.

Lascaratos, J., & Poulakou-Rebelakou, E. (2000). Child sexual abuse: Historical cases in Byzantine empire (324–1453 A.D.). *Child Abuse & Neglect, 24,* 1085–1090.

Laumann, E. O., Leitsch, S. A., & Waite, L. J. (2008). Elder mistreatment in the United States: Prevalence estimates from a nationally representative study. *Journal of Gerontology: Series B: Psychological Sciences and Social Sciences, 63B,* S248–S254.

Lawrence, E., Heyman, R. E., & O'Leary, K. D. (1995). Correspondence between telephone and written assessments of physical violence in marriage. *Behavior Therapy, 26,* 671–680.

Lawson, D. M. (1989). A family systems perspective on wife battering. *Journal of Mental Health Counseling, 11, 359–374.*

Lawson, D. M. (2003). Incidence, explanations, and treatment of partner violence. *Journal of Counseling & Development, 81,* 19–32.

Lawson, D. M. (2008). Attachment, interpersonal problems, and family functioning: Differences between intimate violent versus non-intimate violent men. *Psychology of Men and Masculinity, 9,* 90–105.

Lawson, D. M. (2010). Comparing cognitive behavioral therapy and integrated therapy in group treatment for partner violent men. *Psychotherapy: Theory, Research, Training, Practice, 47,* 122–133.

Lawson, D. M., Dawson, T. E., Kieffer, K. M., Perez, L. M., Burke, J., & Kier, F. J. (2001). An integrated feminist/cognitive–behavioral and psychodynamic group treatment model for men who abuse their partners. *Psychology of Men and Masculinity, 2,* 86–89.

Lawson, D. M., Kellam, M., Quinn, J., & Malnar, S. G. (2012). Integrated cognitive behavioral therapy and psychodynamic psychotherapy for intimate partner violent men. *Psychotherapy, 49,* 190–201.

Lawson, D. M., Weber, D., Beckner, M., Robinson, L., Marsh, N., & Cool, A. (2003). Men who use violence: Intimate vs non-intimate violence profiles. *Violence and Victims, 18,* 259–277.

Lee, M.-Y. (2000). Understanding Chinese battered women in North America: A review of the literature and practice implications. *Psychology of Women Quarterly, 16,* 145–163.

Leisring, P. A., Dowd, L., & Rosenbaum, A. (2003). Treatment of partner aggressive women. *Journal of Aggression, Maltreatment & Trauma, 7,* 257–277.

Leskin, G. A., & Sheikh, J. I. (2002). Lifetime trauma history and panic disorder: Findings from the National Comorbidity Survey. *Journal of Anxiety Disorders, 16,* 599–603.

Letellier, P. (1994). Gay and bisexual domestic violence victimization: Challenges to feminist theory and response to violence. *Violence and Victims, 9,* 95–106.

Leung, A. K.-Y., & Cohen, D. (2011). Within- and between-culture variation: Individual differences and the cultural logics of honor, face, and dignity cultures. *Journal of Personality and Social Psychology, 100,* 507–526

Levenson, H. (1995). *Time-limited dynamic psychotherapy.* New York, NY: Basic Books.

Levy, B., & Lobel, K. (1998). Lesbian teens in abusive relationships. In B. Levy (Ed.), *Dating violence: Young women in danger* (pp. 203–208). Seattle, WA: Seal Press.

Levy, J. Y. (2004). Counselor's corner: Love is not abuse. *The Pacer Online Edition, 77.* Retrieved from http://pacer.utm.edu/2065.htm

Lewis, C. S., Griffing, S., Chu, M., Sage, R. E., Madry, L., & Primm, B. J. (2006). Coping and violence exposure as predictors of psychological functioning in domestic violence survivors. *Violence Against Women, 12,* 340–354.

Lewis, S. F., & Fremouw, W. (2001). Dating violence: A critical review of the literature. *Clinical Psychology Review, 21,* 105–127.

Lieberman, A. F. (2004). Traumatic stress and quality of attachment: Reality and internalization in disorders of infant mental health. *Infant Mental Health Journal. Special: The Added Value of Attachment Theory and Research for Clinical Work, 25,* 336–396.

Linder Gunnoe, M., Hetherington, E. M., & Reiss, D. (1999). Parental religiosity, parenting style, and adolescent social responsibility. *Journal of Adolescence, 19,* 199–225.

Lindgren, A. S., & Renck, B. (2008). "It is still so deep-seated, the fear": Psychological stress reactions as a consequence of intimate partner violence. *Journal of Psychiatric and Mental Health Nursing, 15,* 219–228.

Linehan, M. M. (1993). *Cognitive–behavioral treatment of borderline personality disorder.* New York, NY: Guilford Press.

Liotti, G. (2004). Trauma, dissociation, and disorganized attachment: Three strands of a single braid. *Psychotherapy: Theory, Research, Practice, Training, 41,* 472–486.

Lipsky, S., Caetano, R., Field, C. A., & Larkin, G. L. (2006). The role of intimate partner violence, race, and ethnicity in help-seeking behaviors. *Ethnicity & Health, 11,* 81–100.

Lithwick, M., Beaulieu, M., Gravel, S., & Straka, S. M. (1999). The mistreatment of older adults: Perpetrator–victim relationships and interventions. *Journal of Elder Abuse & Neglect, 11,* 95–112.

Littell, J. (2001). Client participation and outcomes of intensive family preservation services. *Social Work Research, 25,* 103–114.

Lobach, K. S. (2008). Child and adolescence health. *Journal of Urban Health, 85,* 807–811.

Loewenstein, R. J. (1991). An office mental status examination for complex chronic dissociative symptoms and multiple personality disorder. *Psychiatric Clinics of North American, 14,* 567–604.

Loftus, E. (1993). The reality of repressed memories. *American Psychologist, 48,* 518–537.

Loftus, E. (2003). Our changeable memories: Legal and practical implications. *Nature Reviews, 4,* 231–234.

Loseke, D. R., Gelles, R. J., & Cavanaugh, M. M. (Eds.). (2005). *Current controversies on family violence*. Thousand Oaks, CA: Sage.

Loseke, D. R., & Kurz, M. (2005). Men's violence toward women is the serious social problem. In D. R. Loseke, R. J. Gelles, & M. M. Cavanaugh (Eds.), *Current controversies on family violence* (2nd ed., pp. 79–96). Thousand Oaks, CA: Sage.

Luthar, S. S., Cicchetti, D., & Becker, B. (2000). The construct of resilience: A critical evaluation and guidelines for future work. *Child Development, 71,* 543–562.

Luthra, R., & Gidycz, C. A. (2006). Dating violence among college men and women: Evaluation of theoretical model. *Journal of Interpersonal Violence, 21,* 717–731.

Lyons-Ruth, K., Alpern, L., & Repacholi, B. (1993). Disorganized infant attachment classification and maternal psychosocial problems as predictors of hostile–aggressive behavior in the preschool classroom. *Child Development, 64,* 572–585.

Lyons-Ruth, K., & Jacobvitz, D. (1999). Attachment disorganization: Unresolved loss, relational violence, and lapses in behavioral and attentional strategies. In J. Cassidy & P. R. Shaver (Eds.), *Handbook of attachment: Theory, research, and clinical applications* (pp. 520–554). New York, NY: Guilford Press.

Mace, N. L. (1981). *The 36-hour day: A family guide to caring for persons with Alzheimer's disease, related dementing illness, and memory loss in later life*. Baltimore, MD: Johns Hopkins University Press.

Mackey, A. L., Fromuth, M. E., & Kelly, D. B. (2009). The association of sibling relationship and abuse with later psychological adjustment. *Journal of Interpersonal Violence, 25,* 955–968.

MacLeod, J., & Nelson, G. (2000). Programs for the promotion of family wellness and the prevention of child maltreatment. A meta-analytic review. *Child Abuse & Neglect, 24,* 1127–1149.

Magdol, L., Moffitt, T. E., Caspi, A., Newman, D. L., Fagan, J. A., & Silva, P. A. (1997). Gender differences in partner violence in a birth cohort of 21-year-olds: Bridging the gap between clinical and epidemiological approaches. *Journal of Consulting and Clinical Psychology, 65,* 68–78.

Magdol, L., Moffitt, T. E., Caspi, A., & Silva, P. A. (1998). Developmental antecedents of partner abuse: A prospective–longitudinal study. *Journal of Abnormal Psychology, 107,* 375–389.

Mahoney, A., Donnelly, W. O., Boxer, P., & Lewis, T. (2003). Marital and severe parent-to-adolescent physical aggression in clinic-referred family: Mother and adolescent reports on co-occurrence and links to child behavior problems. *Journal of Family Psychology, 17,* 3–19.

Mahoney, A., Pargament, K. I., Jewell, T., Swank, A. B. Scott, E., Emery, E., & Rye, M. (1999). Marriage and the spiritual realm: The role of proximal and distal religious constructs in marital functioning. *Journal of Family Psychology, 13,* 1–18.

Main, M., & George, C. (1985). Response of abused and disadvantaged toddlers to distress in age mates: A study in the day care setting. *Developmental Psychology, 21,* 407–412.

Making Daughters Safe Again (2010). *Statement of purpose.* Retrieved from http://mdsa-online.org/

Malamuth, N. M. (2003). Criminal and noncriminal sexual aggressors: Integrating psychopathy in heirarchial–mediational confluence. In R. A. Prentky, E. S. Janus, & M. C. Seto (Eds.), *Annals of the New York Academy of Sciences: Vol. 989. Sexually coercive behavior: Understanding and management* (pp. 33–58). New York, NY: New York Academy Sciences.

Mallet, C. A., Dare, P. S., & Seck, M. M. (2009). Predicting juvenile delinquency: The nexus of childhood maltreatment, depression and bipolar disorder. *Criminal Behaviour and Mental Health, 19,* 235–246.

Malley-Morrison, K., & Hines, D. A. (2004). *Family violence in a cultural perspective: Defining, understanding, and combating abuse.* Thousand Oaks, CA: Sage.

Malley-Morrison, K., & Hines, D. A. (2007). Attending to the role of race/ethnicity in family violence research. *Journal of Interpersonal Violence, 22,* 943–972.

Malloy, K. A., McCloskey, K. A.., Grigsby, N., & Gardner, D. (2003). Women's use of violence within intimate relationships. *Journal of Aggression, Maltreatment & Trauma, 6,* 37–59.

Mammen, O. K., Kolko, D. J., & Pilkonis, P. A. (2002). Negative affect and parental aggression in child physical abuse. *Child Abuse & Neglect, 26,* 407–424.

Manly, J. T., Kim, J. E., Rogosch, F. A., & Cicchetti, D. (2001). Dimensions of child maltreatment and children's adjustment: Contributions of developmental timing and subtype. *Development and Psychopathology, 13,* 759–782.

Mann, C. R. (1996). *When women kill.* New York: State University of New York Press.

Mann, R., Webster, S., Wakeling, H., & William, M. (2007). The measurement and influence of child sexual abuse supportive beliefs. *Psychology, Crime, & Law, 13,* 443–458.

Mannarino, A. P., & Cohen J. A. (1996). Abuse-related attributions and perceptions, general attributions, and locus of control in sexually abused girls. *Journal of Interpersonal Violence, 11,* 162–180.

March, J. S., Parker, J. D. A., Sullivan, K., Stallings, P., & Conners, C. K. (1997). The Multidimensional Anxiety Scale for Children: Factor structure, reliability and validity. *Journal of the American Academy of Child and Adolescent Psychiatry, 36,* 554–565.

Marcus, R. F., & Swett, B. (2003). Violence in close relationships: The role of emotion. *Aggression and Violent Behavior, 8,* 313–327.

Margolies, L., & Leeder, E. (1995). Violence at the door: Treatment of lesbian relationships. In C. M. Renzetti & C. H. Miley (Eds.), *Violence in gay and lesbian domestic partnerships* (pp. 23–33). New York, NY: Harrington Park Press/Haworth Press.

Margolin, G. (2005). Children's exposure to violence: Exploring developmental pathways to diverse outcomes. *Journal of Interpersonal Violence, 20,* 72–81.

Margolin, G., & Vickerman, K. A. (2011). Posttraumatic stress in children and adolescents exposed to family violence: I. Overview and issues. *Couple and Family Psychology: Research and Practice, 1,* 63–73.

Marquart, B. S., Nannini, D. K., Edwards, R. W., Stanley, L. R., & Wayman, J. C. (2007). Prevalence of dating violence and victimization: Regional and gender differences. *Adolescence, 42,* 645–657.

Marrujo, B., & Kreger, M. (1996). Definition of roles in abusive lesbian relationships. In C. M. Renzetti & C. H. Miley (Eds.), *Violence in gay and lesbian domestic partnerships* (pp. 23–33). New York, NY: Harrington Park Press/Haworth Press.

Marshall, A. D., & Holtzworth-Munroe, A. (2010). Recognition of wives' emotional expressions: A mechanism in the relationship between psychopathology and intimate partner violence perpetration. *Journal of Family Psychology, 24,* 21–30.

Martin, E. K., Taft, C. T., & Resick, P. A. (2007). A review of marital rape. *Aggression and Violent Behavior, 12,* 329–347.

Mason, A., & Blankenship, V. (1987). Power and affiliation motivation, stress, and abuse in intimate relationships. *Journal of Personality and Social Psychology, 52,* 203–210.

Masten, A. (2001). Ordinary magic: Resilience processes in development. *American Psychologist, 56,* 227–238.

Masten, A., & Coatsworth, J. M. (1998). The development of competence in favorable and unfavorable environments: Lessons from research of successful children. *American Psychologist, 53,* 205–220.

Mauricio, A. M., Tein, J. Y., & Lopez, F. G. (2007). Borderline and antisocial personality scores as mediators between attachment and intimate partner violence. *Violence and Victims, 22,* 139–157.

Max, W., Rice, D. P., Finkelstein, E., Bardwell, R. A., & Ledbetter, S. (2004). The economic toll of intimate partner violence against women in the United States. *Violence and Victims, 19,* 259–272.

McCann, J. T. (2003). Stalking and obsessional forms of harassment in children and adolescents. *Psychiatric Annals, 33,* 637–640.

McCarty, L. M. (1986). Mother–child incest: Characteristics of the offender. *Child Welfare, 65,* 447–458.

McCauley, J., Kern, D. E., Kolodner, K., Dill, L., Schroeder, A. F., DeChant, H. K., . . . Bass, E. B. (1997). Clinical characteristics of women with a history of childhood abuse: Unhealed wounds. *Journal of the American Medical Association, 277,* 1362–1368.

McClennen, J. C. (1999). Prevailing theories regarding same-gender partner abuse: Proposing the feminist social–psychological model. In J. C. McClennen & J. Gunther (Eds.), *A professional's guide to understanding gay and lesbian domestic violence: Understanding practice interventions* (pp. 3–12). Lewiston, NY: Edwin Mellen Press.

McClennen, J. C. (2010). *Social work and family violence.* New York, NY: Springer.

McClennen, J. C., Summers, B., & Daley, J. G. (2002). Lesbian Partner Abuse Scale. *Research on Social Work Practice, 12,* 277–292.

McCloskey, L. A., & Bailey, J. A. (2000). The intergenerational transmission of risk for child sexual abuse. *Journal of Interpersonal Violence, 15,* 1019–1035.

McCloskey, L. A., & Lichter, E. L. (2003). The contribution of marital violence to adolescent aggression across different relationships. *Journal of Interpersonal Violence, 18,* 390–412.

McDonald, R., Jouriles, E. N., Ramisetty-Mikler, S., Caetano, R., & Green, C. E. (2006). Estimating the number of American children living in partner-violent families. *Journal of Family Psychology, 20,* 137–142.

McEachern, D., Van Winkle, M., & Steiner, S. (1998). Domestic violence among the Navajo: A legacy of colonization. *Journal of Poverty, 2,* 31–46.

McFarlane, J., Campbell, J. C., & Watson, K. (2002). Intimate partner stalking and femicide: Urgent implications for women's safety. *Behavioral Sciences & the Law, 20,* 51–68.

McFee, R. B., Turano, J. A., & Roberts, S. (2001). Risk factors for dating violence in adolescents. *Journal of the American Medical Association, 286,* 2813.

McGarry, J., & Simpson, C. (2009). Raising awareness of elder abuse in the community practice setting. *British Journal of Community Nursing, 14,* 305–308.

McGloin, J. M., & Widom, C. S. (2001). Resilience among abused and neglected children grown up. *Development and Psychopathology, 13,* 1021–1038.

McKenry, P. C., Serovich, J., Mason, T., & Mosack, K. (2006). Perpetration of gay and lesbian partner violence: A disempowerment perspective. *Journal of Family Violence, 21,* 233–243.

McLaughlin, E. M., & Rozee, P. D. (2001). Knowledge about heterosexual versus lesbian battering among lesbians. In E. Kaschak (Ed.), *Intimate betrayal: Intimate partner abuse in lesbian relationships* (pp. 39–58). New York, NY: Haworth Press.

McNeely, R. L., Cook, P. W., & Torres, J. B. (2001). Is domestic violence a gender issue, or a human issue? *Journal of Human Behavior in the Social Environment, 4,* 227–251.

McNeil, C. B., & Hembree-Kigin, T. L. (2010). *Parent–child interaction therapy* (2nd ed.). New York, NY: Springer.

McVeigh, M. J. (2003). "But she didn't say no": An exploration of sibling sexual abuse. *Australian Social Work, 56,* 116–126.

Medeiros, R. A., & Straus, M. A. (2006). Risk factors for physical violence between dating partners: Implications for gender-inclusive prevention and treatment of family violence. In J. C. Hamel & T. Nicholls (Eds.), *Family approaches to domestic violence: A practitioners guide to gender-inclusive research and treatment* (pp. 59–87). New York, NY: Springer.

Melton, H. C. (2007). Predicting the occurrence of stalking in relationships characterized by domestic violence. *Journal of Interpersonal Violence, 22,* 3–25.

Menio, D., & Keller, B. H. (2000). CARIE: A multifaceted approach to abuse prevention in nursing homes. *Generations, 24,* 28–32.

Merrill, G. S. (1998). Understanding domestic violence among gay and bisexual men. In R. K. Bergin (Ed.), *Issues in intimate violence* (pp. 129–141). Thousand Oaks, CA: Sage.

Merrill, G. S., & Wolfe, V. A. (2000). Battered gay men: An exploration of abuse, help seeking, and why they stay. *Journal of Homosexuality, 39,* 1–30.

Merschman, J. C. (2001). The dark side of the Web: Cyberstalking and the need for contemporary legislation. *Harvard Women's Law Journal, 24,* 255–292.

Meyer, R. G., & Deitsch, S. E. (1996). *The clinician's handbook: Integrated diagnostics, assessment and intervention in adult and adolescent psychopathology.* Boston, MA: Allyn & Bacon.

Miele, D., & O'Brien, E. J. (2010). Under diagnosis of posttraumatic stress disorder in at risk youth. *Journal of Traumatic Stress, 23,* 591–598

Mihalic, S. W., & Elliott, D. (1997). A social learning theory model of marital violence. *Journal of Family Violence, 12,* 21–47.

Milam, J. E., Ritt-Olson, A., & Unger, J. B. (2004). Posttraumatic growth among adolescents. *Journal of Adolescent Research, 19,* 192–204.

Miller, D., & Prentice, D. (1994). Collective errors and errors about the collective. *Personality and Social Psychology Bulletin, 20,* 541–550.

Miller, D. H., Greene, K., Causby, V., White, B. W., & Lockhart, L. L. (2001). Domestic violence in lesbian relationships. *Women and Therapy, 23,* 107–127.

Miller, J., & Bukva, K. (2001). Intimate violence perceptions: Young adults' judgments of abuse escalating from verbal arguments. *Journal of Interpersonal Violence, 16,* 133–150.

Miller, T. W., & Veltkamp, L. K. (1996). *Theories, assessment, and treatment of domestic violence: Directions in clinical and counseling psychology.* New York, NY: Hatherleigh.

Miller, W. R., & Rollnick, S. (2002). *Motivational interviewing: Preparing people for change* (2nd ed.). New York, NY: Guilford Press.

Miller-Perrin, C. L., & Perrin, R. D. (2007). *Child maltreatment: An introduction* (2nd ed.). Thousand Oaks, CA: Sage.

Millon, T. (1983). *Millon Clinical Multiaxial Inventory manual.* Minneapolis, MN: Interpretive Scoring Systems.

Millon, T., & Davis, R. D. (1997). The MCMI-III. Present and future directions. *Journal of Personality, 68,* 69–85.

Mills, R. B., & Malley-Morrison, K. (1998). Emotional commitment, normative acceptability, and attributions for abusive partner behaviors. *Journal of Interpersonal Violence, 13,* 133–150.

Milner, J. S., & Chilamkurti, C. (1991). Physical child abuse perpetrator characteristics: A review of the literature. *Journal of Interpersonal Violence, 6,* 336–344.

Mitchell, K., Finkelhor, D., & Wolak, J. (2003). The exposure of youth to unwanted sexual material on the Internet: A national survey of risk, impact, & prevention. *Youth & Society, 34,* 330–358.

Moffitt, T. E., Caspi, A., Rutter, M., & Silva, P. A. (2001). *Sex differences in antisocial behaviour conduct disorder, delinquency and violence in the Dunedin Longitudinal Study.* Cambridge, England: Cambridge University Press.

Mohandie, K., Meloy, J. R., McGowan, M. G., & Williams, J. (2006). The RECON typology of stalking: Reliability and validity based upon a large sample of North American stalkers. *Journal of Forensic Science, 51,* 147–166.

Molidor, C. E., Tolman, R. M., & Kober, J. (2000). Gender and contextual factors in adolescent dating violence. *Prevention Research, 7,* 1–4.

Moncher, F. J. (1996). The relationship of maternal adult attachment style and risk of physical child abuse. *Journal of Interpersonal Violence, 11,* 335–350.

Money, J. (1961). Sex hormones and other variables in human eroticism. In W. C. Young (Eds.), *Sex and internal secretions* (Vol. 8). Baltimore, MD: Williams & Wilkins.

Monnier, J., Resnick, H. S., Kilpatrick, D. G., & Seals, B. (2002). The relationship between distress and resource loss following rape. *Violence and Victims, 17,* 85–91.

Monson, C. M., Schnurr, P. P., Resick, P. A., Friedman, M. J., Young-Xu, Y., & Stevens, S. P. (2006). Cognitive processing therapy for veterans with military-related posttraumatic stress disorder. *Journal of Consulting and Clinical Psychology, 74,* 898–907.

Moon, A., & Benton, D. (2000). Tolerance of elder abuse and attitudes toward third-party intervention among African American, Korean American, and White elderly. *Journal of Multicultural Social Work, 8,* 283–303.

Moon, A., & Williams, O. (1993). Perceptions of elder abuse and help-seeking patterns among African-American, Caucasian American, and Korean-American elderly women. *Gerontologist, 33,* 386–395.

Moore, T. M., & Stuart, G. L. (2005). A review of the literature on masculinity and partner violence. *Psychology of Men and Masculinity, 6,* 46–61.

Morse, B. J. (1995). Beyond the Conflict Tactics Scale: Assessing gender differences in partner violence. *Violence & Victims, 4,* 251–271.

Murphy, C. M., & Eckhardt, C. I. (2005). *Treating the abusive partner: An individualized cognitive–behavioral approach.* New York NY: Guilford Press.

Murphy, C. M., & Hoover, S. A. (1999). Measuring emotional abuse in dating relationships as a multifactorial construct. *Violence and Victims, 14,* 39–53.

Murphy, C. M., Meyer, S., & O'Leary, K. D. (1994). Dependency characteristics of partner assaultive men. *Journal of Abnormal Psychology, 103,* 729–733.

Murphy, C. M., & O'Leary, K. D. (1989). Psychological aggression predicts physical aggression in early marriage. *Journal of Consulting and Clinical Psychology, 57,* 579–582.

Murray, C. E. (2006). Controversy, constraints, and context: Understanding family violence through family systems theory. *The Family Journal, 14,* 234–239.

Murrell, A. R., Christoff, K. A., & Henning, K. R. (2007). Characteristics of domestic violence offenders: Associations with childhood exposure to violence. *Journal of Family Violence, 22,* 523–532.

Musser, P. H., Semiatin, J. N., Taft, C. T., & Murphy, C. M. (2008). Motivational interviewing as a pregroup intervention for partner-violent men. *Violence and Victims, 23,* 539–557.

Myers, J. E. B. (1992). *Evidence in child abuse and neglect cases.* New York, NY: Wiley.

Myers, J. E. B. (2002). The legal system and child protection. In J. E. B. Myers, L. Berliner, J. Briere, C. T. Hendrix, C. Jenny, & T. A. Reid (Eds.), *The APSAC handbook on child maltreatment* (2nd ed., pp. 305–327). Thousand Oaks, CA: Sage.

Nahmiash, D., & Reis, M. (2000). Most successful intervention strategies for abused older adults. *Journal of Elder Abuse & Neglect, 12,* 53–70.

Najavits, L. M. (2002). *Seeking safety: A treatment manual for PTSD and substance abuse.* New York, NY: Guilford Press.

Nathan, P., & Ward, T. (2002). Female sex offenders: Clinical and demographic features. *Journal of Sexual Aggression, 8,* 5–21.

National Center on Elder Abuse (NCEA). (1998). *National Elder Abuse Incidence Study.* Available at http://aoa.gov/AoARoot/AoA_Programs/Elder_Rights/Elder_Abuse/docs/ABuseReport_Full.pdf

National Center on Elder Abuse (NCEA). (2002). *The National Elder Abuse Incidence Study: Final report.* Madison, WI: Author. Available from http://www.aoa.gov/eldfam/Elder_Rights/Elder_Abuse/ABuseReport_Full.pdf

National Center on Elder Abuse (NCEA). (2012). *Major types of elder abuse.* Retrieved from http://www.ncea.aoa.gov/Main_Site/FAQ/Basics/Types_Of_Abuse.aspx

National Child Traumatic Stress Network (NCTSN). (2012). *National Child Traumatic Stress Network empirically supported treatments and promising practices.* Retrieved from http://www.nctsn.org/sites/default/files/assets/pdfs/CCG_Book.pdf

National Clearinghouse on Child Abuse and Neglect Information (2004). *What is child abuse and neglect?* Retrieved December 2008 from http://nccanch.acf.hhs.gov

National Coalition of Anti-Violence Programs (NCAVP). (1998). *Annual report on lesbian, gay, and transgender domestic violence: 2003 supplement.* Retrieved from http://www.avp.org/publications/reports/2003NCAVPdvrpt.pdf

National Coalition of Anti-Violence Programs (NCAVP). (2004). *Lesbian, gay, bisexual, and transgender domestic violence: 2003 supplement.* Retrieved from http://www.ncavp.org/common/document_files/Reports/2003NCAVPDVRpt.pdf.pdf

National Institute of Justice. (1998). *Stalking and domestic violence: The third annual report to Congress under the Violence Against Women Act* (NCJ 172204). Washington, DC: U.S. Department of Justice.

National Research Council. (2003). *Elder mistreatment: Abuse, neglect, and exploitation in aging America. Panel to review risk and prevalence of elder abuse and neglect.* Washington, DC: National Academies Press.

NBC. (2005). *Female teachers accused of sex with male students.* Retrieved from www.nbc10.com/news/4179284/detail.html.

Neidig, P. H., & Friedman, D. H. (1984). *Spouse abuse: A treatment program for couples.* Champaign., IL: Research Press.

Nelson, D. (2000). Injustice and conflict in nursing homes: Toward advocacy and exchange. *Journal of Aging Studies, 14,* 39–61.

Nelson, D. (2002). Violence against elderly people: A neglected problem. *Lancet, 360,* 1094.

Newby, J. H., Ursano, R. J., McCarroll, J. E., Martin, L. T., Norwood, A. E., & Fullerton, C. S. (2003). Spousal aggression by U.S. Army female soldiers toward employed and unemployed civilian husbands. *American Journal of Orthopsychiatry, 73,* 288–293.

Nishith, P., Resick, P. A., & Griffin, M. G. (2002). Pattern of change in prolonged exposure and cognitive–processing therapy for female rape victims with posttraumatic stress disorder. *Journal of Consulting and Clinical Psychology, 70,* 880–886.

Nolan, P., & Lenski, G. (2004). *Human societies: An introduction to macrosociology.* London, England: Paradigm.

North American Man/Boy Love Association. (2002). *Statement of purpose.* Retrieved from http://qrd.tcp.com/qrd/orgs/NAMBLA/statement.of.purpose.

Oatley, A. (1994). Domestic violence doesn't discriminate on the basis of sexual orientation. *Suncoast News,* 19–21.

O'Donohue, W., Yeater, E. A., & Fanetti, M. (2003). Rape prevention with college males. *Journal of Interpersonal Violence, 18,* 513–531.

Office for Victims of Crime. (2002). *Strengthening antistalking statutes* (NCJ Publication No. 189192). Washington, DC: U.S. Department of Justice.

Okamura, A., Heras, P., & Wong-Kerberg, L. (1995). Asian Pacific Island and Filipino Americans and sexual child abuse. In L. Fontes (Eds.), *Sexual abuse in nine North American cultures* (pp. 67–96). Thousand Oaks, CA: Sage.

O'Keefe, M. (1998). Factors mediating the link between witnessing interpersonal violence and dating violence. *Journal of Family Violence, 13,* 39–57.

O'Leary, K. D. (1993). Through a psychological lens: Personality traits, personality disorders, and levels of violence. In R. J. Gelles & Loseke (Eds.), *Current controversies on family violence* (pp. 7–30). Newbury Park, CA: Sage.

O'Leary, K. D. (1995). Assessment and treatment of partner abuse. *Clinician's Research Digest, 12* (Supplemental Bulletin–July), 1–3.

O'Leary, K. D. (1999). Developmental and affective issues in assessing and treating partner aggression. *Clinical Psychology: Science and Practice, 6,* 400–414.

O'Leary, K. D., Barling, J., Arias, I., Rosenbaum, A., Malone, J., & Tyree, A. (1989). Prevalence and stability of marital aggression between spouses: A longitudinal analysis. *Journal of Consulting and Clinical Psychology, 57,* 263–268.

O'Leary, K. D., & Curley, A. D. (1986). Assertion and family violence: Correlates of spouse abuse. *Journal of Marital and Family Therapy, 12*, 281–289.

O'Leary, K. D., Heyman, R. E., & Neidig, P. H. (1999). Treatment of wife abuse: A comparison of gender specific and couples approaches. *Behavior Therapy, 30,* 475–505.

O'Leary, K. D., & Slep, A. M. S. (2003). A dyadic longitudinal model of adolescent dating aggression. *Journal of Clinical Child and Adolescent Psychology, 32,* 314–327.

O'Leary, K. D., Vivian, D., & Malone, J. (1992). Assessment of physical aggression against women in marriage: The need for a multimodal assessment. *Behavioral Assessment, 14,* 5–14.

Olshen, E., McVeigh, K. H., Wunsch-Hitzig, R. A., & Rickert, V. I. (2007). Dating violence, sexual assault, and suicide attempts among urban teenagers. *Archives of Pediatric and Adolescent Medicine, 161,* 539–545.

Onyskiw, J. E. (2003). Domestic violence and children's adjustment: A review of research. *Journal of Emotional Abuse, 3,* 11–45.

Orsillo, S. M., Roemer, L., & Barlow, D. H. (2003). Integrating acceptance and mindfulness into existing cognitive–behavioral treatment for GAD: A case study. *Cognitive and Behavioral Practice, 10,* 222–230.

Ozer, E. J., Best, S. R., Lipsey, T. L., & Weiss, D. S. (2003). Predictors of posttraumatic stress disorder and symptoms in adults: A meta-analysis. *Psychological Bulletin, 129,* 52–73.

Pagano, N., Mihaly, C., Dauenhauer, A., & Mason, A. (2007, September/October). County-based needs assessment. *Victimization of the Elderly and Disabled, 10,* 44–46.

Pagelow, M. D. (1984). *Family violence*. New York, NY: Praeger.

Pan, H., Neidig, P., & O'Leary, K. D. (1994). Predicting mild and severe husband-to-wife physical aggression. *Journal of Consulting and Clinical Psychology, 62,* 975–981.

Panchanadeswaran, S., El-Bassel, N., Gilbert, L., Wu, E., & Chang, M. (2008). An examination of the perceived social support levels of women in methadone maintenance treatment programs who experience various forms of intimate partner violence. *Women's Health Issues, 18,* 35–43.

Panchanadeswaran, S., & McCloskey, L. A. (2007). Predicting the timing of women's departure from abusive relationships. *Journal of Interpersonal Violence, 22,* 50–65.

Paradis, A., Reinherz, H., Giaconia, R., Beardslee, W., Ward, K., & Fitzmaurice, G. (2009). Long-term impact of family arguments and physical violence on adult functioning at age 30 years: Findings from the Simmons longitudinal study. *Journal of the American Academy of Child & Adolescent Psychiatry, 48,* 290–298. doi: 10.1097/CHI.0b013e3181948fdd

Paredes, M., Leifer, M., & Kilbane, T. (2001). Maternal variables related to sexually abused children's functioning. *Child Abuse & Neglect, 25,* 1159–1176.

Parents Anonymous, Inc. (2008). *Strengthening families around the world*. Retrieved from http://www.parentsanonymous.org/pahtml/parBene.html

Patzel, B. (2006). What blocked heterosexual women and lesbians in leaving their abusive relationships. *Journal of the American Psychiatric Nurses Association, 12,* 208–215.

Paulozzi, L. J., Saltzman, L. E., Thompson, M. P., & Holmgreen, P. (2001). Surveillance for homicide among intimate partners: United States, 1981–1998. *CDC Surveillance Summaries 50,* 1–6.

Paveza, G. J., Cohen, D., Eisdorfer, C., Frells, S., Semla, T., Ashford, J. W., . . . Levy, P. (1992). Severe family violence and Alzheimer's disease: Prevalence and risk factors. *Gerontologist, 32,* 493–497.

Pearce, J. W., & Pezzot-Pearce, T. D. (2007). *Psychotherapy of abused and neglected children* (2nd ed.). New York, NY: Guilford Press.

Pearlman, L. A. (2003). *Trauma and Attachment Belief Scale (TABS) manual.* Los Angeles, CA: Western Psychological Services.

Pearlman, L. A., & Courtois, C. A. (2005). Clinical applications of the attachment framework: Relational treatment of complex trauma. *Journal of Traumatic Stress, 18,* 449–459.

Pelcovitz, D., van der Kolk, B. A., Roth, S., Mandel, F. S., Kaplan, S., & Resick, P. A. (1997). Development of a criteria set and a structured interview for disorders of extreme stress (SIDES). *Journal of Traumatic Stress, 10,* 3–17.

Pence, E., & Paymar, M. (1993). *Education groups for men who batter: The Duluth model.* New York: Springer.

Perilla, J. L., Frndak, K., Lillard, D., & East, C. (2003). A working analysis of women's use of violence in the context of learning, opportunity, and choice. *Violence Against Women, 9,* 10–46.

Perry, B. D. (2001). The neurodevelopmental impact of violence in childhood. In D. Schetky & E. Benedek (Eds.), *Textbook of child and adolescent forensic psychiatry* (pp. 221–238). Washington, DC: American Psychiatric Press.

Perry, B. D. (2002). Childhood experience and the expression of genetic potential: What childhood neglect tells us about nature and nurture. *Brain and Mind, 3,* 79–100.

Peter, T. (2005). *Hearing silent voices: Examining mother–daughter sexual abuse* (Unpublished doctoral dissertation). University of Manitoba, Winnipeg, Canada.

Peter, T. (2009). Exploring taboos: Comparing male- and female-perpetrated child sexual abuse. *Journal of Interpersonal Violence, 24,* 1111–1128.

Peterman, L. M., & Dixon, C. G. (2003). Domestic violence between same-sex partners: Implications for counseling. *Journal of Counseling & Development, 81,* 40–47.

Pfohl, B., Blum, N., & Zimmerman, M. (1997). *Structured Interview for DSM-IV Personality.* Washington, DC: American Psychiatric Press.

Pfohl, S. J. (1977). The "discovery" of child abuse. *Social Problems, 24,* 310–323.

Phillips, L. R., Torres de Ardon, E., & Briones, G. S. (2000). Abuse of female caregivers by care recipients: Another form of elder abuse. *Journal of Elder Abuse & Neglect, 12,* 123–143.

Pierce, L. H., & Peirce, R. L. (1984). Race as a factor in the sexual abuse of children. *Social Work Research & Abstracts, 20,* 9–14.

Piers, M. W. (1978). *Infanticide: Past and present.* New York, NY: Norton.

Pillemer, K. A. (1985). The dangers of dependency: New findings on domestic violence against elderly. *Social Problems, 33,* 146–158.

Pillemer, K. A. (1986). Risk factors in elder abuse: Results from a case-control study. In K. Pillemer & R. S. Wolf (Eds.), *Elder abuse: Conflict in the family* (pp. 236–263). Dover, MA: Auburn House.

Pillemer, K. A. (2005). Elder abuse is caused by the deviance and dependence of abusive caregivers. In D. R. Loseke, R. J. Gelles, & M. Cavanaugh (Eds.), *Current controversies on family violence* (2nd ed., pp. 207–220). Thousand Oaks, CA: Sage.

Pillemer, K., & Bachman-Prehn, R. (1991). Helping and hurting: Predictors of maltreatment of patients in nursing homes. *Research on Aging, 13,* 74–95.

Pillemer, K. A., & Finkelhor, D. (1988). The prevalence of elder abuse: A random sample survey. *Gerontologist, 28,* 128–131.

Pillemer, K., & Finkelhor, D. (1989). Causes of elder abuse: Caregiver stress versus problem relatives. *American Journal of Orthopsychiatry, 59,* 179–187.

Pillemer, K., & Moore, D. W. (1989). Abuse of patients in nursing homes: Findings from a survey of staff. *The Gerontologist, 29,* 314–320.

Pinsof, W. M. (1995). *Integrative problem-centered therapy.* New York, NY: Basic Books.

Pinto, L. A., Sullivan, E. L., Rosenbaum, A., Wyngarden, N., Umhau, J. C., Miller, M. W., & Taft, C. T. (2010). Biological correlates of intimate partner violence perpetration. *Aggression and Violent Behavior, 15,* 387–398.

Pleck, E. (1987). *Domestic tyranny: The making of American social policy against family violence from colonial times to present.* New York, NY: Oxford University Press.

Pleck, E. (1989). Criminal approaches to family violence. In L. Ohlin & M. Tonry (Eds.), *Family violence* (pp. 19–57). Chicago, IL: University of Chicago Press.

Ploeg, J., Fear, J., Hutchison, B., MacMillan, H., & Bolan, G. (2009). A systematic review of interventions for elder abuse, *Journal of Elder Abuse & Neglect, 21,* 187–210.

Plummer, C. A. (2005). Sexual abuse prevention is appropriate and successful. In D. R. Loseke, R. J. Gelles, & M. M. Cavanaugh (Eds.), *Current controversies on family violence* (2nd ed., pp. 257–270). Thousand Oaks, CA: Sage.

Pollack, S., & Gilligan, C. (1982). Images of violence in Thematic Apperception Test stories. *Journal of Personality and Social Psychology, 42,* 159–167.

Pollak, S. D., Cicchetti, D., Hornung, K., & Reed, A. (2000). Recognizing emotion in faces: Developmental effects of child abuse and neglect. *Developmental Psychology, 36,* 679–688.

Pontius, A. S. (2002). Impact of fear-inducing violence on neuropsychological visuo-spatial test in warring hunter-gathers: Analogies to violent Western environments. *Aggression and Violent Behavior, 7,* 69–84.

Power, C., Koch, T., Kralik, D., & Jackson, D. (2006). Lovesick: Women, romantic love and intimate partner violence. *Contemporary Nurse, 21,* 174–185.

Powers, M. N. (1986). *Oglala women.* Chicago, IL: University of Chicago Press.

Prentky, R., Harris, B., Frizzell, K., & Righthand, S. (2000). An actuarial procedure for assessing risk in juvenile sex offenders. *Sexual Abuse: A Journal of Research and Treatment, 12,* 71–93.

Prochaska, J. O., & DiClemente, C. C. (1992). The transtheoretical model. In J. C. Norcross & M. R. Goldried (Eds.), *Handbook of psychotherapy integration* (pp. 300–334). New York NY: Basic Books.

Putallaz, M., & Bierman, K. L. (2004). *Aggression, antisocial behavior and violence amongst girls.* New York, NY: Guilford Press.

Pushkareva, N. (1997). *Women in Russian history: From the tenth to the twentieth century* (Eve Levin, Ed. and Trans.). Armonk, NY: M. E. Sharpe.

Putnam, F. W. (2003). Ten-year update review: Child sexual abuse. *Journal of the American Academy of Child & Adolescent Psychiatry, 42,* 269–278.

Pynoos, R. S., Rodriguez, N., Steinberg, A., Studer, M., & Fredrick, C. (1998). *The UCLA PTSD Index for DSM-IV.* Unpublished instrument that is available from the National Child Traumatic Stress Network website: www.nctsnet.org

Pynoos, R. S., Steinberg, A. M., & Goenjian, A. (1996). Traumatic stress in childhood and adolescence: Recent developments and current controversies. In B. A. van der Kolk, A. C. McFarlan, & L. Weisaeth (Eds.), *Traumatic stress: The effects of overwhelming experience on mind, body, and society* (pp. 331–358). New York, NY: Guilford Press.

Quayhagen, M., Quayhagen, M. P., Patterson, T. L., Irwin, M., Hauger, R. L., & Grant, I. (1997). Coping with dementia: Family caregiver burnout and abuse. *Journal of Mental Health and Aging, 3,* 357–364.

Quigley, B. M., & Leonard, K. E. (1996). Desistance of husband aggression in the early years of marriage. *Violence and Victims, 11,* 355–370.

Quintana, S. M., & Holahan, W. (1992). Termination in short-term counseling: Comparison of successful and unsuccessful cases. *Journal of Counseling Psychology, 39,* 299–305.

Radbill, S. X. (1987). Children in a world of violence: A history of child abuse. In R. E. Helfer & R. S. Kempe (Eds.), *The battered child* (4th ed., pp. 3–22). Chicago, IL: University of Chicago Press.

Rahim, H. (2000). Virtue, gender, and the family: Reflections on religious texts in Islam and Hinduism. *Journal of Social Distress and the Homeless, 9,* 187–199.

Rand, M. R. (2009). *National Crime Victimization Survey, Criminal Victimization, 2008* (NCJ Publication No. 227777). Washington, DC: U.S. Department of Justice, Bureau of Justice Statistics.

Rathus, J. H., & Feindler, E. L. (2004). *Assessment of partner violence: A handbook for researchers and practitioners.* Washington, DC: American Psychological Association.

Reay, A. M., & Browne, K. D. (2002). The effectiveness of psychological interventions with individuals who physically abuse or neglect their elderly dependents. *Journal of Interpersonal Violence, 17,* 416–431.

Reed, J. S. (1981). Below the Smith and Wesson line: Reflections on Southern violence. In M. Black & J. S. Reed (Eds.), *Perspectives on the American South: An annual review of society, politics, and culture* (pp. 9–22). New York, NY: Cordon and Breach Science Publications.

Reis, M., & Nahmiash, D. (1995). Validation of Caregiver Abuse Screen (CASE). *Canadian Journal of Aging, 14,* 45–60.

Reis, M., & Nahmiash, D. (1998). Validation of the Indicators of Abuse (IOA) screen. *Gerontologist, 38,* 471–480.

Reitzel-Jaffe, D., & Wolfe, D. A. (2001). Predictors of relationship abuse among young men. *Journal of Interpersonal Violence, 16,* 99–115.

Rennison, C. M. (2001). *Intimate partner violence and age of victim, 1993–99* (Special Report, NCJ 187635). U.S. Department of Justice, Office of Justice Programs, Bureau of Justice Statistics. Retrieved January 2009 from http://www.ojp.usdoj.gov/bjs/abstract/ipva99.htm

Rennison, C. M., & Welchans, S. (2000). *Intimate partner violence* (Special Report, NCJ 178247). U.S. Department of Justice, Office of Justice Programs, Bureau of Justice Statistics. Retrieved from http://www.ojp.usdoj.gov/bjs/abstract/ipv.htm

Renzetti, C. M. (1989). Building a second closet: Third party responses to victims of lesbian partner abuse. In S. M. Stith & M. A. Straus (Eds.), *Understanding partner violence* (pp. 24–34). Minneapolis, MN: National Council on Family Relations.

Renzetti, C. M, (1992). *Violent betrayal: Partner abuse in lesbian relationships.* Newbury Park, CA: Sage.

Renzetti, C. M. (1996). The poverty of services for battered lesbians. In C. M. Renzetti & C. H. Miley (Eds.), *Violence in gay and lesbian domestic partnerships* (pp. 61–68). New York, NY: Harrington Park Press.

Renzetti, C. M. (1998). Violence and abuse in lesbian relationships: Theoretical and empirical issues. In R. K. Berger (Ed.), *Issues in intimate violence* (pp. 117–127). Thousand Oaks, CA: Sage.

Renzetti, C. M., & Miley, C. H. (Eds.). (1996). *Violence in gay and lesbian domestic partnerships.* Binghamton, NY: Harrington Park Press.

Reynolds, C. R., & Kamphaus, R. W. (2006). *Behavior Assessment System for Children* (2nd ed.). New York, NY: Pearson.

Rhodes, K. V., Cerulli, C., Dichter, M. E., Kothari, C. L., & Barg, F. K. (2010). "I didn't want to put them through that": The influence of children on victim decision-making in intimate partner violence cases. *Journal of Family Violence, 25,* 485–493.

Richie, B. E. (2005). Foreword. In B. E. Richie, N. J. Sokoloff, & C. Pratt (Eds.), *Domestic violence at the margins: Readings on race, class, gender, and culture* (pp. xv–xviii). New Brunswick, NJ: Rutgers University Press.

Rickert, V. I., Sanghvi, R., & Wiemann, C.M. (2002). Is lack of sexual assertiveness among adolescent and young adult women a cause for concern? *Sexual Reproductive Health, 34,* 178–183.

Riedel, M., & Best, J. (1998). Patterns in intimate partner violence homicide: California, 1987–1996. *Homicide Studies, 2,* 305–320.

Riggs, D. S., & O'Leary, K. D. (1996). Aggression between heterosexual dating partners: An examination of a causal model of courtship aggression. *Journal of Interpersonal Violence, 11,* 519–540.

Ristock, J. L. (2003). Exploring dynamics of abusive lesbian relationships: Preliminary analysis of a multisite, qualitative study. *American Journal of Community Psychology, 31,* 329–342.

Rodriquez, C. M. (2010). Personal contextual characteristics and cognitions: Predicting child abuse potential and disciplinary style. *Journal of Interpersonal Violence, 25,* 315–335.

Rodriquez, M. A., Wallace, S. P., Woolf, N. H., & Mangione, C. M. (2006). Mandatory reporting of elder abuse: Between a rock and a hard place. *Annals of Family Medicine, 4,* 403–409.

Roe-Sepowitz, D., & Krysik, J. (2008). Examining the sexual offenses of female juveniles: The relevance of childhood maltreatment. *American Journal of Orthopsychiatry, 78,* 405–412.

Rogosch, F., Cicchetti, D., & Abre, J. L. (1995). The role of child maltreatment in early deviations in cognitive and affective processing abilities and later peer relationship problems, *Development and Psychopathology, 7,* 591–609.

Rose, S. J. (1999). Reaching consensus on child neglect: African American mothers and child welfare workers. *Children and Youth Services Review, 21,* 463–479.

Rosen, K. H., & Stith, S. M. (1995). Women terminating abusive dating relationships: A qualitative study. *Journal of Social and Personal Relationships, 12,* 155–160.

Rosenbaum, A., & Hodge, S. K. (1989). Head injury and marital aggression. *American Journal of Psychiatry, 146,* 1048–1051.

Rosenbaum, A., & Kunkel, T. S. (2009). Group interventions for intimate partner violence. In K. D. O'Leary, & E. M. Woodin (Eds.), *Psychological and physical aggression in couples: Causes and interventions* (pp.191–210). Washington, DC: American Psychological Association.

Rosenbaum, A., & Maiuro, R. D. (1990). Perpetrators of spouse abuse. In R. T. Ammerman & M. Hersen (Eds.), *Treatment of family violence: A sourcebook* (pp. 280–309). New York, NY: Plenum Press.

Rosenfeld, B. D. (2000). Assessment and treatment of obsessional harassment. *Aggression and Violent Behavior, 5,* 529–549.

Rosenfeld, B. (2004). Violence risk factors in stalking and obsessional harassment: A review and preliminary meta-analysis. *Criminal Justice and Behavior, 31,* 9–36.

Rosenman, S. (2002). Trauma and posttraumatic stress disorder in Australia: Findings in the population sample of the Australian National Survey of Mental Health and Wellbeing. *Australian and New Zealand Journal of Psychiatry, 36,* 515–520.

Ross, C. A., Heber, S., Norton, G. R., Anderson, D. Anderson, G., & Barchet, P. (1989). The Dissociative Disorders Interview Schedule: A structured interview. *Dissociation, 2,* 169–189.

Ross, J. M., & Babcock, J. C. (2010). Gender and intimate partner violence in the United States: Confronting the controversies. *Sex Roles, 62,* 194–200.

Rossman, B. B. R., & Ho, J. (2000). Posttraumatic response and children exposed to parental violence. *Journal of Aggression, Maltreatment, & Trauma, 3,* 85–106.

Rothbard, J. C., & Shaver, P. S. (1994). Continuity of attachment across the life span. In M. B. Sperling & W. H. Berman (Eds.), *Attachment in adults: Clinical and developmental perspectives* (pp. 31–71). New York, NY: Guilford Press.

Rothbaum, B. O., & Foa, E. B. (1996). Cognitive–behavioral therapy for posttraumatic stress disorders. In B. A. van der Kolk, A. C. McFarlan, & L. Weisaeth (Eds.), *Traumatic stress: The effects of overwhelming experience on mind, body, and society* (pp. 491–509). New York, NY: Guilford Press.

Rothbaum, B. O., Meadows, E. A., Resick, P., & Foy, D. W. (2000). Cognitive–behavioral therapy. In E. B. Foa, T. M. Keane, & M. J. Friedman (Eds.), *Effective treatments of PTSD: Practice guidelines from the International Society of Traumatic Stress Studies* (pp. 60–83). New York, NY: Guilford Press.

Royce, L., & Coccaro, E. (2001). The neuropsychopharmacology of criminality and aggression. *Canadian Journal of Psychiatry, 46,* 35–43.

Runyon, M. K., Deblinger, E., & Schroeder, C. (2009). Pilot evaluation of outcomes of combined parent–child cognitive–behavioral therapy for families at risk for child physical abuse. *Cognitive and Behavioral Practice, 16,* 101–118.

Russell, D. E. H. (1986). *The secret trauma.* New York, NY: Basic Books.

Russell, D. E. H. (1990). *Rape in marriage.* Indianapolis: Indiana University Press.

Ryan, G. (2002). *Primary, secondary, and tertiary perpetration prevention childhood and adolescence.* Denver, CO: Kempe Center.

Ryan, G. (2005). Preventing violence and trauma in the next generation. *Journal of Interpersonal Violence, 20,* 132–141.

Sackett, L. A., & Saunders, D. G. (2001). The impact of different forms of psychological abuse on battered women. In K. D. O'Leary & R. D. Maiuro (Eds.), *Psychological abuse in violent domestic relations* (pp. 197–212.) New York, NY: Springer.

Safran J. D., Crocker, P., McMain, S., & Murry, P. (1990). The therapeutic alliance rupture as a therapy event for empirical investigation. *Psychotherapy, 27,* 154–165.

Safran, J. D., Muran, J. C., & Eubanks-Carter, C. (2011). Repairing alliance ruptures. *Psychotherapy, 48,* 80–87.

Sagatun, I. J., & Edwards, L. P (1995). *Child abuse and the legal system.* Chicago, IL: Nelson-Hall.

Saigh, P. A. (2004). Assessment of PTSD in children and adolescents. In R. R. Silva (Ed.), *Posttraumatic stress disorder in children and adolescents* (pp. 202–217). New York, NY: Norton.

Saigh, P. A., Yasik, A. E., Oberfield, R. A., Green B. L., Halamandaris, P. V., Rubsenstein, H., . . . McHugh, M. (2000). The Children's PTSD Inventory: Development and reliability. *Journal of Traumatic Stress, 3,* 369–380.

Samuelson, S. L., & Campbell, C. D. (2005). Screening for domestic violence: Recommendations based on a practice survey. *Professional Psychology: Research and Practice, 36,* 276–282.

Sanderson, M., Coker, A. L., Roberts, R. E., Tortolero, S. R., & Reininger, B. M. (2004). Acculturation, ethnic identity, and dating violence among Latino ninth-grade students. *Preventive Medicine: An International Journal Devoted to Practice and Theory, 39,* 373–383.

Sappington, A. A., Pharr, R., Tunstall, A., & Rickert, E. (1997). Relationships among child abuse and psychological problems. *Journal of Clinical Psychology, 53,* 318–329.

Sarantakos, S. (2004). Deconstructing self-defense in wife-to-husband violence. *Journal of Men's Studies, 12,* 277–296.

Saunders, B. E., Berliner, L., & Hanson, R. F. (Eds.). (2004). *Child physical and sexual abuse: Guidelines for treatment (Revised report: April 26, 2004).* Charleston, SC: National Crime Victims Research and Treatment Center. Retrieved from http://www.musc.edu/cvc/

Saunders, D. G. (1992). A typology of men who batter: Three types derived from cluster analysis. *American Journal of Orthopsychiatry, 62,* 264–275.

Saunders, D. G. (1996). Feminist–cognitive–behavioral and process–psychodynamic treatments for men who batter: Interaction of abuser traits and treatment models. *Violence & Victims, 11,* 393–414.

Saunders, D. G., Lynch, A., Grayson, M., & Linz, D. (1987). The Inventory of Beliefs About Wife Beating: The construction and empirical validation of a measure of beliefs and attitudes. *Violence and Victims, 2,* 39–55.

Saunders, D. G., & Parker, J. C. (1989). Legal sanctions and treatment follow-through among men who batter: A multivariate analysis. *Social Work Research & Abstracts, 25,* 21–29.

Saywitz, K. J., Goodman, G. S., & Lyon, T. D. (2002). Interviewing children in and out of court. In J. E. B. Myers, L. Berliner, J. Briere, C. T. Hendrix, C. Jenny, & T. A. Reid (Eds.), *The APSAC handbook on child maltreatment* (2nd ed., pp. 349–377). Thousand Oaks, CA: Sage.

Scheeringa, M. S., Weems, C. F., Cohen, J. A., Amaya-Jackson, L., & Guthrie, D. (2011). Trauma-focused cognitive–behavioral therapy for posttraumatic stress disorder in three through six year-old children: A randomized clinical trial. *Journal of Child Psychology and Psychiatry, 52,* 853–860.

Schiamberg, L. B., Oehmke, J., Zhang, Z., Barboza, G. E., Griffore, R. J., Von Heydrich, L., . . . Mastin, T. (2012). Physical abuse of older adults in nursing homes: A random sample survey of adults with an elderly family member in a nursing home. *Journal of Elder Abuse & Neglect, 24,* 65–83

Schneider, M. W., Ross, A., Graham, J. C., & Zielinski, A. (2005). Do allegations of emotional maltreatment predict developmental outcomes beyond that of other forms of maltreatment? *Child Abuse & Neglect, 29,* 513–532.

Schore, A. N. (2003). Early relational trauma, disorganized attachment, and the development of a predisposition to violence. In M. F. Solomon & D. J. Siegel (Eds.), *Healing trauma: Attachment, mind, body, and brain* (pp. 107–167). New York, NY: Norton.

Schumacher, J. A., Feldbau-Kohn, S., Smith Slep, A., M., & Heyman, R. E. (2001). Risk factors for male-to-female partner physical abuse. *Aggression and Violent Behavior, 6,* 281–352.

Schwartz, J. P., Magee, M. M., Griffin, L. D., & Dupuis, C. W. (2004). Effects of group preventative intervention on risk and protective factors related to dating violence. *Group Dynamics: Theory, Research, and Practice, 8,* 221–231.

Scott, K. L. (2004). Stage of change as a predictor of attrition among men in a batterer treatment program. *Journal of Family Violence, 19,* 37–47.

Scott, K. L., & Wolfe, D. A. (2003). Readiness to change as a predictor of outcome in batterer treatment. *Journal of Consulting and Clinical Psychology, 71,* 879–889.

Seamans, C. L. (2003). A qualitative study of women perpetrators of domestic violence: Comparison with literature on men perpetrators of domestic violence. *Dissertation Abstracts International: Section B. Sciences and Engineering, 64*(3), 1506. (UMI No. 3084187)

Seaver, C. (1996). Muted lives: Older battered women. *Journal of Elder Abuse and Neglect, 8,* 3–21.

Sedlak, A. J. (1991). *National incidence and prevalence of child abuse and neglect: 1988: Revised report*. Rockville, MD: Westat.

Sedlak, A. J., & Broadhurst, D. D. (1996). *Third National Incidence Study on Child Abuse and Neglect*. Washington, DC: U.S. Department of Health and Human Services.

Sedlak, A. J., Mettenberg, J., Basena, M., Petta, I., McPherson, K., Greene, A., & Li, S. (2010). *Fourth National Incidence Study of Child Abuse and Neglect (NIS-4): Report to Congress, executive summary*. Washington, DC: U.S. Department of Health & Human Services, Administration for Children and Families.

Seidman, I., & Pokorak, P. J. (2011). Justice responses to sexual violence. In J. W. White, M. P. Koss, & A. E. Kazdin (Eds.), *Violence against women and children: Navigating solutions* (Vol. 2, pp. 137–157). Washington, DC: American Psychological Association.

Selley, C., King., E., Peveler, R., Osola, K., Martin, N., & Thompson, C. (1997). Posttraumatic stress disorder symptoms and the Clapham rail accident. *British Journal of Psychiatry, 171,* 478–482.

Selzer, M. (1971). The Michigan Alcoholism Screening Test: The quest for a new diagnostic instrument. *American Journal of Psychiatry, 127,* 1653–1658.

Senn, C. Y., Desmarais, S., Verberg, N., & Wood, E. (2000). Predicting coercive sexual behavior across the life span in a random sample of Canadian men. *Journal of Social and Personal Relationships, 17,* 95–113.

Sexual exploitation of children over the Internet, 109th Congress (2007) (U.S. House staff report prepared for the Committee on Energy and Commerce).

Seymour, A. (1998). Aetiology of the sexual abuse of children: An extended feminist perspective. *Women Studies International Forum, 21,* 415–427.

Shackelford, T. K., & Mouzos, J. (2005). Partner killing by men in cohabiting and marital relationship: A comparative, cross-national analysis of data from Australia and the United States. *Journal of Interpersonal Violence, 20,* 1310–1324.

Sharps, P., Campbell, J. C., Campbell, D., Gary, E., & Webster, D. (2003). Risky mix: Drinking, drugs use, and homicide. *National Institute of Justice Journal, 250,* 8–12.

Shaw, J. A., Lewis, J. E., Loeb, A., Rosado, J., & Rodriquez, R. A. (2001). A comparison of Hispanic and African American sexually abused girls and their families. *Child Abuse and Neglect, 25,* 1363–1379.

Sheridan, D. J., & Nash, K. R. (2007). Acute injury patterns of intimate partner violence victims. *Trauma, Violence, & Abuse, 8,* 281–289.

Sheridan, L. P., Gillett, R., Blaauw, E., Davies, D. M., & Patel, D. (2003). There's no smoke without fire: Are male ex-partners perceived as more "entitled" to stalk than stranger or acquaintance stalkers? *British Journal of Psychology, 94,* 87–98.

Sherman, L., & Rogan, D. (1992). *Policing domestic violence: Experiments and dilemmas*. New York, NY: Free Press.

Sherman, L., & Schmidt, J. (1993). Does arrest deter domestic violence? *American Behavioral Scientist, 36,* 601–609.

Short, L. M., McMahon, P. M., Chervin, D. D., Shelley, G. A., Lezin, N., Sloop, K. S., & Dawkins, N. (2000). Survivors' identification of protective factors and early warning signs for intimate partner violence. *Violence Against Women, 6,* 272–285.

Siegel, D. J. (2003). An interpersonal neurobiology of psychotherapy: The developing mind and the resolution of trauma. In M. F. Solomon & D. J. Siegel (Eds.), *Healing trauma: Attachment, mind, body, and brain* (pp. 1–56). New York, NY: Norton.

Siegel, L. W. (1995). The marital rape exemption: Evolution to extinction. *Cleveland State Law Review, 43,* 351–378.

Sigler, T. T. (1989). *Domestic violence in context: An assessment of community attitudes.* Lexington, MA: Lexington Books.

Silverman, A. B., Reinherz, H. Z., & Giaconia, R. M. (1996). The long-term sequelae of child and adolescent abuse: A longitudinal community study. *Child Abuse and Neglect, 20,* 709–723.

Silverman, W. K., Pina, A. A., & Viswesvaran, C. (2008). Evidence based psychosocial treatment for phobic and anxiety disorders in children and adolescents. *Journal of Clinical Child and Adolescent Psychology, 38,* 105–130.

Simonelli, C. J., & Ingram, K. M. (1998). Psychological distress among men experiencing physical and emotional abuse in heterosexual dating relationships. *Journal of Interpersonal Violence, 13,* 667–681.

Skowron, E., & Reinemann, D. H. S. (2005). Effectiveness of psychological interventions for child maltreatment: A meta-analysis. *Psychotherapy: Theory, Research, Practice, Training, 42,* 52–71.

Slade, A., Sadler, L. S., & Mayes, L. (2005). Minding the baby: Enhancing parental reflective functioning in a nursing/mental health home visiting program. In L. J. Berlin, Y. Ziv, L. Amaya-Jackson, & M. T. Greenberg (Eds.), *Enhancing early attachments: Theory, research, intervention, and policy* (pp. 152–177). New York, NY: Guilford Press.

Smith, D. W., Davis, J. L., & Fricker-Elhai, A. E. (2004). How does trauma beget trauma? Cognitions about risk in women with abuse histories. *Child Maltreatment, 9,* 292–303.

Smith, K. P., & Christakis, N. A. (2008). Social networks and health. *Annual Review of Sociology, 34,* 405–429.

Snyder, D .K. (1997). *Marital Satisfaction Inventory–Revised manual* (MSI-R). Los Angeles, CA: Western.

Snyder, D. K., & Snow, A. C. (1996, August). *Evaluating couples' aggression in marital therapy.* Paper presented at the annual convention of the American Psychological Association, New York.

Soler, H., Vinayak, P., & Quadagno, D. (2000). Biosocial aspects of domestic violence. *Psychoneuroendocrinology, 25,* 721–739.

Sonkin, D. J., & Dutton, D. G. (2003). Treating assaultive men from an attachment perspective. In D. G. Dutton & D. J. Sonkin (Eds.), *Intimate violence: Contemporary treatment approaches* (pp. 105–134). New York, NY: Haworth Press.

Sorenson, S. B., & Telles, C. A. (1991). Self-reports of spousal violence in a Mexican-American and Non-Hispanic White population. *Violence and Victims, 6,* 3–15.

Southworth, C., Finn, J., Dawson, S., Fraser, C., & Tucker, S. (2007). Intimate partner violence, technology, and stalking. *Violence Against Women, 13,* 842–856.

Spencer, G. A., & Bryant, S. A. (2000). Dating violence: A comparison of rural, suburban, and urban teens. *Journal of Adolescent Health, 27,* 302–305.

Spielberger, C. D., Edwards, C. D., Montuori, J., & Lushene, R. (1973). *Manual for the State–Trait Anxiety Inventory for Children.* Palo Alto, CA: Consulting Psychologist Press.

Spitzberg, B. (2002). The tactical topography of stalking victimization and management. *Trauma, Violence, & Abuse, 30,* 261–288.

Spohn, C. G., & Holleran, D. (2001). Prosecuting sexual assault: A comparison of changing decisions in sexual assault cases involving strangers, acquaintances, and intimate partners. *Justice Quarterly, 18,* 651–688.

Sprenkle, D. H. (1994). Wife abuse through the lens of "systems theory." *The Counseling Psychologist, 22,* 598–602.

Stahly, G. B. (1996). Battered women: Why don't they just leave? In J. C. Chrisler, C. Golden, & P. D. Rozee (Eds.), *Lectures on the psychology of women* (pp. 289–306). New York, NY: McGraw-Hill.

Stankiewicz, J. M., & Rosselli, E. (2008). Women as sex objects and victims in print advertisement. *Sex Roles, 58,* 579–589.

Stark, E., & Flitcraft, A. (1988). Violence among intimates: An epidemiological review. In V. B. Van Hasselt, R. L. Morrison, A. S. Bellack, & M. Hersen (Eds.), *Handbook of family violence* (pp. 293–317). New York, NY: Plenum.

Stark, E., & Flitcraft, A. (1995). Killing the beast within: Women battering and female suicidality. *International Journal of Health Services, 25,* 43–64.

Starzyk, K. B., & Marshall, W. L. (2003). Childhood family personological risk factors for sexual offending. *Aggression and Violent Behavior, 8,* 93–105.

Statutory Rape Act, California Penal Code § 261.5 (2010).

Stauffer, L. B., & Deblinger, E. (2003). *Let's talk about taking care of you: An educational book about body safety.* Hatfield, PA: Hope for Families.

Stauffer, L. B., & Deblinger, E. (2004). *Let's talk about taking care of you: An educational book about body safety for young children.* Hatfield, PA: Hope for Families.

Steele, K., & van der Hart, O. (2009). Treating dissociation. In C. A. Courtois & J. D. Ford (Eds.), *Treating complex traumatic stress disorders* (pp. 145–165). New York, NY: Guilford Press.

Stein, M. B., Jang, K. L., Taylor, S., Vernon, P. A., & Livesley, W. J. (2002). Genetic and environmental influences on trauma exposure and posttraumatic stress disorder symptoms: A twin study. *American Journal of Psychiatry, 159,* 1675–1681.

Steinberg, M. (1994). *Interviewer's guide on the Structural Clinical Interview for DSM-IV Dissociative Disorders–Revised (SCID-E-R).* Washington, DC: American Psychiatric Association Press.

Steinmetz, S. K. (1977–1978). The battered husband syndrome. *Victimology: An International Journal, 2,* 499–509.

Steinmetz, S. K. (1983). Dependency, stress and violence between middle-aged care-givers and their elderly parents. In J. I. Kosberg (Ed.), *Abuse and maltreatment of the elderly: Causes and interventions* (pp. 134–139). Little, MA: John Wright.

Steinmetz, S. K. (1988). *Duty bound: Elder abuse and family care.* Newbury Park, CA: Sage.

Steinmetz, S. K. (2005). Elder abuse is caused by the perception of stress associated with providing care. In D. R. Loseke, R. J. Gelles, & M. M. Cavanaugh (Eds.), *Current controversies on family violence* (2nd ed., pp. 191–206). Thousand Oaks, CA: Sage.

Stermac, L., Del Bove, G., & Addison, M. (2001). Violence, injury, and presentation patterns in spousal sexual assaults. *Violence Against Women, 7,* 1218–1233.

Stets, J. E. (1990). Verbal and physical aggression in marriage. *Journal of Marriage and the Family, 52,* 501–514.

Stets, J. E., & Hammons, S. A. (2002). Gender, control, and marital commitment. *Journal of Family Issues, 23,* 3–25.

Stets, J. E., & Straus, M. A. (1990). Gender differences in reporting marital violence and its medical and psychological consequences. In M. A. Straus & R. J. Gelles (Eds.), *Physical violence in American families: Risk factors and adaptations to violence in 8,145 families* (pp. 151–166). New Brunswick, NJ: Transaction.

Stiegel, L. A. (2003, July/August). Washington report. *Victimization of the Elderly and Disabled, 6,* 19–20.

Stith, S. M. (2000). Prevalence and costs of domestic violence. *Clinical Update: Domestic Violence, 2,* 1–8.

Stith, S. M., & Farley, S. C. (1993). A predictive model of male spousal violence. *Journal of Family Violence, 8,* 183–201.

Stith, S. M., & McCollum, E. E. (2009). Couples treatment for psychological and physical aggression. In K. D. O'Leary & E. M. Woodin (Eds.), *Psychological and physical aggression in couples: Causes and interventions* (pp. 233–250). Washington, DC: American Psychological Association.

Stith, S. M., McCollum, E. E., Rosen, K. H., & Locke, L. D. (2002). Multicouple group treatment for domestic violence. In F. Kaslow (Ed.), *Comprehensive textbook of psychotherapy* (Vol. 4, pp. 499–520). New York, NY: Wiley.

Stith, S. M., McCollum, E. E., Rosen, K. H., Locke, L, & Goldberg, P. (2005). Domestic violence focused couples treatment. In J. Lebow (Ed.), *Handbook of clinical family therapy* (pp. 406–430). New York, NY: Wiley.

Stith, S. M., & McMonigle, C. L. (2009). Risk factors associated with intimate partner violence. In D. J. Whitaker & J. R. Lutzker (Eds.), *Preventing partner violence: Research and evidence-based intervention strategies* (pp. 67–92). Washington, DC: American Psychological Association.

Stith, S. M., Rosen, K. H., & McCollum, E. E. (2003). Effectiveness of couples' treatment for spouse abuse. *Journal of Marital & Family Therapy, 29,* 407–426.

Stith, S. M., Rosen, K. H., McCollum, E. E., & Thomsen, C. J. (2004). Treating intimate partner violence within intact couple relationships: Outcomes of multi-couple versus individual couple therapy. *Journal of Marital and Family Therapy, 30,* 305–318.

Stith, S. M., Smith, D. B., Penn, C. E., Ward, D. B., & Tritt, D. (2004). Intimate partner physical abuse perpetration and victimization risk factors: A meta-analytic review. *Aggression and Violent Behavior, 10,* 65–98.

Stoddard, J. P., Dibble, S. L., & Fineman, N. (2009). Sexual and physical abuse: A comparison of lesbians and their heterosexual sisters. *Journal of Homosexuality, 56,* 407–420.

Straus, M. A. (1979). Measuring intrafamily conflict and aggression: The Conflict Tactics Scale (CTS). *Journal of Marriage and the Family, 41,* 75–88.

Straus, M. A. (1990). Injury and frequency of assault and the 'representative sample fallacy' in measuring wife beating and child abuse. In M. A. Straus & R. J. Gelles (Eds.), *Physical violence in American families: Risk factors and adaptations to violence in 8,145 families* (pp. 75–89). New Brunswick, NJ: Transaction.

Straus, M. A. (1994). *Beating the devil out of them: Corporal punishment in American families.* New York, NY: Lexington Books.

Straus, M. A. (1999). The controversy over domestic violence by women: A methodological, theoretical, and sociology of science analysis. In X. B. Arriaga & S. Oskamp (Eds.), *Violence in intimate relationships* (pp. 17–44). Thousand Oaks, CA: Sage.

Straus, M. A. (2004). Prevalence of violence against dating partners by male and female university students worldwide. *Violence Against Women, 10,* 790–811.

Straus, M. A. (2005). Women's violence toward men is a serious social problem. In D. R. Loseke, R. J. Gelles, & M. M. Cavanaugh (Eds.), *Current controversies on family violence* (2nd ed., pp. 55–78). Thousand Oaks, CA: Sage.

Straus, M. A. (2007). Processes explaining the concealment and distortion of evidence on gender symmetry in partner violence. *European Journal of Criminal Policy and Research, 13,* 227–232.

Straus, M. A. (2008). Dominance and symmetry in partner violence by male and female university students in 32 nations. *Children Youth Services Review, 30,* 252–275.

Straus, M. A. (2009). Current controversies and prevalence concerning female offenders on intimate partner violence: Why the overwhelming evidence on parent physical violence by women has not been perceived and is often denied. *Journal of Aggression, Maltreatment & Trauma, 18,* 552–571.

Straus, M. A., & Donnelly, D. A. (2008). *Beating the devil out of them: Corporal punishment in American families and its effects on children* (2nd ed.). New Brunswick, NJ: Transaction Books.

Straus, M. A., & Gelles, R. J. (1986). Societal change and change in family violence from 1975 to 1985 as revealed by two national surveys. *Journal of Marriage and the Family, 48,* 465–479.

Straus, M. A., & Gelles, R. J. (1988). How violent are American families? Estimates from the National Family Violence Resurvey and other studies. In G. T. Hoteling, D. Finkelhor, J. T. Kirkpatrick, & M. A. Straus (Eds.), *Family abuse and its consequences: New directions in research* (pp. 14–36). Beverly Hills, CA: Sage.

Straus, M. A., & Gelles, R. J. (1990). How violent are American families? Estimates from the National Family Violence Resurvey and other studies. In M. A. Straus & R. J. Geles (Eds.), *Physical violence in American families: Risk factors and adaptations to violence in 8,145 families* (pp. 95–112). New Brunswick, NJ: Transaction Books.

Straus, M. A., Gelles, R. J., & Steinmetz, S. (1980). *Behind closed doors: Violence in the American family*. Garden City, NY: Anchor.

Straus, M. A., Hamby, S. L., Boney-McCoy, S., & Sugarman, D. B. (1995). *The Revised Conflict Tactics Scales (CTS2): Development and preliminary psychometric data.* Durham, NH: Family Violence Research Laboratory.

Straus, M. A., Hamby, S. L., Finkelhor, D., Moore, D. W., & Runyan, D. (1998). Identification of child maltreatment with the Parent Child Conflict Tactics Scale: Development and psychometric data for a national sample of American parents. *Child Abuse & Neglect, 22,* 249–270.

Straus, M. A., & Smith, C. (1990). Violence in Hispanic families in the United States. In M. A. Straus & R. J. Gelles (Eds.), *Physical violence in American families: Risk factors and adaptations to violence in 8,145 families* (pp. 341–367). New Brunswick, NJ: Transaction.

Straus, M. A., & Sweet, S. (1992). Verbal/symbolic aggression in couples: Incidence rates and relationships to personal characteristics. *Journal of Marriage and the Family, 54,* 346–357.

Stroshine, M. S., & Robinson, A. L. (2003). The decision to end abusive relationships: The role of the offender characteristics. *Criminal Justice and Behavior, 30,* 97–117.

Stroufe, L. A., Egeland, B., Carlson, E. A., & Collins, W. A. (2005). *The development of the person: The Minnesota study of risk and adaptation from birth to adulthood.* New York, NY: Guilford Press.

Strupp, H. H., & Binder, J. L. (1984). *Psychotherapy in a new key.* New York, NY: Basic Books.

Studer, M. (1984). Wife-beating as a social problem: The process of definition. *International Journal of Women's Studies, 7,* 412–422.

Sue, D. W., & Torino, G. C. (2005). Racial–cultural competence: Awareness, knowledge, and skills. In R. T. Carter (Ed.), *Handbook of racial–cultural psychology and counseling: Vol. 2. Training and practice* (pp. 3–18). Hoboken, NJ: Wiley.

Suitor, J., Pillemer, K., & Straus, M. A. (1990). Marital violence in a life course perspective. In M. A. Straus & R. J. Gelles (Eds.), *Physical violence in American families* (pp. 305–317). New Brunswick, NJ: Transaction Books.

Sullivan, J., & Beech, A. (2004). A comparative study of demographic data relating to intra- and extra-familial child sexual abusers and professional perpetrators. *Journal of Sexual Aggression, 10,* 39–50.

Sullivan, P. M., & Knutson, J. E. (1998). The association between child maltreatment and disabilities in a hospital-based epidemiological study. *Child Abuse & Neglect, 22,* 271–288.

Swan, N. (1998). Exploring the role of child abuse on later drug abuse: Researchers face broad gaps in information. *NIDA Notes, 13.* Retrieved from the National Institute of Drug Abuse, http://www.nida.nih.gov/NIDA_Notes/NNVol13N2/exploring

Swan, S. C., & Snow, D. L. (2002). A typology of women's use of violence in intimate relationships. *Violence Against Women, 8,* 286–319.

Swan, S. C., & Snow, D. L. (2003). Behavioral and psychological differences among abused women who use violence in intimate relationships. *Violence Against Women, 9,* 75–109.

Swan, S. C., & Snow, D. L. (2006). The development of a theory of women's use of violence in intimate relationships. *Violence Against Women, 12,* 1026–1045.

Taft, C. T., Murphy, C. M., Elliott, J. D., & Keaser, M. C. (2001). Race and demographic factors in treatment attendance for domestically abusive men. *Journal of Family Violence, 16,* 385–400.

Taft, C. T., Murphy, C. M., Elliott, J. D., & Morrel, T. M. (2001). Attendance enhancing procedures in group counseling for domestic abusers. *Journal of Counseling Psychology, 48,* 51–60.

Taft, C. T., Murphy, C. M., King, D. W., Musser, P. H., & DeDeyn, J. M. (2003). Process and treatment adherence factors in group cognitive behavioral therapy for partner violent men. *Journal of Consulting and Clinical Psychology, 71,* 812–820.

Tatara, T., Kuzmeskus, L. B., Duckhorn, E., Bivens, L., Thomas, C., Gertig, J., . . . Rust, K. (1998). *The National Elder Abuse Incidence Study* (Final report by the National Center of Elder Abuse, the American Public Human Service Association [Grant No. 90-AM-0660]). Washington, DC: U. S. Department of Health and Human Services.

Teasdale, J. D., Segal, S. V., Williams, J. M., Ridgeway, V. A., Soulsby, J. M., & Lau, M. A. (2000). Prevention of relapse/recurrence in major depression by mindfulness-based cognitive therapy. *Journal of Consulting and Clinical Psychology, 68,* 615–623.

Teaster, P. B., Dugar, T. A., Mendiondo, M. S., Abner, E. L., Cecil, K. A., & Otto, J. M. (2006). *The 2004 survey of state adult protection services: Abuse of adults 60 years of age and older.* Washington, DC: National Center on Elder Abuse. Retrieved from http://www.edlerabusecenter.org

Teaster, P. B., Nerenberg, L., & Stansbury, K. L. (2003). A national look at elder abuse multidisciplinary teams. *Journal of Elder Abuse & Neglect, 15,* 91–107.

Tedeschi, R. G., & Calhoun, L. G. (2004). Posttraumatic growth: Conceptual foundations and empirical evidence. *Psychological Inquiry, 15,* 1–18.

Thompson, E. H., Jr. (1991). The maleness of violence in dating relationships: An appraisal of stereotypes. *Sex Roles, 24,* 261–278.

Thompson, K. M. (2009). Sibling incest: A model for group practice with adult female victims of brother–sister incest. *Journal of Family Violence, 24,* 531–537.

Tjaden, P., & Thoennes, N. (1998). *Prevalence, incidence, and consequences of violence against women: Findings from the National Violence Against Women Survey* (NCJ Publication No. 172837). Washington, DC: U.S. Department of Justice.

Tjaden, P., & Thoennes, N. (2000). *Extent, nature, and consequences of intimate partner violence* (NCJ Publication No. 181867). Washington, DC: U.S. Department of Justice.

Tolman, R. M. (1989). The development of a measure of psychological maltreatment of women by their male partners. *Violence and Victims, 4,* 159–178.

Torres, S. (1987). Hispanic-American battered women: Why consider cultural differences? *Response, 10,* 20–21.

Triandis, H. C. (1994). *Culture and social behavior.* New York, NY: McGraw-Hill.

Triandis, H. C., & Suh, E. M. (2002). Cultural influences on personality. *Annual Review of Psychology, 53,* 133–160.

Trull, T. J. (2001). Structural relations between borderline personality disorder features and putative etiological correlates. *Journal of Abnormal Psychology, 110,* 471–481.

Turell, S. C. (2000). A descriptive analysis of same-sex relationship violence for a diverse sample. *Journal of Family Violence, 15,* 281–294.

Tutty, L. M., Babins-Wagner, R., & Rothery, M. A. (2006). Group treatment for aggressive women: An initial evaluation. *Journal of Family Violence, 21,* 341–349.

Tweed, R., & Dutton, D. G. (1998). A comparison of impulsive and instrumental subgroups of batterers. *Violence and Victims, 13,* 217–230.

Ullman, S. E., & Brecklin, L. R. (2002). Sexual assault history and suicidal behavior in a national sample of women. *Suicide and life-threatening behavior, 32,* 117–130.

Ullman, S. E., & Filipas, H. H. (2001). Predictors of PTSD symptom severity and social reactions in sexual assault victims. *Journal of Traumatic Stress, 14,* 393–413.

Ullman, S. E., & Filipas, H. H. (2005). Ethnicity and child sexual abuse experience of female college students. *Journal of Child Sexual Abuse Research, & Program Innovations for Victims, Survivors, & Offenders, 14,* 67–89.

Ulrich, L. T. (1991). *Good wives: Image and reality in the lives of women in Northern New England, 1650–1750.* New York, NY: Vantage Books.

U.S. Census Bureau. (2011). *U.S. Census 2010.* Retrieved November 28, 2011, from http://www.census.gov/prod/cen2010/briefs/c2010br-09.pdf

U.S. Department of Health and Human Services. (2007). *Child maltreatment 2005.* Washington, DC: Government Printing Office. Retrieved from http://acf.hhs.gov/programs/cb/stats_research/index.htm#cam

U.S. Department of Health and Human Services, Administration for Children and Families. (1981). *Study findings: National study of the incidence and severity of child abuse and neglect* (DHHS Publication No. OHDS 81-30325). Washington, DC: Government Printing Office.

U.S. Department of Health and Human Services, Administration for Children and Families, Administration on Children, Youth and Families, Children's Bureau. (2010). *Child maltreatment 2009.* Available from http://www.acf.hhs.gov/programs/cb/stats_research/index.htm#can

U.S. Department of Health and Human Services, Administration on Children, Youth and Families. (2005). *Child maltreatment 2003.* Washington, DC: Government Printing Office.

U.S. Department of Health and Human Services, National Center on Child Abuse, Neglect. (1996). *Third national incidence study of child abuse and neglect: Final report.* Washington, DC: Government Printing Office.

U.S. Department of Justice, Federal Bureau of Investigation. (2010). *Crime in the United States 2008* (Expanded homicide data, Table 10—Murder circumstances). Washington, DC: Author.

Vandecar-Burdin, T., & Payne, B. K. (2010). Risk factors for victimization of younger and older persons: Assessing differences in isolation, intra-individual characteristics, and health factors. *Journal of Criminal Justice, 38,* 160–165.

Vandello, J. A., Bosson, J., Cohen, D., Burnaford, R., & Weaver, J. (2008). Precarious manhood. *Journal of Personality and Social Psychology, 95,* 1325–1339.

Vandello, J. A., & Cohen, D. (2003). Male honor and female fidelity: Implicit cultural scripts that perpetuate domestic violence. *Journal of Personality and Social Psychology, 84,* 997–1010.

Vandello, J. A., Cohen, D., Grandon, R., & Franiuk, R. (2009). Stand by your man: Indirect prescriptions for honorable violence and feminine loyalty in Canada, Chile, and the United States. *Journal of Cross-Cultural Psychology, 40,* 81–104.

van der Kolk, B. A. (1988). Trauma in men: Effects on family life. In M. B. Straus (Ed.), *Abuse and victimization across the life span* (pp. 170–185). Baltimore, MD: Johns Hopkins University Press.

van der Kolk, B. A. (1996). The complexity of adaptation to trauma: Self-regulation, stimulus discrimination, and characterological development. In B. A. van der Kolk, A. C. McFarlan, & L. Weisaeth (Eds.), *Traumatic stress: The effects of overwhelming experience on mind, body, and society* (pp. 182–213). New York, NY: Guilford Press.

van der Kolk, B. A. (2005). Developmental trauma disorder: Toward a rational diagnosis for children with complex trauma histories. *Psychiatric Annals, 35,* 401–408.

van der Kolk, B. A., Hostetler, A., Herron, N., & Fisler, R. (1994). Trauma and the development of borderline personality disorder. *Psychiatric Clinics of North America, 17,* 715–730.

van der Kolk, B. A., & McFarlane, A. C. (1996). The black hole of trauma. In B. A. van der Kolk, A. C. McFarlan, & L. Weisaeth (Eds.), *Traumatic stress: The effects of overwhelming experience on mind, body, and society* (pp. 3–23). New York, NY: Guilford Press.

van der Kolk, B. A., McFarlane, A. C., & van der Hart, O. (1996). A general approach to treatment of posttraumatic stress disorder. In B. A. van der Kolk, A. C. McFarlane, & L. Weisaeth (Eds.), *Traumatic stress: The effects of overwhelming experience on mind, body, and society* (pp. 417–440). New York, NY: Guilford Press.

van der Kolk, B. A., Pelcovitz, D., Sunday, S., & Spinazzola, F. (2005). Disorders of extreme stress: The empirical foundation of a complex adaptation to trauma. *Journal of Traumatic Stress, 18,* 389–399.

Vandiver, D. M., & Kercher, G. (2004). Offender and victim characteristics of registered female sexual offenders in Texas: A proposed typology of female sexual offenders. *Sexual Abuse: Journal of Research and Treatment, 16,* 121–137.

Villarreal, G., & King, C. Y. (2004). Neuroimaging studies reveal brain changes in posttraumatic stress disorder. *Psychiatric Annals, 34,* 845–856.

Vinton, L. (1992). Battered women's shelters and older women: The Florida experience. *Journal of Family Violence, 7,* 63–72.

Vladescu, D., Eveleigh, Ploeg, J., & Patterson, C. (1999). An evaluation of a client-centered case management program for elder abuse. *Journal of Elder Abuse & Neglect, 11,* 5–22.

Waldner-Haugrud, L. K., Gratch, L. V., & Magruder, B. (1997). Victimization and perpetration rates of violence in gay and lesbian relationships: Gender issues explored. *Violence and Victims, 12,* 173–184.

Walker, C. E., Bonner, B. L., & Kaufman, K. L. (1988). *The physically and sexually abused child.* New York: Pergamon.

Walker, L. E. (1979). *The battered woman.* New York, NY: Harper Perennial.

Walker, L. E. (1984). *The battered woman syndrome.* New York, NY: Springer-Verlag.

Walker, L. E. (1993). The battered woman syndrome is a psychological consequence of the abuse. In R. J. Gelles & D. L. Loseke (Eds.), *Current controversies on family violence* (pp. 133–153). Newbury Park, CA: Sage.

Walker, L. E. (1995). Current perspectives on men who batter women— Implications for intervention and treatment to stop violence against women: Comment on Gottman et al. (1995). *Journal of Family Psychology, 9,* 264–271.

Walker, L. E. A. (1999). Psychology and domestic violence around the world. *American Psychologist, 54,* 21–29.

Walker, L. E. A. (2000). *The battered woman syndrome* (2nd ed.). New York, NY: Springer.

Walker, L. E. A. (2009). *The battered woman syndrome* (3rd ed.). New York, NY: Springer.

Wallace, H. (2005). *Family violence: Legal, medical and social perspectives* (4th ed.). New York, NY: Allyn & Bacon.

Walsh, F. (1996). Partner abuse. In D. Davies & C. Neal (Eds.), *Pink therapy: A guide for counselors and therapists working with lesbian, gay, and bisexual clients* (pp. 187–198). Philadelphia, PA: Open University Press.

Waltz, J., Babcock, J. C., Jacobson, N. S., & Gottman, J. M. (2000). Testing a typology of batterers. *Journal of Consulting and Clinical Psychology, 68,* 658–669.

Wang, C., & Holton, J. K. (2007). *Total estimated cost of child abuse and neglect in the United States.* Chicago, IL: Prevent Child Abuse America.

Waters, M. (2000, June). Guidelines urge researcher to take a less superficial look at minorities. *APA Monitor on Psychology, 3,* 12.

Watson, J. M., Cascardi, M., Avery-Leaf, S., & O'Leary, K. D. (2001). High school students' responses to dating aggression. *Violence and Victims, 16,* 339–348.

Watts-English, T., Fortson, B. L., Gibler, N., Hooper, S. R., & De Bellis, M. D. (2006). The psychobiology of maltreatment in childhood. *Journal of Social Issues, 62,* 717–736.

Weinberg, S. K. (1955). *Incest behavior.* New York, NY: Citadel.

Weiss, D. S., & Marmar, C. R. (1997). *The Impact of Event Scale–Revised*. In J. P. Wilson & T. M. Keane (Eds.), *Assessing psychological trauma and PTSD* (pp. 399–411). New York, NY: Guilford Press.

Weisz, A. N., Tolman, R. M., & Saunders, D. G. (2000). Assessing the risk of severe domestic violence: The importance of survivors' predictions. *Journal of Interpersonal Violence, 15,* 75–90.

Wekerle, C., & Avgoustis, E. (2003). Child maltreatment, adolescent dating, and adolescent dating violence. In P. Florsheim (Ed.), *Adolescent romantic relations and sexual behavior* (pp. 213–242). Mahwah, NJ: Erlbaum.

Werner, E. E. (1989). High-risk children in young adulthood: A longitudinal study from birth to 32 years. *American Journal of Psychiatry, 59,* 72–81.

West, M., & George, C. (1998). *Abuse and violence in intimate adult relationships: New perspectives from attachment theory*. Unpublished manuscript.

Weston, R., Marshall, L. L., & Coker, A. L. (2007). Women's motives for violent and nonviolent behaviors in conflict. *Journal of Interpersonal Violence, 22,* 1043–1065.

Whaley, A. L., & Davis, K. E. (2007). Cultural competence and evidence-based practice in mental health services. *American Psychologist, 62,* 563–574.

Whipple, E. E., & Webster-Stratton, C. (1991). The role of parental stress in physically abusive families. *Child Abuse & Neglect, 15,* 279–291.

Whitaker, D. J., Haileyesus, T., Swahn, M., & Saltzman, L. S. (2007). Differences in frequency of violence and reported injury between relationships with reciprocal and nonreciprocal intimate partner violence. *American Journal of Public Health, 97,* 941–947.

Whitaker, D. J., Le, B., Hanson, R. K., Baker, C. K., McMahon, P. M., Ryan, G., . . . Rice, D. (2008). Risk factors for the perpetration of child sexual abuse: A review and meta-analysis. *Child Abuse & Neglect, 32,* 529–548.

White, J. W., Smith, P. H., Koss, M. P., & Figueredo, A. J. (2000). Intimate partner aggression: What have we learned? Comment on Archer (2000). *Psychological Bulletin, 126,* 690–696.

White, R. J., & Gondolf, E. W. (2000). Implications of personality profiles for batterer treatment. *Journal of Interpersonal Violence, 15,* 467–488.

Widom, C. S. (1989). Does violence beget violence? *Psychological Bulletin, 106,* 3–28.

Widom, C. S. (1995). Victims of childhood sexual abuse: Later criminal consequences. *NIJ Research in Brief*. Retrieved January 2008 from http://www.ncjrs.org/txfo;es/abise.txt

Widom, C. S., & Ames, M. A. (1994). Criminal consequences of childhood sexual victimization. *Child Abuse & Neglect, 18,* 303–318.

Widom, C. S., & Maxfield, M. G. (2001). *An update on the "Cycle of Violence"* (NCJ Publication No. 184894). Washington, DC: U.S. Department of Justice. Retrieved May 2009 from http://www.acf.hhs.gov/programs/cb/pubs/cm04/cm04.pdf

Wiglesworth, A., Mosqueda, L., Mulnard, R., Liao, S., Gibbs, & Fitzgerald, W. (2010). Screening for abuse and neglect of people with dementia. *Journal of the American Geriatric Society, 58,* 493–500.

Wigman, S. A., Graham-Kevan, N., & Archer, J. (2008). Investigating subgroups of harassers: The roles of attachment, dependency, jealousy and aggression. *Journal of Family Violence, 23,* 557–568.

Wilcox, W. B. (1998). Conservative Protestant parenting: Authoritarian or authoritative? *American Sociological Review, 63,* 796–809.

Williams, T. S., Craig, W., Connolly, J., Pepler, D., & Laporte, L. (2008). Risk models of dating aggression across different adolescent relationships: A developmental psychopathology approach. *Journal of Consulting and Clinical Psychology, 76,* 622–632.

Williamson, G. M., & Shaffer, D. R. (2001). Caregiver loss and quality of care provided: Pre-illness relationship makes a difference. In J. H. Harvey & E. D. Miller (Eds.), *Loss and trauma: General and close relationship perspectives* (pp. 307–330). Philadelphia, PA: Brunner/Mazel.

Wilson, J., & Keane, T. (Eds.). (2004). *Assessing psychological trauma and PTSD: A practitioner's handbook* (2nd ed.). New York, NY: Guilford Press.

Winnicott, D. W. (1965). *The maturational process and the facilitating environment.* London, England: Hogarth Press.

Winston, A., Laikin, M., Pollack, J., Samstag, L., McCullough, L., & Muran, J. C. (1994). Short-term psychotherapy of personality disorders. *American Journal of Psychiatry, 151,* 190–194.

Wolak, J., Finkelhor, D., Mitchell, K. J., & Ybarra, M. (2008). Online 'predators' & their victims: Myths, realities, & implications for prevention & treatment. *American Psychologist, 63,* 111–128.

Wolak, J., Mitchell, K., & Finkelhor, D. (2003). Escaping or connecting? Characteristics of youth who form close online relationships. *Journal of Adolescence, 26,* 105–119.

Wolf, R. S., & Pillemer, K. (1989). *Helping elderly victims: The reality of elder abuse.* New York, NY: Columbia University Press.

Wolf, R. S., Strugnell, C. P., & Godkin, M. A. (1982). *Preliminary findings from three model projects on elderly abuse, Center on Aging.* Worcester: University of Massachusetts Medical Center.

Wolfe, D. A. (1991). *Preventing physical and emotional abuse of children.* New York, NY: Guilford Press.

Wolfe, D. A. (2003). Elder abuse intervention: Lessons from child abuse and domestic violence initiatives. In R. J. Bonnie & R. B. Wallace (Eds.), *Elder maltreatment: Abuse, neglect, and exploitation in an aging America* (pp. 501–525). Washington, DC: National Academy Press.

Wolfe, D. A. (2006). Preventing violence in relationships: Psychological science addressing complex social issues. *Canadian Psychology/Psychologie Canadienne, 47,* 44–50.

Wolfe, D., Crooks, C., Hughes, R., & Jaffe, P. (2009). *Youth Relationships Program: Featuring the Fourth R for Healthy Relationships: A relationship-based program for 8th grade physical and health education.* London, Canada: Centre for Addiction and Mental Health, Centre for Prevention Science.

Wolfe, D. A., Crooks, C. V., Lee, V., McIntryre-Smith, A., & Jaffe, P. G. (2003). The effects of children's exposure to domestic violence: A meta-analysis and critique. *Clinical Child and Family Psychology Review, 6,* 171–187.

Wolfe, D. A., Fairbank, J. A., Kelly, J. A., & Bradlyn, A. S. (1983). Child abusive parents' physiological responses to stressful and non-stressful behavior in children. *Behavioral Assessment, 5,* 363–371.

Wolfe, D. A., & Jaffe, P. G. (1999). Emerging strategies in the prevention of domestic violence. *Future of Children, 9,* 133–141.

Wolfe, D. A., Scott, K., Wekerle, C., & Pittman, A. L. (2001). Child maltreatment: Risk of adjustment problems and dating violence in adolescence. *Journal of American Academy of Child and Adolescent Psychiatry, 40,* 282–289.

Wolfe, D. A., Wekerle, C., Gough, R., Reitzel-Jaffe, D., Grasley, C, Pittman, A., . . . Stumph, J. (1996). *The Youth Relationships Manual: A group approach with adolescents for the prevention of woman abuse and the promotion of healthy relationships*. Thousand Oaks, CA: Sage.

Wolfe, D. A., Wekerle, C., Scott, K., Straatman, A., & Grasley, C. (2004). Predicting abuse in adolescent dating relationships over 1 year: The role of child maltreatment and trauma. *Journal of Abnormal Psychology, 113,* 406–415.

Wolfe, D. A., Wekerle, C., Scott, K., Straatman, A., Grasley, C., & Reitzel-Jaffe, D. (2003). Dating violence prevention with at-risk youth: A controlled outcome evaluation. *Journal of Consulting and Clinical Psychology, 71,* 279–291.

Wolfsdorf, B. A. (2001). Affect management in group therapy for women with posttraumatic stress disorder and histories of childhood sexual abuse. *Journal of Clinical Psychology, 57,* 2001, 169–181.

Wolitzky-Taylor, M. A., Ruggleio, K. J., Danielson, C. K., Resnick, H. S., Hanson, R. F., Smith, D.W., . . . Kilpatrick, D. G. (2008). Prevalence and correlates of dating violence in a national sample of adolescents. *Journal of the American Academy of Child and Adolescent Psychiatry, 47,* 755–762.

Woodin, E. M., & O'Leary, K. D. (2010). A brief motivational intervention for physically aggressive dating couples. *Prevention Science, 11,* 371–383.

Woods, S. J. (2000). Prevalence and patterns of posttraumatic stress disorder in abused and postabused women. *Issues in Mental Health Nursing, 21,* 309–324.

Woods, S. J., & Isenberg, M. A. (2001). Adaptation as a mediator of intimate abuse and traumatic stress in battered women. *Nursing Science Quarterly, 14,* 213–221.

Worcester, N. (2001). What is the battered women's movement saying about women who use force? Women who use force in heterosexual domestic violence: Putting the context (back) in the picture. *Wisconsin Coalition Against Domestic Violence Newsletter, 21,* 2–5.

Worell, J., & Remer, P. (2002). *Feminist perspectives in therapy: Empowering diverse women* (2nd ed.). New York, NY: Wiley.

Worrall, J. L., Ross, J. W., & McCord, E. S. (2006, July). Modeling prosecutors' charging decisions in domestic violence cases. *Crime & Delinquency, 52,* 472–503.

Wright, L. M., Watson, W. L., & Bell, J. M. (1990). Brain density and symmetry in pedophilic and sexually aggressive offenders. *Annals of Sex Research, 3,* 319–328.

Wyman, P. A., Sandler, I., Wolchik, S., & Nelson, K. (2000). Resilience as cumulative competence promotion and stress protection: Theory and intervention. In D. Cicchetti & Rappaport (Eds.), *The promotion of wellness in children and adolescents* (pp. 133–184). Washington, DC: Child Welfare League of America.

Yan, E., & Tang, C. S. (2003). Proclivity to elder abuse: A community study on Hong Kong Chinese. *Journal of Interpersonal Violence, 18,* 999–1017.

Yates, T. M., Carlson, E. A., & Egeland, B. (2008). A prospective study of child maltreatment and self-injurious behavior in a community sample. *Development and Psychopathology, 20,* 651–671.

Yllo, K. (2005). Through a feminist lens: Gender, diversity, and violence. In D. R. Loseke, R. J. Gelles, & M. M. Cavanaugh (Eds.), *Current controversies on family violence* (2nd ed., pp. 19–34). Thousand Oaks, CA: Sage.

Yoshioka, M. R., & Choi, D. Y. (2005). Culture and interpersonal violence research. *Journal of Interpersonal Violence, 20,* 513–519.

Young, J. E. (1999). *Cognitive therapy for personality disorders: A schema-focused approach* (3rd ed.). Sarasota, FL: Professional Resource Press.

Youth Risk Behavior Surveillance. (2004). Youth Risk Behavior Surveillance—United States, 2003. *Morbidity and Mortality Weekly Report, 53,* no. 22-2.

Yuan, N. P., Koss, M. P., Polacca, M., & Goldman, D. (2006). Risk factors for physical assault and rape among six Native American tribes. *Journal of Interpersonal Violence, 21,* 1566–1590.

Zeldin, S. (2004). Preventing youth violence through the promotion of community engagement and membership. *Journal of Community Psychology, 32,* 623–641.

Zhang, A., Snowden, L., & Sue, S. (1998). Differences between Asian and White Americans' help-seeking and utilization patterns in the Los Angeles area. *Journal of Community Psychology, 26,* 317–326.

Zielinski, D. S., & Bradshaw, C. P. (2006). Ecological influences on the sequelae of child maltreatment: A review of the literature. *Child Maltreatment, 11,* 49–62.

Zlotnick, C., Johnson, D. M., & Kohn, R. (2006). Intimate partner violence and long-term psychosocial functioning in a national sample of American women. *Journal of Interpersonal Violence, 21,* 262–275.

Zlotnick, C., Zakariski, A. L., Shea, M. T., & Costello, E. (1996). The long-term sequelae of sexual abuse: Support for a complex posttraumatic stress disorder. *Journal of Traumatic Stress, 9,* 195–205.

Zorza, J. (1998, June/July). Batterer manipulation and retaliation in the courts. A largely unrecognized phenomenon sometimes encouraged by court practices. *Domestic Violence Report, 2,* 67–68, 75–76.

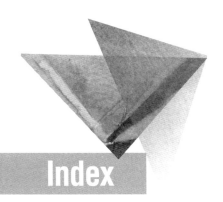

Index

Boxes and tables are indicated by b and t following page numbers.

F

W

Y

Z